Trial Practice Series

PSYCHIATRIC AND PSYCHOLOGICAL EVIDENCE

Daniel W. Shuman
Professor of Law
School of Law
Southern Methodist University
Dallas, Texas

SHEPARD'S/McGRAW-HILL
P.O. Box 1235
Colorado Springs, Colorado 80901

McGRAW-HILL BOOK COMPANY
New York ● St Louis ● San Francisco ● Colorado Springs
Auckland ● Bogotá ● Hamburg ● Johannesburg ● London
Madrid ● Mexico ● Milan ● Montreal ● New Delhi ● Panama ● Paris
São Paulo ● Singapore ● Sydney ● Tokyo ● Toronto

12345678910   SHKP   895432109876

Library of Congress Cataloging-in-Publication Data

Shuman, Daniel W.
  Psychiatric and psychological evidence.

  (Trial practice series)
  Includes index.
  1. Evidence, Expert—United States. 2. Forensic
psychiatry—United States. 3. Psychology, Forensic.
I. Title. II. Series.
KF8965.S57 1986   347.73'6   86-11915
ISBN 0-07-057179-1   347.3076

ISBN 0-07-057179-1

To my daughters,
   Brooke and Lindsy

Acknowledgments

Dr. Kevin Karlson, my contributing author for Part One (Chapters 1-5), not only provided invaluable assistance in his work on those chapters, but also provided helpful comments to me on work throughout the book. In addition, my research assistants, Mike Chambers, Michelle Daniels, and Elizabeth Ruman provided much useful assistance.

Numberous psychiatrists and psychologists provided me with extremely helpful insights into the problems and the use of psychiatrists and psychologists in civil and criminal litigation. My thanks to Dr. Saleem Ateek, Dr. Jim Grigson, Dr. John Looney, Dr. Robert Sadoff, and Dr. Lisa Blue. Jan DeLipsey, an experienced therapist, gave me invaluable assistance on issues relating to sexual abuse.

My colleague Ellen Solender provided me with insightful comments on Chapter 13 for which I am deeply indebted. William Bridge and Fred Moss, fellow teachers of evidence, often found me camped in their offices seeking their good counsel on questions of evidence and criminal law. I am extremely grateful for their patience and expertise.

Professor David Wexler of the University of Arizona College of Law, my mental health law mentor, reviewed the manuscript and as always, shed new light for me with his comments.

The Southern Methodist University School of Law, through a Dr. Don Smart Research Grant, provided me with financial support to enable me to work at a pace that kept my editors happy.

Preface

The impetus for this book comes from the increased use of and increased public attention to the use of psychiatric and psychological evidence in judicial proceedings along with the increased skepticism about the use of this evidence. Unfortunately, much of the response to this dichotomy in the literature has argued that psychiatric and psychological evidence is unreliable and ought to be excluded from judicial proceedings or, in the alternative, that this evidence is extremely valuable and ought to be received by courts. The difficulty with this all or nothing approach is that it fails carefully to distinguish that psychiatric and psychological evidence which is valuable from that which is not. In addition, it fails to recognize that while an attorney may seek to exclude this evidence one week, that same attorney may wish it admitted in another case that following week.

This is a practitioner's book. It is designed to explain each side of the questions it addresses, the reasoning underlying inclusion or exclusion of this evidence, the responses of courts to these questions, and arguments about the appropriate weight of this evidence. It explains the relevant psychiatric and psychological knowledge, relevant legal rules, and the meshing of the two.

The book is not designed to transform an attorney into a psychiatrist or psychologist, or to make a psychiatrist or psychologist into an attorney. However, it proceeds on the assumptions that an attorney seeking to present or exclude psychiatric or psychological evidence requires certain basic knowledge about these disciplines and that a psychiatrist or psychologist participating in litigation requires certain basic knowledge about relevant legal rules. Part One of the book is designed to provide this basic knowledge about psychiatry and psychology to attorneys. It was prepared by Dr. Kevin Karlson, a contributing author, who is a clinical and forensic psychologist. It explains, in language understandable to one not possessed of a degree in psychology or medicine, the basic operating assumptions and structures in the fields of psychiatry and psychology.

Part Two deals generally with rules governing the use of psychiatric and psychological evidence and Part Three deals with issues raised by the use of this evidence in particular proceedings. In both later parts the basic psychiatric and psychological knowledge articulated in Part One is applied to the legal rules discussed. For example, the discussion about the education and training of a psychologist in Chapter 4 is integrated into the qualifications for psychological expert testimony in Chapter 7. Although the individual chapters or sections may be considered separately, the whole is greater than the sum of its parts. The greatest benefit from the use of the book will be obtained by reading Parts One and Two in their entirety and then reading portions of Part Three relevant to the reader.

No single-volume treatise can hope to cover all the relevant law in all states or represent changes in the law following the date of its publication. To remedy these limitations, in cooperation with West Publishing Company, references to WESTLAW are provided where relevant at the conclusion of each chapter. After reading the relevant sections, an attorney may find cases in a given jurisdiction or discover the latest cases through the WESTLAW search references provided.

Contents

Detailed Contents

4 The Professions of Psychiatry and Psychology

5 Researching Psychiatric and Psychological Literature

8 Qualification of the Expert

9 Form and Mode of Presentation of Psychiatric and Psychological Evidence

Part One

Introduction to Psychiatry and Psychology*

* Kevin W. Karlson, J.D., Ph.D., the contributing author for Part I of this book, is a forensic and clinical psychologist in Dallas, Texas. He received his Ph.D. from the University of Texas Health Science Center at Dallas and his J.D. from Southern Methodist University School of Law. Special thanks to John Kennedy, Psychology Intern at the University of Texas Health Science Center at Dallas & Terrell State Hospital Program, for his invaluvable research assistance.

1

Theories of Mental Illness

§1.01   Introduction

The prevalent model in thinking about mental disorder is the medical model. The medical model approaches problems in behavior in the same way it approaches problems in body function. First, there is an assumed *normal* or disease-free state that exists in the absence of an identifiable disease or cause for deviation from the normal state. Changes in behavior that deviate from the norm are seen as symptoms of a disease for which etiological (causal) factors can be found and treated to ameliorate the disease state and return the patient to normal. In the same way that a runny nose is viewed as a symptom of a viral infection, the medical model of mental disorder views everything from anxiety to hallucination as a symptom, not as the problem.[1]

In stark contrast, the recently emergent behavioral theories explicitly

---

[1] See §§1.02 and 1.03 for further elaborations of this basic concept.

3

reject the medical model of mental disorder. American psychology, which is heavily empirical in its emphasis, has attacked the medical model as invalid for mental and behavioral problems, and as counter-productive to the development of effective methods of changing behavior.[2] To behaviorists, the disordered behavior is the problem. There is no need to postulate an underlying disorder to treat the problem behavior. Consequently, a system of classification and diagnosis that assumes that behaviors are symptoms of diseases is viewed as unnecessary, or not scientifically defensible.[3]

The next seven sections of this chapter are discussions of theories that are explicitly or implicitly based on the medical model. Section **1.09** is a discussion of various behavioral theories, all of which reject the medical model, either largely or entirely.

§1.02   Organic Theories

Although most psychiatrists and psychologists agree that a number of mental disorders are directly attributable to injury to the brain itself, one school of thought ascribes the cause of all mental disorders to these factors, not just the organic brain syndromes. These theories of the etiology of mental disorders are the *organic theories.*

The organic theories of mental disorder grew out of the observation of unusual behavior in brain-damaged individuals.[4] The basic assumption is that damage to the brain itself causes abnormal behavior. Two major schools evolved among the organic theorists: the globalists and the localizationists. Both of these groups developed competing ideas about the nature of brain organization and function.

The globalists contend that brain function is dependent on the interaction of various parts of the brain. Their contention is that damage to a part of the brain interferes with the brain's ability to form a complete Gestalt (whole) of a particular function, such as memory. For example, injuries to the brain in a wide variety of locations, both to the cortex (the outer layer) and to subcortical structures, have been observed to result in problems in learning new information or in making new

---

[2] D. Rimm & J. Masters, Behavior Therapy 6 (2d ed 1979).

[3] *Id* 5.

[4] Albert, *Critique of Neurobiologic Paradigm,* in Models for Clinical Psychopathology 133 (1981).

memories. Brain function is thought to depend not on particular brain areas, but on the functioning of the whole.[5]

The localizationists, on the other hand, studied the effect of damage to particular areas of the brain on behavior. They marshaled a body of observations which supported their position, especially by studying patients with limited injuries to specific brain areas. They found that damage to one area of the temporal lobe (the area of the brain beneath the temple) resulted in loss of ability to produce speech while damage to another area of the same lobe led to loss of speech comprehension. Damage to the same area on the other side had little effect on speech at all. These observations produced theoretical speculation about centers in the brain which govern complex behavior.[6]

Other support for the organic theories has come from spectacular cases. Charles Whitman, the sniper who shot 14 people from the tower at the University of Texas before killing himself, was found upon autopsy to have a malignant tumor deep in his brain. The location of the tumor was in an area of the brain which, when stimulated in animal experiments, resulted in aggressive behavior. The inference that was drawn was that the tumor was a cause of the violence.[7]

The use of computerized axial tomography (CAT) scans in research on mental disorders has recently given organic theorists new ammunition. CAT scans have revealed certain cerebral abnormalities in some patients suffering from mental disorders. A high percentage of chronic alcoholic patients has been found to manifest detectable cortical shrinkage and enlargement of the cerebral ventricles,[8] even when the patients appear externally intact.[9]

Another group of studies has focused on the brain structure of patients with schizophrenic disorders.[10] A recent review of these studies concluded that a number of clinical manifestations were associated with

---

[5] *Id.*

[6] *Id* 134.

[7] N. Carlson, Physiology of Behavior 455 (1977).

[8] The cerebral ventricles are fluid-filled cavities located deep in the interior of the brain which can be seen and measured using special CAT scanning techniques.

[9] Lishman, *Cerebral Disorder in Alcoholism: Syndromes of Impairment,* 104 Brain 1 (1981); Ron, Acker, & Shaw, *Computerized Tomography of the Brain in Chronic Alcoholism: A Survey and Follow-up Study,* 105 Brain 497 (1982).

[10] See §2.03 for the criteria for a schizophrenic disorder. The use of CAT scan findings as diagnostic technique was at issue in the trial of President Reagan's would-be assassin, John Hinckley. L. Caplan, The Insanity Defense and The Trial of John Hinckley, Jr. (1984).

CAT scan findings of ventricular enlargement. These included cognitive impairment,[11] poor response to antipsychotic medication, and a history of poor premorbid adjustment extending back to childhood.[12]

For these two mental disorders, at least some of the patients seem to have identifiable structural organic features which are associated with clinical symptomatology. Other groups of patients manifest symptoms of these disorders even without the anatomical anomalies. The implications are twofold: the current psychiatric diagnostic system is insufficiently precise to allow distinction of these two groups of patients,[13] and the organic theories may account for the etiology of some mental disorders, but probably not for all of them.

Other mental disorders that have been traditionally attributed to social or cultural conditions are being reevaluated as increasingly sophisticated research methodology becomes available. The prevailing view of borderline mental retardation[14] has been that social and cultural deprivation and its resulting dearth of environmental stimulation and opportunity were the primary causal factors. A recent study of mental retardation concluded that the main cause of mild mental retardation may be brain damage resulting from prenatal and birth difficulties rather than social or other biological factors.[15]

§1.03   Psychological Theories

A number of psychological theories have developed to attempt to explain abnormal behavior. The oldest is psychoanalytic theory, the most recent humanistic theories. Neither of these is a single theory, rather both are groups of theories with shared assumptions about human behavior.

§1.04   —Psychoanalytic Theories

Psychoanalytic theory was born in 1895 with the publication of

---

[11] Cognitive impairment is a measurable decline in thinking ability, usually measured on psychological tests of abstract thinking and problem solving.

[12] Lishman, *The Apparatus of Mind: Brain Structure and Function in Mental Disorder,* 24 Psychosomatics 699 (1983).

[13] *See* **§2.04.**

[14] Borderline mental retardation is defined by the Diagnostic and Statistical Manual of Mental Disorders (3d ed 1980) as IQ scores on standardized intelligence tests between 70 and 84.

[15] Costeff, Cohen, & Weller, *Biological Factors in Mild Mental Retardation,* 75 Dev Med & Child Neurology 580 (1983).

Sigmund Freud's first paper on hysteria.[16] For most of the first half of the twentieth century, Freud continued to develop his theory about the operation of the human psyche. The last 30 years have seen further elaboration of psychoanalytic theory and technique, as analysts have begun to treat more seriously disturbed individuals.[17]

The basic assumptions of psychoanalytic theory revolutionized thinking about mental disorders and profoundly affected both psychology and psychiatry. Freud observed that feelings and memories of which his patients were unaware often seemed to exert a marked influence on how they behaved. He postulated that unconscious psychological processes were important in the development of mental disorders.[18] Another assumption of psychoanalytic theory is that symptoms develop when strongly conflicting internal motives cannot be satisfactorily resolved by the individual. The manifestation of conflict is anxiety, which is a signal of psychological distress.[19] Freud assumed that all behavior was psychologically motivated, including symptoms. He further assumed that quantitative differences in the intensity of drives were crucial in distinguishing health from illness; the distinction between normal and abnormal was a matter of degree, not kind.[20]

Because of Freud's interest in the effect of past experience on current behavior, he became interested in infant development. He advanced a theory of psychological development which postulated that problems at different developmental phases would manifest themselves in different types of psychopathology. Problems during the oral phase of psychosexual development were associated with psychosis, the anal phase with obsessive-compulsive neurosis, and the phallic phase with hysteria. The process which explained those relationships was called fixation and was thought to involve the freezing of aims or drives at early stages as a result of psychological trauma.[21]

Freud organized the mind into a three-part structure. The id was understood as being the biological substrate out of which the two major drives, sex and aggression, emerged. It was also postulated to be the

---

[16] Freud, *Studies on Hysteria,* in Standard Edition of the Complete Psychological Works of Sigmund Freud (1953-1966).

[17] *See* **§3.08.**

[18] Michels, *The Psychoanalytic Paradigm,* in Models for Clinical Psychopathology (1981).

[19] Freud, *Inhibitions, Symptoms and Anxiety,* in Standard Edition of the Complete Psychological Works of Sigmund Freud (1953-1966).

[20] R. Price, Abnormal Psychology: Perspectives in Conflict 28-56 (1978).

[21] *Id* 35.

source of psychic energy. The id was assumed to be unaffected by external reality, and to remain unorganized and unable to distinguish between objective and subjective reality.

The ego was understood to develop out of the id as a result of interaction with the external world. The ego acts as a mediator between the impulses of the id and external reality. Where the id is governed by the pleasure principle, the ego is governed by the reality principle. The ego must also balance the demands of the third mental agency, the superego.

The superego represents the domain of moral values in the mind. The superego develops out of the ego through interactions with parents and others who reward and punish children's behavior. This part of the superego corresponds roughly to conscience. The other part of the superego consists of the ego ideal—the image of the person one strives to become.[22]

The mechanisms used by the ego to cope with the internal and external demands are called defense mechanisms. Defense mechanisms are thought to be unconscious and to deny or distort some facet of reality in order to minimize the experience of painful anxiety. Defense mechanisms have been categorized along a continuum from primitive to mature. Primitive defenses include denial ("No! it didn't happen"), distortion ("I'm Jesus Christ because I'm an only son"), and projection ("I'm not angry at them, they're angry with me"). Mature defenses include altruism (giving a gift to someone who's hurt your feelings), humor (finding something funny in a stressful situation) and conscious suppression of impulses ("I'm so angry I could hit her, but that's not a good idea").[23]

The emergence of symptoms (like anxiety, depression, or hallucinations) mark a failure of the ego to cope effectively with the demands made on it. A symptom may also be interpreted as a compromise between the id's demand for unrestrained drive expression and the superego's moral imperatives. Symptoms result when the intensity of the conflict overwhelms the ego's capacity for managing it without interfering with day-to-day functioning of the individual. Conflict itself is not seen as pathological, but rather as a reality of living.[24]

Ego psychology is one of the major elaborations of Freudian theory.

---

[22] Freud, *The Ego and the Id*, in Standard Edition of the Complete Psychological Works of Sigmund Freud (1953-1966).

[23] Meissner, *Theories of Personality and Psychopathology: Classical Psychoanalysis*, in Comprehensive Textbook of Psychiatry/IV 389-90 (4th ed 1985).

[24] R. Price, *supra* note 20, at 55.

Ego psychologists downplay the importance of the id and its drives and emphasize the development and function of the ego in normal development and psychopathology. Vagaries of ego development, influenced by both the individual's genetically inherited vulnerabilities and other early environment and parenting, are thought to account for a spectrum of disorders between neurosis and psychosis which have become the focus of treatment.[25] These personality disorders (also called character disorders) are notable for their *stable instability*, and were recently added to DSM-III[26] as new diagnoses: borderline personality disorder, schizotypal personality disorder, and narcissistic personality disorder.[27]

Another group of theories that evolved out of traditional psychoanalytic thought are designated Neo-Freudian. These include theories of Jung and Adler, both disciples of Freud, and other writers like Horney and Sullivan. These theories retain some key Freudian concepts, especially a psychodynamic approach to mental disorder and its treatment. However, each of these theorists differed sharply with Freud on the role of instinctual drives in mental disorder and on the basic nature of man, which Freud thought was *bad*.[28]

§1.05 —Humanistic Theories

The other major group of psychological theories of mental disorder has been called the *third force* in psychology along with psychoanalytic and behavioral theories.[29] The humanistic theories also share some values and assumptions about human nature. The major contrast between the humanistic theories and the others is their emphasis on positive human potentialities.[30]

Carl Rogers, a clinical psychologist, has been one of the primary thinkers of the humanistic school. Rogers posits that vulnerability to anxiety develops out of what he calls *conditions of worth* that result from children experiencing being valued for *good* but not *bad* behavior. This lack of *unconditional positive regard* from others leads to a lack of unconditional positive self-regard. A child who experiences a large

---

[25] R. Blanck & G. Blanck, Ego Psychology: Theory and Practice (1974).

[26] Diagnostic and Statistical Manual of Mental Disorders (3d ed 1980) (DSM-III).

[27] See §2.01 for discussion of DSM-III.

[28] Meissner, *supra* note 23, at 419-40.

[29] R. Price, Abnormal Psychology: Perspectives in Conflict 180 (1978).

[30] *Id* 181.

number or intense *conditions of worth* develops vulnerability to anxiety which arises when experiences occur that do not fit with the self-concept. Defenses are seen as attempts to make the experience fit the self-concept.[31]

A simplistic example may help clarify these concepts. Suppose a young boy is caught in a struggle between his divorcing parents. Each time he expresses some concern about or love for his absent father, his mother punishes or ignores him. The mother's positive regard of her child is conditioned on his expressing dislike toward his father or keeping quiet. Should this situation continue for a very long time, or result in an expression of anger by his mother, the child will develop anxiety since he cannot make the experience of hating his father fit with his self-concept, which is that he is a boy who loves his father.

Defenses are categorized as either disorganized behaviors or defensive behaviors. Disorganized behaviors are those typically considered as acutely psychotic.[32] For Rogers, disorganized behavior represents an opportunity for denial of the individual's current self-concept or adoption of an altered self-concept. Defensive behaviors, on the other hand, correspond roughly to psychoanalytic neurotic defenses. These defenses operate to distort the experience to resolve the incongruence between the individual's self-concept and experience.[33]

Humanistic theory is rooted in the traditions of existential philosophy and phenomenology, which emphasize the value and importance of an individual's immediate experience. The humanistic theorists have, therefore, been interested in altered states of consciousness as sources of growth experiences. The most radical of these thinkers, R.D. Laing, suggests that schizophrenia is merely an altered state of consciousness.[34] The humanists suggest that labeling an unusual experience, such as schizophrenia, as pathological is antitherapeutic. They insist that the experience presents an opportunity for personal growth which may be interrupted if it is devalued by labeling it as *sick*.[35]

---

[31] *Id* 187.

[32] *Psychotic* refers to a severe mental disorder characterized by loss of contact with reality and accompanied by disintegration of the personality.

[33] R. Price, *supra* note 29, at 187.

[34] R. Laing, The Divided Self (1965).

[35] R. Price, *supra* note 29, at 188.

§1.06 Biological Theories

Biological theories of mental disorder can be divided into two major groups: genetic and biochemical. In fact, these are related since an individual's genetic makeup also influences brain biochemistry. For clarity, each group of theories is examined separately.

§1.07 —Genetic Theories

The genetic theories have been more successful in accounting for familial contribution to risk for serious disorders like schizophrenic disorders and bipolar affective disorders than for less debilitating disorders.[36] The genetic theories postulate that an individual can inherit a predisposition to mental disorders, but that the genetic predisposition is insufficient in itself to develop the disorder.[37]

A number of arguments have been made that support the genetic theory of schizophrenia. No environmental causes of the disorder have been found that produce schizophrenic disorders in persons who have no relatives with schizophrenic disorders. The risk of schizophrenic disorders increases with the degree of genetic relatedness. The identical twin of a schizophrenic has a threefold greater risk of developing the disorder than a fraternal twin, and is more than 35 times more likely to develop the disorder than the general population. Studies conducted on children of schizophrenic parents who have been reared in homes of nonrelatives suggest that these children have rates of schizophrenic disorders much higher than the rest of the population, and sometimes the rate is about equal to that of children raised by their schizophrenic parents.[38]

Genetic studies of affective (mood) disorders[39] have been plagued by difficulties with diagnosis, since the diagnostic criteria have been the subject of considerable debate.[40] Generally, bipolar disorders[41] are thought to be genetically transmitted. Twin-family studies revealed that the probability of developing bipolar disorder ranges from about 17 per cent in half-siblings to nearly 100 per cent in identical twins. Other

---

[36] See **§2.03** for the diagnostic criteria and definitions of these disorders.

[37] Nicol & Gottesman, *Clues to the Genetics and Neurobiology of Schizophrenia*, 71 Am Scientist 398 (1983).

[38] *Id* 399.

[39] *See* **§2.03**.

[40] *See* **§2.04**.

[41] See **§2.03** for definition of bipolar disorders.

studies have found evidence ranging from 34 per cent for parents to 50 per cent of children of patients with the disorder.[42]

Family studies indicate that alcoholism may also be genetically transmitted. Studies of alcoholic parents and their children separated early in life suggest that being the biological child of an alcoholic is more predictive of later alcoholism than is growing up with an unrelated alcoholic parent.[43]

Genetic studies of psychopathic or antisocial behavior are less easily interpreted. Antisocial personality disorder is defined by DSM-III[44] as repeated antisocial conduct of various types beginning before age 15 and must be evident without any symptoms of severe mental retardation, schizophrenic, or bipolar disorders.[45] Research into the genetic contributions to antisocial personality disorder has been complicated by difficulty in controlling family and social environmental effects in the research design. The problems of collecting information about criminal behavior from, or about, these individuals has also made this research very difficult in this country, although it is somewhat easier in the more socialized Scandinavian countries with national registers. In any case, rates of criminality based on police records have usually been used in this research as indicative of antisocial personality.[46]

Rates of criminality among fraternal and identical twins, along with those of siblings, are so similar that environmental factors seem to play a major role. A recent adoption study, however, found that the rate of psychopathy, as defined by criminality, was five times greater in the biological fathers of *psychopathic* adoptees than in adoptive fathers or the biological fathers of *nonpsychopathic* control adoptees.[47] The genetic component of antisocial behavior remains unclear.

One genetic abnormality has been suggested as the cause of some violent behavior. The syndrome, marked by the presence of any extra Y chromosome in men, is found in some very tall, very aggressive men with low intelligence. These men are often the only criminal individuals

---

[42] Nicol & Gottesman, *supra* note 37, at 399.

[43] Winokur, Reich, Rimmer, & Pitts, *Alcoholism III. Psychiatric and Familial Psychiatric Illness in 259 Alcoholic Probands,* 23 Archives Gen Psychiatry 104 (1970).

[44] Diagnostic and Statistical Manual of Mental Disorders (3d ed 1980) (DSM-III).

[45] *See* §2.01.

[46] *See* Valliant & Perry, *Personality Disorders,* in Comprehensive Textbook of Psychiatry/IV 958-86 (4th ed 1985).

[47] Rainer, *Genetics & Psychiatry,* in Comprehensive Textbook of Psychiatry/IV 40 (4th ed 1985).

in their families, which tends to distinguish this disorder from antisocial behavior in general. At this point, very little else is known. The incidence of the 47 XYY disorder[48] is estimated to be in the range of 1 in 250 to 1 in 2000 infants, and there are a number of reports of individuals with the 47 XYY anomaly who have no history of antisocial behavior.[49] The current state of knowledge appears to place the relationship between the disorder and the behavior in the hypothetical but unproven category.

As the severity of the mental disorder decreases, the contribution of genetic factors seems to be less easily determined. However, a recent study of panic disorder found that the increasing risks of developing the disorder among first-degree relatives of panic disorder patients suggested a genetic component.[50] Panic disorder is characterized as an anxiety disorder by DSM-III and is marked by three panic attacks in a three-week period accompanied by a cluster of psychological and physical symptoms during the episode.[51]

Another study found a genetic component in the development of schizotypal, but not borderline, personality disorder.[52] Schizotypal personality disorder is characterized by the presence of peculiarities in thinking and a certain interpersonal aloofness while borderline personality disorder is marked more by the presence of impulsive behavior and intense, unstable interpersonal relationships along with problems tolerating being alone.[53]

§1.08 —Biochemical Theories

The biochemical theories of mental disorder have arisen from two primary sources. The first is experimentally induced psychoses using drugs. The second is the action of antipsychotic drugs on psychotic symptoms and brain chemistry.[54] As in the genetic research, more is known about the more serious disorders.

Theorizing about the biochemical basis of schizophrenic disorders

---

[48] Normal genotype is 46-Chromosome XY for males and 46-XX for females.

[49] Rainer, *supra* note 47, at 31.

[50] Crowe, Pauls, & Slymen, *A Family Study of Anxiety Neurosis: Morbidity Risk in Families of Patients With and Without Imitral Value Prolapse* 37 Archives Gen Psychiatry 77 (1980).

[51] DSM-III, *supra* note 44, at 231-32.

[52] Torgersen, *Genetic and Nosological Aspects of Schizotypal and Borderline Personality Disorders,* 41 Archives Gen Psychiatry 546 (1984).

[53] *See* DSM-III, *supra* note 44, at 311-12, 322-23.

[54] *See* §3.04.

has recently concentrated on the action of dopamine, a neurotransmitter. Dopamine is one of the chemicals responsible for transmitting nerve impulses over the microscopic distances between individual neurons in the brain. Dopamine is manufactured and stored in vesicles at the end of the neuron and is released when the neuron fires. It then crosses over to the *receiver* neuron and binds to a receptor site, like a key fitting into a lock. The more rapidly the neuron fires, the more dopamine is produced. Schizophrenic disorders are thought to be associated with an excess of dopamine.[55]

The evidence for the hypothesis is increasingly compelling. Antipsychotic drugs block dopamine receptor sites.[56] Drugs with stronger dopamine blocking properties are more potent antipsychotics. Antipsychotic medications produce side effects similar to Parkinson's disease, a syndrome known to be related to insufficient dopamine in specific brain areas.[57] Research which has induced schizophrenic-like psychoses has used amphetamines, drugs known to release stored dopamine and stimulate dopamine synthesis.[58]

The biochemistry of affective disorders[59] is somewhat more complicated, as several different theories have been proposed to explain the causes of depression and mania. The catecholamine hypothesis suggests that lowered brain levels of the neurotransmitter substance norepinephrine (NE) are associated with depression while elevated levels are associated with mania.[60] Two classes of antidepressant medications, tricyclics and monoamine oxidase inhibitors (MAOIs), both increase the levels of NE in the brain.[61]

The second theory proposes that depression is associated with decreases in serotonin, another neurotransmitter also called an indoleamine.[62] Both the catecholamine and the indoleamine hypotheses have

---

[55] Nicol & Gottesman, *Clues to the Genetics and Neurobiology of Schizophrenia*, 71 Am Scientist 398, 400 (1983).

[56] *Id*

[57] *Id.*

[58] *Id.*

[59] Affective disorders are disorders of mood, that is, mania or depression. *See* §2.03.

[60] Taska & Brodie, *New Trends in the Diagnosis and Treatment of Depression*, 44 J Clinical Psychiatry 11 (1983).

[61] *Id.*

[62] *Id.*

problems in that research hypotheses derived from the theories have not been supported by the research data.[63]

The third biochemical theory of depression suggests that yet another neurotransmitter is implicated in affective disorders. Increased levels of brain acetylcholine are associated with depression, and depletion is associated with mania. Neurons which use acetylcholine for their neurotransmitter substance are called cholinergic neurons. The action of tricyclic antidepressants, which are anticholinergic, supports this hypothesis.[64]

Recently, theories proposing that interactions between two or more neurotransmitters could account for affective disorders have been developed. One theory suggests that decreased serotonin levels account for the development of the illness, while the nature of the illness, whether manic or depressive, is determined by the level of activity of neurons using NE as a transmitter substance. Reduced NE results in a depressive illness, increased NE in mania.[65] Another interactionist theory postulates that the balance between the level of activity of cholinergic neurons and the NE neurons determines the individual's affective state.[66]

§1.09 Behavioral Theories

Behavioral theories reject the notion of underlying causes to mental disorders and focus instead on behavior. Within the behavioral school, a range of philosophical positions can be found. For the strict Skinnerian[67] behaviorist, the medical model is completely rejected and the behavior is identified as the problem. For other more moderate behaviorists, anxiety is seen as a symptom of an underlying problem, which can be alleviated by learning to reduce the maladaptive anxiety.[68] The cognitive behavior theorists have postulated that irrational self-verbalizations are the basis of maladaptive behavior.[69]

The primary assumption of the behavioral theories is that maladap-

---

[63] *Id.*

[64] *Id.*

[65] Prange, Wilson, & Lynn, *L-trytophan in Mania,* 30 Archives Gen Psychiatry 56 (1974).

[66] Mendels, Stern, & Frazer, *Biochemistry of Depression,* 37 Diseases Nervous System 3-9 (1976).

[67] B.F. Skinner is the leading American psychologist associated with contemporary operant behavior theory. *See* B.F. Skinner, About Behaviorism (1974). *See also* **§3.10.**

[68] D. Rimm & J. Masters, Behavior Therapy 4 (2d ed 1979).

[69] *Id* 5.

tive behavior is learned. Healthy and maladaptive behavior differ in their impact on the individual and others, but are fundamentally alike otherwise. However, modern behaviorists do not contend that behavior whose origin is traumatic head injury or genetic disorder is learned. Some theorists even acknowledge certain biological predispositions.[70]

One of differences among the behavioral theories is in their explanation of the way that maladaptive behavior is learned. The major dichotomy is between the operant learning school[71] and the classical conditioning school.[72] Each school is identified with a specific experimental methodology and a specific paradigm for the development of a problem behavior.

Classical conditioning was discovered and extensively explored by the Russian physiologist Pavlov. He was investigating the digestive system using dogs when he found that he could condition a salivary response to previously neutral stimuli, like bells or lights, by presenting both food and the bell together for several trials. Then he would just ring the bell and the dog would salivate just as if the food were present. Later, Pavlov investigated experimental neuroses by training his dogs to distinguish between two shapes. For example, presentation of a circle would be accompanied by food, and, therefore, salivation, while presentation of an ellipse would not. With each succeeding trial, the ellipse would become more and more round. Finally, the dog could no longer make the discrimination and would become very agitated, barking, biting the apparatus, and struggling to escape.[73]

Other theorists took this paradigm and applied it to problems of human behavior. Paralyzing anxiety was seen as a conditioned response, and phobias were thought to have been classically conditioned by some accidental event. In one controversial demonstration, a young child was placed in a room with a white rabbit. The child evidenced no fear and petted and played with the bunny without any behavioral disruption. The experimenter then made a very loud noise behind the child, sufficient to startle him and make him cry. The next time the child was placed in the room with the rabbit, he would not approach the animal

---

[70] *Id* 7.

[71] Operant learning is based on the principle that behavior which is rewarded will be repeated. An *operant* is a discrete bit of behavior.

[72] D. Rimm & J. Masters, *supra* note 68, at 2. *See also* **§3.10.**

[73] 1 I. Pavlov, Lectures on Conditioned Reflexes (1928).

and was apparently quite afraid of it. The experimenter had induced a *rabbit phobia* by classical conditioning in one trial.[74]

The other behavioral school utilized a different experimental paradigm. The operant conditioning paradigm used a rat in a Skinner box, named for the famous American psychologist who designed it. The basic box contained a lever which, when pushed by the animal, dispensed a food pellet to the hungry rat. The rate of reinforcement, that is, how many lever presses were required for a pellet, could be adjusted by the experimenter. The wire mesh grid upon which the rat stood could be electrified to give the rat a shock as a punishment. The operant theorists were interested in how the consequences of a behavior affected the probability of a behavior occurring again. They found that when a behavior is rewarded (positive reinforcement) it tends to be repeated.[75]

Applying the operant paradigm to problem behavior led to the development of behavior modification techniques. The operating assumption is that if a problematic behavior is being repeated frequently, it is being rewarded somehow. For example, if a child is playing and every time she begins to bother another child, the teacher comes over to talk to her, and she likes having the teacher talk to her, she will probably bother the other children more often. The teacher's attention is the positive reinforcement maintaining the problem behavior.

Since behaviorists reject trait theories of personality, they also reject the utility of psychological tests that measure traits.[76] Behavioral assessment techniques measure behavior which is the target of change. For example, an individual with complaints of anxiety might be hooked up to a biofeedback device[77] to obtain a baseline reading of muscle tension or galvanic skin response (GSR), both of which are physiological measures of anxiety, or might fill out a behavior checklist or take one home to be filled out by a teacher, parent, or friend based on observations of the individual's behavior.[78]

---

[74] Watson & Ranor, *Conditioned Emotional Reactions*, 3 J Experimental Psychology 1 (1920).

[75] *See* B.F. Skinner, About Behaviorism (1974).

[76] *See* **§2.10.**

[77] Biofeedback devices electronically amplify a signal from a device which records a biologically generated signal and feed it back to the patient as a visual or audio signal.

[78] *See* D. Rimm & J. Masters, *supra* note 68, at 18.

§1.10   Suggested Reading

Books

R. Blanck, & G. Blanck, *Ego Psychology: Theory and Practice* (1974).

N. Carlson, *Physiology of Behavior* (1977).

Diagnostic and Statistical Manual of Mental Disorders (3d ed 1980) (DSM-III).

H. Kaplan & B. Sadock, *Comprehensive Textbook of Psychiatry/IV* (1985).

R. Laing, *The Divided Self* (1965).

1 I. Pavlov, *Lectures on Conditioned Reflexes* (1928).

R. Price, *Abnormal Psychology: Perspectives in Conflict* (1978).

D. Rimm & J. Masters, *Behavior Therapy* (2d ed 1979).

B.F. Skinner, *About Behaviorism* (1974).

Articles

Albert, *Critique of Neurobiologic Paradigm,* in Models for Clinical Psychopathology 133 (1981).

Costeff, Cohen, & Weller, *Biological Factors in Mild Mental Retardation,* 75 Dev Med & Child Neurology 580 (1983).

Crowe, Pauls, & Slymen, *A Family Study of Anxiety Neurosis: Morbidity Risk in Families of Patients With and Without Imitral Value Prolapse,* 37 Archives Gen Psychiatry 77 (1980).

Freud, *The Ego and the Id,* in Standard Edition of the Complete Psychological Works of Sigmund Freud (1953-1966).

Freud, *Inhibitions, Symptoms and Anxiety,* in Standard Edition of the Complete Psychological Works of Sigmund Freud (1953-1966).

Freud, *Studies on Hysteria,* in Standard Edition of the Complete Psychological Works of Sigmund Freud (1953-1966).

Lishman, *The Apparatus of Mind: Brain Structure and Function in Mental Disorder,* 24 Psychosomatics 699 (1983).

Lishman, *Cerebral Disorder in Alcoholism. Syndromes of Impairment,* 104 Brain 1 (1981).

Meissner, *Theories of Personality and Psychopathology: Classical Psychoanalysis,* in Comprehensive Textbook of Psychiatry/IV 389-90 (4th ed 1985).

Mendels, Stern, & Frazer, *Biochemistry of Depression,* 37 Diseases Nervous System 3 (1976).

Michels, *The Psychoanalytic Paradigm,* in Models for Clinical Psychopathology (1981).

Nicol & Gottesman, *Clues to the Genetics and Neurobiology of Schizophrenia*, 71 Am Scientist 398 (1983).

Prange, Wilson, & Lynn, *L-trytophan in Mania*, 30 Archives Gen Psychiatry 56 (1974).

Rainer, *Genetics & Psychiatry*, in Comprehensive Textbook of Psychiatry/IV 40 (4th ed 1985).

Ron, Acker, & Shaw, *Computerized Tomography of the Brain in Chronic Alcoholism: A Survey and Follow-up Study*, 105 Brain 497 (1982).

Taska & Brodie, *New Trends in the Diagnosis and Treatment of Depression*, 44 J Clinical Psychiatry 11 (1983).

Torgersen, *Genetic and Nosological Aspects of Schizotypal and Borderline Personality Disorders*, 41 Archives Gen Psychiatry 546 (1984).

Valliant & Perry, *Personality Disorders*, in Comprehensive Textbook of Psychiatry/IV 958-86 (4th ed 1985).

Watson & Ranor, *Conditioned Emotional Reactions*, 3 J Experimental Psychology 1 (1920).

Winokur, Reich, Rimmer, & Pitts, *Alcoholism III: Psychiatric and Familial Psychiatric Illness in 259 Alcoholic Probands*, 23 Archives Gen Psychiatry 104 (1970).

2 Psychiatric and Psychological Diagnosis

§2.01 Introduction

The prevailing model of mental disorder in the United States is the medical or disease model. Its assumptions are inherent in the prevailing techniques for the diagnosis of mental disorders. The problem definition phase of this process is termed a diagnostic evaluation. Once a diagnosis is reached, a treatment should logically follow from that diagnosis. Finally, the diagnosis should suggest a prognosis, that is, what the outcome and consequences of the illness will be.

Diagnosis in medicine is the equivalent of classification and identification in biology. Diagnosis is the initial attempt to apply the scientific method of identification and classification of the *disease* to the difficulties of the individual patient. In psychiatry, diagnosis has been the subject of heated controversy, both inside and outside mental health professions, because of the potential social consequences of a psychiatric diagnosis. Most of the problems seem to occur at the interface of the mental health system and other social systems, such as the legal system. The evolution of a more complex diagnostic system in medicine has been cause for little legal concern, however, the evolution of a psychiatric diagnostic system has had direct legal consequences.

The law and psychiatry interface is complicated by different classification systems and different terminology. Insanity has no diagnostic classification that always fits the various legal criteria. An individual with a schizophrenic disorder may be legally responsible for criminal behavior, despite suffering from a major mental disorder. An individual who is not competent to stand trial may be retarded, schizophrenic, or delirious. The failure of legal and mental health professionals to recognize the difference in classification systems and the reasons for those differences can be a vicious trap for the unwary.

This chapter is a discussion and explanation of the diagnostic system currently in use by mainstream mental health professionals and is intended to give the reader a general understanding of diagnostic concepts and practices.

§2.02   Diagnostic Categories: DSM-III

The first edition of the Diagnostic and Statistical Manual (DSM-I) of the American Psychiatric Association (APA) was published in 1952. DSM-I was a pioneering effort to standardize psychiatric nomenclature and diagnosis in the United States. An increasingly international outlook in psychiatry prompted the APA to participate in the revision of the International Classification of Diseases, eighth edition (ICD-8), and this became the basis of DSM-II in 1968. As the work on ICD-9 neared completion, the APA decided that the ICD-9 classification of mental disorders was unsatisfactory for use in the United States and began work to expand and refine it for use by American psychiatrists.[1]

The Diagnostic and Statistical Manual-III (DSM-III) became the standard diagnostic system in the United States upon its approval in June of 1979 by the APA. Certain features of the new system provoked considerable controversy in the mental health community while other features were acknowledged as responsive to criticisms of the DSM-II diagnostic system which it replaced.

The introduction to DSM-III describes mental disorders as:

> [A] clinically significant behavioral or psychological syndrome or pattern that occurs in an individual and that is typically associated with either a painful symptom (distress) or impairment in one or more important areas of functioning (disability). In addition, there is an inference that there is a behavioral, psychological, or biological dysfunction, and that the disturbance is not only in the relationship between the individual and society.[2]

The consequence of this definition is that breaking a law is not in itself a mental disorder, nor is dropping out of society to live the life of a hermit because one believes that the quality of one's life is more important than money or power. A mental disorder is either subjectively uncomfortable to the individual who is ill or to those with whom the person has contact. For example, an individual with a bipolar disorder, manic type, might not feel any subjective distress, but her pacing, incessant talking, inability to sleep, and impulsive behavior would be disabling to her and troublesome to others.

The DSM-III takes a descriptive approach, since etiological (causal) factors for many disorders are unknown. The descriptive approach extends to the classification system as well, with disorders grouped together on the basis of shared clinical features when the etiology is unknown. The descriptive approach requires rather low-level inferences to make diagnostic decisions, which contributes to improved reliability over systems that require more and higher order inferences.[3]

§2.03 —Multiaxial Diagnosis

The DSM-III[4] inaugurated the use of a multiaxial diagnostic system

---

[1] Diagnostic and Statistical Manual of Mental Disorders 1 (3d ed 1980) (DSM-III).

[2] *Id* 6.

[3] *Id* 7.

[4] Diagnostic and Statistical Manual of Mental Disorders (3d ed 1980) (DSM-III).

as an aid to prognostic decision making and treatment planning. An individual receives a diagnosis on each of five axes, each of which communicates different information about the individual's clinical status and the history of the present problem.[5] A brief explanation of each axis follows:

> Axis I: Clinical Syndromes, that is symptom clusters, appear on this axis along with some other situations which are not mental disorders (e.g., malingering).
> Axis II: Personality Disorders in adults and Developmental Disorders in children appear on this axis.
> Axis III: Physical Disorders and Conditions are coded on this axis which are relevant to the management or treatment planning of the individual (e.g., diabetes).[6]

These three axes constitute the diagnosis for each individual. This system allows the clinician to report the complaints, symptoms, and psychological disturbances on Axis I, the patient's personality style on Axis II, and any relevant physical illness on Axis III.

An example of a diagnosis from a recent case might help to clarify the DSM-III system. After the commission of a serious crime, a man is interviewed by a psychologist in jail. During the interview, the man reveals that he does not remember the events surrounding the crime and has a history of violent episodes, none of which he remembers afterwards. He states that he believes that he will be released from jail and become President of the United States. He relates how all his employers have cheated him, and how women have used him for sex. He also relates that he has suffered numerous head injuries. Psychological testing and collateral interviews confirm this information. Neuropsychological testing reveals diffuse organic brain damage. The diagnosis arrived at from this information is:

> Axis I - 295.30 Organic Personality Syndrome
> Axis II - 301.00 Paranoid Personality Disorder
> Axis III - Diffuse Organic Brain Damage-Rule out Seizure Disorder

As is evident from this example, the major mental disorder was coded on Axis I, the personality style on Axis II, and the medical condition which could account for the syndrome on Axis III.

The two additional axes are intended to be used in research and

---

[5] *Id* 8.
[6] *Id* 23.

special clinical settings to provide additional information for treatment planning:

> Axis IV: Severity of Psychosocial Stressors. This axis allows coding of a rating of the level of stress the individual has experienced during the previous year (usually) on an eight-point scale. A rating of 1 is no stress while a 7 is given for catastrophic stress levels.
>
> Axis V: Highest Level of Adaptive Functioning Past Year. This axis contains a rating of the highest level of functioning in work, family and social relationships and psychological functioning during the preceding year.[7]

The five axes are a concise summary of a large amount of information regarding the individual's psychological status and social history.

§2.04   —Hierarchy of Disorders

The DSM-III[8] is organized in a hierarchical fashion so that disorders higher in the hierarchy and closer to the front of the manual may have clinical features similar to those lower in the hierarchy, but not the reverse. Accordingly, disorders that are more complex, that is, have more symptoms or clusters of symptoms necessary to the diagnosis, come first.[9] For example, anxiety is a symptom of many mental disorders, but if anxiety is the only symptom, then the clinician would rule out organic mental disorders, schizophrenic disorders, or affective disorders since each of these requires additional symptoms besides anxiety. This system allows construction of a series of clinical decision trees, that prevent multiple diagnoses from different classes of disorders, but allow multiple diagnoses within some classes of disorders. For example, since psychoses are higher in the decision tree than antisocial personality, any psychotic features such as delusions or hallucinations preclude a diagnosis of antisocial personality. One individual cannot be both in this system.

The DSM-III divides the mental disorders into a handful of larger categories under which the diagnostic classifications are clustered. The

---

[7] *Id* 26-30.

[8] Diagnostic and Statistical Manual of Mental Disorders (3d ed 1980) (DSM-III).

[9] *Id* 8.

major headings are themselves fairly descriptive and are listed below in the order in which they appear in the DSM-III.

Disorders Usually First Evident in Infancy, Childhood, or Adolescence

These disorders are those which typically affect children. They include mental retardation, autism, disorders affecting attention, conduct, eating, movement difficulties, or those with physical manifestations (e.g., stuttering or sleepwalking).[10]

Specific Developmental Disorders (Coded on Axis II)

This group of disorders is commonly called *learning disabilities* and they are commonly coded in Axis II.[11] It includes identifiable and delimited problems with reading, arithmetic, language, or combinations of these which are usually diagnosed by psychological testing.[12]

Organic Mental Disorders

The organic mental disorders are classified in two sections. One section contains disorders with causes that are other physical disorders or processes, like a fever-induced delirium, for example, caused by an infection. The other section contains mental disorders where the pathophysiological process is listed as part of the disorder. An example of this group would be alcohol hallucinosis, where alcohol ingestion leads to hallucinations.[13]

Substance Use Disorders

This group of disorders is listed by type of substance being abused, from alcohol to tobacco, and includes both abuse and dependence.[14]

Schizophrenic Disorders

These are the disorders usually identified by the layperson as making people *crazy*. The schizophrenic disorders include five subtypes from disorganized to residual. These disorders are manifested by peculiarities in thinking, by hallucinations (hearing voices) or delusions (mistak-

---

[10] *Id* 35.

[11] *See* **§2.02.**

[12] Diagnostic and Statistical Manual of Mental Disorders 92 (3d ed 1980) (DSM-III).

[13] *Id* 101.

[14] *Id* 128.

en beliefs about the nature of reality), and sometimes by bizarre speech or movements.[15]

Paranoid Disorders

The paranoid disorders are characterized by paranoid delusions or paranoid jealousy. A firmly held belief that someone is actively attempting to hurt the patient constitutes a paranoid delusion, provided there is no factual basis for the belief. One form of this delusion would be the belief that the CIA, FBI, or some other agency is monitoring the patient's activities because he heard some static on his telephone.[16]

Psychotic Disorders Not Elsewhere Classified

The disorders in this category are those for which the duration of the symptoms is insufficient to classify the disorder as schizophrenia, or those that do not fit the criteria for any other major psychotic disorder.[17]

Affective Disorders (Disorders of Mood)

The disorders of mood include elevated mood (mania) as well as depressed mood (depression), or a combination of both (bipolar disorder or cyclothymic disorder, if not as severe). What used to be called neurotic depression is classified here as dysthymic disorder.[18]

Anxiety Disorders

The anxiety disorders include anxiety attacks, panic attacks, and the phobias (irrational fears), such as social phobia and agoraphobia (fear of open spaces). Also grouped here is the post-traumatic stress disorder, the so-called combat fatigue disorder that has been used in criminal defense cases of Vietnam veterans.[19]

Somatoform Disorders

These disorders are characterized by physical symptoms for which no organic cause can be found and for which there is a strong presumption of psychological causation. The disorders range from vague complaints to dramatic paralysis of arms or legs. These disorders should not be confused with malingering or faking, as there is no conscious awareness

---

[15] *Id* 181.
[16] *Id* 195.
[17] *Id* 199.
[18] *Id* 205.
[19] *Id* 225.

of or intent to manifest these symptoms.[20]

Dissociative Disorders

The essential feature of this group of disorders is a loss of integration and conscious control of motor behavior, identity, or consciousness. This problem might be manifested by the complete loss of one's identity and the assumption of an entirely new one, either for a short time, as in multiple personality, or for a long period, as in psychogenic fugue. Alternatively, it could be manifested as loss of memory for important events, as in psychogenic amnesia.[21]

Psychosexual Disorders

The difficulties in sexual identification or sexual functioning for which no organic etiology exists are listed here. This may range from transsexualism (wishing to be a member of the opposite sex), transvestism (cross-dressing for sexual excitement), or inhibited sexual desire.[22]

Factitious Disorders

Factitious symptoms are those produced by an individual under voluntary control. It is the voluntary control that separates these disorders from the somatoform disorders. The lack of obvious goals or gains to be derived from the symptoms distinguishes these disorders from malingering, where the payoff may be quite evident.[23]

Disorders of Impulse Control Not Elsewhere Classified

These disorders are characterized by the inability to control impulses to steal, set fires, gamble, or explode in a rage. There is usually increasing tension prior to these acts with a sense of relief afterwards, and there may or may not be feelings of guilt or regret as well.[24]

Adjustment Disorder

An adjustment disorder is a maladaptive response to an identifiable psychosocial stressor that occurs within three months of the stressor. The result is a problem in occupational or personal functioning out of

---

[20] *Id* 241.
[21] *Id* 253.
[22] *Id* 261.
[23] *Id* 285.
[24] *Id* 291.

proportion to the stressor. The symptom or symptoms do not meet the criteria for any other mental disorder discussed above.[25]

Psychological Factors Affecting Physical Condition

This category allows the clinician to indicate that psychological factors may be interacting with a physical illness in some way which has important implications for the individual. For example, an individual with a paranoid disorder may refuse to take her insulin for her diabetes because she thinks it is poison.[26]

Personality Disorders (Coded on Axis II)

These disorders may be diagnosed in children and adolescents in unusual cases, but usually cannot be diagnosed until adulthood when the individual's patterns of relating have solidified. Personality disorders must be distinguished from personality traits, which are characteristic patterns of thinking and relating which are not so inflexible as to cause the individual problems. A personality disorder is an exaggerated and problematic version of a trait.[27]

Codes for Conditions Not Attributable to a Mental Disorder That Are a Focus of Attention or Treatment

DSM-III recognizes that problems exist that might prompt an individual to seek professional consultation which are not mental disorders. These include such difficulties as borderline intellectual functioning, bereavement, marital problems, or parent-child problems.[28]

The major diagnostic categories are explained in some detail in **§2.06**. The terms used as headings are defined and clarified there as well.

§2.05   Basic Diagnostic Theory

There are certain characteristics that are fundamental to the evolution of a discipline from a philosophy into a science. Development of a classification system is one of those characteristics, since the ability to sort objects or disorders into classes is a first step to the study and understanding of the basic processes of nature. The social sciences (psychology, anthropology, sociology) are confronted with difficulties not usually faced in the natural sciences (biology, physics, geology),

---

[25] *Id* 299.

[26] *Id* 303.

[27] *Id* 305.

[28] *Id* 331.

although they are shared with other clinical sciences, such as medicine. While there is general agreement among biologists about the differences between pine trees and oak trees, and the characteristics of each species that define it, similar agreement is much less frequent in the social sciences. This lack of agreement arises from difficulties in defining, reproducing, and recording the phenomena which are the object of study, discrete bits of human behavior. The lack of agreement about the nature of reality gives rise to two major classes of diagnostic problems in psychiatry: validity and reliability.

As in any science, classification, called diagnosis in psychiatry, relies on the observations of a trained observer. What distinguishes psychiatry and psychology from the natural sciences is that what is being observed may be profoundly affected by the actions of the observer.[29] In addition, no biologist has to cope with a leaf capable of hiding its shape or color because it does not want to be observed. Furthermore, few biologists have such strong feelings about pines or oaks that those feelings are likely to affect substantially their perceptions or memories of their observation of a tree. However, that is precisely what can happen to a diagnostician, and these individual variations in perception and memory can introduce uncertainty into classification systems.

Consequently, there is a need to quantify both the amount and the kind of uncertainty. Uncertainty in psychiatry has profound human consequences, since accurate diagnosis (problem definition) is essential to good treatment (problem solution). Accurate diagnosis is also essential to making good prognostic judgments. Uncertainty therefore makes psychiatry a probabilistic science. While the apple will always drop from the tree, a drop in mood is not always depression; but, a drop in mood increases the odds that the individual is depressed.

Validity is a determination of whether a set of characteristics defines what it is supposed to define, or for a test, whether it measures the characteristic it is intended to measure.[30] Reliability, on the other hand, is a determination of how often there is agreement about whether those characteristics are present. For a test, reliability is a measure of the tendency to get the same score when repeatedly measuring the same thing.[31]

A concrete metaphor will help clarify the distinction between validity and reliability. Assume that the psychiatric diagnosis in question is the bull's eye on a target, and the diagnostic process is a dart game. The

---

[29] *See* S. Garfield, Clinical Psychology 93-99 (1983).

[30] *Id* 111.

[31] *Id* 32.

validity of the dart toss is measured by how close to the bull's eye the dart hits, while the reliability is measured by how close together the darts cluster. High reliability can be attained by having all the darts within the same small circle at the edge of the target, since reliability is independent of validity.

DSM-III[32] leans in the direction of of improving the reliability of the psychiatric diagnostic system by making diagnostic criteria more concrete, behavioral, and observable, and by attempting to reduce to a minimum the amount of inference required to make a diagnosis. For the first time, videotaping of interviews allowed the developers of DSM-III to train clinicians to use the system uniformly, thus increasing reliability.[33] The question of validity of the DSM-III diagnostic system has been the subject of much debate, which is summarized in §2.11.

§2.06 Major Disorderes

The major psychiatric disorders are discussed below in order of decreasing severity, with the most severe and disruptive disorders first. The defining criteria are those listed in DSM-III.[34] This is not intended to be a comprehensive treatise on psychopathology. For further information, the reader should consult Chapter 5 for research literature in the mental health field.

§2.07 —Schizophrenic Disorders

The psychoses are the most severe mental disorders in the diagnostic system. A *psychosis* is defined as the loss of contact with reality accompanied by personality disintegration.[35] The schizophrenic disorders are the largest class of psychoses. DSM-III[36] considers the schizophrenic disorders to be defined by onset before age 45, duration of at least six months, deterioration from a previous level of functioning, characteristic symptoms during the active phase of the illness, and

---

[32] Diagnostic and Statistical Manual of Mental Disorders (3d ed 1980) (DSM-III).

[33] Lerman, *The Advantages of DSM-III*, 141 Am J Psychiatry 541 (1984).

[34] Diagnostic and Statistical Manual of Mental Disorders (3d ed 1980) (DSM-III).

[35] See Diagnostic and Statistical Manual of Mental Disorders (3d ed 1980) (DSM-III) for types of mental disorders which may be so classified: schizophrenic disorders, organic mental disorders, affective disorders.

[36] *Id.*

psychotic features.[37] Onset of the same symptoms after age 45 is diagnosed as atypical psychosis.[38] Duration of symptoms of less than six months is diagnosed as schizophreniform disorder, while duration of two weeks or less is diagnosed as brief reactive psychosis according to DSM-III.[39] Thus, even though the introduction to the section in DSM-III indicates that the boundaries of the disorder are unclear, the criteria draw clear demarcations for purposes of diagnostic reliability. The DSM-III criteria for schizophrenic disorders follow as they appear in the manual:

Diagnostic criteria for Schizophrenic Disorder
A. At least one of the following during a phase of the illness:
    (1) bizarre delusions (content is patently absurd and has no possible basis in fact), such as delusions of being controlled, thought broadcasting, thought insertion, or thought withdrawal
    (2) somatic, grandiose, religious, nihilistic, or other delusions without persecutory or jealous content
    (3) delusions with persecutory or jealous content if accompanied by hallucinations of any type
    (4) auditory hallucinations in which either a voice keeps up a running commentary on the individual's behavior or thoughts, or two or more voices converse with each other
    (5) auditory hallucinations on several occasions with content of more than one or two words, having no apparent relation to depression or elation
    (6) incoherence, marked loosening of associations, markedly illogical thinking, or marked poverty of content of speech if associated with at least one of the following:
        (a) blunted, flat, or inappropriate affect
        (b) delusions or hallucinations
        (c) catatonic or other grossly disorganized behavior
B. Deterioration from a previous level of functioning in such areas as work, social relations, and self-care.
C. Duration: Continuous signs of the illness for at least six months at some time during the person's life, with some signs of the illness present. The six-month period must include an active

---

[37] *Id* 182-88.
[38] *Id* 202.
[39] *Id* 201-02.

phase during which there were symptoms from A, with or without a prodromal or residual phase, as defined below.

> Prodromal phase: A clear deterioration in functioning before the active phase of the illness not due to a disturbance in mood or to a Substance Use Disorder and involving at least two of the symptoms noted below. Residual phase: Persistence, following the active phase of the illness, of at least two of the symptoms noted below, not due to a disturbance in mood or to a Substance Use Disorder.

Prodromal or Residual Symptoms
(1)   social isolation or withdrawal
(2)   marked impairment in role functioning as wage earner, student, or homemaker
(3)   markedly peculiar behavior (e.g., collecting garbage, talking to self in public, or hoarding food)
(4)   marked impairment in personal hygiene and grooming
(5)   blunted, flat, or inappropriate affect
(6)   digressive, vague, overelaborate, circumstantial, or metaphorical speech
(7)   odd or bizarre ideation, or magical thinking, e.g., superstitiousness, clairvoyance, telepathy, "sixth sense", "others can feel my feelings", overvalued ideas, ideas of reference
(8)   unusual perceptual experiences, e.g., recurrent illusions, sensing the presence of a force or person not actually present

Examples: Six months of prodromal symptoms with one week of symptoms from A; no prodromal symptoms with six months of symptoms from A; no prodromal symptoms with two weeks of symptoms from A and six months of residual symptoms; six months of symptoms from A, apparently followed by several years of complete remission, with one week of symptoms in A in current episode.

D.   The full depressive or manic syndrome (criteria A and B of major depressive or manic episode), if present, developed after any psychotic symptoms, or was brief in duration relative to the duration of the psychotic symptoms in A.

E.   Onset of prodromal or active phase of the illness before age 45.

F.   Not due to any Organic Mental Disorder or Mental Retardation.[40]

Notice that the criteria for the disorder encompass inclusion and exclusion items.

The DSM-III includes five types of schizophrenic disorders into which the individual's current symptom picture is to be classified. They are: disorganized type, catatonic type, paranoid type, undifferentiated type, and residual type.[41] Individuals with schizophrenic disorders usually manifest those symptoms that laypeople consider crazy: auditory hallucinations (hearing voices) and a variety of delusions; bizarre and frequently ritualistic behavior; and, in the case of the paranoid type, violence may be present. Those who are not in the active phase of the illness may not seem ill at all, as only a skilled interviewer may be able to elicit the signs of the disorder.

§2.08   —Organic Mental Disorders

The next most serious group of disorders is organic mental disorders. DSM-III[42] divides them into two traditional groups: those attributable to the aging of the brain itself, and those whose cause is the ingestion of some substance.[43] The former group are chronic and irreversible; the latter, acute and generally treatable.

Organic brain syndrome refers to a cluster of symptoms without reference to cause in DSM-III and should not be confused with the organic mental disorder where an etiology is either known or assumed. The organic brain syndromes are grouped into six types depending on the types of symptom clusters which are present. In both delirium and dementia, global impairment of thinking ability (cognitive impairment) is present. In the amnestic syndrome (loss of of memory) and organic hallucinosis, specific cognitive areas are adversely affected. The organic delusional syndrome and the organic affective syndrome resemble schizophrenic and affective disorders, respectively, in their clinical presentation but are distinguished by an identifiable organic etiology. Organic personality syndrome is characterized by changes in personality as a result of toxic or traumatic injury to the brain. Disorders related to intoxication and withdrawal are always associated with ingestion of

---

[40] *Id* 188-90 reprinted by permission.

[41] *Id* 190-93.

[42] Diagnostic and Statistical Manual of Mental Disorders (3d ed 1980) (DSM-III).

[43] *Id* 101.

an identifiable substance. The final organic brain syndrome in DSM-III is the residual category for disorders which do not fit elsewhere: atypical or mixed organic brain syndrome.[44] Diagnostic criteria for each of these syndromes are given in the beginning of the section on organic mental disorders in the DSM-III. The name of a syndrome plus an identifiable etiology usually are combined to form the names of the organic mental disorders.

One specific organic brain syndrome which may be encountered by an attorney in estate planning practice is dementia. The DSM-III criteria for a dementia are reproduced below.

Diagnostic criteria for Dementia

A.   A loss of intellectual abilities of sufficient severity to interfere with social or occupational functioning.

B.   Memory impairment.

C.   At least one of the following:
   (1)   impairment of abstract thinking, as manifested by con-crete interpretation of proverbs, inability to find similari-ties and differences between related words, difficulty in defining words and concepts, and other similar tasks
   (2)   impaired judgment
   (3)   other disturbances of higher cortical function, such as aphasia (disorder of language due to brain dysfunction), apraxia (inability to carry out motor activities despite intact comprehension and motor function), agnosia (fail-ure to recognize or identify objects despite intact sensory function), "constructional difficulty" (e.g., inability to copy three dimensional figures, assemble blocks, or arrange sticks in specific designs)
   (4)   personality change, i.e., alteration or accentuation of premorbid traits

D.   State of consciousness not clouded (i.e., does not meet the criteria for Delirium or Intoxication, although these may be superimposed)

E.   Either (1) or (2):
   (1)   evidence from the history, physical examination, or laboratory tests, of a specific organic factor that is judged to be etiologically related to the disturbance
   (2)   in the absence of such evidence, an organic factor necessary for the development of the syndrome can be

---

[44] *Id* 103.

presumed if conditions other than Organic Mental Disorders have been reasonably excluded and if the behavioral change represents cognitive impairment in a variety of areas[45]

Once a dementia is diagnosed, then the clinician must decide which kind it is. The criteria for one type follow:

Diagnostic criteria for Primary Degenerative Dementia
A. Dementia.
B. Insidious onset with uniformly progressive deteriorating course.
C. Exclusion of all other specific causes of Dementia by the history, physical examination, laboratory tests.[46]

The same diagnostic process applies for the rest of the organic disorders, with the organic brain syndrome being delimited first, and then fit into an etiology to make the organic mental disorder diagnosis.

§2.09 —Affective Disorders

In order of decreasing severity, the affective disorders are the next group of disorders defined by DSM-III.[47] An affective disorder is a disorder of mood, usually resulting in depression, but sometimes in mania. To be classified as an affective disorder in DSM-III, the cause of the mood disturbance must not be any other physical or mental disorder. Three groups of affective disorders appear in DSM-III: major affective disorder, other specific affective disorders, and atypical affective disorders.[48]

The major affective disorders are bipolar disorder and major depression which are distinguished by whether the individual has ever had a manic episode; if so, the diagnosis is bipolar disorder. Diagnostic criteria for both manic and depressive episodes are included in the DSM-III, along with a discussion of factors to aid in differential diagnosis from the organic and schizophrenic disorders.[49]

---

[45] *Id* 111-12 reprinted by permission.

[46] *Id* 126 reprinted by permission.

[47] Diagnostic and Statistical Manual of Mental Disorders (3d ed 1980) (DSM-III).

[48] *Id* 205.

[49] *Id* 207-08.

The criteria for a major depressive disorder in DSM-III are listed below:

Diagnostic criteria for Major Depressive Disorder

A. Dysphoric mood or loss of interest or pleasure in all or almost all activities or pastimes. The dysphoric mood is characterized by symptoms such as the following: depressed, sad, blue, hopeless, low, down in the dumps, irritable. The mood disturbance must be prominent and relatively persistent, but not necessarily the most dominant symptom, and does not include momentary shifts from one dysphoric mood to another dysphoric mood, e.g., anxiety to depression to anger, such as are seen in states of acute psychotic turmoil. (For children under six, dysphoric mood may have to be inferred from a persistently sad facial expression.)

B. At least four of the following symptoms have each been present nearly every day for a period of at least two weeks (in children under six, at least three of the first four).

(1) poor appetite or significant weight loss (when not dieting) or increased appetite and significant weight gain (in children under six, failure to make expected weight gains)

(2) insomnia or hypersomnia

(3) psychomotor agitation or retardation (but not merely subjective feelings of restlessness or being slowed down) (in children under six, hypoactivity)

(4) loss of interest or pleasure in usual activities, or decrease in sexual drive not limited to a period when delusional or hallucinating (in children under six, signs of apathy)

(5) loss of energy; fatigue

(6) feelings of worthlessness, self-reproach, or excessive or inappropriate guilt (either may be delusional)

(7) complaints or evidence of diminished ability to think or concentrate, such as slowed thinking, or indecisiveness not associated with marked loosening of associations or incoherence

(8) recurrent thoughts of death, suicidal ideation, wishes to be dead, or suicide attempt

C. Neither of the following dominate the clinical picture when an affective syndrome (i.e., criteria A and B above) is not present, that is, before it developed or after it remitted:

(1) preoccupation with a mood-incongruent delusion or

hallucination (definition given elsewhere in DSM-III, Ed.)

(2)   bizarre behavior

D.   Not superimposed on either Schizophrenia, Schizophreniform Disorder, or a Paranoid Disorder.

E.   Not due to any Organic Mental Disorder or Uncomplicated Bereavement.[50]

The next category of disorders would have been called neuroses in DSM-II. Now, cyclothymic disorder, characterized by mood swings, but not severe enough to be a bipolar disorder, and dysthymic disorder, formerly called depressive neurosis, are grouped together in the category of other specific affective disorders. These two disorders are substantially less disruptive of an individual's functioning than the major affective disorders, but the boundaries between the two classes of affective disorders are hard to define.[51]

As in the other categories of disorders, the atypical affective disorder is a catchall category for those disorders which do not fit the criteria for the other affective disorders.[52]

§2.10   —Other Mental Disorders

Moving further up the ladder in the direction of increasing mental health and decreasing severity of illness, the anxiety disorders are a new category inaugurated by DSM-III.[53] They encompass those disorders usually described as neuroses whose primary unifying characteristic is the presence of severe anxiety as one of the primary complaints.[54]

Somatoform disorders are those psychological disorders which manifest themselves as physical symptoms for which no physical etiology can be found and for which some evidence exists that there is a link to some psychological conflict. These disorders range from hypochondriasis to conversion disorder, and, because of the nature of the disorders, are usually discovered in a medical context. For example, the victim of an automobile accident may be found to be unable to walk in the hospital even though no organic injury can be found after

---

[50] *Id* 213-15 reprinted by permission.

[51] *Id* 218-23.

[52] *Id* at 223-24.

[53] Diagnostic and Statistical Manual of Mental Disorders (3d ed 1980) (DSM-III).

[54] *Id* 225.

extensive testing. Psychological testing may reveal the test pattern characteristic typical of a conversion disorder.[55] The DSM-III criteria are reproduced below:

Diagnostic criteria for Conversion Disorder
A. The predominant disturbance is a loss of or alteration in physical functioning suggesting a physical disorder.
B. Psychological factors are judged to be etiologically involved in the symptom, as evidenced by one of the following:
   (1) there is a temporal relationship between an environmental stimulus that is apparently related to a psychological conflict or need and the initiation or exacerbation of the symptom
   (2) the symptom enables the individual to avoid some activity that is noxious to him or her
   (3) the symptom enables the individual to get support from the environment that otherwise might not be forthcoming
C. It has been determined that the symptom is not under voluntary control.
D. The symptom cannot, after appropriate investigation, be explained by a known physical disorder or pathophysiological mechanism.
E. The symptom is not limited to pain or to a disturbance in sexual functioning.
F. Not due to Somatization Disorder or Schizophrenia.[56]

All of the disorders discussed above are coded on Axis I in the DSM-III system.[57] Axis II is reserved for coding of personality disorders in adults, as an individual can receive an Axis II diagnosis even if no diagnosis is given for Axis I.

Personality traits are patterns of thinking, acting, and relating to self and others that are relatively constant regardless of situation or social context. When these traits are so inflexible or problematic as to cause difficulties for the individual or for those who have contact with the individual, then they constitute personality disorders. Isolated episodes of a problematic behavior are not sufficient to diagnose a personality disorder; the pattern must have emerged during adolescence and

---

[55] *Id* 244.
[56] *Id* 247 reprinted by permission.
[57] *See* §2.03.

continued into adulthood. DSM-III allows the clinician to diagnose more than one personality disorder if the evidence warrants multiple diagnoses. Some of the adult personality disorders have childhood precursors since maladaptive styles may emerge during childhood or adolescence in sufficient intensity to make them the focus of professional attention.[58] DSM-III recognizes 11 types of personality disorders and one residual category for those not classifiable as one of the other 11.

§2.11 Criticisms of DSM-III

The adoption of the DSM-III[59] by the American Psychiatric Association (APA) capped a long period of intensive debate both within and without the association. The debate produced some rather stinging criticisms of the new diagnostic system. Some of those criticisms are outlined below.

It has been argued that DSM-III places too much emphasis on reliability at the expense of validity.[60] DSM-III incorporates a fixed-rule diagnostic approach that is the natural outgrowth of the assumption that individuals manifesting similar clinical pictures should receive the same diagnosis regardless of the geographical location or clinical setting. This fixed-rule system is composed of a list of symptoms for a given disorder, along with a rule that provides that if an individual manifests, for example, for or more of the symptoms listed, that individual will receive that diagnosis. An individual with the same cluster of symptoms minus one will receive a different diagnosis even though the same treatment may be indicated for the problem.[61] Thus, a basic goal of any diagnostic system, classification for treatment, is not accomplished.

Some critics contend that DSM-III takes a reductionistic approach by ignoring the reality of continua in psychological phenomena. In contrast to some medical problems, like pregnancy, where clear distinctions are possible (pregnant or not pregnant) few mental disorders are so clearly defined.[62] Fixed-rule diagnosis and symptom lists led to an increase in the number of categories of diagnoses which is needlessly complex. At the same time, the term *neurosis* was

---

[58] DSM-III, *supra* note 53, at 305.

[59] Diagnostic and Statistical Manual of Mental Disorders (3d ed 1980) (DSM-III).

[60] Valliant, *The Disadvantages of DSM-III*, 141 Am J Psychiatry 545 (1984).

[61] Finn, *Base Rates, Utilities, and DSM-III: Shortcomings of Fixed Rule Systems of Psychodiagnosis*, 91 J Abnormal Psychology 294 (1982).

[62] *Id* 543.

abandoned even though it had a long history because of its association with Freud and psychoanalytic theory.[63]

DSM-III emphasizes current symptoms at the expense of long-term clinical course. As noted in the section on schizophrenic disorders, an individual with exactly the same symptoms will change diagnoses from brief reactive psychosis to schizophreniform psychosis to schizophrenic disorder with no change in symptoms at all as the duration of symptoms moves from two weeks to six months.[64]

DSM-III's attempts to improve reliability confuses symptoms with diseases and fails to acknowledge the role of psychodynamics in the development of symptoms. And, it ignores the significance of symptoms as attempts at communication, particularly within the family context.[65]

The implications of these criticisms for the legal practitioner may be difficult to understand, but they may have significant consequences. First, the DSM-III is a descriptive diagnostic system as contrasted with a dynamic diagnostic system. When presenting an individual's story in litigating a case, the DSM-III diagnosis is not likely to communicate much in the way of understandable human pathos. It does not help to explain the *why* the individual is suffering, only the *what*. A dynamic diagnostic system would focus more on the *why* at the expense of consensus about the *what*.

The more severe the disorder, the greater the reliability of the diagnosis. The highest rate of agreement among clinicians in the DSM-III field trials was for the affective disorders, then the schizophrenic disorders, followed by the substance use disorders. The reliability of personality disorders diagnosis is much lower, and the reliability for the dissociative disorders is very low.[66] These data suggest that the DSM-III is not equally reliable across the diagnostic spectrum, and this must be recognized when presenting or impeaching psychiatric testimony.

More restrictive and definitive diagnostic protocols are being used by researchers but were not adopted by the APA. Since the DSM-III was drafted by a committee and adopted by a professional organization, it is, to some extent, a politicized document.[67] Physicists do not vote on

---

[63] Valliant, *supra* note 60, at 543.

[64] *Id* 544.

[65] *Id* 545.

[66] DSM-III, *supra* note 59, at 470. *See* Frances, *DSM-III Personality Disorders Section: A Commentary*, 137 Am J Psychiatry 1050 (1980).

[67] Schacht, *DSM-III and the Politics of Truth*, 40 Am Psychologist 513 (1985). *But see* Spitzer, *DSM-III and the Politics-Science Dichotomy Syndrome*, 40 Am Psychologist 522 (1985).

whether some phenomenon should be included in the body of physical fact, but psychiatrists did vote to include tobacco and caffeine abuse as mental disorders and to exclude egosyntonic homosexuality.[68]

§2.12   Diagnostic Procedures

Diagnostic techniques in psychiatry depend to a large extent on reports from the patient, and to a lesser extent on observable signs and symptoms. Diagnosis is complicated by a number of factors that may lead to distortions, omissions, or outright falsification of crucial information by the patient for any number of conscious or unconscious reasons. Diagnosis of some severe psychoses may be made quite reliably on the basis of observing acute symptoms while diagnosis of a personality disorder could almost never be made without the information acquired from a history and interview.

Since the diagnostic system requires the elimination of physical causes as etiological factors to make psychiatric diagnoses, routine physical and neurological examinations may be necessary first steps in psychiatric diagnosis. The steps in an ideal diagnostic procedure are outlined in the sections that follow. In practice, very few diagnostic procedures encompass all these steps, unless there are indications along the way that all these procedures are necessary to a diagnosis and formulation of a treatment plan.

§2.13   —Medical Examinations

Physical Examination

Physical examinations are nearly always necessary precursors to psychiatric diagnostic procedures to rule out a physical etiology for the presenting complaints or symptoms. For example, consider a patient seeking psychotherapy after suffering *panic attacks* at work. After about three months of psychotherapy, the patient suffered an automobile accident after *blacking out.* A series of tests including a detailed computerized axial tomography (CAT) scan of her brain revealed a very small temporal lobe tumor, which had been triggering seizure activity that had been mistaken for panic attacks.

Secondarily, some widely prescribed medications for chronic health

---

68 *See* DSM-III, *supra* note 60, at 16-18. *See* Spitzer, *The Diagnostic Status of Homosexuality in DSM-III: A Reformulation of the Issues,* 138 Am J Psychiatry 210 (1981).

difficulties, such as hypertension, have side effects in some patients that resemble mental disorders.[69] Thorough and systematic elimination of probable physical etiology prior to beginning the psychiatric diagnostic process is essential to good diagnosis.

The standard physical examination consists of a systematic examination of all the major organ systems, routinely including examination of the eyes, ears, mouth, and throat. Respiration rate, pulse rate, and blood pressure are measured and recorded. Heart, lungs, and other internal organs are examined by auscultation using a stethoscope. Blood and urine samples may be collected and analyzed.[70] This analysis is usually performed by an internist, although it could be performed by a psychiatrist or neurologist.

If the physical examination reveals no physical problem or disease which accounts for the symptoms of which the patient complains, then the referral for psychiatric/psychological evaluation can be made. If the physical examination reveals signs or symptoms of problems in the brain or spinal cord which could account for the patient's difficulties, the patient should be referred for neurological evaluation.

Neurological Examination

Where the presenting complaint suggests the possibility of a neurological disorder as the etiology of the symptoms, the physician who performs the physical examination may refer the patient for neurological evaluation. The boundary between neurology and psychiatry is not clearly defined, but any disorder that may have as its etiology a change in brain structure is usually considered the province of a neurologist. That change may be the result of a disease, such as Alzheimer's disease, or of an accident or tumor.

The standard neurological examination consists of a detailed examination of the patient's nerves and reflexes, as well as the patient's sensory system and motor abilities. Tests of coordination and of stance and gait are included. Speech is evaluated along with level of consciousness, orientation, and attitude toward being examined. The skull and the spine are inspected, and the carotid pulse is palpated and observed via stethoscope. (The carotid artery runs through the neck to the head.) A thorough neurological examination attempts to identify indications of damage to the brain and spinal cord which may be causes of psychiatric symptoms. If the examination reveals abnormalities which cannot definitively be diagnosed, then more intensive testing will be

---

[69] See J. Allen & B. Allen, Guide to Psychiatry 39 (1978).
[70] See, e.g., G. Wolf, Collecting Data from Patients (1977).

done. These tests might range from electromyography (EMG) to check muscle functions to a CAT scan to look for tumors or lesions in the brain.[71]

§2.14   —Clinical Psychiatric Interview

History

History taking serves two important purposes during the clinical interview. The first is to gather important information about the presenting complaint and its course as well as the patient's background and family without which diagnosis is impossible. The second is to establish rapport with patients to enable them to tell even those things which make them uncomfortable.[72]

A systematically acquired history would include the following information:

1. When the difficulties started.

2. What precipitated the disorder, if anything. Stressful life events are frequently identifiable.

3. How the symptoms developed. The prognostic implications may be entirely different if the onset was slow and insidious rather than acute.

4. The current severity of the disorder and the amount of subjective distress reported by the patient. These factors have important implications for both treatment and prognosis.[73]

In addition to defining these elements of the presenting complaint, the history should examine the patient's personal history in detail. Each of the following areas should be the subject of inquiry:

1. Infancy and early childhood. This information is sometimes difficult to ascertain, as patients are frequently unable to remember much about their early years. Any family or medical difficulties should be noted along with any psychological difficulties dating from this period.

2. Childhood and adolescence. This period is centered around

---

[71] E. Bickerstaff, Neurological Examination in Clinical Practice 338 (3d ed 1978).

[72] J. Leff & A. Isaacs, Psychiatric Examination in Clinical Practice 8 (1981).

[73] *Id* 9-11.

school, family, and friends for most individuals, and each of these areas should be discussed. Adolescence brings expanded social and sexual awareness, and these factors should be examined also.

3.   Occupational history. This period begins at the end of formal schooling for most individuals. Patterns in types of jobs, job difficulties and achievements, work style, income levels and job satisfaction all may be important.

4.   Sexual adjustment and relationship history. A thorough dating and sexual history may reveal patterns important to diagnosis. If married, the patient's courtship and current marital and sexual relationship should be discussed. Current status of any children may be relevant.

5.   Present social circumstances. Occupation, income, hobbies, leisure activities, and living arrangements all help to paint the picture of the patient's current life.[74]

The history will be complete when the patient's health history has been discussed, with special emphasis on any personal or family psychiatric history. An inquiry into any past or current legal difficulties is always indicated.

Mental Status Examination

The mental status examination (MSE) is a structured format for the comprehensive evaluation of the patient's current psychological functioning by means of an interview and a few simple tests.[75] Since this is often the primary basis for expert testimony by a psychiatrist, the MSE will be examined in detail. The MSE begins when the interviewer first sees the patient. Observations about the patient's style and manner of dress are noted. Of interest are unusual combinations of clothing, clothing that is not appropriate to the age or sex of the patient, that is excessively revealing, or that is accompanied by unusual accessories. The individual's personal hygiene is also noted. An attempt is made to observe the patient's gait. Abnormal movements or unusual speed (very fast or very slow) are noted. The quality of the patient's motor behavior may be revealing. This behavior could range from fidgeting to stereotyped movements or posturing to incessant pacing.[76]

The social behavior and style of personal interaction is usually tracked

---

[74] *Id* 15-20.
[75] *Id* 25.
[76] *Id* 25-29.

throughout the interview along with the patient's verbal behavior. The rate and quality of speech is noted for unusual features. The volume and tonal quality may give important clues about mood disorders or about affective blunting. Unusual speech may be present, as in psychotic patients who may make up new words called neologisms. Unusual speech patterns may be indicative of unusual thinking patterns, especially in the more severe disorders. Vague speech is characteristic of schizophrenic disorders.[77]

The patient should be questioned about hallucinations and delusions. Visual and auditory hallucinations should be clearly distinguished, and their frequency and duration should be determined if possible. Sometimes hallucinations may be experienced in other sensory modalities, such as taste (gustatory), touch (tactile), or smell (olfactory). Delusions may be paranoid, grandiose, religious, nihilistic, sexual, or hypochondriacal.[78]

An assessment of the patient's judgment should be made to evaluate self care ability and avoid harm to oneself or others. The patient's insight into personal psychological difficulties should also be assessed and included in the report of the MSE.[79]

To assess the patient's current cognitive functioning, most clinicians recite a proverb and ask the patient to explain it. Vague or concrete responses are characteristic of those with below average intelligence or severe thinking difficulties. Acutely psychotic individuals may give bizarre responses.

Another test of cognitive ability is a series of questions regarding the way in which two objects are similar, for example an apple and a banana. Here again, responses that focus on concrete or unusual aspects of the objects may reveal intellectual deficits or psychotic thinking difficulties.

To assess short-term memory and concentration, the patient may be asked to repeat a series of digits of increasing length, and then to repeat a different series backwards from the order of presentation. Another task frequently used is asking the patient to count backwards by sevens from 100. Recent memory may be tested by giving the patient three unrelated words to remember and letting a few minutes of the interview elapse before asking the patient to repeat them.[80]

---

[77] *Id* 38-39.

[78] *Id* 54-64.

[79] *See* J. Allen & B. Allen, Guide to Psychiatry 40 (1978).

[80] One procedure involves three different types of stimuli, e.g., *red elephant, blue chair, 1983*. The unusual stimuli reduce the probabilities of guessing correctly.

Traditionally, the MSE includes the interviewer's assessment of the patient's mood (unremarkable, elated, depressed, etc.) and affective expression (appropriate to mood, blunted, inappropriate, etc.). Suicidal ideation and intent should also be noted.[81]

As should be obvious, the MSE is highly subjective and the amount of useful information gained is dependent on a number of factors, including the setting in which the interview is conducted and the rapport established by the interviewer. Furthermore, much of the information contained in the report is based on the interviewer's interpretation of what transpired. A review of a huge body of psychological research concluded that an individual's behavior in any given setting is determined by the following three factors: one-third by the individual's personality traits, one-third by the environment, and one-third by the interaction of the individual and the environment.[82] This conclusion suggests that the environment of the mental status examination (private physician's office, jail, or state hospital) and the individual's manner of interacting with it will constitute about two thirds of the variability of the information obtained. A careless or biased interviewer can literally create the kind of patients expected.

Even a relatively neutral interviewer cannot counteract all the effects of the setting of the interview.[83] Interviews conducted in a jail are not likely to be the same as interviews conducted in an outpatient clinic. Court-ordered evaluations usually evoke guarded, even hostile, behavior from the person being interviewed and may evoke heightened vigilance and scepticism in the clinician that can further antagonize the person being evaluated.

Differences in socioeconomic status and cultural background between interviewer and patient can lead to faulty conclusions in an MSE. Unthinking criticism of the patient's dress, without regard to cultural context, may result in an overly harsh evaluation of the patient's personal hygiene or grooming, suggesting lower levels of psychological functioning than are in fact evident.[84]

The overall utility of the MSE is dependent on the amount of accurate information obtained during the interview.[85] For a cooperative, verbal, talkative patient, a tentative diagnosis can be made within the course of

---

[81] J. Allen & B. Allen, *supra* note 79, at 39.

[82] *See* W. Mischel, Personality and Assessment (1968).

[83] S. Garfield, Clinical Psychology 98 (1983).

[84] This issue is particularly relevant in forensic settings where the motivation to *fake bad* may be great.

[85] S. Garfield, *supra* note 83, at 95-96.

a 60-to-90-minute interview. For patients who are acutely and severely disturbed and are seen in a hospital or clinic setting, a shorter interview may be sufficient. For those being evaluated in jail or juvenile detention centers, who are nonverbal or uncooperative, an MSE may be of virtually no utility, and collateral interviews, history, and psychological testing may be required.

Social Workup

In agencies that are organized along the traditional psychiatric service model, social histories are the province of the clinic social worker. The family and social factors that have contributed to the development of symptoms will typically be elicited from the members of the patient's family. Family reports of significant events, as well as the patient's medical, personal, and occupational history can be explored in some detail and then compared to the patient's report for discrepancies and distortions. In some forensic settings, the social workup entails a home visit so the social worker can personally inspect the home environment, especially when the safety of small children is at issue. When the social worker is taking a social history, the psychiatrist or psychologist who is interviewing the patient may abbreviate history taking and focus more on the mental status examination.[86]

§2.15   Psychological Testing

Psychological tests are a standardized way of sampling a segment of an individual's behavior and comparing it to that of a group with known characteristics. Psychological tests are categorized by the psychological factors they measure, such as intelligence tests, personality tests, achievement tests, and neuropsychological tests. Cases that involve psychological issues usually require testimony about intelligence and personality, so the sections that follow examine the major tests in these areas.

§2.16   —Intelligence Tests

Wechsler Adult Intelligence Scale-Revised

The original Wechsler scale was devised in 1939, but has been revised

---

[86] *See* Ginsberg, *Psychiatric Interview,* in Comprehensive Textbook of Psychiatry/IV 488-89 (4th ed 1985).

twice since then, the last time in 1981.[87] A recent survey of practicing clinicians revealed it to be the most widely administered adult intelligence test in the United States.[88] The latest version of the Wechsler scale is called the Wechsler Adult Intelligence Scale-Revised (WAIS-R).[89]

While the purpose of any intelligence test is to measure intelligence, the WAIS-R provides more than just an IQ. The test is divided into two categories of tasks, verbal and performance. Each is composed of individual subtests which measure a different ability. Consequently, the clinician can analyze the pattern of scores across subtests in addition to the verbal, performance, and full-scale IQs in making diagnostic determinations. WAIS-R performance can assist in the diagnosis of psychiatric disorders, chronic alcoholism, and brain damage.[90]

The WAIS-R consists of eleven subtests, six of which are designated as verbal and five as performance subtests. In contrast to the WAIS, the WAIS-R order of administration alternates from verbal to performance subtests, instead of administering all the verbal subtests first. Within each subtest, items are arranged so that the easy items are at the beginning and hardest items at the end, gradually increasing in difficulty.[91] Ethical prohibitions prevent disclosure of the items themselves as availability of the items would invalidate the test.[92] However, the general content of each subtest will be discussed below.

Each of the subtests is listed below in the order in which it appears in the test and is designated as a verbal (V) or performance (P) subtest:

> Information - V
>
> Picture Completion - P
>
> Digit Span - V
>
> Picture Arrangement - P
>
> Vocabulary - V
>
> Block Design - P

---

[87] S. Garfield, Clinical Psychology 127 (1983).

[88] Lubin, Larson, & Matarazzo, *Patterns of Psychological Test Usage in the United States: 1935-1982*, 39 Am Psychologist 452-53 (1984).

[89] D. Wechsler, WAIS-R Manual: Wechsler Adult Intelligence Scale-Revised (1981).

[90] *See* C. Golden, Clinical Interpretation of Objective Psychological Tests 2 (1979).

[91] D. Wechsler, *supra* note 89, at 24.

[92] *See* American Psychological Assn, *Ethical Principles of Psychologists*, 36 Am Psychologist 633-38 (1981).

Arithmetic - V

Object Assembly - P

Comprehension - V

Digit Symbol - P

Similarities - V

The information subtest is a test of knowledge of specific facts. It serves primarily as a test of general knowledge. Poor performance is associated with low intelligence, but may also be the result of an alternate cultural background, poor educational background, or severe mental disorder.[93]

Digit span is a subtest of immediate auditory memory. It is a standardized version of the test typically given during the mental status examination (MSE).[94] Good performance is dependent on concentration and attention as well as memory. Separate scores for digits forward and digits backward are combined to give the score for digit span.[95]

Vocabulary is the best estimate of intelligence. An individual's performance on this subtest may also be adversely affected by differences in cultural or socioeconomic background, however, so the presence of these factors affects the interpretation of low scores. High scores are generally obtained by those with high verbal intelligence and advanced education.[96]

The arithmetic subtest examines an individual's ability to deal with number concepts in the context of problems confronted in daily living. Problems are presented orally and must be solved without using pencil and paper. The test requires attention, memory, and verbal understanding in addition to arithmetic skills. Problems with any one of those abilities may result in lowered scores.[97]

The comprehension subtest is a measure of social judgment and understanding of social customs. Socialization is a major factor in scores on this subtest. Since this subtest elicits remarks from the patient, it can give valuable diagnostic clues if the responses are unusual or bizarre.[98]

The similarities subtest is another standardized version of a test frequently included in the mental status exam. This subtest requires the

---

[93] C. Golden, *supra* note 90, at 14.

[94] *See* **§2.14.**

[95] C. Golden, *supra* note 90, at 18.

[96] *Id* 19.

[97] *Id* 16.

[98] *Id* 15.

individual to tell how two objects are alike. The individual's ability to classify objects, along with concentration and memory, is tested. Low scores are related to concrete thinking.[99]

The performance subtests are less dependent upon verbal skills and more dependent on visual, spatial, and sequential abilities. However, the dichotomy is not complete, as verbal abilities are required for nearly all these subtests.[100]

The picture completion subtest consists of a series of drawings with an important detail missing. It is the patient's task to find the missing detail. There is a cultural component to this task, as lack of experience with the items will contribute to low scores. Ability to organize visual information and screen out distractions are essential to good performance on this task.[101]

Block design is a subtest that requires the individual to duplicate designs constructed by the examiner or presented in a test booklet with red and white blocks. This test is the purest measure of spatial reasoning on the WAIS-R. Visual perception and visual-motor coordination are necessary on this task. This test is quite sensitive to brain injury.[102]

Object assembly requires visual and visual-motor skills as well, but, rather than abstract designs, the individual must reconstruct puzzles of familiar objects. Good scores depend on accuracy and speed, as in block design.[103]

The WAIS-R and its predecessor, the WAIS, represent a number of advantages as measures of intelligence. They are widely used and a large amount of normative data is available. The WAIS-R is the standard against which virtually all other intelligence tests are measured. The subtest scores provide data about discrete abilities as well as overall functioning.[104]

The disadvantages of the WAIS-R (and WAIS) include its unsuitability for group administration, and thus increased cost of administration, its bias toward average American cultural experience, its tendency to give higher scores on retesting, and its tendency to be inaccurate for very high and very low intelligence individuals.[105]

---

[99] *Id* 17.

[100] *Id* 28.

[101] *Id* 20.

[102] *Id* 21.

[103] *Id* 22.

[104] *Id* 33.

[105] *Id* 34.

Stanford Binet

The Stanford Binet test was first developed before the WAIS as a measure of children's intelligence and later extended to measure adult intelligence. The original test divided the mental age, based on test results, by the chronological age to get the intelligence quotient (IQ). The current version of the test arrives at IQ in the same manner as the WAIS, however.[106]

The tests in the Stanford Binet are arranged in groups by year level. The test is difficult to administer since there are a number of different kinds of items, and more small pieces of material to present. The Stanford Binet relies more on verbal functions than the WAIS. Unlike the WAIS, subtest scores are not developed individually.[107]

The advantage of the Stanford Binet is that it may be used to establish IQs for adults suspected of being mentally retarded. The major disadvantages come from the difficulty in administration and the difficulty in evaluating differences in performance between types of items.[108]

§2.17 —Personality Tests

Personality tests are designed to measure various aspects of a person's emotional and social, as opposed to intellectual, functioning. They are generally of two types: objective and projective. Objective tests, like the Minnesota Multiphasic Personality Inventory, present the individual with questions or statements to which it is necessary to reply by choosing among a set of alternative responses. These may be True-False, Sometimes-Always-Never, Agree-Disagree, or the like. Projective tests, on the other hand, present the individual with a stimulus and ask for a response. These tests are much less structured and therefore more stressful to take. Differences among the projective tests are related to the types of stimuli used. With some notable exceptions, the projective tests are more difficult to validate and less reliable than the objective tests.

Rorschach Inkblot Technique

The Rorschach was first introduced more than 50 years ago and has been widely used and researched since that time. Over the years, a number of different systems have been used to classify and score the

---

[106] *Id* 36.
[107] *Id* 38.
[108] J. Exner, The Rorschach: A Comprehensive System 7 (1974).

responses to this projective test. These scoring techniques have some similarities, but enough differences to prompt one writer to suggest that each constitutes a different Rorschach.[109] Although widely criticized because of problems with reliability and validity, the Rorschach continues to be frequently utilized by clinical psychologists.[110]

The test consists of 10 plates with designs on them. Five of the cards are black and white and five are colored. The cards are numbered and administered one at a time in the sequence dictated by the number of the card. Generally, the individual is shown the card and asked to tell the clinician what he sees. After all 10 cards have been shown, the clinician exposes the cards again and reads the responses back to the patient. During this period, called the inquiry, the patient is asked to point out which portions of the blot were used to form the percept and to articulate, if possible, which qualitative features of the blot contributed to making the percept.[111]

The different scoring systems share some common characteristics. The responses are scored based on which part of the blot was used (all or some part), whether the form is judged good or bad, whether there is movement in the response, whether other stimulus features were used (color, shading, texture, etc.) and the content of the percept (human, animal, anatomy, etc.). Other features may be scored as well depending on the scoring system used by the clinician.[112]

The development of the Exner system of administration and scoring represented a substantial improvement in the reliability and validity of the Rorschach technique. Exner collected and published normative data for normal individuals and various diagnostic groups from age five years through adult. Consequently, using this system it is now possible to compare an individual's Rorschach performance to that of normal people as well as those with mental disorders. Therefore, although still a projective technique, these improvements in its psychometric characteristics have increased its utility.[113]

Exner also conducted a large number of research studies exploring various features of the test as a means of validating clinical hypotheses generated from the test data. These clinical and experimental studies

---

[109] J. Exner, The Rorschach: A Comprehensive System 26 (1974).

[110] Lubin, Larson, & Matarazzo, *Patterns of Psychological Test Usage in the United States: 1935-1982*, 39 Am Psychologist 452 (1984).

[111] J. Exner, *supra* note 108, at 35.

[112] *Id* 42.

[113] *Id* 44.

form the basis of a growing body of validity data for the Rorschach.[114]

The multiplicity of scoring systems and differences in reliability and validity among systems make it imperative that any challenge to Rorschach testing testimony be specific, as general attacks on the Rorschach may be irrelevant to the scoring system used. Given the sophistication necessary to mount this challenge properly, consultation with a forensic or clinical psychologist may be necessary.

Thematic Apperception Test (TAT)

The Thematic Apperception Test (TAT) is another projective test frequently used by clinicians. It consists of 30 cards with black and white drawings depicting people in various situations. A few of the plates contain other types of scenes, some without people. Usually the examiner will select cards to present, which may come from the standard set or be selected by the clinician to investigate a particular area of interest. The patient is asked to look at each card and make up a story about the picture. The content of the pictures *pulls* different attitudes depending on the scene. Some elicit stories about achievement, others about the nature of male-female relationships, others about family relationships.[115]

The patient's stories are analyzed by noting the quality of the relationships between characters in the stories and by the various needs and external forces experienced by the *hero* of each story. The basic assumption of the test is that the patient must project personal feelings into the stories. A number of different scoring systems have been developed, and normative data have been collected which allow comparison of TATs obtained from patients with those obtained from normal individuals.[116]

The TAT is designed to be used for diagnosis of mental disorders as well as for understanding the patient's attitudes. This information may be useful, even crucial, to diagnosis and treatment planning when combined with other test data and the history. There has been some concern among clinicians that the pictures that compose the TAT pull negatively toned stories. Since that concern has been confirmed by recent research, a clinician must take the stimulus characteristics of the test into account when interpreting data derived from the TAT.[117]

---

[114] *See* II J. Exner, The The Rorschach: A Comprehensive System (1978).

[115] H. Murray, Explorations in Personality (2d ed 1947).

[116] Kraiger, Hakel, & Cornelius, *Exploring Fantasies of TAT Reliability,* 48 J Pers Assessment 365 (1984).

[117] Ritzler, Sharkey, & Chudy, *A Comprehensive Projective Alternative to the TAT,* 44 J Pers Assessment 358 (1980).

Sentence Completion Test (SCT)

The sentence completion test (SCT) is another projective test ranked in the top 10 most used tests in surveys of practicing clinical psychologists.[118] Actually the SCT is not one test, but a type of test. There are many versions which share the same basic design but differ in their item content. A number of scoring systems have been devised for research purposes, but none is widely used for diagnostic purposes.[119]

The test consists of a list of incomplete sentence stems which the patient is instructed to complete in any manner the patient wishes. The content of the stems and their order of presentation varies from version to version of the SCT. Once again, the emphasis in evaluating test responses is on understanding the subjective reality of the patient and not on diagnostic categorization. It is this feature that makes inferences drawn from the test dependent on the skill of the clinician doing the analysis and opens the door for questions about the reliability and validity of the test.

The Minnesota Multiphasic Personality Inventory (MMPI)

The Minnesota Multiphasic Personality Inventory (MMPI) is the most frequently utilized psychological personality test in the United States.[120] Developed in the 1930s, it has become the premier diagnostic and screening device in clinical psychology. The test was developed not on the basis of any particular theory, but rather on the basis of empirically derived objective items which, it was hoped, would differentiate patients into diagnostic categories consistent with the name of the particular scale to which the item belonged. Although psychiatric diagnosis proved to be more complex than physical diagnosis in that respect, the MMPI has been used in so many clinical and research settings that a vast body of literature is available regarding diagnostic and treatment implications of various MMPI profiles.[121]

The test itself consists of 550 true-false items, 16 of which are repeated to make a total of 566. There are four basic forms of the test. One version consists of cards containing one item per card. These cards

---

[118] Lubin, Larson, & Matarazzo, *supra* note 110, at 452.

[119] *See, e.g.,* J. Loevinger, R. Wessler, & C. Redmore, Measuring Ego Development 2 (1970).

[120] Lubin, Larson, & Matarazzo, *supra* note 110, at 452.

[121] C. Golden, Clinical Interpretation of Objective Psychological Tests 57 (1979).

are sorted into stacks for true, false, and cannot say items. This version is used for those individuals who cannot complete the answer sheet, but are lucid enough to complete the test. The second version contains all the items on audiotape for those with reading problems. The third version is the booklet form which contains 566 items, with 16 being repeated for scoring purposes. The answers are marked on an IBM answer sheet which can be scored by computer. The fourth version, Form R, consists of a hard cover spiral-bound booklet with an answer sheet which fits over pegs on the back cover. This version is frequently used to administer a 399-item version of the MMPI which allows scoring of all the clinical and validity scales.[122]

The test is scored either by computer or by using scoring templates which fit over the answer sheet, one for each validity and clinical scale. The scores are then plotted on a graph which converts the raw scores into T scores which allows comparison with the normative group. A T score is a distribution of scores with a mean of 50 and standard deviation of 10. A T score of 70, for example, on any scale means that score is higher than 98 per cent of the scores of the people in the normative group.

The MMPI profile consists of scores on four validity scales and 10 clinical scales. The clinical scales were named for the disorders which they were intended to differentiate when initially developed; as previously noted, that goal was not attained. Consequently, the names of the scales are currently somewhat misleading. Each of these scales is listed below, followed by its abbreviation, if any:

Validity Scales:
   Cannot Say (?)
   Lie (L)
   F
   K
Clinical Scales:
1. Hypochondriasis (Hs)
2. Depression (D)
3. Hysteria (Hy)
4. Psychopathic Deviate (Pd)
5. Masculinity-Feminity (Mf)
6. Paranoia (Pa)

---

[122] *Id* 59-60.

7.   Psychasthenia (Pt)

8.   Schizophrenia (Sc)

9.   Hypomania (Ma)

10. Social Introversion (Si)[123]

Most interpretation of MMPI profiles is done by examining the highest two points in the profile. A number of interpretation manuals are available which provide information about diagnosis, personality, symptom patterns, quality of relationships with others, and probable need for and response to medication. Since the test lends itself to computerized scoring, a number of computerized interpretation services are available to clinicians.[124]

The advantages of the MMPI include its ease of administration in most circumstances and its minimal demands on professional time since it can be administered by a layperson. The research data base is huge and still growing, and provides good evidence of reliability and validity for both diagnosis and prognosis. The disadvantages include the necessity of about a seventh grade reading level and the temptation to make interpretations without a history and diagnostic interview. The development of computerized interpretation systems has aggravated the temptation to misuse the test by relying exclusively on the computer printout.[125]

§2.18   —Neuropsychological Tests

Neuropsychological tests are those tests designed to detect brain dysfunction. A number of tests have been devised and are frequently used by psychologists in everyday evaluation practice. Two of these, the Bender Gestalt and the Benton Visual Retention Test, are used individually as neuropsychological screening devices.[126] When more extensive evaluation is required, a battery of neuropsychological tests will usually be given. The two batteries most frequently used are the Halsted-Reitan Neuropsychological Battery and the newer standardized version of Luria's Neuropsychological Battery.

---

[123] *Id* 61.

[124] *Id* 64.

[125] *Id* 65.

[126] *Id* 121-42.

Halsted-Reitan Neuropsychological Battery

The Halstead-Reitan Battery consists of a number of independent tests, including two tests discussed above—the Wechsler Adult Intelligence Scale-Revised (WAIS-R) and the Minnesota Multiphasic Personality Inventory (MMPI).[127] In addition, the test contains a number of tests designed to test a specific area of brain function. Each of these tests is briefly explained below.

The Halstead Category Test is designed to test an individual's abstract thinking ability in the area of logical deduction. The individual is presented with cards depicting the items to be categorized into one of four categories, each of which is represented by a lever numbered one through four. A correct categorization results in a bell ringing after the patient pulls the lever; an incorrect response is followed by a buzzer. There are seven different subtests, each with its own underlying principle to guide the categorization process. It is the patient's task to discover the underlying principle. The score is based on the number of items correctly categorized.[128]

The Speech Sounds Perception Test consists of a number of nonsense syllables that are presented orally. The patient must pick the correct, written version of the nonsense syllable from four possible choices. The score is based on the number of items correctly matched with those on the audiotape. The actual score is the number of errors out of 60 items.[129]

Another test presented on audiotape is the Seashore Rhythm Test. This test requires the patient to judge whether two rythymic patterns are alike or different.[130]

The Tactual Performance Test requires the patient to be blindfolded and to place geometrically shaped blocks into a form board that has indentations that match the shape of the blocks. Three trials are run, one with the dominant hand (right hand for right-handed people), one with the nondominant hand, and the third using both hands. After these trials, the patient is asked to draw a picture of the board with the shapes in their correct locations. This drawing is scored for correct shape and

---

[127] *Id* 161. *See* §§**2.16-2.17.**

[128] C. Golden, *Clinical Interpretation of Objective Psychological Tests* 161-62 (1979).

[129] *Id* 163.

[130] *Id* 163-64.

location. The earlier trials are scored based on the time required to complete the task.[131]

The Trail-Making Test consists of two parts. This test is similar to a child's connect-the-dot coloring book. Part A is identical to the coloring book task, while part B requires alternating between numbers and letters while connecting the dots. The score is dependent on the time required to complete each part.[132]

The Reitan-Klove Sensory Perceptual Exam is composed of a number of tasks that measure sensory functions. The first measures touch by having the clinician alternately touch the backs of the patient's hands in a random pattern when the patient's eyes are closed. The second test repeats the procedure for auditory perception using sounds presented on alternate sides of the body in a random pattern. The patient must correctly identify on which side of the body the stimulus was presented. The third procedure tests visual perception and visual field abnormalities by presenting moving stimuli on the edge of the patient's visual field. Then the examiner tests whether the patient can correctly identify which finger is being touched when the patient's eyes are closed. Next, the patient is tested for fingertip number writing recognition. Following that test, the patient is asked to identify three coins, a dime, a nickel, and a penny by touch only. Finally, the patient is given four geometrically shaped blocks to place in the correct slot on a form board, two trials for each hand.[133]

The Aphasia Screening Test requires the patient to name objects, spell words, draw shapes, read words, and so forth. Each item is related to symptoms of some form of aphasia, a disorder of language production or comprehension.[134]

The Lateral Dominance Exam tests for dominance in use of eyes and hands. This test consists of a series of tasks that determine which eye is used on various tasks and a measure of comparative grip strength.[135]

The Halstead Fingertapping Test uses an apparatus like a Morse code key. The patient taps the counter as fast as possible with each hand for five trials of 10 seconds.[136]

Scores from all the exams and the WAIS-R and MMPI are evaluated to determine whether brain damage is present and whether it is localized

---

131 *Id* 164.
132 *Id* 166.
133 *Id* 167-69.
134 *Id* 170.
135 *Id* 170-71.
136 *Id* 171-72.

or diffuse. This test battery has been extensively validated and has been used in a wide variety of research and clinical applications. This body of validation data allows a clinician to compare the pattern of scores from an individual patient with those scores obtained from patients in various diagnostic groups to increase the accuracy of the diagnosis.[137]

The major disadvantage of this test battery is that it takes a very long time to administer. In addition, some areas of neuropsychological functioning, such as speech expression, are not tested or are tested only briefly. The test does not discriminate well between chronic schizophrenics and organic mental disorders.[138]

Luria's Neuropsychological Investigation

The Luria is a standardized version of a group of specific items used by the Russian neuropsychologist, A. R. Luria. Luria's approach was to devise items to test specific brain functioning, while the Halstead-Reitan studies took a more global approach to construction of the battery of tests. The Luria battery consists of 269 items covering 10 areas of neuropsychological functioning. The items are organized into 11 scales which are briefly explained here.[139]

The motor function scale includes simple and complex motor skills, ranging from imitating of simple motor acts to drawing of geometric shapes to completing complex motor movements directed by verbal commands. Mouth and tongue movements are also evaluated.[140]

Rhythmic and pitch skills are evaluated by a series of items which are scored on this scale. The first section evaluates the patient's ability to reproduce an increasingly complex series of pitches which are administered via audiotape. The rhythmic skills section requires the patient to discriminate between different rhythmic patterns as well as to reproduce patterns from verbal commands.[141]

A series of items evaluates tactile functions and that is the name of the scale. All items are administered blindfolded. The patient must identify objects by touch, reproduce arm movement in one arm which

---

[137] Boll, *The Halstend-Reitan Neuropsychology Battery,* in Handbook of Clinical Neuropsychology 597-603 (1981).

[138] C. Golden, Clinical Interpretation of Objective Psychological Tests 196 (1979).

[139] *Id* 203.

[140] *Id.*

[141] *Id* 204.

has been produced by the examiner in the patient's other arm, and identify letters and numbers written on the hands.[142]

Visual functions are examined by a series of items which require the patient to identify objects, line drawings, and photographs. Problems are presented using blocks and jumbled pictures.[143]

Two scales evaluate speech functions, receptive speech and expressive speech. The receptive speech scale evaluates the patient's ability to comprehend correctly a variety of verbal material. The items range from presentation of phonemes to complex sentences. The expressive speech scale items also range from phonemes to statements, but the patient must actually produce them for this scale. Other items test production and logical organization of speech.[144]

Three subtests evaluate the patient's reading, writing, and arithmetic skills. The reading items require basic reading skills for letters, words, sentences, and short stories. The writing items are analogous to those for reading. The arithmetic items range from number recognition to simple arithmetic skills to simple algebra.[145]

The memory section evaluates memory of verbal and visual information as well as the ability to memorize with and without interference. The ability to associate labels with pictures is also examined.[146]

The intellectual processes scale contains items similar to that on the WAIS-R. Additional items require the patient to find the humor in a picture, to describe the theme of a picture, and to make comparisons between two objects.[147]

Three summary scales are also calculated, one for the left hemisphere of the brain, one for the right hemisphere, and one called the pathognomonic scale. The first two help to indicate which side of the brain is damaged. The pathognomonic scale consists of 31 items which are almost never missed by normal people, so a high score on this scale is highly suggestive of some brain injury.[148]

The Luria has been found to discriminate between brain damaged and normal people from 74 to 96 per cent of the time, and between brain

---

[142] *Id.*

[143] *Id.*

[144] *Id* 204-05.

[145] *Id* 205.

[146] *Id* 205-06.

[147] *Id* 206.

[148] *Id* 207.

damaged and schizophrenic patients about 58 to 78 per cent of the time.[149] The advantages of the Luria include its relatively short administration time (two and one-half hours) and its specificity for individual functions. The disadvantages include the smaller body of validation data and a requirement of a knowledge of Luria's theory to interpret the data.

§2.19 —Mental or Emotional Disabilities

The DSM-III[150] contains a diagnostic category that is likely to be directly related to civil actions for damages for mental disabilities, post-traumatic stress disorder.[151] The essential elements include a precipitating stressor, re-experiencing the event long after it is over, emotional numbness, and some other symptoms which are associated with acute emotional distress. This disorder, which has been called traumatic neurosis in the past, may be so intense as to be nearly incapacitating and may not emerge until months or years after the traumatic event.

The other group of mental disabilities is likely to constitute those injuries to the brain itself which result from a toxic substance or a traumatic blow to the head, such as might be suffered in a car accident. Because these injuries might be so diffuse as to defy detection by X-ray or CAT scan, neuropsychological testing may be the only way to document deficits in intellectual or emotional functioning which result from such an accident. These problems may range from memory problems to episodic rage to profound personality changes. The injuries thus diagnosed fall into the category of the organic mental disorders in DSM-III.[152]

§2.20 Criticism of Psychological Tests

No psychological test should be considered for use in the judicial process until its validity is adequately demonstrated by empirical studies. Beyond the question of facial validity, one legitimate criticism of psychological tests emerges from attempts to use tests beyond their limits. These tests are the tools of psychologists, and as tools, their usefulness is limited by the knowledge, skill, and integrity of the user

---

[149] *Id* 206.

[150] Diagnostic and Statistical Manual of Mental Disorders (3d ed 1980) (DSM-III).

[151] *Id* 238.

[152] *Id* 101.

and the purpose of the test. Failure of the test developer or the test user to understand the following concepts can lead to abuses of tests and test data.[153]

Psychological tests used in the United States are usually based on *typical* Americans as the norms, and that means middle class and Caucasian individuals. Thus, a test may be valid when used to evaluate individuals similar to this group but invalid when used for members of any other cultural or subcultural group. There is a potential for cultural bias in virtually any test.[154]

The validity of any test is dependent on standard administration by the examiner. Failure to follow the standard instructions to any significant degree may invalidate an otherwise valid test. Disruption of the standard administration procedure may be inadvertantly caused by either the examiner or the patient, and the effects of the disruption on the test results may be quite difficult to ascertain.[155]

Test performance is sensitive to the setting in which the test is administered. Performance on the same test may be quite different for individuals with quite similar psychological characteristics depending on whether the test is given in a hospital, a private practitioner's office, or a jail. These differences may be the result of deliberate faking or malingering or the result of subtle unintentional, or unconscious, situational factors.[156]

Personality tests are constructed on the assumption that an individual's behavior is characterized by consistency in different situations. While cognitive abilities are fairly consistent regardless of situation, individual behavior shows considerable variability from one situation to another. Thus, tests that identify individual traits without qualifying the situations in which they are likely to be manifest are probably misleading if not invalid.[157]

§2.21 Suggested Reading

Books

J. Allen & B. Allen, *Guide to Psychiatry* (1978).

A. Anastasi, *Psychological Testing* (5th ed 1982).

---

[153] *See* A. Anastasi, Psychological Testing 22-44 (5th ed 1982).

[154] *Id* 343.

[155] *Id* 24.

[156] *Id* 33.

[157] *Id* 526-32.

E. Bickerstaff, *Neurological Examination in Clinical Practice* (3d ed 1978).

Diagnostic and Statistical Manual of Mental Disorders (3d ed 1980) (DSM-III).

J. Exner, *The Rorschach: A Comprehensive System* (1974).

S. Garfield, *Clinical Psychology* (1983).

C. Golden, *Clinical Interpretation of Objective Psychological Tests* (1979).

J. Leff & A. Isaacs, *Psychiatric Examination in Clinical Practice* (1981).

J. Loevinger, R. Wessler, & C. Redmore, *Measuring Ego Development* (1970).

W. Mischel, *Personality and Assessment* (1968).

H. Murray, *Explorations in Personality* (2d ed 1947).

D. Wechsler, *WAIS-R Manual: Wechsler Adult Intelligence Scale-Revised* (1981).

G. Wolf, *Collecting Data from Patients* (1977).

Articles

American Psychological Assn, *Ethical Principles of Psychologists*, 36 Am Psychologist 633 (1981).

Boll, *The Halstend-Reitan Neuropsychology Battery*, in Handbook of Clinical Neuropsychology (1981).

Finn, *Base Rates, Utilities, and DSM-III: Shortcomings of Fixed Rule Systems of Psychodiagnosis*, 91 J Abnormal Psychology 294 (1982).

Frances, *DSM-III Personality Disorders Section: A Commentary*, 137 Am J Psychiatry 1050 (1980).

Ginsberg, *Psychiatric Interview*, in Comprehensive Textbook of Psychiatry/IV 488-89 (4th ed 1985).

Kraiger, Hakel, & Cornelius, *Exploring Fantasies of TAT Reliability*, 48 J Pers Assessment 365 (1984).

Lerman, *The Advantages of DSM-III*, 141 Am J Psychiatry 541 (1984).

Lubin, Larson, & Matarazzo, *Patterns of Psychological Test Usage in the United States: 1935-1982*, 39 Am Psychologist 452 (1984).

Ritzler, Sharkey, & Chudy, *A Comprehensive Projective Alternative to the TAT*, 44 J Pers Assessment 358 (1980).

Spitzer, *DSM-III and the Politics-Science Dichotomy Syndrome*, 40 Am Psychology 522 (1985).

Spitzer, *The Diagnostic Status of Homosexuality in DSM-III: A Reformulation of the Issues*, 138 Am J Psychiatry 210 (1981).

Valliant, *The Disadvantages of DSM-III*, 141 Am J Psychiatry 545 (1984).

3

Treatment

§3.01　Introduction

Once the diagnostic process is completed, the information learned is used to formulate a treatment plan. Two sets of considerations should have a major bearing on the treatment plan. One is the condition of the patient. The other is the theoretical orientation of the clinician. The treatment recommended will be influenced by the clinician's attitude about the etiology of the illness as discussed in Chapter 1.

The clinician should integrate the information about the patient's condition from the interviews, social history, physical examination, neurological examination, and psychological evaluation and make a preliminary determination whether inpatient or outpatient treatment is indicated. The more disorganized and out of control the patient is, the more external structure and control will be required to aid in the process of reorganization. Inpatient treatment, psychiatric hospitalization, is discussed in **§3.02.**

The other methods of treatment, depending on the severity of the mental disorder, may be an adjunct to hospitalization or an alternative method of treatment, administered on an outpatient basis. If the diagnosis reveals a disorder with known biological or biochemical causes, it is more likely a biological treatment will be required. If the disorder is viewed as primarily behavioral, a behavioral treatment will be instituted.

Regardless of the etiology of the disorder, most mental disorders have social consequences for the patient and family, and a comprehensive treatment plan should attempt to ameliorate those social consequences.

§3.02 Hospitalization

Hospitalization is the treatment of choice for individuals who have lost the ability to control their own behavior. This behavioral dyscontrol may be the result of psychosis, drug or alcohol abuse, or severe depression. Psychiatric hospitalization may be voluntary or involuntary.[1]

A number of factors should be considered on the question of hospitalization. The patient's current level of functioning, mental and physical status, social support system, judgment, and ability to be managed as an outpatient should be evaluated by the clinician. A patient who is still able to work, or at least feed herself and maintain personal hygiene, is physically healthy, has a supportive family, and seems unlikely to act impulsively or self-destructively and likely to keep her outpatient appointments probably should not be hospitalized and should be treated as an outpatient.[2]

---

[1] *See* **ch 16.**

[2] This area of psychiatric practice has been so affected by court constraints that legal, rather than clinical, judgments prevail in difficult cases. For the

Conversely, hospitalization is indicated for a patient so disorganized or out of control that the patient is in physical danger. Hospitalization is also indicated when the nature of the patient's mental disorder suggests that others may be in danger of being harmed by the patient, as in the case of violent individuals with paranoid delusions.[3] When substance abuse is the presenting problem, hospitalization may be the only way to interrupt the pattern of substance abuse while treatment is being initiated.[4]

Psychiatric wards are usually of two types: open and closed. The open or unlocked wards are for those patients for whom the acute crisis has passed, but who are not yet ready to leave the security of the structured hospital environment. Closed wards are required for patients whose agitation and disorganization requires more structure for the safety of the patient or for the protection of society.

Psychiatric facilities in the United States may be either public or private. Private facilities tend to be oriented toward more intensive, long-term, and expensive treatment. The resources available to private facilities and their patients increase the odds that acute disorders will be treated properly, and that chronic problems will be managed in a manner that minimizes repeated rehospitalization by providing high quality aftercare.[5]

Inpatient psychiatric treatment shares one important feature with inpatient medical treatment: it is very expensive. Public policy trends toward reducing social service agency budgets and lawsuits that mandate a minimum patient to staff ratio at state hospitals have placed administrators in a serious treatment dilemma that has generated pressures for shorter hospital stays for patients. Facilities operated by state and county governments, operating under political and fiscal constraints, tend to focus on shorter length of hospital stay and rapid reintegration into the community. At the same time, the ability of the community mental health centers to provide adequate follow-up care necessary to prevent rehospitalization has been strained by falling

---

clinical standards, *see, e.g.,* L. Kolb, Modern Clinical Psychiatry 428 (9th ed 1977). *But see* A. Stone, Psychiatry, Law and Morality (1984). The admitting criteria may vary significantly between psychiatrists. *See* McRae, *Seen But Not Admitted at the State Hospital,* 7 Psychosocial Rehabilitation J 21 (1983).

[3] W. Reid, Treatment of the DSM-III Psychiatric Disorders 124 (1983).

[4] Balis, *Substance Use Disorders,* in W. Reid, Treatment of the DSM-III Psychiatric Disorders 81 (1983).

[5] Reid, *supra* note 3, at 115-18, 122.

budgets and the difficulty in overcoming community resistance to having "crazy" people in their neighborhoods.[6]

§3.03 —Basic Technique

The current prevailing philosophy of inpatient treatment is that of the ward as a therapeutic community or milieu. The ward is recognized as a social system that can be used to aid patients to regain their internal behavior controls and their rational thinking abilities while improving the quality of their personal relationships. The philosophy is translated into operational terms by setting the following goals for the community:

Direct and open communication between patient and staff.

Active encouragement of patient participation in their own treatment.

Provision of a system of ward government that offers opportunities for participation in both administrative and therapeutic decisions by patients and staff.

Maximum patient control of unit operations with final authority vested in the staff.

Democratically oriented patient government.

Frequent open and close contact between the unit and hospital with an emphasis on collaborative relationships between patients and staff.

An open door to the unit and patient access to the hospital grounds.[7]

These principles are designed to encourage patients to establish and maintain positive and meaningful human relationships, to discourage social withdrawal, and to avoid the dehumanization of large, impersonal institutions.

The staff designs the structure of the program and participates with the patients in working out how the program will be implemented. The entire staff, from aides to psychiatrists and psychologists, should be involved in the decision making. Staff intervention in ward problems should be limited to those situations where the community cannot solve the difficulty or where a patient's safety demands intervention.

---

[6] *See* Jerrell & Larsen, *Policy Shifts and Organizational Adaption: A Review of Current Developments,* 20 Community Mental Health J 282 (1984).

[7] Katz, *Psychiatric Hospitalization,* in Comprehensive Textbook of Psychiatry/IV 1576-82 (4th ed 1985).

The structure of the ward program is as important to treatment as the structure of the ward government. Daily activities should be designed to provide the patient opportunities for social interaction with other patients, occupational therapy suited to the patient's needs, recreational therapy, group therapy or individual therapy, and meetings with the treatment team for treatment and discharge planning. Medical rounds should be provided to manage any physical complaints and psychotropic medications.[8]

Occupational therapy (OT) has become an integral part of psychiatric hospitalization. Occupational therapy is a mode of treatment employing useful work as a treatment modality. The goals are to spark interest in the patient, to restore self-esteem through accomplishment, to occupy mind and body in healthy activity, and to improve human relationships through interactions with other patients and staff in a work setting. For severely disorganized individuals with schizophrenic disorders, OT may involve relearning basic personal hygiene and social skills, vocational rehabilitation, high school equivalency (GED) classes, or vocational training.[9]

§3.04   —Limitations

While hospitalization does provide the necessary structure and safety for the disorganized and out-of-control patient, hospitalization is not the answer for every type of patient. For example, a recent research study comparing the effectiveness of various treatment modalities concluded that hospitalization was contraindicated for patients suffering from temporary, situational, or maladjustment disorders.[10] An example of such a disorder would be the acute, catastrophic reaction to the death of a loved one which incapacitates the patient. In these circumstances, even though the patient may be manifesting rather severe symptoms, and may even be psychotic, if friends or relatives can provide the necessary supervision and support, these arrangements are preferable to hospitalization. In these cases, the stability of the environment, that is, the presence of familiar things and people, is likely to encourage recovery, while a major change of environment, even to

---

8 *Id* 1003.

9 *Id* 1007-08.

10 Lantz, Carlberg, & Wilson, *Mental Health Treatment Outcome by Sex, Diagnosis, and Treatment Agency*, 14 Prof Psychology 308 (1983). *See also* Shuman & Hawkins, *The Use of Alternatives to Institutionalization of the Mentally Ill*, 33 Sw LJ 1181 (1980).

a supportive hospital setting, may encourage regressive, helpless behavior and retard the process of recovery.

Advances in the technology of treatment evaluation research have facilitated analysis of the factors constituting effective treatment programs. The most effective inpatient treatment settings are characterized by a high percentage (44 per cent) of long-term patients on the ward, a higher percentage (33 per cent) of young, single patients, and a physical environment that encourages interaction with both staff and other patients and discourages social withdrawal like solitary television watching. Treatment programs in hospitals that do not provide a milieu like the one described are likely to be much less effective.[11] This research suggests that just being in the hospital is not as helpful as being in a hospital with a good physical and treatment-oriented environment.

A controversy over the pathological effects of hospitalization on the social functioning of chronic patients has been fought within the mental health professions and in the courts. It has been frequently contended that involuntary hospitalization is an unconstitutional abrogation of personal freedom under any circumstances and that this deprivation is particularly egregious where treatment programs are inadequate to provide rehabilitation services leading to eventual discharge. It is difficult to resolve this controversy, since some chronic patients, especially those suffering from schizophrenic disorders of the chronic variety, apparently suffer cortical deterioration that would render rehabilitation increasingly fruitless.[12] In these cases, an extensive evaluation of the patient, as well as a comprehensive evaluation of the treatment program as actually implemented, may be required to resolve these important questions. For some other patients, the hospital environment may support dependent and helpless behavior, and adoption of a sick role that interferes with acquisition of the skills necessary to independent functioning outside the hospital.

Involuntary hospitalization has been recognized by the Supreme Court as a deprivation of liberty cognizable under the due process clause[13] and is now limited in most states to instances in which a person suffers from a major mental disorder and is consequently dangerous to

---

[11] Ellsworth, Collins, Casey, Schoonover, Hickey, Hyer, Twemlow, & Nesselroade, *Some Characteristics of Effective Psychiatric Treatment Programs*, 47 J Consulting & Clinical Psychology 813-15 (1979).

[12] *See* **§1.03.**

[13] O'Connor v Donaldson, 422 US 563 (1975).

self or others.[14] Several states have recently adopted a version of the standard set forth in the American Psychiatric Association Model State Law on Civil Commitment of the Mentally Ill[15] that permits involuntary hospitalization of persons suffering from a major mental disorder who require available treatment but lack the capacity to make an informed decision about treatment. Persons who do not satisfy the applicable criteria may only be hospitalized voluntarily.

§3.05   Medication

The introduction of phenothiazines in the early 1950s marked a major advance in the treatment of schizophrenic disorders.[16] Since that time, the number of psychotropic medications available has mushroomed. This rapid proliferation of drugs produced both more alternatives for patients who had been nonresponsive to other drugs in the same class and more confusion about drug effectiveness as drug availability often preceded extensive research on drug efficacy and side effects.[17]

Drug selection is influenced not only by the action of the drug, but also by its side effects. Side effects are the result of drug action at sites in the body in addition to the target sites for which the drug is prescribed. Since introduction of a drug into the body usually means that the drug, or some of its chemical components, circulate in the bloodstream all over the body, other parts of the body may be affected, sometimes adversely. Psychotropic drug side effects range from the transitory to the debilitating and fatal. Some drugs have side effects that mimic psychiatric symptoms, so increasing the dosage to eliminate a symptom that is assumed to be caused by the disorder may only make the symptom worse.[18]

The decision when to medicate and which medication to use should be predicated on an accurate diagnosis of the patient's mental disorder.

---

[14] Beis, *State Involuntary Commitment Statutes*, 7 Mental Disability L Rep 350 (1983).

[15] Stromberg & Stone, *A Model State Law on Civil Commitment of the Mentally Ill*, 20 Harv J Legis 275 (1983). *See, e.g.*, NC Gen Stat §122-58.2(1)(a); Tex Civ Code Ann art 5547-50(b) (Vernon Supp 1985); Wash Rev Code Ann §71.05.020(1) (Supp 1985).

[16] Davis, *Antipsychotic Drugs*, in Comprehensive Textbook of Psychiatry/IV 1481 (4th ed 1985).

[17] *See* C. Bowden & M. Giffen, Psychopharmacology for Primary Care Physicians 4 (1978).

[18] Kessler & Waletzky, *Clinical Use of the Antipsychotics*, 138 Am J Psychiatry 202 (1981).

The discussion that follows is organized by diagnosis, roughly in the order in which the disorder appears in DSM-III.

§3.06 —Basic Technique

The most frequently treated organic mental disorder that involves psychiatric administration of medication is alcohol withdrawal and its associated delirium. The patient is almost always concurrently hospitalized in a special detoxification unit. The patient is sedated with a benzodiazepine (e.g., Valium) given orally or intramuscularly (IM) every two to four hours until the withdrawal symptoms are suppressed. The drug may also be administered intravenously (IV) when delirium is impending. Since thiamine deficiency usually accompanies alcohol abuse, thiamine, a B vitamin, usually is administered concurrently.[19]

The other drug that may be used in the treatment of alcohol abuse is disulfiram, Antabuse. This drug is given during later phases of treatment to discourage further drinking. Ingestion of alcohol within four days of taking the drug makes the patient violently ill.[20]

Schizophrenic disorders nearly always are treated with medication along with hospitalization in the acute phases. Recent advances in drug therapy have developed a technique of drug administration called a rapid neuroleptization schedule. A neuroleptic medication is primarily antipsychotic in its effect. The patient is admitted to a quiet milieu and given haloperidol (Haldol) IM every hour until symptoms improve, the patient is sedated, or the cumulative dose over 12 hours is 100 milligrams. Haldol is a high potency antipsychotic medication with a high incidence of extra-pyramidal side effects, which will be discussed below. Haldol is the drug of choice for treating agitated or violent patients, especially when the history is insufficiently detailed to reveal successful past treatment with some other antipsychotic medication.[21]

Antipsychotic medications do not cure schizophrenic disorders, they merely suppress the symptoms. Therefore, once the acute episode is past, a maintenance dose of the medication is sought by reducing the dose in steps until the lowest effective dosage is found. For patients who have had previous hospitalizations, this may require switching to the drug and dosage they have used before. Patients should be routinely taking medication on their own prior to discharge. Recent research

---

[19] Balis, *Substance Abuse Disorders,* in W. Reid, Treatment of the DSM-III Psychiatric Disorders 83-84 (1983).

[20] *Id* 99.

[21] W. Reid, Treatment of the DSM-III Psychiatric Disorders 113 (1983).

suggests that drug maintenance after discharge is essential to avoiding further hospitalization since two of three patients who discontinue their medication are rehospitalized within a year. Patients who continue taking their medication have relapse rates less than one-half that of patients who stop taking their medication.[22]

The next major diagnostic category treated with drugs is the affective disorders. Once again, accurate diagnosis is important, since different types of disorders respond to different types of medication. The bipolar disorder, manic type, is initially treated using the rapid neuroleptization schedule outlined above. After the acute manic behavior is controlled, the patient should be evaluated for the initiation or resumption of lithium administration. Adjustment of the dosage is normally done while in the hospital because of side effects and toxicity problems associated with lithium administration. Outpatient management of lithium dosage and periodic lab tests of serum lithium levels may be all that is required to prevent relapse.[23]

Treatment of the other group of affective disorders, the major depressions, requires a different class of drugs. The tricyclic antidepressants are effective in treating depressive symptoms about 60 to 70 per cent of the time, usually within about four weeks. Some of the newer drugs purport to work more rapidly; however, clinical experience with these drugs in the United States is currently limited. Since some patients with severe depressions may be suicidal, inpatient management may be required until the drug takes effect.[24]

Another class of antidepressants, the tetracyclics, has recently been introduced. These drugs (e.g., Ludiomil) have significantly fewer cardiotoxic effects than the tricyclics and are preferred for patients with cardiovascular problems. Antidepressant drugs also have side effects which must be considered when choosing a specific drug from the class.[25]

The anxiety disorders are sometimes treated with medication. Panic disorders in particular may be treated with benzodiazepines (e.g., Valium) for a brief period, usually coupled with psychotherapy and reassurance.[26] Obsessive compulsive disorder has been successfully

---

[22] Kessler & Waletzky, *Clinical Use of the Antipsychotics*, 138 Am J Psychiatry 202, 204 (1981).

[23] W. Reid, *supra* note 21, at 129-32.

[24] *Id* 135-37.

[25] *Id* 135.

[26] *Id* 143.

treated with clomipramine, a tricyclic antidepressant.[27] Generalized anxiety disorder may be treated with benzodiazepines and psychotherapy.[28]

The other group of disorders for which drug treatment may be effective, though controversial, is the paraphilias (i.e., pedophilia and exhibitionism). The drug normally used in such treatment is an antiandrogenic medication (i.e., medoxyprogesterone acetate-MPA). The action of this drug is to reduce the blood levels of male sex hormone testosterone and therefore reduce sex drive. The effectiveness of these drugs in treating cases of deviant hypersexuality has been demonstrated in research and clinical trials.[29]

§3.07 —Limitations

The therapeutic limitations of drug treatment of mental disorders fall into three major categories: noncompliance, side effects, and drug dependence. Some classes of psychotropic drugs have problems with more than one of these limitations; nearly all have side effects.

Medications will not work if they are not taken. Patients with chronic and severe disorders such as schizophrenic disorders and bipolar disorders[30] often stop taking medications after hospital discharge or even before, when the acute and distressing symptoms are no longer evident.[31] This problem is exacerbated if the patient lacks family or social supports to help monitor compliance or a follow-up physician who has a genuine interest in the patient. Most state hospital systems transfer patients to a community mental health center clinic for follow-up care. Usually that results in transfer to a medication clinic and an unknown physician with very limited time to spend with each patient.

The other group for whom noncompliance is likely to be a problem is the group of patients undergoing court-ordered treatment for hypersexuality or paraphilias with an antiandrogenic medication. There is a great temptation among these patients to deny that they suffer from any disorder and discontinue the medication.[32]

Side effects are a major consideration in the choice of medication by

---

[27] *Id* 145.

[28] *Id* 144.

[29] *Id* 161-64.

[30] See **§2.03** for discussions of these disorders.

[31] Kessler & Waletzky, *Clinical Use of the Antipsychotics,* 138 Am J Psychiatry 202, 204 (1981).

[32] W. Reid, Treatment of the DSM-III Psychiatric Disorders 164 (1983).

a psychiatrist. Different classes of drugs have different types of side effects, some relatively benign, others quite serious.

The benzodiazepines', widely prescribed by nonpsychiatric physicians to treat anxiety, most frequently observed side effect is drowsiness, which occurs in about 10 per cent of patients. This may represent a life- or limb-threatening problem for those who must drive or operate dangerous equipment. Other side effects noted include movement difficulties, confusion, and sometimes hostile, aggressive behavior.[33]

The antipsychotic (neuroleptic) medications cause side effects that fall into two classes, reversible and irreversible. Reversible side effects of the antipsychotic drugs include one group called extrapyramidal syndromes. These syndromes are more frequently observed with Haldol and other similar highly potent drugs than with other less potent antipsychotic medications. The symptoms of these side effects include muscle rigidity (dystonic reaction), restlessness and inability to sit still (akasthisia), resting tremor and movement difficulties (parkinsonian reaction), or catatonia. Treatment of these symptoms by first reducing the dosage of the medication and then, if that fails to alleviate the symptoms, prescribing an anticholinergic drug (e.g., Artane) is usually effective. Drug treatment of the side effects can be discontinued in three months for 60 to 90 per cent of patients.[34]

The group of irreversible side effects tends to be associated with neuroleptic drug treatment that continues for several years. One potentially fatal syndrome is called the neuroleptic malignant syndrome. This syndrome is characterized by muscle rigidity, lowered body temperature (hypothermia), altered level of consciousness, and potential for cardiac and respiratory failure. This syndrome is estimated to be fatal in about 20 per cent of the reported cases, but it is probably unrecognized in many cases. There are no proven, recognized treatments except discontinuation of the medication and supportive medical treatment of the associated symptoms. Respiratory, renal (kidney), and cardiovascular complications are frequently noted. The syndrome usually lasts from five to ten days after stopping oral medications, and two to three times longer after long-acting injections.[35]

Tardive dyskinesia is a potentially irreversible syndrome that is characterized by repetitive jaw movements, tongue thrusting, lip

---

[33] C. Bowden & M. Giffen, Psychopharmacology for Primary Care Physicians 10-11 (1978).

[34] Kessler & Waletzky, *supra* note 31, at 205-06.

[35] *Id* 206. *See also* Carnoff, *The Neuroleptic Malignant Syndrome*, 41 J Clinical Psychiatry 79-82 (1980).

smacking, and sometimes, jerky involuntary movements of limbs and trunk as well. Older chronic patients with a long history of antipsychotic medication maintenance have about a 20 per cent chance of experiencing the syndrome. Treatment involves discontinuation of the medication. Remission of symptoms occurs about 30 per cent of the time. Remission rates are better for younger patients with shorter durations of antipsychotic use and earlier diagnosis of the symptoms. There is currently no other satisfactory treatment and no method of determining who is at risk.[36] Because this syndrome is so dramatic in its clinical presentation, a number of patients have refused antipsychotic medication when hospitalized involuntarily,[37] in some instances citing the risk of tardive dyskinesia. The courts have generally recognized that in nonemergency situations, because an order of commitment does not typically entail a finding of incompetence, a patient may refuse antipsychotic medication; however, this refusal may be overridden by a constitutionally adequate surrogate decision-making process.[38]

The marked effectiveness of lithium in the treatment of the bipolar manic disorders is somewhat tempered by the seriousness of its side effects. This drug has quite a narrow range of therapeutic effectiveness and a rather low threshhold of toxicity which is just above the therapeutic range. In short, too much lithium is a poison, although just enough is therapeutic. Symptoms of drug toxicity include confusion, sluggishness, tremor, coma, and eventually, seizures and death. Another difficulty is that lithium therapy can trigger a syndrome resulting in salt (electrolyte) loss, also leading to seizures and coma. The least serious side effect is gastric irritability which can occur at therapeutic levels.[39]

The major class of side effects caused by the antidepressant drugs are shared with some of the antipsychotic drugs: anticholinergic side effects. These include dry mouth, blurred vision, drowsiness, constipation, problems with urine retention, and sweating. Other problematic side effects include the cardiac (cardiotoxic) effects noted above, weight gain, and increased risk of seizures. The cardiotoxic effect results from interference with normal transmission of nerve impulses regulating

[36] Kessler & Waletzky, *supra* note 31, at 205.

[37] Rennie v Klein, 653 F2d 836 (3d Cir 1981), *vacated & remanded*, 458 US 1119 (1982), *on remand*, 720 F2d 266 (3d Cir 1983); Rogers v Okin, 634 F2d 650 (1st Cir 1980), *vacated & remanded sub nom* Mills v Rogers, 457 US 291 (1982).

[38] Rennie v Klein, 653 F2d 836 (3d Cir 1981), *vacated & remanded*, 458 US 1119 (1982), *on remand*, 720 F2d 266 (3d Cir 1983).

[39] C. Bowden & M. Giffen, *supra* note 33, at 33-36.

heart rate. Because severely depressed patients may be suicidal, another danger is fatal overdose of antidepressant medication. This problem is usually managed by restricting the amount of medication the patient can obtain by prescription at one time.[40]

The third type of limitation on treatment with medication is drug dependence for some types of drugs. This problem is most dramatic in methadone treatment of heroin addiction, but can also be a problem in prolonged unsupervised use of antianxiety drugs (e.g., Valium).[41]

§3.08   Psychotherapy

Psychotherapy is an interpersonal process in which one person communicates understanding, respect, and a wish to help to another. While most treatment of mental disorders is predicated on the desire to be understanding and helpful, when the primary mode of treatment is medication, electroshock therapy, or behavior therapy, the implicit message is that the understanding is secondary to the effects expected from the other therapeutic modalities. In psychotherapy, on the other hand, this communication of understanding in the context of a helping relationship is explicit and is the central feature of this method of treatment.[42]

Although the treatment of mental disorders by talking is probably as old as time, the modern era of talk therapy began about 80 years ago. Practiced almost exclusively by physicians for the first 40 years, psychologists became involved in psychotherapy in the late 1940s and have devoted an increasing proportion of their professional time to its practice. The entry of psychologists into the practice of psychotherapy was the high water mark of psychoanalytic theoretical influence on psychotherapy technique and theory, and marked the beginning of a rapid diversification in both areas.[43]

The increasing pressure by third-party payors, insurance companies and the federal government, for accountability and efficacy has sparked renewed interest in psychotherapy outcome research. Recent reviews suggest that, regardless of the theoretical orientation of the therapist, in general, about two-thirds to three-fourths of those who receive psychotherapeutic treatment are rated as functioning better at follow-

---

[40] *Id* 27-32.

[41] *Id* 15.

[42] I. Weiner, Principles of Psychotherapy 3 (1975).

[43] *See* Garfield, *Psychotherapy: A 40-year Appraisal*, 36 Am Psychologist 174-83 (1981).

up than those who suffer from a similar disorder but were not treated.[44] The various treatment techniques are not uniformly effective for all mental disorders, however.[45]

To understand the research on the effectiveness of psychotherapy, it is necessary to understand the standard research methodology. Most research involves two groups of patients, one of which is treated, while the other serves as a control. In clinical research settings, the patients on the waiting list serve as a control group. After a certain length of time determined by the investigator, the two groups are tested, interviewed, or rated as to their psychological state. Statistical comparisons of the two groups are used to evaluate the effectiveness of the treatment. More sophisticated research designs are usually elaborations and refinements of this basic paradigm.[46]

Just as medical treatment of minor physical disorders tends to be more successful than treatment of severe or chronic diseases, the same principle holds for mental disorders. People suffering from acute, situational, adjustment difficulties may be readily treated with outpatient psychotherapy and usually recover quite quickly. The more chronic, severe, or disabling the disorder, the more likely that treatment will be correspondingly prolonged and a successful result more in doubt. A recent survey found that the average length of treatment for outpatients receiving individual psychotherapy was six sessions, which suggests that for the most part these patients were treated for acute, situational difficulties.[47]

§3.09 —Basic Technique

Although most laypersons think of lying on a couch and engaging in free association as the usual manner in which psychotherapy is conducted, this traditional method of therapy, called psychoanalysis, accounts for a rather small percentage of treatment. Three major psychotherapeutic treatment techniques are currently in use: individual

---

[44] *See* Smith & Glass, *Meta-analysis of Psychotherapy Outcome Studies,* in Evaluation Studies Review Annual (1978).

[45] Epstein & Vlok, *Research on the Results of Psychotherapy: A Summary of the Evidence,* 138 Am J Psychiatry 1027-35 (1981).

[46] *Id* 1027.

[47] Garfield, *Research on Client Variables in Psychotherapy,* in Handbook of Psychotherapy and Behavior Change 191-232 (2d ed 1978).

psychotherapy, group psychotherapy, and marital/family therapy.[48]

Individual psychotherapy is conducted in private meetings between the the patient and the therapist. Typically, outpatient appointments are scheduled once per week, although more frequent appointments may be necessary for personality disorder patients or for those in acute crisis without adequate social supports. Appointments usually last 15 minutes to an hour.[49]

Individual psychotherapy has been found to be effective in the treatment of a wide range of mental disorders when three conditions are met. The patient must be motivated to engage in psychotherapeutic treatment. The patient must be able to talk and engage in self-reflection. Notwithstanding the disorder, the patient must have retained a generally well integrated level of personality functioning. None of these criteria is essential to the initiation of treatment; however, they are related to the patient's ability to use and profit from individual psychotherapy.[50]

The therapy process varies from therapist to therapist depending on the therapist's style and on the patient. Most therapists now consider themselves eclectic in their theoretical orientation, an adjective with meanings as diverse as the therapists themselves. In spite of that ambiguity, the techniques can be broadly categorized as psychodynamic, humanistic-existential, and behavioral. The behavior therapy techniques will be covered in §3.11.

Psychoanalysis is a treatment technique that is usually distinguished from psychotherapy by the mental health community because of significant differences in the technique from garden variety psychotherapy. Psychoanalysis is practiced only by psychoanalysts and involves one-hour sessions four to five times per week for three to five years. The patient lies on a couch and engages in free association, that is, says whatever comes to mind. The goal is personality restructuring through insight into intrapsychic conflicts. Analysis is a treatment intended for people with neurotic disorders, that is, those disorders caused by psychological conflicts. Psychoanalysis is not a treatment of choice for psychotic disorders, like schizophrenia, because the treatment itself is quite stressful, and requires a rather well-integrated patient to use and benefit from treatment.[51]

Psychodynamically oriented therapists discriminate between two

---

48 Epstein & Vlok, *Research on the Results of Psychotherapy: A Summary of the Evidence*, 138 Am J Psychiatry 1027-28 (1981).

49 *See* I. Weiner, Principles of Psychotherapy 91-96 (1975).

50 *Id* 61.

51 S. Garfield, Clinical Psychology 259-64 (2d ed 1983).

different approaches to psychotherapy: supportive and uncovering. Supportive psychotherapy involves the attempt by the therapist to help the patient deal with real world problems without exploring unconscious conflicts. Uncovering approaches attempt to help the patient reorganize or restructure personality through the recognition and understanding of unconscious conflicts and maladaptive defenses.

Supportive psychotherapy is appropriate for the treatment of schizophrenic disorders once the acute symptomatology is controlled. Bipolar disorders and major depressive disorders may also be treated supportively to help the patient regain the ability to cope and function effectively in the aftermath of an acute episode.

Uncovering approaches, regardless of the theoretical orientation of the therapist, attempt to modify the patient's personality structure through a process which involves encouraging one to step back for a moment and look at one's manner of relating to others. Thus, uncovering approaches may be necessary for patients with personality disorders since, usually, it is their characteristic way of relating that causes them difficulty.[52]

For example, if the patient suffers from a compulsive personality disorder and complains of difficulty in making an important decision, supportive and uncovering approaches would dictate different therapeutic interventions. A supportive approach would help the patient to make the decision. An uncovering approach would encourage the patient to figure out why decision making is so difficult. The supportive approach accepts the patient's personality structure as is and helps the patient to live with it, while the uncovering approach challenges the patient's characteristic style by exploring the functions the maladaptive behavior serves in coping with the patient's internal psychological conflicts about decision making.

Humanistic/existential therapists share the goal of communicating their understanding of the patient's psychological condition with the psychodynamically oriented therapists. The techniques emphasize understanding and change in the *here and now,* and, therefore, include recreation of and reexperiencing of troublesome situations in the session through role playing or use of an empty chair to create the experience of confronting a significant person in the patient's life. The emphasis is on seeing available choices and actively choosing what the patient wants, rather than passively accepting things as they are.[53]

Group psychotherapy, the second major psychotherapeutic treatment

---

[52] I. Weiner, *supra* note 49, at 40-43.

[53] *See* S. Garfield, *supra* note 51, at 288-96.

modality, may be conducted in either inpatient or outpatient settings. The group, rather than the therapist, is viewed as the therapeutic agent. Outpatient groups usually meet once or twice per week for 60 to 90 minutes at a time.[54]

Group psychotherapy is typically utilized in the hospital treatment of drug and alcohol abuse where other group members can confront a patient about behavior in a way that the therapist could not. A more supportive approach to group therapy may be utilized to help psychotic patients regain reality contact and reestablish social relationships.[55] Outpatient group therapy might be recommended for someone who identifies relationships with others as the area of greatest distress.[56]

Psychodynamic and humanistic-existential theoretical positions predominate in the thinking about how to conduct group psychotherapy as well. The dynamically oriented therapists tend to be less interactive in groups, preferring to establish initial guidelines which facilitate the interaction of group members with each other and then let group dynamics determine the course of the group. The assumption is that problematic relationships will be unconsciously recreated with the therapist and other group members and that the group members will both confront and interpret these conflicts for each other.[57] The existentially oriented therapists sometimes use the group as a setting for conducting individual therapy with the rest of the group observing the patient who is *working*. As in individual therapy, the emphasis is on *here and now* experiencing and change.[58]

The third major treatment technique is marital/family treatment. The therapeutic assumption is that the symptoms of the *identified patient* are symptoms of pathological family interactions, and, therefore, the real patient is the family. The goal of treatment is to change the nature of the family interactions to enable the *identified patient* to give up the exhibited symptoms. Theoretical approaches to family therapy range from behavioral to psychodynamic to systems theory. Systems theory postulates that the interactions of family members constitute a system in which certain patterns of interacting are maintained by the responses

---

[54] I. Yalom, The Theory and Practice of Group Psychotherapy 278 (2d ed 1975).

[55] Epstein & Vlok, *supra* note 48, at 1029.

[56] I. Yalom, *supra* note 54, at 232.

[57] *Id* 195.

[58] *Id* 447.

of other people in the system. The therapist's task is to intervene in those patterns and change them in the treatment setting.[59]

Family therapy is often used in conjunction with other modes of treatment in treating hospitalized adolescents and children as well as adult substance abusers. Family therapy in outpatient settings has been used to treat child and sexual abuse, as well as marital difficultie s. Family therapy may also be recommended when two divorced parents with custody of their children marry, to aid the *blending* of the two families. The sessions are usually 60 to 90 minutes long once per week. Treatment may last from two months to a year or more depending on the severity of the difficulties.[60]

§3.10 —Limitations

Each type of psychotherapy has strengths and weaknesses, indications and contraindications for its use. Limitations on the use of any type of psychotherapy are based sometimes on practical considerations and sometimes on research data on outcome of various modes of treatment with various types of patients. Because of the nature of the therapy it has a limitation not found with hospitalization or medication: a patient cannot effectively be compelled to participate in psychotherapy. To benefit, at some point, the patient must be willing to be treated.

As noted above, a majority of patients treated with psychotherapy improved and were better off compared to those who were not treated. The range of improvement in the reported studies is 0 to 100 per cent, which suggests that the techniques and practitioners are not uniformly efficacious. For example, psychotherapy with patients with schizophrenic disorders seems to be useful when the focus of treatment is on reality-oriented problem solving combined with drug therapy. Patients who received these treatments were less likely to relapse, or if they did relapse, were able to stay out of the hospital longer and function better socially and vocationally.[61] For depressed patients, individual therapy that allowed the patients to express negative affect and talk about their symptoms resulted in higher relapse rates than therapy in which the patients talked more about problems in living and expressed more positive affect during treatment.[62]

For certain other disorders, individual therapy has not been shown

---

[59] *See* S. Minuchin, Families and Family Therapy (1974).

[60] Epstein & Vlok, *supra* note 48, at 1029-30.

[61] Epstein & Vlok, *Research on the Results of Psychotherapy: A Summary of the Evidence,* 138 Am J Psychiatry 1027, 1030-31 (1981).

[62] *Id* 1032.

to be effective regardless of technique. There is little research to suggest that outpatient treatment of alcoholism is effective in doing more than reducing drinking problems. Since alcoholism has debilitating and potentially fatal physical concomitants that are exacerbated by continued ingestion of alcohol, treatment that fails to stop the patient's drinking cannot be considered effective.[63] Individual psychotherapy for marital problems is effective in resolving those marital problems less than half the time.[64] Outpatient individual psychotherapy with sociopathic personalities seems to have little effect and if it is to have a chance at all, must be initiated while the patient is confined to a residential setting.[65]

The outcome research for outpatient group psychotherapy is even less encouraging. Although there are indications that group psychotherapy aimed at specific problems may be a useful adjunct to other forms of treatment for patients with schizophrenic disorders, little else is available to recommend it at this time. Perhaps group psychotherapy is an effective treatment, but there is little research support for that contention.[66]

Family therapy has emerged as a very effective treatment modality. When compared to individual and group psychotherapy for family-related problems, family therapy is more effective in alleviating the distress of the family members and improving the mental health of the family unit in 73 per cent of the cases and equally effective in the remaining 27 per cent. Positive results have been reported about 65 per cent of the time family treatment is initiated. Positive outcome is associated with more experienced therapists, regular therapy attendance by both spouses, the quality of family interaction, and the therapist's ability to build positive relationships with the family.[67] It may be that family therapy will be more frequently utilized when third-party payors recognize it as a cost-effective treatment alternative to individual psychotherapy.

---

[63] *Id* 1033.

[64] *Id* 1029.

[65] Frosch, *The Treatment of Antisocial and Borderline Personality Disorders,* 34 Hosp & Community Psychiatry 245 (1983).

[66] Epstein & Vlok, *supra* note 61, at 1029.

[67] *Id* 1029-30.

§3.11   Behavioral Therapies

The behavioral therapies are the most recently developed treatment technique, having emerged within the last 25 years. Although popularly referred to as a single therapy—behavior modification or *B-Mod*—there are really four different groups of behavioral therapies, each having developed independently of the others. In spite of their differences in technique, the behavioral approaches share some common assumptions and goals.

The behavior therapies are empirically derived, that is, based on research data. In contrast to the psychodynamic theories and therapies that rely on high-level inferences to explain therapeutic techniques and outcomes, behavior therapists disavow such concepts as *conflicts* and *defenses* as not capable of validation by research and, therefore, as useless in changing behavior. Instead, they posit that treatment is intended to result in observable changes in behavior. Therefore, assessment, both pretreatment and posttreatment, is designed to provide objective behavioral measures rather than measures of *personality*. The medical model of psychopathology is overtly or indirectly rejected, since it provides no information about what behaviors need to be changed or which reinforcers are maintaining the maladaptive behavior.[68]

§3.12   —Basic Technique

The first of the four groups of behavior therapies is called *applied behavior analysis,* and is the outgrowth of the operant learning research.[69] Operant conditioning is popularly recognized by the experiments where rats push a lever to receive a food pellet reward. Human operant conditioning programs utilize tokens or, sometimes, *M&M* candies. As in the experimental research, the focus of assessment and treatment is on observable behavior and the consequences which maintain that behavior. For the strict behaviorist, if the behavior cannot be seen, heard, or measured, it does not exist and cannot be the focus of treatment.

Treatment technique usually involves an observation period during which the target behavior is charted to establish a baseline frequency and to discover the environmental events that sustain the target behavior.[70] Once the program is initiated, the target behavior is either rewarded, not rewarded, or punished. The target behavior is charted

---

[68] D. Rimm & J. Masters, Behavior Therapy 4-28 (2d ed 1979).

[69] Also called *contingency management.*

[70] D. Rimm & J. Masters, Behavior Therapy 156-59 (2d ed 1979).

during this period as well, and its frequency recorded. Usually the program will be suspended, and the target behavior observed and recorded again. Return to baseline frequency during the interruption of the program confirms that the behavior is controlled by the program. The operant program is then reinstated and maintained.[71] This kind of approach has been successfully used to treat autistic children, mentally retarded children and adults, chronically psychotic patients, and children with behavior problems in school.[72]

For example, if a child's temper tantrums are the target behavior, the parents might be instructed to construct a chart on which to record the number of times a tantrum occurs each day, what action preceded the tantrum, and what the parents did in response to the child's behavior. If the charting reveals that when the child seeks attention from her parents and is ignored, she has a tantrum which one or both parents seek to stop by talking, holding, or hugging the child, the program would seek to stop the reinforcement of the tantrum behavior with attention. The program would reward the child's nontantrum behavior with parental attention. Tantrum behavior would be ignored or result in immediate punishment like being sent to her room for five minutes.

The second major group in the behavioral school is an outgrowth of classical conditioning research. Classical conditioning principles were discovered by Pavlov by presenting meat powder to his dogs at the same time a bell was rung. After a few trials where the bell and meat powder were presented together, just ringing the bell would produce the same involuntary salivation as presenting the meat.[73] That experimental procedure and its results form the basis of understanding of neurosis for this group of practitioners. Anxiety is understood to be a conditioned response, and treatment is oriented toward the reduction of anxiety through counterconditioning.[74]

Treatment techniques that have evolved from this research include systematic desensitization, implosive therapy, and flooding. Systematic desensitization involves the teaching of a progressive relaxation procedure that is mastered during the first phase of treatment. A hierarchy of anxiety-producing situations is constructed by the patient and the therapist, with the lowest anxiety item first and the highest anxiety item last. The items are presented one at a time, and followed by rehearsal of the relaxation technique. The item is repeated until it no longer

---

[71] *Id* 159-82.

[72] *Id* 197-98.

[73] *See* 1 I. Pavlov, Lectures on Conditioned Reflexes (1928).

[74] D. Rimm & J. Masters, *supra* note 70, at 58.

causes anxiety, and then the next higher item is presented, and so on until the hierarchy is completed and the anxiety-producing situations no longer have their old effect. This treatment has been successfully used to treat phobias and some anxiety disorders.[75] This technique is the treatment of choice for obsessive-compulsive disorders.[76]

Implosive therapy and flooding are techniques that involve exposure to the stimulus that provokes the phobic response. Thus, a person who is afraid of heights might be taken up to the top of a very tall building by the therapist and encouraged to stay there until the fear subsides.[77]

The third group of behavioral therapies is based on social learning theory. In this theoretical system, behavior is influenced by stimulus control, that is, by being paired with some environmental event; by operant contingencies, that is, *If I do this, I'll get an M&M;* and by cognitive (mental) processes. Observational learning is important in these procedures, and modeling is an important component of behavior change.[78]

Assertiveness and social skills training is an outgrowth of this theoretical orientation. Assertiveness training is intended to teach people to be honest and straightforward in the expression of thoughts and ideas, to do so in a socially appropriate way, and to take other people's feelings and welfare into account while acting assertively. This training is thought to increase feelings of well-being and to increase the individuals' social success, thus improving the quality of their lives. It might be recommended for any patients, regardless of diagnosis, who seem to have difficulty in expressing themselves effectively in social or intimate relationships.[79]

Assertiveness training has been conducted both in individual treatment settings and in groups. A technique called *behavioral rehearsal* is frequently utilized in either setting. Behavioral rehearsal involves role playing the desired behavior while the therapist or another group member role plays the person from whom some action is desired or to whom some thought or feeling is expressed. Behavioral rehearsal by the patient may be preceded by modeling by the therapist, that is, the therapist may demonstrate the assertive behavior first. After the rehearsal, the patient receives feedback from the therapist or other

---

[75] *Id* 41-42.

[76] W. Reid, Treatment of the DSM-III Psychiatric Disorders 145 (1983).

[77] D. Rimm & J. Masters, *supra* note 70, at 297-313.

[78] *Id* 103-23.

[79] *Id* 63-102.

patients about which behaviors were assertive and which need to be changed to be more assertive.[80]

The final group of behavior therapies is the cognitive/behavioral therapies. The assumption of this group of therapies is that faulty cognitive processes (irrational thoughts) are the cause of disordered behavior. The goal of therapy is to change cognitive events, that is, the patients' thoughts, and, consequently, their behavior.[81]

Therapy consists of learning to correct irrational thoughts, beliefs, and assumptions. Some therapists go one step further and direct behavior change as well through *homework assignments*. These are behavioral exercises to be completed between therapy sessions. The treatment is usually highly structured during the sessions, the number of sessions is limited, and the therapist actively engages in teaching the patient new verbal and behavioral strategies.[82] This treatment technique has been utilized to treat major depressive disorders with considerable success. Some research suggests that this technique is more effective than medication in reducing symptoms of depression and preventing relapse in moderately depressed outpatients.[83] Treatment sessions are usually scheduled twice per week for about one hour each. Some practitioners limit the length of treatment to 12 to 16 sessions, while others will continue beyond that time if the depression does not remit.[84]

Another cognitive technique has been utilized in the treatment of obsessive thoughts, that is, thoughts which recur over and over again and over which the patient usually feels no control. The technique, called *thought stopping*, involves having the patient concentrate on the recurring thought during the treatment session until the therapist says *stop* or perhaps administers a mild shock. After several repetitions of this procedure, the patient is then encouraged to take over the task of saying *stop*. Sometimes the patient is instructed to wear a rubber band on his wrist, and to snap himself on the wrist while saying *stop* as a first step in this process. Treatment is continued until the patient can stop the

---

[80] *Id* 133-39.

[81] *Id* 377-78.

[82] *Id* 379-90.

[83] Epstein & Vlok, *Research on the Results of Psychotherapy: A Summary of the Evidence*, 138 Am J Psychiatry 1027, 1030 (1981).

[84] D. Rimm & J. Masters, *supra* note 70, at 409. *See also* Kovacs, *The Efficacy of Cognitive and Behavior Therapies for Depression*, 137 Am J Psychiatry 1495-501 (1980).

obsessive and troublesome thoughts without difficulty and without the external aids.[85]

§3.13 —Limitations

Behavioral therapies have some important limitations. Behavior changes effected in the treatment setting, especially in schools or hospitals, frequently do not generalize to other settings. In addition, the behavior changes frequently do not last very long after treatment is completed.[86] The cognitive behavior therapies seem to be less prone to such problems, however.[87]

The use of punishment to modify behavior is particularly fraught with difficulty. The use of physical punishment of aggressive behavior, for example, may result in the elimination of the aggressive behavior in the setting where it is punished while increasing the frequency of such behavior in other settings where punishment is impossible. This process, called *negative modeling,* is the behavioral equivalent of the old proverb *What you do speaks so loudly I cannot hear what you are saying.*[88]

The use of operant behavior management programs in prisons and juvenile detention facilities has been highly controversial. In these settings, target behaviors such as performing routine maintenance tasks or attending educational programs are rewarded with such reinforcers as cigarettes, leisure time, or access to television. These programs have been quite effective in managing the behavior of inmates on these units. However, the potential for abuse has been demonstrated in several instances when the control of the program is in the hands of the correctional staff or administration, as the emphasis usually swings to punishment of undesirable behavior through loss of already accrued reinforcers rather than through reward of desirable behavior.[89] Where access to food, law libraries, or other constitutionally guaranteed protections are made contingent on institutionally defined desirable behavior, these programs may be a violation of the prisoners' constitutional rights.[90]

---

[85] D. Rimm & J. Masters, *supra* note 70, at 396.

[86] D. Rimm & J. Masters, Behavior Therapy 265 (2d ed 1979).

[87] *Id* 395.

[88] *Id* 323-24.

[89] *Id* 255-56.

[90] Wexler, *Token and Taboo: Behavior Modification, Token Economies, and the Law,* 61 Cal L Rev 81 (1973).

§3.14   Electroconvulsive Therapy

Electroconvulsive therapy (ECT) has been a controversial treatment for mental disorders. Therapeutically induced seizures as a treatment for severe mental disorders grew out of the observations of a physician that depression and schizophrenia were very rare in patients with seizure disorders. The physician reasoned that induced seizures might ameliorate the symptoms of the other disorders.[91] For severe depressions, the hypothesis seems to be true. Seizures were initially introduced by drug injection, but the use of electric current proved to be superior since it could be controlled as to dose, duration, and site of administration.[92]

§3.15   —Basic Technique

Electroconvulsive therapy (ECT) is usually administered while the patient is hospitalized. A thorough medical workup is essential prior to initiating a course of ECT to assess the risk of physical complications from the procedure. Ordinary ECT is administered only to the nondominant side of the brain (right side of the head in righthanded people). ECT is given while the patient is under a general anesthetic. In addition to the sedative, other drugs are administered to reduce muscular contractions and salivation. Treatments are given three times per week until eight to twelve have been completed. Several administrations of ECT beyond the remission of symptoms are usually given to minimize the occurrence of relapse.[93]

ECT is effective in alleviating symptoms of major depression within four weeks about 80 per cent of the time. This rapid alleviation of symptoms may be an important consideration in treating a suicidal patient.[94] Although ECT has been used to treat schizophrenic disorders, especially those patients with severe affective components (mania or depression superimposed on a schizophrenic disorder), withdrawn patients who have been nonresponsive to other treatment, or patients who have been catatonic for an extended period, medication is the preferred treatment and ECT the last resort.[95]

---

[91] Fink, *Medina and the Origins of Convulsive Therapy*, 141 Am J Psychiatry 1034-40 (1984).

[92] *Id* 1039.

[93] W. Reid, Treatment of the DSM-III Psychiatric Disorders 135-36 (1983).

[94] *Id* 135.

[95] *Id* 119.

§3.16   —Limitations

The limitations of electroconvulsive therapy (ECT) have to do with its side effects. Because it involves the administration of electric current, patients with cardiac problems are at some risk for cardiac complications. ECT typically induces confusion, short-term memory loss, slurred speech, and disorientation, which, even though temporary, can be very frightening for patients.[96] Some patients refuse to give consent for ECT because of these effects.[97] In the absence of the consent of a competent patient, some constitutionally adequate substitute decision-making process is required to implement this treatment.[98] Other complications that were a problem in the past, like bone fractures secondary to muscle contractions, have been virtually eliminated by the administration of prophylactic medication.

Recent follow-up research has investigated the long-term after-effects of ECT using neuropsychological test batteries. These test batteries are very sensitive to organic brain damage and include tests of memory function. A recent review of that research concluded that, in spite of pronounced memory deficits found during the first several weeks after administration of ECT, the bulk of the research suggests that these symptoms disappear completely within a few weeks, leaving no residual effects. That review found two studies that indicated residual organic deficits after ECT, one with depressed patients and the other with chronic schizophrenic patients with 50 or more ECT treatments. Those studies were criticized because of methodological flaws in the design of the research that made interpretation of the findings difficult.[99]

§3.17   Psychosurgery

Modern surgical intervention in mental disorders was begun by the Portuguese surgeon, Moniz, in 1935. This technique involved the surgical disconnection of the prefrontal lobes from the remainder of the brain and resulted in his being awarded a Nobel Prize in 1948. The technique was introduced in the United States by Freeman and Watts

---

[96] Heaton & Crowley, *Effects of Psychiatric Disorders and Their Somatic Treatments on Neuropsychological Test Results,* in Handbook of Clinical Neuropsychology 512-16 (1981).

[97] Winslade, *Medical, Judicial and Statutory Regulation of ECT in the United States,* 141 Am J Psychiatry 1349 (1984).

[98] *See, e.g.,* Deering v Johnson, 307 Minn 250, 239 NW2d 905 (1976).

[99] Heaton & Crowley, *supra* note 96, at 516. *See also* Holden, *A Guarded Endorsement for Shock Therapy,* 228 Sci 1510 (1985).

and a number of variations of techniques and locations of incisions were developed. Various techniques have been introduced for different types of mental disorders, with chronic schizophrenia, obsessive-compulsive disorders, and violent behavior being most frequent target syndromes.[100] Psychosurgery has been seen as a last-ditch effort to prevent the patient from spending a lifetime confined in an institution.

§3.18   —Basic Technique

The traditional prefrontal leucotomy consisted of neurosurgical cuts across the white matter in both sides of the brain which disconnected the very front of the brain from portions to the rear. The technique introduced in the United States involved cutting both sides of the connecting pathways just in front of the lateral ventricles, two fluid-filled cavities deep in the interior of brain.

Recent technical advances use stereotaxic techniques to locate precise areas of the brain to be destroyed using electric current passed through a very fine needle. A small hole is drilled in the skull and the needle is guided into precise position using X-ray monitors. The stereotaxic device allows control of the needle in its spatial orientation on any axis.[101] Other areas of the brain are now targeted for surgical ablation (destruction) in addition to prefrontal cortex. Techniques recently have centered on subcortical areas, such as the thalamus and amygdala. These structures, located deep in the brain, are currently understood to be involved in regulating basic physiological processes like hunger and thirst, and arousal in response to danger. These two structures have been implicated as having a role in disordered behavior in animal research.[102]

The research documenting the efficacy of psychosurgery has been plagued by poor planning and execution. Therefore, it is not possible to confirm or deny the proposition that these techniques are a reasonable alternative to permanent hospitalization for some patients.[103]

---

[100] Earp, *Psychosurgery: The Position of the Canadian Psychiatric Association,* 24 Can J Psychiatry 356 (1977).

[101] Donnelly, *Psychosurgery,* in Comprehensive Textbook of Psychiatry/IV 1564 (4th ed 1985).

[102] N. Carlson, Physiology of Behavior 455-56 (1977).

[103] *Id* 455.

§3.19 —Limitations

Psychosurgery is seldom currently utilized as a treatment technique in the United States. Most of the research is being conducted in England and Japan, since public reaction in the United States has been vehement in its opposition to psychosurgery. Concern about selective utilization of the techniques on individuals confined to prisons or institutions has raised ethical and legal concern about informed consent.[104]

Apart from these public policy concerns, other problems have been raised. Any neurosurgical technique carries a risk, and a high degree of neurosurgical skill and good postoperative care is essential if the technique is to have a chance of being successful.[105] Psychosurgery remains an experimental or research technique, and specific indications for psychosurgery are indefinite.[106] Finally, there is a real difficulty in evaluating the outcome of the surgery since pre- and postoperative evaluations have not generally been adequate to assess the results.[107]

Acute side effects of psychosurgery resemble those of other brain surgery. Transitory disorientation, memory loss, and emotional blunting may be present for a few days to a few weeks. The extent of these postoperative symptoms is dependent on the extent of the surgery, although with current procedures, long-term complications appear to occur in less than one per cent of cases.[108]

§3.20 Suggested Reading

Books

C. Bowden & M. Giffen, *Psychopharmacology for Primary Care Physicians* (1978).

N. Carlson, *Physiology of Behavior* (1977).

A. Freedman, H. Kaplan, & B. Sadock, *Modern Synopsis of Comprehensive Textbook of Psychiatry/II* (2d ed 1976).

S. Garfield, *Clinical Psychology* (2d ed 1983).

---

[104] *See, e.g.,* Kaimowitz v Department of Mental Hygiene, Circuit Ct of Wayne County, Michigan (1973), *reprinted in* F. Miller, R. Dawson, G. Dix, & R. Parnas, The Mental Health Process 567 (1976).

[105] Donnelly, *Psychosurgery,* in Comprehensive Textbook of Psychiatry/IV 1564 (4th ed 1985).

[106] *Id* 1566.

[107] N. Carlson, Physiology of Behavior 456-67 (1977).

[108] Donnelly, *supra* note 105, at 1567.

L. Kolb, *Modern Clinical Psychiatry* (9th ed 1977).

F. Miller, R. Dawson, G. Dix, & R. Parnas, *The Mental Health Process* (1976).

S. Minuchin, *Families and Family Therapy* (1974).

1 I. Pavlov, *Lectures on Conditioned Reflexes* (1928).

W. Reid, *Treatment of the DSM-III Psychiatric Disorders* (1983).

D. Rimm & J. Masters, *Behavior Therapy* (2d ed 1979).

A. Stone, *Psychiatry, Law and Morality* (1984).

I. Weiner, *Principles of Psychotherapy* (1975).

I. Yalom, *The Theory and Practice of Group Psychotherapy* (2d ed 1975).

Articles

Balis, *Substance Abuse Disorders*, in W. Reid, Treatment of the DSM-III Psychiatric Disorders 81 (1983).

Carnoff, *The Neuroleptic Malignant Syndrome*, 41 J Clin Psychiatry 79 (1980).

Donnelly, *Psychosurgery*, in Comprehensive Textbook of Psychiatry/IV (4th ed 1985).

Earp, *Psychosurgery: The Position of the Canadian Psychiatric Association*, 24 Can J Psychiatry 358 (1979).

Ellsworth, Collins, Casey, Schoonover, Hickey, Hyer, Twemlow, & Nesselroade, *Some Characteristics of Effective Psychiatric Treatment Programs* 47 J Cons & Clinical Psychology 813 (1979).

Epstein & Vlok, *Research on the Results of Psychotherapy: A Summary of the Evidence*, 138 Am J Psychiatry 1027 (1981).

Fink, *Medina and the Origins of Convulsive Therapy*, 141 Am J Psychiatry 1034 (1984).

Frosch, *The Treatment of Antisocial and Borderline Personality Disorders*, 34 Hosp & Comm Psychiatry 245 (1983).

Garfield, *Psychotherapy: A 10-year Appraisal*, 36 Am Psychologist 174 (1981).

Garfield, *Research on Client Variables in Psychotherapy*, in Handbook of Psychotherapy and Behavior Change 191 (2d ed 1978).

Heaton & Crowley, *Effects of Psychiatric Disorders and Their Somatic Treatments on Neuropsychological Test Results*, in Handbook of Clinical Neuropsychology 512 (1981).

Jerrell & Larsen, *Policy Shifts and Organizational Adaptation: A Review of Current Developments*, 20 Community Mental Health J 282 (1984).

Katz, *Psychiatric Hospitalization,* in Comprehensive Textbook of Psychiatry/IV (4th ed 1985).

Kessler & Waletzky, *Clinical Use of the Antipsychotics,* 138 Am J Psychiatry 202 (1981).

Kovacs, *The Efficacy of Cognitive and Behavior Therapies for Depression,* 137 Am J Psychiatry 1495 (1980).

Lantz, Carlberg, & Wilson, *Mental Health Treatment Outcome by Sex, Diagnosis, and Treatment Agency,* 14 Prof Psychology 308 (1983).

McRae, *Seen But Not Admitted at the State Hospital,* 7 Psychosocial Rehabilitation J 21 (1983).

Shuman & Hawkins, *The Use of Alternatives to Institutionalization of the Mentally Ill,* 33 Sw LJ 1181 (1980).

Smith & Glass, *Meta-Analysis of Psychotherapy Outcome Studies,* in Evaluation Studies Review Annual (1978).

Wexler, *Token and Taboo: Behavior Modification, Token Economies, and the Law,* 61 Cal L Rev 81 (1973).

Winslade, *Medical, Judicial and Statutory Regulation of ECT in the United States,* 141 Am J Psychiatry 1349 (1984).

Cases

Kaimowitz v Department of Mental Hygiene, (Mich 1973), *reprinted in* F. Miller, R. Dawson, G. Dix, & R. Parnas, *The Mental Health Process* 567 (1976).

Rennie v Klein, 653 F2d 836 (3d Cir 1981), *vacated & remanded,* 458 US 1119 (1982), *on remand,* 720 F2d 266 (3d Cir 1983).

Rogers v Okin, 634 F2d 650 (1st Cir 1980), *vacated & remanded sub nom Mills v Rogers,* 457 US 291 (1982).

4   The Professions of Psychiatry and Psychology

§4.01   Introduction

Although laypersons frequently confuse psychiatrists with psychologists, the undergraduate and the graduate educations of these two professions are different. These differences in education and orientation have important implications for attorneys who contemplate consulting or cross-examining them. Failure to distinguish these two professions can result in embarrassment, at the least, and may even lead to disaster in a critical case.

The following sections summarize the critical components of the educational and licensing process for both psychiatrists and psychologists. This information is intended to allow the attorney to evaluate critically the vita of the professional he is hiring or confronting and to be able to quality or challenge her.

§4.02   Psychiatrists

Benjamin Rush, a physician in colonial Philadelphia, is considered the father of American psychiatry. He was a pioneer in treatment of the mentally ill and wrote the first American psychiatric text, in which he classified insanity as a brain disease. No other American figure exerted such an influence on the course of psychiatric thinking and practice. Early psychiatric theorizing was dominated by the idea that mental disorders had a physiopathological etiology, an idea that held sway until Freud published his first paper in the late nineteenth century.[1]

There are currently 31,000 practicing psychiatrists in the United States. Most of these practice in urban areas.[2]

§4.03   —Definition

A psychiatrist is a *physician,* either allopathic (M.D.) or osteopathic (D.O.), who specializes in the study and treatment of mental disorders.

§4.04   —Education

Undergraduate Education

In medicine, the four years of medical school are referred to as the *undergraduate education,* with the four years of college necessary to enter most medical schools referred to as *premedical education.* Both the premedical and the undergraduate medical educational curricula are discussed below.

In the United States, premedical education in the vast majority of colleges and universities is fairly standard. This trend toward increasing homogeneity in premedical education resulted from increasing competition for entry into medical schools in the 1960s and 1970s. Most entering medical students have had courses in the following areas as requirements for admission to medical school:

---

[1] Comprehensive Textbook of Psychiatry/III 60-62 (Freedman, Kaplan, & Sadock eds 1980).

[2] American Psychiatric Assn, APA (1984).

Biology

Inorganic chemistry

Organic chemistry

Quantitative analysis

Biochemistry

Advanced mathematics

Physics

Zoology

Some social science

Some literature and humanities

The emphasis in the premedical curriculum is on the natural sciences.

The undergraduate medical training of psychiatrists is the same as for any other physician. The emphasis during the first two years is on classroom and laboratory education in the basic medical sciences such as gross anatomy, pathology, biochemistry, microbiology, and microanatomy.

Most medical schools require introductory psychiatry during this period, but it is generally a survey course. The third and fourth years of medical school are usually devoted to clinical training. During this period, one three-month rotation in psychiatry is generally required. This rotation usually consists of assignment to a psychiatric service under the supervision of a psychiatric resident and a member of the psychiatric faculty. The emphasis is on firsthand experience interviewing psychiatric patients or medical patients with psychiatric complications. Some programs require experience in a psychiatric emergency room during this period. Since this is the only psychiatric training most physicians receive, the goal is to teach physicians to recognize the symptoms of a mental disorder to facilitate referral to a psychiatrist during the course of their medical practice. The remainder of this 24 months is devoted to other specialties such as internal medicine, surgery, pediatrics, obstetrics-gynecology, and orthopedics with some limited opportunity for electives in areas of interest to the individual student.[3]

---

[3] See A. Flexner, Medical Education in the United States and Canada (1972).

The following medical school curriculum, taken from the catalogue of the Southwestern Graduate School of Biomedical Sciences, The University of Texas Health Science Center of Dallas, Texas illustrates a representative course of study.

Graduate Education

Once an individual has graduated from medical school, formal training in psychiatry or some other specialty can begin. The physician in specialty training is designated a *resident*. Residency training programs

FIRST-YEAR CURRICULUM

Course	Approximate Total Hours	Credits*
Medical Biochemistry	160	2.0
Biology of Cells and Tissues	130	1.5
Medical Genetics	40	0.5
Human Anatomy and Embryology	200	2.0
Psychiatry	60	0.5
Medical Physiology	160	2.0
Neurobiology	100	1.0
Endocrinology and Human Reproduction	70	1.0

SECOND-YEAR CURRICULUM

Introduction to Clinical Medicine	320	3.5
Immunology and Medical Microbiology	170	2.0
Anatomic and Clinical Pathology	390	4.0
Medical Pharmacology	130	1.5
Psychiatry	40	0.5

THIRD-YEAR CURRICULUM

Surgery	8 (weeks)	4.0
Pediatrics	8	4.0
OB/Gyn	8	4.0
Internal Medicine	16	8.0
Psychiatry	4	2.0
(One month unscheduled.)		

FOURTH-YEAR CURRICULUM

Neurology	4	2.0
Internal Medicine Selective	4	2.0
Surgery Selective	4	2.0
OB/Gyn Selective	4	2.0
Four (4) Other Electives	16	2.0

* Credit units are not to be confused with traditional semester hours. One (1) unit is approximately 100 contact hours.

are monitored by the Department of Graduate Medical Education of the American Medical Association and the Accreditation Council for Graduate Medical Education Residency Review Committees. These two professional associations may be excellent sources of information about the quality of an expert witness's residency training.[4]

The first year of postgraduate medical education is designated the *internship* year. There are currently four different types of first-year training that are generally accepted as appropriate training for future psychiatrists:

1. Categorical first year. These residency programs are planned, sponsored, and conducted by the approved program and limited to one medical specialty—Internal Medicine, Family Practice, Pediatrics, Surgery, or Obstetrics and Gynecology.

2. Categorical* first year. These residency programs are planned, sponsored, and supervised by the approved residency program and include experience not only in the field of the sponsoring department but also from medical specialty fields outside the sponsoring department. Generally this means a minimum of four months direct patient care experience in Internal Medicine, Family Practice, or Pediatrics.

3. Flexible First Year (*Flex*). These programs are sponsored by two or more residency programs (i.e. Family Practice and Pediatrics) and allow the student who is undecided as to a specialty to sample from several fields during their first year. Minimum requirements are usually to spend at least four months in Internal Medicine during this period.

4. Transitional Programs. Transitional programs provide physicians who decide to gain experience in other specialty fields during their first or later years of residency training to do that prior to further training in a single specialty.[5]

These requirements have been shifting toward more training in primary care medicine in the first year. As psychiatric thinking swings back toward a more biological, as opposed to psychological approach

---

[4] The American Medical Association publishes an annual Directory of Residency Training Programs. This can be obtained at most medical school libraries or from the AMA, P.O. Box 10946, Chicago, IL 60610. This directory contains a listing of programs accredited by the Accreditation Council for Graduate Medical Education of the AMA.

[5] American Board of Psychiatry and Neurology, Inc, Information for Applicants 6A-7, (1983).

to mental disorders, the emphasis is increasingly toward a more medical approach to first-year training in psychiatry. Consequently, first-year residency training in psychiatry is now usually advanced training in clinical medicine, with intensive training in psychiatry beginning in the second year of the four-year program.

The second through the fourth years in a psychiatry residency typically involve seminars and colloquia in psychopathology, diagnostic interviews, psychopharmacology, and neurology. In addition, psychiatry residents provide clinical services to patients in both inpatient and outpatient settings, along with training in various treatment approaches and techniques. The training settings range from state mental hospitals to medical school outpatient clinics to social service agency mental health clinics and facilities.[6]

Fellowships

Once a psychiatrist has completed a residency program, more advanced training in a particular area of interest within psychiatry is then available. This period of advanced training in psychiatry is termed a *fellowship*. It might involve, for example, research in depression or sleep disorders. Commonly, psychiatrists wishing to be trained as specialists in child psychiatry will take advanced training in child diagnostics and treatment and will be called *child fellows*. The lengths of fellowships range from one to three years. Research fellowships are most often sought by physicians pursuing careers in academic medicine.

A research fellowship usually provides a promising research scientist an opportunity to work closely with a physician who is also involved in research in some highly specialized area, and to receive the financial and professional support necessary to investigate a problem of interest to the fellow. The fellow thus usually gains considerable expertise in this area.

The child fellow, on the other hand, receives basic training in child psychiatry in addition to training in child psychiatry. During this period, the child fellow learns diagnostic techniques unique to assessing children, and gains supervised experience in the treatment of children and their families.[7]

---

[6] *See, e.g.,* Southwestern Medical School, University of Texas Health Sciences Center at Dallas, SW Med Sch Bull 1984-87, (1984).

[7] *Id* 62.

§4.05 —Licensing

Licensing of physicians is regulated by state law. The licensing acts usually establish a state board of medical examiners to act as the regulatory agency in the state. The state board then promulgates rules to aid in carrying out its regulatory function and acts on complaints about medical practice.[8]

All states require that an applicant for licensure demonstrate some minimal competence in the practice of medicine and good character. Most state licensing boards now accept the results of the Federal Licensing Examination (FLEX), a standardized comprehensive examination covering all aspects of medicine, as proof of competence. The FLEX is the medical equivalent of the Multistate portion of the bar exam. Part I is a two-day written test covering the basic medical sciences and is usually taken after the completion of the second year of medical school. Part II is a two-day written examination covering basic clinical medicine and is usually taken after completion of medical school. Part III is an objective test of clinical competence. To be eligible to sit for Part III, the candidate must have passed parts I and II, received a medical degree, and have served six months in an approved residency or internship. In addition, to be licensed, the applicant must furnish proof of graduation from an accredited medical school, and evidence of good moral character. Some states require completion of one year of graduate medical education to receive an unrestricted license, although, as noted above, an applicant need not have completed that year of training to sit for the examination.[9]

There is no separate licensing for psychiatrists. Psychiatrists are licensed as physicians by the state in which they practice. Beyond this general licensing, no special training or education is necessary to represent oneself as a psychiatrist.[10] One does not have to have completed a psychiatry residency program to practice psychiatry. It is not necessary to be *board certified* by the American Board of Psychiatry and Neurology to practice psychiatry or to represent oneself as a psychiatrist. The specialty designation is self-imposed and approximately two thirds of practicing psychiatrists are not board certified.

The impetus to continue on to graduate medical training is primarily

---

[8] *See, e.g.,* Medical Practice Act, Tex Rev Civ Stat Ann art 4495b (Vernon 1983).

[9] *Id* **§3.01.** *See also* Rypin's Medical Licensure Examinations 1-18 (13th ed 1984).

[10] Taylor & Torrey, *The Pseudo Regulation of American Psychiatry,* 129 Am J Psychiatry 658 (1972).

a matter of professional custom and economics. There is considerable distrust and even prejudice among physicians toward those who practice a specialty for which they have no specialty training. And, since psychiatrists usually depend on referrals from primary care physicians (internists and family practitioners), failure to be accepted by one's medical colleagues has potentially adverse economic effects. The lack of specialty training is also likely to cause difficulties in acquiring hospital privileges, particularly in urban areas, and consequently may limit the psychiatrist's practice to outpatient treatment.

§4.06 —Specialty Certification

Psychiatry

Specialty certification in psychiatry is awarded by the American Board of Psychiatry and Neurology.[11] To be eligible for certification, an applicant must be a physician with an unlimited license to practice medicine in a state and have satisfactorily completed a specialized training in psychiatry approved by the board. At least 24 months of the four years of specialized postgraduate training must have been in psychiatry.[12]

The examination in psychiatry consists of two parts and each applicant must pass both parts. Part I is a written examination that covers all areas of psychiatry and some areas of neurology, since the board requires proficiency in neurology as well as psychiatry. Passing part I of the exam entitles the applicant to apply to take part II of the exam, which consists of a one-hour examination in clinical psychiatry during which the applicant interviews a patient under the supervision of the examiners for 30 minutes. During the next 30 minutes the candidate is interviewed by the examiners to evaluate the candidate's knowledge of diagnostics, therapeutic techniques, as well as an ability to make prognostic and management decisions. Next, each applicant is required to view a 20-minute videotaped psychiatric examination and is examined by the board as to the contents of the tape. This portion of the exam also takes approximately one hour.[13]

Prior to 1981, candidates in psychiatry had to pass a one-hour examination in clinical neurology in addition to the two-hour examina-

---

[11] *See* **§4.13.**

[12] American Board of Psychiatry and Neurology, Inc, Information for Applicants 7 (1983).

[13] *Id* 10.

tion in psychiatry. In October 1984, the videotaped segments of the exam were replaced with *multiple written patient encounters* to be used by the examiners as a basis for discussion of issues related to diagnosis and treatment.[14] The exam is given four times per year. The pass rate for this examination in 1984 ranged from 50 to 58 per cent of those psychiatrists taking the examination.[15]

The implications of being *board certified* are unclear. Although board certification adds to a psychiatrist's prestige, the exam is a test of basic psychiatric knowledge, not of particular expertise or advanced skills.[16] Most hospitals currently require board eligibility, not certification, for the granting of staff or admitting privileges. Board certification, however, may be necessary for those in academic or administrative positions in some institutions. The trend seems to be toward requiring board certification, especially in high-status hospitals in urban areas where the supply of psychiatrists is great and competition is keen.

Neurology

Neurology is the medical specialty that deals with diseases of the nervous system. Neurology and psychiatry are closely related branches of medicine, and it is common for neurology residents to receive psychiatric training during their residency, as it is common for psychiatry residents to train in neurology. Sigmund Freud was a neurologist when he became interested in psychological phenomena.

Specialty certification in neurology is also awarded by the American Board of Psychiatry and Neurology. The general requirements for application to take the examination are the same as for psychiatry: an unlimited license to practice medicine and successful completion of an approved training program. The examination consists of two parts and both must be passed to be board certified as a neurologist. Part I includes questions across the field of neurology from neuroanatomy to neuro-virology and neuro-endocrinology. Part I also includes questions in some areas of psychiatry including growth and development, psychopathology, biological psychiatry, psychosocial psychiatry, and

---

14 *Id* 12.

15 American Board of Psychiatry and Neurology, Inc, Personal Communication (Nov 16, 1984).

16 Margenstern, *A Criticism of Psychiatry's Board Examinations*, 127 Am J Psychiatry 33 (1970).

diagnostic procedures. Finally, questions are also included that bridge clinical material common to both psychiatry and neurology.[17]

Part II of the exam is oral and may be taken after passing part I. This part of the exam consists of three one-hour exams: two in clinical neurology and one in clinical child neurology. As in psychiatry, one of the clinical exams involves examination of a patient and subsequent discussion with the examiners of the findings and management implications for the patient, and the other involves evaluation of clinical material without a patient being present.

Prior to 1982, neurology candidates had to take a one-hour oral exam in clinical psychiatry during part II. However, for those applicants who successfully completed part I of the exam after April 1, 1982, the oral exam in clinical psychiatry is no longer required. As in psychiatry, the format for the examination when the patient is not present was changed in October of 1984 to *multiple written simulated patient encounters* instead of videotape.[18]

The pass rate for those taking the exam during one of the four administrations in 1983-84 ranged from 63 to 68 per cent.[19]

Forensic Psychiatry

Forensic psychiatry is a subspecialty in psychiatry that relates psychiatric knowledge to legal problems. Forensic psychiatrists have studied not only the psychiatric aspects of problems that have legal consequences, but the legal aspects of these problems as well. Diplomate status in forensic psychiatry is awarded by the American Board of Forensic Psychiatry upon successful completion of oral and written examinations testing substantive legal knowledge and clinical skills. Certification began in 1979 when the American Board of Forensic Psychiatry was formed by the American Academy of Forensic Science, the Forensic Sciences Foundation, and the American Academy of Psychiatry and Law.[20] Eligibility for the examinations requires licensure in the jurisdiction in which the applicant resides, five years of residency training, and *substantial experience* in forensic psychiatry. There are currently about 80 diplomates in forensic psychiatry in the country.[21]

---

[17] American Board of Psychiatry and Neurology, *supra* note 15, at 11.

[18] *Id* 12.

[19] American Board of Psychiatry and Neurology, *supra* note 15.

[20] *See* §6.07.

[21] 1 Encyclopedia of Associations (19th ed 1984).

Child Psychiatry

Child psychiatry is a subspecialty in psychiatry whose practitioners are trained in the diagnosis and treatment of mental disorders in children and adolescents. Children with behavior problems, learning difficulties, emotional problems, or psychological adjustment difficulties secondary to chronic physical handicaps are those who might be evaluated or treated by a child psychiatrist.

Diplomate status in child psychiatry is awarded by the American Board of Psychiatry and Neurology. Each applicant for certification in child psychiatry must pass the exam in psychiatry before applying to take the exam in child psychiatry. The process of the examination is similar to that for certification in psychiatry with the content of the examination limited to the special problems of children's development, diagnosis, and treatment.[22] This examination, like the one in psychiatry, is designed to test basic competence in child psychiatry, not special expertise.

§4.07 —Psychoanalytic Training

Psychoanalytic treatment technique differs substantially from other forms of psychotherapy.[23] Standard psychoanalysis involves four to five visits per week for a number of years. The analysand (patient) lies on a couch, and the analyst sits behind the patients, out of the patient's field of vision. The patient is expected to engage in free association, to say whatever comes to mind. Because of these differences in treatment technique, the training of analysts differs in some important respects from standard psychiatric training. Psychoanalytic training is conducted at accredited training institutes, staffed by training analysts. Although analytic training may be a part of a psychiatric residency, it usually begins after the completion of a psychiatric residency.

The standards for the training of psychoanalysts are established by the Board on Professional Standards of the American Psychoanalytic Association. These standards are currently being revised, but major changes are not anticipated. To be accepted into an institute which offers analytic training accredited by the association, the following criteria must be met:

1.   Graduation from a Class A medical school
2.   Completion of one year of internship at a hospital approved by

---

[22] American Board of Psychiatry and Neurology, *supra* note 15, at 8.
[23] *See* **§3.08.**

the Council on Medical Education and Hospitals of the American Medical Association (AMA)

3. Completion of at least one year of psychiatric training unless the first year of training is included in the institutes training program and takes place in a psychiatric facility approved by the Council on Medical Education and Hospitals[24]

The applicant must also present evidence of integrity of character, maturity of personality, and the capacity to be analyzed. The analytic candidate must receive three years of psychiatric training prior to the completion of psychoanalytic training. During the course of the analytic training, the trainee will undergo *preparatory analysis.* Minimum requirements are for 300 hours, but most analytic candidates have two to three times that number before graduation from the institute.

The curriculum consists of reading, lectures, and seminars along with supervised clinical work. Students are expected to have read Freud's work and other relevant psychoanalytic literature. Students are expected to have treated a minimum of three patients during training. Candidates are furnished with a written statement upon the completion of training.[25]

Some analytic institutes accept Ph.D. clinical psychologists as analytic candidates, but most analysts are psychiatrists. Completion of analytic training is still considered quite prestigous in the medical community. Since psychoanalytic practice is not regulated by medical practice legislation beyond that of any other physician or psychologist, there are no direct legal implications of this training.

§4.08 Psychologists

Psychology was primarily an academic discipline until World War II, when psychological tests were developed to help screen potential pilots for flight training. This large-scale application of psychological knowledge opened the door to other applications, including treatment of mental disorders. Clinical psychology emerged during the 1950s and expanded rapidly during the 1960s.[26]

In addition to psychologists with doctoral degrees, there are a large number of psychologists with master's degrees working under the

---

[24] American Psychoanalytic Assn, Standards for Training in Psychoanalysis (1977).

[25] *Id* 8.

[26] *See* S. Garfield, Clinical Psychology 8-10 (1983).

supervision of the doctoral-level psychologists in schools, hospitals, and clinics. This two-tiered system of professionals, both of whom may be legally called psychologists in some circumstances, has created some confusion about the qualifications of someone who is labeled a psychologist. There are currently more than 25,000 doctoral-level psychologists in the United States, and the majority of those are clinical psychologists.[27]

§4.09   —Definition

A psychologist is a person who is trained to study and measure mental processes, and to diagnose and treat mental disorders. The use of the title *psychologist* is regulated by state law in all 50 states.[28]

§4.10   —Education

Undergraduate Education

Undergraduate education for psychologists, leading to a bachelor's degree, includes a major in psychology, as most graduate psychology schools require an undergraduate degree in psychology as a condition of admission. Undergraduate psychology curricula usually include the following courses:

1.   General (introductory) psychology
2.   Developmental psychology
3.   Social psychology
4.   Experimental psychology
5.   Physiological psychology
6.   Learning theories
7.   Abnormal psychology
8.   Behavior modification
9.   Introduction to psychological testing
10.   Statistics

---

[27] *Id* 449.

[28] See Laliotis & Grayson, *Psychologist Heal Thyself,* 40 Am Psychologist 34 (1985) for a succinct discussion of the regulatory practice.

Most undergraduate curricula allow the student to pursue areas of interest through participation in faculty research projects and seminars in upper-division classes.

The remainder of the undergraduate curriculum is usually heavily concentrated in other social sciences and humanities, with relatively little emphasis in natural sciences beyond those generally required for the bachelor's degree. These general rules may not apply to those who are intending to pursue graduate degrees in experimental or biological psychology and who may focus more on mathematics and natural or biological sciences as undergraduates.

Graduate Education

Graduate education in psychology is provided by two different types of institutions, graduate schools and professional schools. The graduate schools are usually located on the campuses of major universities and account for the largest number of graduating doctoral psychologists in all specialties. Professional schools of psychology graduate clinical psychologists almost exclusively. Professional schools may be affiliated with a college or university or may be free-standing and self-supporting. Faculty and administration may be practicing clinicians who teach part-time in addition to their practice.

Graduate programs in psychology in the United States typically award a Doctor of Philosophy (Ph.D.) degree upon completion of a dissertation and class work. However, within the last 15 years, training programs in clinical psychology have begun to grant the Doctor of Psychology degree (Psy.D.) instead of the traditional Ph.D. The training programs granting the Psy.D. have dropped the requirement of completion of a dissertation, and have emphasized the training of clinicians rather than scientist-practitioners.[29] In the past, some educational psychology departments granted Doctor of Education degrees (Ed.D.) to students trained as educational or counseling psychologists. Recent trends toward tightening of licensure requirements have made licensure as a psychologist more difficult for those with Ed.D. degrees.

The distinction between the Psy.D. and the Ph.D. in psychology may be important in making initial determinations of qualifications of experts. If the legal issue requires the expert to have training and experience conducting psychological research, a Ph.D. psychologist would very likely be better qualified than a Psy.D. psychologist. In other situations where clinical training and experience are relevant, a Psy.D.

---

[29] S. Garfield, Clinical Psychology 10-18 (1983).

psychologist may have more clinical experience than a Ph.D. psychologist with the same number of years of training.

Graduate training in psychology may be broadly categorized into five major specialty areas: Clinical, Counseling, School, Industrial/Organizational, and Experimental. Although the training in each of these areas is quite different, graduates from all types of programs may be licensed as psychologists. Consequently, it is important to understand the type of training conducted in each specialty area.

Training in clinical psychology is monitored by the Education and Training Board of the American Psychological Association, which sets standards for training and grants approval to programs which meet those standards.[30] Therefore, American Psychological Association approval is one measure of the quality of a training program in clinical psychology. Training in clinical psychology prepares the future practitioner to evaluate and treat patients with severe psychological difficulties. Advanced graduate training is usually oriented toward diagnosis and treatment in both outpatient and inpatient settings, including state and private psychiatric facilities.

Counseling psychology training is oriented toward preparing psychologists who intend to work with less severely disturbed individuals, usually in outpatient and higher educational settings. This emphasis affects the content of the graduate curriculum as well as the choice of training sites. Training of counseling psychologists is also evaluated by the American Psychological Association, which grants its approval to training programs which meet its standards.

School psychologists are trained to evaluate, treat, and consult in areas directly related to educational problems of children and adolescents. The training emphasis is less on severe emotional problems and more on evaluation and remediation of learning problems. School psychology programs are also approved by the American Psychological Association.

Each of the graduate programs outlined above consists of three years of academic work in psychology with emphasis in the specialty area, totaling 90 semester hours (or equivalent). In addition, the fourth year is devoted to a full-time predoctoral internship, generally in an institution other than the graduate school from which the degree will be received. The American Psychological Association (APA) has also established guidelines for institutions providing internship training to psychologists, and, therefore, internships may also be *APA approved.* The

---

[30] American Psychological Assn, *APA Approved Doctoral Programs in Clinical, Counseling, and School Psychology*, 36 Am Psychologist 1516-18 (1981).

internship year is usually devoted to supervised practice in a clinic, hospital, school, or counseling center, or some combination of these.[31]

Programs in experimental psychology and industrial/organizational psychology do not require internships and are not granted APA approval. Experimental psychology programs prepare psychologists for careers in teaching or research. The emphasis in these programs is on statistical methods, experimental design, and investigation into basic psychological and biopsychological processes.[32] Programs in industrial/organizational psychology usually emphasize the application of psychological knowledge in social, learning, and psychometric areas to business problems. These programs are usually more training-oriented than experimental psychology programs, but should not be confused with programs that train clinicians.

Postgraduate Education

Postgraduate training experiences in psychology are usually referred to as postdoctoral fellowships or *post-docs*. These advanced training courses may be broadly classified as either research or clinical in their emphasis. They are usually one to two years in duration, and postdoctoral fellows are usually paid a stipend during their training. No additional degrees are awarded upon completion. As in the case of psychiatrists, most postdoctoral fellowships are sought with the intention of pursuing an academic career in psychology.[33]

Postdoctoral training in psychology, like fellowships in psychiatry, provides the fellow with the opportunity to work closely with experienced clinicians or researchers in the area of interest. Depending on whether the purpose of the fellowship is training in clinical practice or research, the fellow will receive advanced training and supervised experience in a specialized area of psychology. Fellowships usually impart a certain status to the fellow which may be a competitive advantage in the academic or clinical job market and among professional peers.

---

[31] See American Psychological Assn, Graduate Training in Psychology and Associated Fields (1984) for a complete listing of APA approved programs.

[32] American Psychological Assn, *Education and Training Board, Education for Research in Psychology* 19 Am Psychologist 167-69 (1959).

[33] *See, e.g., Announcements,* 39 Am Psychologist 1331 (1984).

§4.11 —Licensing

Licensing is a prerequisite to holding oneself out to the public as a psychologist in all 50 states.[34] Psychologists are regulated under the provisions of licensing acts separate from those which regulate physicians. Therefore, each state has a state board of examiners of psychologists or similar administrative body empowered to regulate the practice of psychology in the state.[35]

Most licensing acts delineate some entities that are exempt from the requirements of the licensing act; usually these are schools, hospitals, and government agencies. Psychologists employed by these entities need not be licensed by the state to practice in that setting. The protective umbrella does not cover services performed outside the scope of that exempt relationship with the agency, for example, in private practice.[36]

Licensing and certification of psychologists are separate processes. Certification empowers the practitioner to use the title *psychologist*, while licensure allows independent practice. Certification is usually obtained by applying to the licensing agency to take the examination. This exam covers all areas of psychological knowledge. The vast majority of state boards obtain the examination from the same source, so this portion of the exam is relatively uniform. Some states add additional exams in ethics or law.[37]

Once a psychologist is certified, there is usually a requirement for a period of postdoctoral supervised practice prior to licensure. The minimum period is usually about one year of full-time practice with regular supervision by a licensed psychologist. Once the license is granted, the psychologist may practice independently.[38]

The licensing of psychologists is further complicated by certification of subdoctoral psychologists under the titles of psychological associate, psychological assistant, or psychological technician. These individuals, who have completed a Master's Degree in psychology, typically are not allowed to practice independently or to represent themselves as psychologists, and must perform their services under the direction of a licensed psychologist. The majority of these individuals work in public

---

[34] *See* Laliotis & Grayson, *Psychologist Heal Thyself,* 40 Am Psychology 89-90 (1985).

[35] *See, e.g.,* Psychologists' Certification and Licensing Act, Tex Rev Civ Stat, Ann art 4512c (Vernon Supp 1985).

[36] *Id* §22.

[37] *Id* §14(c).

[38] *Id* §21.

agencies and schools (exempt agencies in most states) and, therefore, may have the title of psychologist conferred by the agency for work performed in the agency.

States that certify subdoctoral psychological associates usually require completion of a Master's Degree in psychology, proof of a minimum number of hours of supervised clinical practical experience, and an examination.[39] The examination covers the broad spectrum of psychological knowledge, from general psychology to learning theory, and does not focus on applied clinical psychology.

§4.12   —Specialty Certification

Licensing of psychologists is generic, that is, no specialty designation of counseling, clinical, or forensic psychologist is recognized by the licensing laws, although a practitioner may designate an area of specialization. Some states do recognize a specialty called *health service provider in psychology.* This usually means that the applicant has met the requirements for listing in the National Register of Health Service Providers that include completion of an internship approved by the American Psychological Association or equivalent including supervised experience in a health care setting and a minimum of 1500 hours of postdoctoral experience, 25 per cent of which must have been in direct patient contact.[40]

Clinical Psychology

Specialty certification in clinical psychology is regulated by the profession itself, acting through the American Board of Professional Psychology (ABPP). Diplomate status is conferred by the board after the candidate has met the requirements of training and experience that are prerequisites to sitting for the examination. A minimum of four years of postdoctoral experience is required. The examination is conducted by a panel of five diplomates who rate the candidate in the following areas of professional competence: evaluative skills, intervention skills, depth and currency of professional and scientific knowledge, ethics and social responsibility, and professional commitment. These ratings are based on observation of a work sample of the candidate, usually a

---

[39] *Id* §19.

[40] *See, e.g.,* Rules and Regulations of The Texas State Board of Examiners of Psychologists, Specialty Certification §§469.1-469.3 (Dec 1983).

recording of a treatment session or a psychological evaluation.[41] There are currently more than 1800 diplomates in clinical psychology.[42] Like diplomate status in psychiatry, the conferring of diplomate status in psychology is peer recognition of professional competence.[43]

Forensic Psychology

Diplomate status in forensic psychology is conferred by the American Board of Forensic Psychology (ABFP). The minimum postdoctoral experience required to sit for the examination is the same as for clinical psychologists, four years. The candidate is also required to document experience in forensic psychology through letters from those familiar with the applicant's work. This examination also includes evaluation of a work sample in some area of forensic psychology. There are currently approximately 100 diplomates in forensic psychology in the United States.[44]

The applicant submits the application and documentation to the board, which then determines if the applicant is qualified to sit for the oral examination. The applicant presents a sample of forensic work to a panel of three examiners who are board members. These examiners then evaluate the applicant's work sample along with the applicant's sensitivity to legal and ethical issues.[45]

Others

The ABPP also confers diplomate status to psychologists in four other specialties: industrial/organizational, school, counseling, and neuro-psychology. There is currently no diplomate status conferred in the area of experimental psychology. The requirements and examination processes for these psychological specialties are similar to those for diplomates in clinical psychology.[46]

---

[41] *See* S. Garfield, Clinical Psychology 453-54 (1983).

[42] Robyak & Goodyear, *Graduate School Origins of Diplomates and Fellows in Professional Psychology*, 15 Prof Psychology 380 (1984).

[43] *Id* 379.

[44] *See* §6.07. *See also* Monahan & Loftus, *The Psychology of Law*, 33 Ann Rev Psychology 441-42 (1982).

[45] American Board of Forensic Psychology, Personal Communication (Nov 15, 1984).

[46] The ABPP, 2100 E. Broadway, Suite 313, Columbia, MO 65201, publishes an annual Manual for Oral Examinations, a Policies and Procedures Annual, and a Triennial Directory of Diplomates.

§4.13   Psychiatric and Psychological Organizations

Examination of expert witnesses frequently includes a litany of the organizations to which the expert belongs. These organizations may be important for two reasons. First, they may identify a pool of potential expert witnesses. Second, membership in the organization may imply that the expert has been selected for membership by peer review, recognizing excellence. As with the legal profession, some psychiatric and psychological organizations do select members based on a demonstration of excellence, while others are open to any members of the profession willing to pay dues. If so, the attorney, judge, and jury should be aware of these criteria.

Psychiatric Organizations

The *American Psychiatric Association* is a nonprofit corporation founded in 1844. According to a pamphlet published by the association, it is "a society of medical specialists brought together by a common interest in the continuing study of psychiatry, the search for more effective application of psychiatric knowledge to combat mental illness, and the promotion of mental health for all citizens."[47] In 1981, there were more than 26,000 members of the American Psychiatric Association, which represented about 70 per cent of the psychiatrists in the United States. All members, other than honorary members, must be physicians with some training and experience in psychiatry who pay their annual dues.[48]

Fellows must have been members of the association for at least eight years and have made significant contributions to psychiatry and to the association. Diplomate status is also a factor in the decision.[49]

The association publishes the *American Journal of Psychiatry* and *Hospital and Community Psychiatry*. The association requires continuing medical education in order to maintain membership status. The Association also publishes DSM-III.[50]

The *American Board of Psychiatry and Neurology, Inc* is a nonprofit corporation founded in 1934 by committees from the American Psychiatric Association, the American Neurological Association, and the American Medical Association. The board itself is composed of representatives from the American Psychiatric Association, the Ameri-

---

[47] American Psychiatric Assn, APA (1984).

[48] *Id.*

[49] *Id.* To obtain a copy of the Biographical Directory, contact the American Psychiatric Association, 1400 K Street NW, Washington, DC 20005.

[50] Diagnostic and Statistical Manual of Mental Disorders (3d ed 1980) (DSM-III).

can Medical Association, the American Neurological Association, and the American Academy of Neurology, with psychiatrists and neurologists equally represented. The board established a Committee on Certification in Child Psychiatry in 1959. The board establishes criteria for certification in psychiatry, neurology, and child psychiatry and publishes a list of diplomates in each specialty which it will make available upon request.[51]

The *American Psychoanalytic Association* is a nonprofit corporation whose membership is limited to psychoanalysts. Current membership is listed at more than 2700. The association publishes the *Journal of the American Psychoanalytic Association,* which is a monthly journal of articles reporting developments in psychoanalytic theory and practice.[52]

The *American Board of Forensic Psychiatry* was founded by the American Academy of Forensic Sciences, the Forensic Sciences Foundation, and the American Academy of Psychiatry and Law[53] in 1978, and currently has 80 members. Certification requires prior certification by the American Board of Psychiatry and Neurology, five years of residency training, licensure, and substantial experience in and passage of the board oral and written exam, testing legal knowledge and clinical skills.[54] The board publishes an annual directory of diplomates.[55]

Founded in 1969, the *American Academy of Psychiatry and Law* is an organization of psychiatrists interested in the practice of, and training in, legal psychiatry. Only practicing psychiatrists are eligible for membership, since membership in the American Psychiatric Association is a requirement for membership. The only other requirement is payment of a membership fee.

The academy publishes the *Bulletin of the American Academy of Psychiatry and the Law,* and sponsors the American Board of Forensic Psychiatry. There are currently about 800 members.[56]

---

[51] American Board of Psychiatry and Neurology, Inc, Personal Communication 2 (Nov 16, 1984).

[52] 1 Encyclopedia of Associations (19th ed. 1984). The Directory of Medical Specialists published by the American Board of Medical Specialties publishes a directory for all board specialties. To obtain this directory, contact Marquis Who's Who, Inc., 200 E Ohio Street, Chicago, IL 60611.

[53] *Forensic Certification Begins,* 11 Psychiatric News 1, 16 (1976).

[54] McGarry, *Operational Aspects, Training and Qualifications in Forensic Psychiatry,* in Modern Legal Medicine, Psychiatry, and Forensic Science 648-49 (1980).

[55] To obtain this directory, contact the American College of Forensic Psychiatry, 26701 Quail Creek, Number 295, Laguna Hills, CA 92653.

[56] American Academy of Psychiatry and Law (1984).

Psychological Organizations

The *American Psychological Association* is the major professional organization for psychologists in the United States, with more than 53,000 members. Full membership in the association is limited to psychologists with doctoral degrees (Ph.D. or Psy.D.) who pay the annual membership fee. Specialty areas are represented by separate divisions within the organization, i.e., Division 12 for clinical psychology, and Division 41 for law and psychology.[57]

The association also confers *fellow* status upon those psychologists able to document "unusual and outstanding contributions or performance in the field of psychology."[58] The criteria for fellow status have been continuously upgraded since their inception; consequently, fellow status recently conferred probably reflects greater competence than that conferred in the more distant past.[59]

The *American Board of Professional Psychology* was founded in 1947 to promote the recognition of advanced professional achievement in psychology. There are currently more than 2,500 diplomates in the four areas of psychology, with the largest number being in clinical psychology. The policies and practices of the board have been the subject of some controversy in the past, especially regarding the criteria and peer evaluation process. The board annually awards a distinguished professional achievement Award to a psychologist whose professional accomplishments it deems laudable.[60]

The *American Board of Forensic Psychology* was founded in 1978 by the Committee on Certification of the American Psychology-Law Society to recognize special competence in the area of forensic psychology. Recognition of diplomate status by this board requires licensure, graduation from an approved doctoral program, 1000 hours of forensic psychology experience, submission of written work samples, and passage of an oral examination.[61] Effective in January, 1987, the

---

[57] American Psychological Assn, Directory of the American Psychological Association (1984).

[58] Bylaws of the American Psychological Association, art II, ¶ 3 (1984). To obtain this directory, contact the American Psychological Organization, 1200 Seventeenth St, NW, Washington, DC 20036.

[59] Robyak & Goodyear, *Graduate School Origins of Diplomates and Fellows in Professional Psychology*, 15 Professional Psychology 379 (1984).

[60] *Id* 379.

[61] American Board of Forensic Psychology, Summary Brochure (1983). The American Board of Forensic Psychology is being acquired by the American Board of Professional Psychology as this book goes to press.

applicant will be required to have received 200 hours of supervision in her field.

The *American Psychology-Law Society* (AP-LS) was founded in 1968 to promote exchanges of law-psychology information in teaching, research, and the administration of justice. AP-LS was recently acquired by the American Psychological Association (APA) and has now become Division 41 of the APA. The society publishes the *Journal of Law and Human Behavior,* a quarterly. Membership is open to those with interests in law and psychology who pay the membership fee.[62]

§4.14   Suggested Reading

Books

American Board of Forensic Psychology, *Summary Brochure* (1983).

American Board of Psychiatry and Neurology, Inc, *Information for Applicants* 6A-7 (1983).

American Psychoanalytic Assn, *Standards for Training in Psychoanalysis* (1977).

American Psychological Assn, *Directory of the American Psychological Association* (1984).

American Psychological Assn, *Graduate Training in Psychology and Associated Fields* (1984).

Comprehensive Textbook of Psychiatry/III (Freedman, Kaplan, & Sadock eds 1980).

Diagnostic and Statistical Manual of Mental Disorders (3d ed 1980) (DSM-III).

1 *Encyclopedia of Associations* (19th ed 1984).

A. Flexner, *Medical Education in the United States and Canada* (1972).

S. Garfield, *Clinical Psychology* (1983).

Rypin's Medical Licensure Examinations (13th ed 1984).

Articles

American Psychological Assn, *APA Approved Doctoral Programs in Clinical, Counseling, and School Psychology,* 36 Am Psychologist 1516 (1981).

American Psychological Assn, *Education and Training Board, Education for Research in Psychology,* 19 Am Psychologist 167 (1959).

---

[62] Encyclopedia of Associations (19th ed 1984).

Forensic Certification Begins, 11 Psychiatric News 1, 16 (1976).

Laliotis & Grayson, *Psychologist Heal Thyself,* 40 Am Psychologist 34 (1985).

Margenstern, *A Criticism of Psychiatry's Board Examinations,* 127 Am J Psychiatry 33 (1970).

McGarry, *Operational Aspects, Training and Qualifications in Forensic Psychiatry,* in Modern Legal Medicine, Psychiatry, and Forensic Science 648 (1980).

Monahan & Loftus, *The Psychology of Law,* 33 Ann Rev of Psychology 441 (1982).

Robyak & Goodyear, *Graduate School Origins of Diplomats and Fellows in Professional Psychology,* 15 Professional Psychology 380 (1984).

Taylor & Torrey, *The Pseudo Regulation of American Psychiatry,* 129 Am J Psychiatry 658 (1972).

5

Researching Psychiatric and Psychological Literature

§5.01 Introduction

Whenever a case involves psychiatric or psychological evidence, thorough preparation involves a review of the relevant recent literature. This review should familiarize the attorney with the issues and experts in the area, as well as information necessary for effective direct or cross-examination. For the expert, it will provide a chance to anticipate potential areas for cross-examination and prepare responses in advance.

The process of conducting research in the psychiatric and psychological literature is very much the same as the process of conducting research in the legal literature on a topic about which the attorney has no prior knowledge. The first step is to define the question or problem being investigated using psychological or psychiatric terms, just as conducting legal research requires definition of a question in legal terms. This step is crucial in minimizing the number of dead ends confronted. Problem definition may be aided by consulting a general treatise like the *Comprehensive Textbook of Psychiatry*[1] or by consulting with a knowledgeable expert.[2]

Once the general parameters of the search have been established, the next step is to locate a library that has the relevant books and journals. Usually, this will be a college or university with a psychology department or medical school. Discovering relevant treatises that provide a broad and authoritative overview of a particular area involves, as in legal research, a review of the card catalog. However, because of the speed with which new discoveries occur in psychiatry and psychology, research cannot end here. A review of the periodical literature is obligatory.

There are two major indexes to periodical literature in the fields of psychiatry and psychology: *Index Medicus* and its computerized data base, MEDLINE; and *Psychological Abstracts* and its computerized data base, PsycINFO. Both of these resources are discussed in the sections that follow.

§5.02   *Index Medicus*/MEDLINE

The National Library of Medicine compiles about 300,000 articles per year and continuously updates the various data bases which it manages. One of these contains recently published articles in psychiatry and psychology, along with those from other medical specialties and allied health sciences. The legal analogue to MEDLINE is services like WESTLAW and Lexis. Access to the data base is gained through a computer terminal and modem.

The MEDLINE data base contains more than 700,000 references to biomedical journals for the current year and the two preceding years. MEDLINE articles come from 3000 journals in the United States and 70 foreign countries. Beginning with 1966, the total number of references on file now totals more than four million. The MEDLINE data base is used to publish *Index Medicus*.[3]

Index Medicus is a widely used periodical index to health sciences literature. The legal analogue to *Index Medicus* is the *Index to Legal Periodicals,* and the indexes are used generally in the same way. *Index Medicus* is published in bound volumes through which a user may scan relevant headings for articles of interest.

Index Medicus covers about 2,500 journals in English and 40 foreign

---

[1] Comprehensive Textbook of Psychiatry/IV (4th ed 1985).

[2] Special Thanks to Susan G. Bader, Librarian at the University of Texas Health Sciences Center at Dallas for her assistance.

[3] Medline, National Library of Medicine (1983).

languages. It is published monthly and cumulated annually. This index is available at most medical school libraries and may be available at college libraries with premedical or allied health curricula.[4]

§5.03 — Organizational Format

The MEDLINE data base is organized into subject headings that are contained in an auxiliary publication to *Index Medicus* called *Medical Subject Headings (MeSH)*. *MeSH* contains alphabetical and hierarchical lists of terms under which references are grouped in the subject sections. References can also be researched by author.

The procedure for gaining access to the MEDLINE data base will vary somewhat depending on the vendor who provides access. One of the larger vendors is DIALOG.[5] This vendor provides services to users who have personal computers with modems for a monthly fee.

Index Medicus is organized using the same format as MEDLINE.[6] Each issue of the index includes articles, listed by subject and author. *MeSH* divides the references into categories.[7] *MeSH* Category F contains *Psychologic and Psychiatric Behavior, Processes, Disorders, and Technics.*

Within each major category, a number of major and minor descriptors exist, under which more specific topic areas are listed along with

---

[4] *Id.*

[5] DIALOG is a trademark of Dialog Information Retrieval Services, Inc, 1983.

[6] S. Bader, Index Medicus (unpublished handout 1984).

[7]   **MeSH CATEGORIES**

Category A – Anatomy (organs, cells, tissues, regions)
Category B – Living Organisms
Category C – Diseases, Abnormalities, Signs & Symptoms
Category D – Chemicals and Drugs
Category E – Procedures & Technics, Equipment & Supplies
Category F – Psychologic & Psychiatric Behavior, Processes, Disorders, and Technics
Category G – Biological Sciences, Health Occupations, Environment & Public Health, and *Physiological Processes*
Category H – Physical Sciences
Category I – Social Sciences, Education, and Human Activities
Category J – Technology, Industry, Agriculture, & Food
Category K – Humanities
Category L – Information Sciences & Communication
Category M – Named Groups
Category N – Health Care
Category Z – Geographic Names

references to the data files where they are located. The organizational format of *Index Medicus* is very similar, since it is a subset of MEDLINE.

The first step in conducting a search is to pick the most specific term that applies to the topic being researched. *MeSH* is located in the front of the annual cumulations of *Index Medicus,* and should be the first place to look for references to other terms which may be relevant to the search.

An example of the *MeSH* subject headings appears in Figure 1.

Figure 1 Medical Subject Headings Annotations

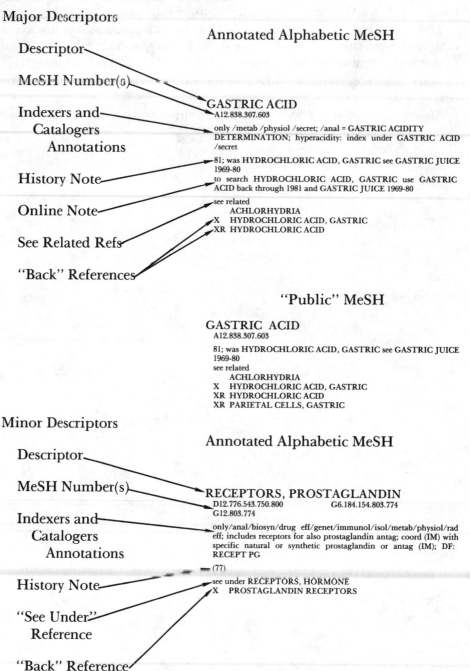

Major Descriptors

Descriptor

McSH Number(s)

Indexers and Catalogers Annotations

History Note

Online Note

See Related Refs

"Back" References

Annotated Alphabetic MeSH

GASTRIC ACID
A12.838.307.603

only /metab /physiol /secret; /anal = GASTRIC ACIDITY
DETERMINATION; hyperacidity: index under GASTRIC ACID
/secret

81; was HYDROCHLORIC ACID, GASTRIC see GASTRIC JUICE
1969-80
to search HYDROCHLORIC ACID, GASTRIC use GASTRIC
ACID back through 1981 and GASTRIC JUICE 1969-80

see related
    ACHLORHYDRIA
X   HYDROCHLORIC ACID, GASTRIC
XR HYDROCHLORIC ACID

"Public" MeSH

GASTRIC ACID
A12.838.307.603

81; was HYDROCHLORIC ACID, GASTRIC see GASTRIC JUICE
1969-80
see related
    ACHLORHYDRIA
X   HYDROCHLORIC ACID, GASTRIC
XR HYDROCHLORIC ACID
XR PARIETAL CELLS, GASTRIC

Minor Descriptors

Descriptor

MeSH Number(s)

Indexers and Catalogers Annotations

History Note

"See Under" Reference

"Back" Reference

Annotated Alphabetic MeSH

RECEPTORS, PROSTAGLANDIN
D12.776.543.750.800   G6.184.154.803.774
G12.803.774

only/anal/biosyn/drug eff/genet/immunol/isol/metab/physiol/rad
eff; includes receptors for also prostaglandin antag; coord (IM) with
specific natural or synthetic prostaglandin or antag (IM); DF:
RECEPT PG

(77)

see under RECEPTORS, HORMONE
X   PROSTAGLANDIN RECEPTORS

"Public" MeSH

RECEPTORS, PROSTAGLANDIN see under RECEPTORS,
ENDOGENOUS SUBSTANCES
X   PROSTAGLANDIN RECEPTORS

In the example reproduced here, the listing is for Gastric Acid, stomach acid. Notice that immediately under the index word, the *MeSH* number is listed after the category, which is *A* for *Anatomy* in this case. Below that are listed other index terms where information relevant to this topic is located. This line is labeled *Indexers and catalogers annotations.* The next line tells how this topic may have been cataloged or indexed in the past, if different from the current system. In this example, gastric acid was previously called gastric juice from 1969 to 1980 in *Index Medicus.* The remainder of the information relates to use of the MEDLINE system and is explained on the diagram in Figure 1.

Another auxilary publication, *Permuted MeSH,* is a key word version of *MeSH,* similar to legal key word indexes. *Permuted MeSH* will direct a researcher to the words in *MeSH* which are index terms for the information sought.

The next step is to locate in *MeSH* the terms the key word index (*Permuted MeSH*) suggested. The list of terms in each category should be scanned to narrow the search to those in which the researcher is specifically interested. Once the terms are located, *MeSH* will direct the researcher to an *Index Medicus* section that contains the list of references related to that term.

The sample that is reproduced in Figure 2 is based on the search for information for a particular type of cancerous tumor.

Figure 2 MeSH Trees

UROGENITAL NEOPLASMS

C4.588.945 +   C12.878+
C13.371.830
GEN or unspecified but must be both uro + genital: prefer specific precoord:
/anal /blood supply /secret /ultrastruct permitted; coord IM with histol type
of neopl (IM)

RESPIRATORY TRACT NEOPLASMS	C4.588.894.797
LUNG NEOPLASMS	C4.588.894.797.520
BRONCHIAL NEOPLASMS	C4.588.894.797.520.140
CARCINOMA, BRONCHIOLAR	C4.588.894.797.520.140.180
CARCINOMA, BRONCHOGENIC	C4.588.894.797.520.140.280
COIN LESION, PULMONARY	C4.588.894.797.520.405
PANCOAST'S SYNDROME	C4.588.894.797.520.734
TRACHEAL NEOPLASMS	C4.588.894.797.838
UROGENITAL NEOPLASMS	C4.588.945
GENITAL NEOPLASMS, FEMALE	C4.588.945.418
FALLOPIAN TUBE NEOPLASMS	C4.588.945.418.365
OVARIAN NEOPLASMS	C4.588.945.418.685
KRUKENBERG'S TUMOR	C4.588.945.418.685.538
MEIGS' SYNDROME	C4.588.945.418.685.595
UTERINE NEOPLASMS	C4.588.945.418.948
CERVIX NEOPLASMS	C4.588.945.418.948.170
CERVIX DYSPLASIA	C4.588.945.418.948.170.170
VAGINAL NEOPLASMS	C4.588.945.418.955
VULVAR NEOPLASMS	C4.588.945.418.968
GENITAL NEOPLASMS, MALE	C4.588.945.440
PENILE NEOPLASMS	C4.588.945.440.715
PROSTATIC NEOPLASMS	C4.588.945.440.770
TESTICULAR NEOPLASMS	C4.588.945.440.915
UROLOGIC NEOPLASMS	C4.588.945.947
BLADDER NEOPLASMS	C4.588.945.947.125
KIDNEY NEOPLASMS	C4.588.945.947.535
URETERAL NEOPLASMS	C4.588.945.947.940
URETHRAL NEOPLASMS	C4.588.945.947.945
VENEREAL TUMORS, VETERINARY	C4.588.945.956
NEOPLASMS, EXPERIMENTAL	C4.619
CARCINOMA 256, WALKER	C4.619.45
CARCINOMA, BROWN–PEARCE	C4.619.124
POLYURIA	C12.777.934.616
URINARY INCONTINENCE	C12.777.934.852
URINARY INCONTINENCE, STRESS	C12.777.934.852.727
UROGENITAL NEOPLASMS	C12.878
UROLOGIC NEOPLASMS	C12.878.950
SEX DISORDERS	C13.371.665
DYSPAREUNIA	C13.371.665.313
FRIGIDITY	C13.371.665.520
TUBERCULOSIS, UROGENITAL	C13.371.803
TUBERCULOSIS, FEMALE GENITAL	C13.371.803.040
UROGENITAL NEOPLASMS	C13.371.830
UTERINE DISEASES	C13.371.852
CERVIX DISEASES	C13.371.852.150
CERVICITIS	C13.371.852.150.150
CERVIX DYSPLASIA	C13.371.852.150.190
CERVIX EROSION	C13.371.852.150.220
CERVIX HYPERTROPHY	C13.371.852.150.250
CERVIX INCOMPETENCE	C13.371.852.150.280
CERVIX NEOPLASMS	C13.371.852.150.310
ENDOMETRIAL HYPERPLASIA	C13.371.852.228
ENDOMETRITIS	C13.371.852.299

Notice the section reproduced comes from Category C *Diseases, Abnormalities, Signs and Symptoms* on the MeSH category list. Then, since the type of tumor being investigated is located in the urogenital system, the search proceeds in alphabetical order within Category C until the *U* section is found. The subtypes of urogenital neoplasms (tumors) are listed along with their reference numbers to *Index Medicus.* Turning to *Index Medicus* at the reference numbers listed, one will find a listing of articles written on this topic.

§5.04   —Sample Search

Figure 3 is an actual MEDLINE search.[8] If the issue facing an attorney involves civil commitment of mentally ill[9] persons who suffer from bipolar disorders,[10] the following search process may be used. After logging in, the attorney searches for articles on bipolar disorders and is told that 678 citations are indexed under this heading. Next, the attorney searches for articles on commitment of the mentally ill and is told that 253 citations are indexed under this heading. Thereafter, the attorney searches for articles including both topics, and is told that four citations are indexed.

Search Statement 4 requests the authors, titles, and available author's abstracts for these four articles. In the next step, the MeSH headings for the four citations are retrieved so that the search can be broadened or narrowed. For example, if the researcher wanted to expand the search, selection of *MeSH* in the article most on point would provide the basis for an additional search.

---

[8] Special thanks for providing this example to Sheldon Kotzin, Chief Biographical Services Division, National Institutes of Health, National Library of Medicine.

[9] *See* §16.01.

[10] *See* §2.09.

Figure 3 Sample MEDLINE Search

```
PLEASE ENTER /LOGIN
/login
PLEASE ENTER USERID/PASSWORD OR LOGON
********************
OSRLINE/TOXLINE UPDATED; POPLINE UPDATE DELAYED;

ACCESS FILE INFORM & TYPE NEWS.

NLM TIME 12:02:10 DATE 84:353 LINE 08A

WELCOME TO THE NATIONAL LIBRARY OF MEDICINE'S ELHILL
RETRIEVAL SYSTEM. YOU ARE NOW CONNECTED TO THE MEDLINE
FILE.

SS 1 /C?
USER:
bipolar disorder
PROG:
SS (1) PSTG (678)

SS 2 /C?
USER:
commitment of mentally ill
PROG:
SS (2) PSTG (253)

SS 3 /C?
USER:
1 and 2
PROG:
SS (3) PSTG (4)

SS 4 /C?
USER:
print include ab
PROG:


1
AU  - Bluestone H
AU  - Travin S
TI  - Murder: the ultimate conflict.
SO  - Am J Psychoanal 1984 Summer;44(2):147-67
```

2
AU   - Marder SR
AU   - Swann E
AU   - Winslade WJ
AU   - Van Putten T
AU   - Chien CP
AU   - Wilkins JN
TI   - A study of medication refusal by involuntary
       psychiatric patients.
AB   - The authors evaluated 31 patients consecutively
       admitted to a locked acute treatment unit in
       California to determine the severity of their
       symptomatology, their attitudes toward treat-
       ment, and whether they would refuse medication
       if they had the opportunity (patients in California
       do not have the right to refuse). Fifteen patients
       indicated that they would refuse medication if
       given the opportunity. Although they did not differ
       in diagnosis from the other patients, they showed
       evidence of more severe psychosis and higher mood
       elevation and had less positive attitudes toward
       treatment. Two-week follow-up of 12 patients in the
       refuser group showed that they were less likely to
       refuse drugs and were clinically improved; however,
       six of the patients still preferred to refuse medi-
       cation despite their clinical improvement. The
       authors discuss their findings in the context of
       the broader issue of when a mentally ill person
       should be forced to give up the power to make
       decisions about drug treatment.
SO   - Hosp Community Psychiatry 1984 Jul;35(7):724-6

3
AU   - Chapelsky D
TI   - Patient's right to refuse psychotherapeutic
       medications. Case for discussion.
SO   - Prog Clin Biol Res 1983;139:11-2

4
AU   - Keisling R
TI   - Characteristics and outcome of patients who refuse
       medication.
SO   - Hosp Community Psychiatry 1983 Sep;34(9):847-8

```
SS 4 /C?
USER:

prt mh
PROG:


1
MH  - Adult
MH  - Aggression/PSYCHOLOGY
MH  - Alcohol Drinking
MH  - Anger
MH  - Bipolar Disorder/PSYCHOLOGY
MH  - Case Report
MH  - Commitment of Mentally Ill
MH  - *Conflict (Psychology)
MH  - Depressive Disorder/PSYCHOLOGY
MH  - Dissociative Disorders/PSYCHOLOGY
MH  - Female
MH  - Forensic Psychiatry
MH  - *Homicide
MH  - Human
MH  - Male
MH  - Middle Age
MH  - *Psychoanalytic Theory
MH  - Schizophrenic Psychology
MH  - Stress, Psychological/COMPLICATIONS


2
MH  - Adult
MH  - Bipolar Disorder/DRUG THERAPY
MH  - California
MH  - *Commitment of Mentally Ill
MH  - Female
MH  - Follow-Up Studies
MH  - Human
MH  - Male
MH  - Mental Disorders/*DRUG THERAPY
MH  - Organic Mental Disorders, Psychotic/DRUG THERAPY
MH  - *Patient Compliance
MH  - Psychotic Disorders/DRUG THERAPY
MH  - Psychotropic Drugs/*THERAPEUTIC USE
MH  - Schizophrenia/DRUG THERAPY
```

3
MH   - Adult
MH   - Bipolar Disorder/DRUG THERAPY
MH   - Case Report
MH   - Commitment of Mentally Ill/LEGISLATION & JURISPRUD.
MH   - *Ethics, Medical
MH   - Female
MH   - Human
MH   - Patient Advocacy/*LEGISLATION & JURISPRUD.
MH   - *Patient Compliance
MH   - Psychotropic Drugs/*THERAPEUTIC USE

4
MH   - Adult
MH   - Bipolar Disorder/DRUG THERAPY
MH   - Case Report
MH   - Commitment of Mentally Ill
MH   - Emergencies
MH   - Female
MH   - Human
MH   - Mental Disorders/*DRUG THERAPY
MH   - Outcome and Process Assessment (Health Care)
MH   - *Patient Compliance
MH   - Pregnancy
MH   - Psychotropic Drugs/*THERAPEUTIC USE
MH   - Schizophrenia, Catatonic/DRUG THERAPY
MH   - Schizophrenia, Paranoid/DRUG THERAPY

SS 4 /C?
USER:
stop y
TIME   0:05:09   NLM TIME 12:07:20
. . .

PROG:

GOOD-BYE!
THE ESTIMATED TOTAL ONLINE COST FOR THIS 5 MINUTE TERMINAL
SESSION IS $1.36.

*** END OF SESSION ***

§5.05   *Psychological Abstracts*/PsycINFO

Psychological Abstracts is an index to periodical literature in psychology and related behavioral and social sciences. It is published by the American Psychological Association and reviews more than 1400 journals and technical reports as well as monographs. PsycINFO, the computerized data base, contains all the information in *Psychological Abstracts* plus information from *Dissertation Abstracts International* and other sources. The total number of sources indexed in PsycINFO is more than 1400. PsycINFO is updated monthly, and currently contains more than 520,000 references compiled since its initiation in 1967.[11]

§5.06   —Organizational Format

Psychological Abstracts is indexed by author and subject sections. Indexes are published annually, although each monthly edition contains an index to that issue. The abstracts are organized by topic in each monthly edition. Each abstract is assigned a number to aid in locating it from the index. The abstracts include the name of the author, the title of the article or monograph, the author's institutional affiliation, a complete citation, and the abstract itself.

PsycINFO is organized into three categories of search options. The basic index includes everything in the abstract in *Psychological Abstracts*. However, searches can be conducted using titles, topic headings, identifiers, or descriptors given in the Thesaurus. Searches can be limited to English or non-English language articles, or to animal or human subjects. Additional indexes are also available.

The *Thesaurus of Psychological Index Terms* is a compilation of terms used to index references in the data base and is the analogue of *Permuted MeSH* for MEDLINE. The *Thesaurus* contains 4300 terms in two sections.

§5.07   —Sample Search

Figure 4 is a sample PsycINFO search with an explanatory introduction.[12]

---

[11] *See* American Psychological Assn, PsycINFO users Reference Manual (1981). These citations are reprinted with permission (fee-paid) of the American Psychological Association, publisher of *Psychological Abstracts* and the PsycINFO Database (Copyright © by the American Psychological Association), and may not be reproduced without its prior permission.

[12] PsycINFO, Sample Search 11 (1984). These citations are reprinted with permission (fee-paid) of the American Psychological Association, publisher of *Psychological Abstracts* and the PsycINFO Database (Copyright © by the American Psychological Association), and may not be reproduced without its prior permission.

Figure 4 Sample PsycINFO Search

This sample search was executed on DIALOG.

Topic: Information concerning testing or screening procedures to determine legal insanity or criminal responsibility.

Discussion: One prominent issue in the psycholegal field is criminal responsibility or the insanity defense. Most of the literature on this subject is indexed in the PsycINFO Database under broad index terms, such as Adjudication, Legal Processes and Expert Testimony. For a precise search of the topic, therefore, it is necessary to use free-text search techniques. Our search strategy contains a variety of free-text combinations that have been limited to the title (TI) and index phrase or identifier (ID) fields for precision. To further narrow our search to documents on the insanity defense related to testing, the classification category or section heading code for psychometrics was used. A list of these categories can be found in the *Thesaurus of Psychological Index Terms,* Appendix E and in the *PsycINFO Users Reference Manual* on Page IV-5.

```
File 11*:PSYCINFO-67-83/Dec
(Copr. Am. Psych. Assn.)
  Set Items Description

? SS COMPETEN? (F) TRIAL/TI, ID OR INSANITY (W) PLEA/TI, ID
OR INSANITY (F) DEFENSE/TI, ID OR CRIMINAL (W)
RESPONSIBILITY/TI, ID OR GUILTY (F) INSANITY/TI, ID OR
ACQUIT? (F) INSANITY/TI, ID
    1    28 COMPETEN? (F) TRIAL/TI, ID, DE
    2    13 INSANITY (W) PLEA/TI, ID
    3    31 INSANITY (F) DEFENSE/TI, ID, DE
    4    38 CRIMINAL (W) RESPONSIBILITY/TI, ID
    5     9 GUILTY (F) INSANITY/TI, ID
    6     6 ACQUIT? (F) INSANITY/TI, ID
    7   116  1 OR 2 OR 3 OR 4 OR 5 OR 6
?SS S7 AND SH=22
    8 18792 SH=22
    9     7 7 AND 10
? T9/3/1-7
9/3/1
70-54304 Vol No: 70 Abstract No: 54304
  An investigation of the Megargee MMPI typology in a
  forensic setting.
  Hawk, Gary L.
  Kent State U
  Dissertation Abstracts International  1983 May Vol
  43(11-B) 3732  ISSN: 04194209

9/3/2
70-09368 Vol No: 70 Abstract No: 09368
  The RCRAS and legal insanity: A cross-validation study.
  Rogers, Richard; Seman, William; Wasyliw, Orest E.
```

Rush Medical Coll
Journal of Clinical Psychology   1983 Jul Vol 39(4)
554-559   CODEN: JCPYAO   ISSN: 00219762

9/3/3
68-02538 Vol No: 68 Abstract No: 02538
The Competency Screening Test: A replication and
extension.
Randolph, John J.; Hicks, Terry; Mason, David
Chester Mental Health Ctr, IL
Criminal Justice & Behavior   1981 Dec Vol 8(4) 471-481
CODEN: CJBHAB   ISSN: 00938548

9/3/4
67-08898 Vol No: 67 Abstract No: 08898
Schedule of affective disorders and schizophrenia, a
diagnostic interview in evaluations of insanity: An
exploratory study.
Rogers, Richard; Cavanaugh, James L.; Dolmetsch, Robert
Rush Medical Coll
Psychological Reports   1981 Aug Vol 49(1) 135-138
CODEN: PYRTAZ   ISSN: 00332941

This sample search was executed on KNOWLEDGE INDEX.

```
? BEGIN PSYC
1/18/84 11:05:11 EST
Now in PSYCHOLOGY (PSYC) Section
  PsycINFO (PSYC1) Database
  (Copyright 1983 American Psychological Association)
? FIND COMPETEN? AND STAND AND TRIAL OR INSANITY PLEA OR
INSANITY DEFENSE
     4769 COMPETEN?
      423 STAND
     6255 TRIAL
       18 INSANITY PLEA
       40 INSANITY DEFENSE
  S1  100   COMPETEN? AND STAND AND TRIAL OR INSANITY PLEA
  OR INSANITY DEFENSE
? FIND CRIMINAL RESPONSIBILITY OR GUILTY AND INSANITY OR
ACQUIT? AND INSANITY
       59 CRIMINAL RESPONSIBILITY
      273 GUILTY
      228 INSANITY
       30 ACQUIT?
  S2  98   CRIMINAL RESPONSIBILITY OR GUILTY AND INSANITY
  OR ACQUIT? AND INSANITY
? FIND S1 OR S2
  S3  167   S1 OR S2
? FIND S3 AND SH=22
    18792 SH=22
  S4  7  S3 AND SH=22
```

? DISPLAY 4/L/1
   Display 4/L/1
70-54304 Vol No: 70 Abstract No: 54304
  An investigation of the Megargee MMPI typology in a
  forensic setting.
  Hawk, Gary L.
  Kent State U
  Dissertation Abstracts International 1983 May Vol
  43(11-B) 3732 ISSN: 04194209
  Language: ENGLISH Document Type: DISSERTATION
  Descriptors: MINN MULTIPHASIC PERSONALITY INVEN,
  PSYCHODIAGNOSTIC TYPOLOGIES, FORENSIC PSYCHIATRY,
  CRIMINALS
  Identifiers: validity of Megargee MMPI typology, males
  referred for criminal responsibility evaluations
  Section Headings: 2220. (TEST CONSTRUCTION &
  VALIDATION), 3230. (BEHAVIOR DISORDERS & ANTISOCIAL
  BEHAVIOR)

? SET V 0
Horizontal line length remains 64
Vertical line count changed from 24 to 0
? DISPLAY 4/MEDIUM/2-5
4/M/2
70-09368 Vol No: 70 Abstract No: 09368
  The RCRAS and legal insanity: A cross-validation study.
  Rogers, Richard; Seman, William; Wasyliw, Orest E.
  Rush Medical Coll
  Journal of Clinical Psychology 1983 Jul Vol 39(4)
  554-559 CODEN: JCPYRO ISSN: 00219762

4/M/3
68-02538 Vol No: 68 Abstract No: 02538
  The Competency Screening Test: A replication and
  extension.
  Randolph, John J.; Hicks, Terry; Mason, David
  Chester Mental Health Ctr, IL
  Criminal Justice & Behavior 1981 Dec Vol 8(4) 471-481
  CODEN: CJBHAB ISSN: 00938548

4/M/4
67-08898 Vol No: 67 Abstract No: 08898
  Schedule of affective disorders and schizophrenia, a
  diagnostic interview in evaluations of insanity: An
  exploratory study.
  Rogers, Richard; Cavanaugh, James L.; Dolmetsch, Robert
  Rush Medical Coll
  Psychological Reports 1981 Aug Vol 49(1) 135-138
  CODEN: PYRTAZ ISSN: 00332941

§5.08   Specialty Legal Journals

There are numerous journals and periodicals that specialize in issues raised by the interface of law and psychiatry or psychology. These journals are worthy of consideration for the attorney's library, should be available at the local law library, and are obligatory reading to keep current in the field. They are discussed in alphabetical order.

The Bulletin of the American Academy of Psychiatry and the Law

This periodical is published quarterly by the American Academy of Psychiatry and the Law,[13] an organization comprising psychiatrists who are selected for admission based on forensic expertise. The academy meets, and papers are prepared for those meetings that are often published in the *Bulletin,* in conjunction with the spring meeting of the American Psychiatric Association. The *Bulletin* contains articles from highly regarded academics and practitioners in the field of law and psychiatry. Editing of the *Bulletin* and selection of articles for publication is performed by members of the academy.

International Journal of Law and Psychiatry

This journal publishes articles from an international coterie of authors in the field of law and psychiatry and related social sciences. It is published by Pergamon Press and edited by an international board of academic and practicing lawyers and psychiatrists. Although many of the articles discuss local questions, the journal's orientation tends to be theoretical questions that transcend national boundaries.

Journal of Psychiatry and Law

This journal has been published since 1973 and is edited by a group of psychiatrists and lawyers, some of whom teach and some of whom practice. Articles cover a broad range of topics, although a review of recent issues indicates that criminal topics tend to predominate.

Law and Psychology Review

This review is a periodical publication edited by law students of the University of Alabama. Material published in the *Review* is prepared by both students at the University of Alabama and authorities in law, psychology, and related disciplines from around the country. The *Review* publishes articles and commentary on issues of common concern

---

[13] *See* §4.13.

to the law and the behavioral sciences. The fundamental purpose of the *Review* is to report the present status of the law in the fields of corrections and mental health, and to explore other topics concerning the interfacing of psychology and law.

Law and Human Behavior

This periodical publication is the official journal of the American Psychology-Law Society/Division 41 of the American Psychological Association.[14] The journal was established in 1977 as a multidisciplinary forum for articles and discussions of issues arising out of the relationship between human behavior and the law, legal system, and legal process. Submitted manuscripts are reviewed without identifying information about the author by two members of the editorial board or outside consultants who have expertise on the topic of the article. Their recommendations are then used by the editor who makes the final decision as to acceptance.

Lawyers Medical Digest

This relatively new monthly publication digests articles appearing in hundreds of medical journals. One of its many headings, Psychiatry and Psychology, is worth regular review to keep current with new research in these fields.

Mental and Physical Disability Law Reporter

This publication of the American Bar Association, in conjunction with its Committee on the Mentally Disabled, should be a part of the library of any attorney, psychiatrist, or psychologist whose workload involves law and psychiatry or psychology. This bimonthly publication contains case law developments, legislative and regulatory developments, plus short topical articles. It is an invaluable tool for keeping up with new developments in the field.

---

[14] *Id.*

Part Two

General Considerations for Use of Psychiatric and Psychological Evidence

6 Obtaining Psychiatric and Psychological Evidence

§6.01   Introduction

Between an attorney's recognition that psychiatric or psychological evidence would assist or is necessary in a particular case and the examination of a psychiatrist or psychologist on the witness stand, there is a broad and potentially intimidating gap. To bridge that gap requires a calculation of the legal and tactical qualifications of the appropriate witnesses; identification of the sources of potential witnesses; contact, evaluation, and selection of the potential witnesses; pretrial preparation of these witnesses; and, ultimately, their presentation at trial. This chapter is designed to make the whole process more careful and less intimidating by its treatment of its pretrial phases.

§6.02   The Fallacy of the Impartial Expert

Critical to the method an attorney employs to search for potential psychiatric and psychological expert witnesses and to the rules of evidence that govern the presentation and challenge of these witnesses are assumptions about their impartiality.[1] Some people assume from the existance of pitched legal battles with armies of psychiatrists and psychologists on both sides that these witnesses, or at least the half on the other side, have sold their testimony and abandoned any semblance of scientific objectivity or impartiality.[2] From this assumption, it follows that a system of presenting expert psychiatric and psychological witnesses in which the witnesses' compensation is unaffected by the party whom it favors would lead to an increase in objective, impartial expert testimony.

The use of court-appointed experts as found in Rule 706 of the Federal Rules of Evidence[3] and the New York Plan[4] responds to these

---

[1] Diamond, *The Fallacy of the Impartial Expert*, 3 Archive Crim Psychodynamics 221 (1959). The title of this section, and many of the ideas discussed within it, are taken from this excellent article by Dr. Bernard Diamond, a prominent forensic psychiatrist. *See also* Gorman, *Are There Impartial Psychiatric Witnesses?*, 11 Bull Am Acad Psychiatry & L 379 (1983).

[2] Foster, *Expert Testimony—Prevalent Complaints and Proposed Remedies*, 11 Harv L Rev 169 (1897); Graham, *Impeaching the Professional Witness by a Showing of Financial Interest*, 53 Ind LJ 35 (1977-78).

[3]   Rule 706.

COURT APPOINTED EXPERTS

(a)   Appointment. The court may on its own motion or on the motion of any party enter an order to show cause why expert witnesses should not be appointed, and may request the parties to submit nominations. The court may appoint any expert witnesses agreed upon by the parties, and may appoint expert witnesses of its own selection. An expert witness shall not be appointed by the court unless he consents to act. A witness so appointed shall be informed of his duties by the court in writing, a copy of which shall be filed with the clerk, or at a conference in which the parties shall have opportunity to participate. A witness so appointed shall advise the parties of his findings, if any; his deposition may be taken by any party;

concerns. A version of these plans exists in most states and permits the court to appoint an expert witness nominated by the parties.[5] The expert is then compensated by the court which, in most civil actions, assesses the parties for this compensation. However, because these plans do not limit the parties' rights to call their own experts or the rights of the parties to scrutinize the qualifications or biases of the experts nominated by the other parties, this approach has not abated the underlying problem and has not been heavily utilized.[6]

Other observers of pitched legal battles of psychiatric and psychological experts have concluded that, although there are undoubtedly some experts who sell their testimony, the divisions among highly reputable psychiatrists and psychologists in some cases stem from another cause unrelated to compensation for testimony.[7] Psychiatrists and psychologists come in all shapes and sizes—some are liberal and some are conservative, some are Democrats and some are Republicans, and some are white and some are black. Psychiatry and psychology are not value-free and the particular school of thought a psychiatrist or psychologist chooses to embrace is a function of a multitude of considerations, some of which involve personal values. Psychiatrists and psychologists disagree among themselves even when attorneys are not

---

and he may be called to testify by the court or any party. He shall be subject to cross-examination by each party, including a party calling him as a witness.

(b) Compensation. Expert witnesses so appointed are entitled to reasonable compensation in whatever sum the court may allow. The compensation thus fixed is payable from funds which may be provided by law in criminal cases and civil actions and proceedings involving just compensation under the fifth amendment. In other civil actions and proceedings the compensation shall be paid by the parties in such proportion and at such time as the court directs, and thereafter charged in like manner as other costs.

(c) Disclosure of appointment. In the exercise of its discretion, the court may authorize disclosure to the jury of the fact that the court appointed the expert witness.

(d) Parties' experts of own selection. Nothing in this rule limits the parties in calling expert witnesses of their own selection.

[4] Report by Special Committee of the Association of the Bar of the City of New York: *Impartial Medical Testimony* (1956). *See also* Van Dusen, *A United States District Judge's View of the Impartial Medical Expert System*, 32 FRD 498 (1963).

[5] J. Weinstein & M. Berger, Weinstein's Evidence §706[04] (1982).

[6] *See, e.g.*, Note, *The Doctor in Court: Impartial Medical Testimony*, 40 S Cal L Rev 728 (1967).

[7] Diamond, *supra* note 1.

around and no one is paying for their opinions;[8] thus, it is also reasonable to expect these professions to include individuals with a diversity of opinions on any given question of legal consequence.

If it is true that psychiatrists and psychologists may hold diverse opinions on professional questions for reasons unrelated to the source of their compensation, then the search for an expert witness entails something more than a trip to the bank to acquire sufficient funds to purchase an expert. Instead, it requires a thorough search of the sources for these experts to identify those whose preexisting professional positions are sympathetic.

§6.03 Sources of Experts

To assist the attorney in a thorough search for potential expert psychiatric and psychological witnesses, the potential sources of experts are broken down into categories that may occasionally overlap.

§6.04 —The Grapevine

The most obvious, and perhaps the most accessible, source of information about expert witnesses is the courthouse corridors and neighboring coffee shops. A particular expert's reputation may in fact accurately reflect effectiveness as a witness. Attorneys and other regular courthouse observers may well know who does a good job on the witness stand in a particular situation.

The problem with this source is not that it is not valuable, but that it is limited, and that its limits may not be recognized by an attorney. First, this source relies on the work of other attorneys in discovering potential experts. Courthouse reputations may accurately reflect who are the best and the worst of those who have testified, but they say nothing about other experts not identified or called by these other attorneys. Thus, exclusive reliance upon this source may preclude an attorney from discovering even more effective expert witnesses. Second, if an attorney can learn about this witness from the grapevine, so, too, can an opponent, judge, and jury. Included within the courthouse reputation may be the knowledge of biases or weak spots in the expert's armor. Finally, while some reputations are deserved, others are not.

---

[8] See discussion of various theories of mental illness discussed in **ch 1.**

§6.05 —Professional Literature

The test of expertise in the scientific community is professional publication. Publication not only demonstrates the author's experience with a particular subject, but submits that experience to peer criticism. Unlike most legal journals, which are student edited, most scientific journals are edited by other members of the professional community who generally submit proposed articles for external peer review. Thus, publication in a high-quality scientific journal is, itself, some minimum indication of an author's competence as reflected by peer review. More importantly, publication then subjects the author's research to criticism by other members of the scientific community who may cite this author's work as authoritative in their own publications, publish critical reviews of this research, or consequently change their opinion of the author.

Utilizing the techniques for researching the psychiatric and psychological literature described in Chapter 5, an attorney may discover the persons most knowledgeable on the issues raised by the case and the opinions about these persons held by others in the same field. There are, of course, limits to this information. While the grapevine will reveal who is thought to be an effective witness, but is not systematic in identifying the pool of potential experts, a review of the professional literature is a systematic method of identifying expertise on a given subject, but provides no information about the expert's effectiveness as a witness.

§6.06 —Academic Institutions

Faculty members of colleges and universities who have the desired expertise for a particular case are relatively easy to identify and enjoy a certain prestige associated with their academic status. Frequently, a look in the telephone book and a few telephone calls will permit the identification of faculty members with expertise in a desired area. Because the hiring, promotion, and tenure decisions of colleges and universities involve screening by other academic colleagues, faculty status is likely to imply some degree of acceptance of expertise by others in the same field. Similarly, the status of the college or university is a function of the quality of its faculty; therefore, membership on the faculty of a prestigious university is thought to imply a higher degree of professional acceptance.

As college students quickly learn, however, substantive knowledge in a particular field does not necessarily result in the ability to communicate that knowledge effectively. Therefore, academics must also be evaluated for their potential as effective communicators. When these experts lack the attributes of an effective witness, but nonetheless are extremely knowledgeable in the field, their use in pretrial preparation should be considered.[9]

§6.07   Professional Societies

Professional organizations[10] are an extremely important source of information about potential expert witnesses. Those organizations that have meaningful selection criteria have screened the experts, and their membership rolls therefore identify numerous potential witnesses with expertise and the prestige associated with membership in that particular organization. Other organizations, analogous to the American Bar Association, that do not impose tests for admissibility beyond basic licensure and a membership fee, make available membership lists that provide much useful data for an attorney. Discussion of several of these organizations and the data they provide follows.[11]

The American Psychiatric Association[12] publishes a *Biographical Directory* and a *Quick Reference to the American Psychiatric Association Biographical Directory*.[13] Included within the *Directory* is an alphabetical listing of members, with education, postgraduate training, specialties, publications, address, and telephone number. Included within the *Quick Reference* is an alphabetical listing of members; a listing of board certified specialists[14] (*By Criterion of Certification*), including forensic, child, adolescence, and neurology, by state; and a similar listing of specialty by practice in these same categories (*By Criterion of Special Interest Endorsement*). In addition, these listings indicate members' addresses, telephone numbers, and employment.

The *Directory of Medical Specialists,*[15] published under the direction of the American Board of Medical Specialties, contains a listing of board certified specialists, by city and by specialty. Included within this directory are individuals certified by the American Board of Psychiatry

---

[9] *See* §**18.01.**

[10] *See generally* §**4.13.**

[11] *See generally* 2 Am Jur *Trials* §§46, 47 (1964).

[12] *See* §**4.13.**

[13] To obtain these directories, contact the American Psychiatric Assn, 1400 K Street N.W., Washington, DC 20005.

[14] *See* §§**4.06, 4.12.**

[15] To obtain this directory, contact Marquis Who's Who, Inc, 200 E Ohio Street, Chicago, IL 60611.

and Neurology[16] and a brief biographical sketch including name, specialty, type of practice, age, education, career history, teaching positions, professional memberships, address, and telephone number.

The American Psychological Association[17] publishes a *Directory*[18] of its members that includes an alphabetical listing of members, their address and telephone number, age, specialty, diplomate status, and employment. The directory provides a list of members by city and areas of interest including psychology and law.

The American Board of Forensic Psychology,[19] which evolved from the Committee on Certification of the American Psychology-Law Society, publishes a *Directory of Diplomates.*[20] The individuals listed in the directory are all licensed, doctoral-level psychologists, with at least one thousand hours of experience in forensic psychology, who have submitted work samples for review by the board and passed an oral examination administered by the board. The directory lists diplomates alphabetically by forensic specialty (e.g., child custody, civil psychological injury) and by state of residence. It also contains the diplomates' addresses, telephone numbers, education, and current posts.

The American College of Forensic Psychiatry publishes *The Attorney's Directory of Forensic Psychiatrists in the United States and Canada.*[21] This directory lists alphabetically, by specialty and by residence, biographical information about psychiatrists who are interested in the practice of forensic psychiatry. The directory does not purport to screen the forensic qualifications of those it lists.

Frequently, state psychiatric and psychological associations also publish directories of their members with biographical and educational information.

§6.08 —Professional Witnesses

Professional witnesses is a term often applied to experts who regularly make themselves available to litigants for testimony. Excluded from

---

[16] *See* §4.13.

[17] *Id.*

[18] To obtain this directory, contact the American Psychological Assn, 1200 Seventeenth Street, NW, Washington, DC 20036.

[19] *See* §4.13.

[20] To obtain this directory, contact the American Board of Forensic Psychology, Center for Forensic Psychiatry, PO Box 2060, Ann Arbor, MI 48106.

[21] To obtain this directory, contact the American College of Forensic Psychiatry, 26701 Quail Creek, Number 295, Laguna Hills, CA 92653.

discussion here are witnesses employed and regularly used by the government, such as the county pathologist or state hospital psychiatrist. Identification of these witnesses is not a problem for the government and there may be little choice between calling this or another similar witness. Instead, the focus of this section is on those witnesses available who are not permanently employed by one party, but who, by word of mouth or formal advertising, make their availability as witnesses known. Many, but not all, of these individuals in the fields of psychiatry and psychology give up or substantially limit their activities in patient treatment and concentrate on participation in the judicial process.

The advantages of these witnesses are that they are experienced and tested—they are familiar with courtroom logistics and the relevant legal rules and process, not as easily intimidated by opposing counsel as inexperienced witnesses, and often very good with juries. If these witnesses were not effective, competent attorneys would not continue to use them. The disadvantages of these witnesses are that this same experience may identify them ideologically or financially with one side, thereby limiting their credibility, and provide a broad base of trials from which opposing counsel can review successful and unsuccessful impeachment strategies. In addition, by reducing their patient treatment activities these witnesses may become vulnerable to attack on this aspect of their experience.

Another type of professional witness is one who participates in an expert witness service whose availability is made known through advertisements in publications such as bar journals and trial lawyer magazines. These witness services will, for a fee, send reports and records provided by the attorney to their consulting experts for review. The attorney is provided with a written report and, if the attorney chooses, the expert will be available to testify at trial. One apparent advantage of these services is that the attorney will not know and, therefore, cannot be compelled to disclose[22] the names of experts consulted by the service but whose reports were not sent to the attorney because they were unfavorable.

When expert testimony is, as a matter of law or tactics, required in a case and the other methods of locating an expert have not yielded a satisfactory expert, this sort of service may be the only alternative. Although these services tout their effectiveness in settlements and jury verdicts as indicated by letters of praise from individual attorneys, their overall quality is difficult to evaluate systematically. The experts these

---

[22] *See* §§6.17–6.19.

services choose may not be the quality the requesting attorney would otherwise require. And, although an attorney may choose not to use one of their experts and request another, these services choose the next expert for the attorney to accept or reject. Finally, there is the underlying fear that a jury learning of the service and its method of operation may assume it is simply a *buy a witness* service and disregard the testimony.

§6.09 Getting the Expert to Court

After having been identified by reputation, writing, or professional status, a potential witness must be contacted, persuaded to evaluate the case, be evaluated as a witness, agree to be a witness, and be prepared for testimony in advance of taking the stand. As with all other aspects of trial preparation, the thoroughness of these activities will determine the effectiveness of the presentation at trial. It is these pretrial activities to which the following sections are devoted.

§6.10 —Initial Contact

Contact with experts who may testify at trial or assist in case preparation should occur very early in the attorney's handling of the case. If possible, this contact should occur prior to filing the action so that the experts' opinions may be considered in determining the structure and theory of the case. For example, if, in a personal injury action following an automobile accident, the plaintiff's mental and emotional damages are not the inevitable result of a particular type of injury, it may be necessary to allege these as special rather than general damages.[23] Similarly, an opinion that particular injuries do not seem to have been caused by the automobile accident in question may result in a decision not to proceed with the case or a decision to consider proceeding against another defendant.

The form of the initial contact with the expert may affect the tenor of the communication. A personal interview with the expert may increase the likelihood of complete concentration on the attorney's presentation of the case, a sympathetic presentation of the case, and the establishment of a good working relationship between the expert and the attorney.[24] A personal interview may necessitate some flexibility in

---

[23] *See, e.g.,* Ziervogel v Royal Packing Co, 225 SW2d 798 (Mo 1949).

[24] Annot, 2 Am Jur *Trials* §31 (1964).

scheduling around the expert's time constraints, but should be worth the effort.

If the potential psychiatrist or psychologist witness has seen the client as a patient, an ethical duty of confidentiality prohibits any extrajudicial discussion involving knowledge gained in this capacity in the absence of a release or consent by the patient.[25] The release or consent need not be overly formal, but should be in writing and include the name of the patient, relevant patient identifying information such as birth date or social security number, a direction from the patient to the psychiatrist or psychologist to release records and reports and to discuss the case with the specified individuals, the name of the person or persons to whom the information may be released, and the signature of the patient.[26] Although an attestation is not legally required, it may reassure the psychiatrist or psychologist that the patient's signature is authentic.

If the potential psychiatric or psychological witness has not previously seen the client as a patient, then the attorney must provide the expert with the factual basis for an opinion. This may entail an examination of the client and should, in any event, include background information about the client and the case. How much information should be provided? Should it be shaded to sway the expert and to obtain a favorable opinion?

The expert, if called to testify, will be subject to cross-examination. Since the validity of the expert's opinion is a function of the facts on which it is based, an accepted ground for cross-examination is to confront the expert with evidence supporting another version of the facts and to ask how the expert's opinion would be affected if these were the facts found by the jury. If, for the first time on cross-examination, the expert is presented with an additional or conflicting version of the facts damaging to the client, it may then be too late to respond

---

[25] *The Principles of Medical Ethics,* 24 JAMA 2187-88 (1981); Principle 5, *Ethical Principles of Psychologists,* 36 Am Psychologist 633 (1981).

[26] A sample release follows:

MEDICAL RELEASE
OF
PAT PATIENT

I, Pat Patient, social security number 123-45-6789, authorize Dr. S. Freud to release to my attorneys, McCormick, Ray and Sutton, all information related to my injuries on or about July 12, 1983, whether in the form of records, charts, or other reports for inspection or copying and to discuss this information with my attorneys.

July 28, 1983   /s/ Pat Patient

Attestation

effectively. If, alternatively, this information is presented to the expert initially, a strategy for minimizing the effect of this damaging information at trial may be developed. Should it be discovered that the effect of the damaging information cannot be minimized, it would be important for counsel to take this into account in the decision to institute litigation or recommend settlement.

One additional consideration in the decision of what to disclose to the expert is the compellability of this information at trial. If the expert's opinion is not favorable and a decision is made not to use the expert, can the opponent compel that expert's testimony? If the consulting attorney does call the expert, may the opposing attorney force the expert to disclose damaging information about the case revealed by the consulting attorney? These questions are treated in Chapter 10, and the answer as to a particular situation should be ascertained before communicating with the expert.

The expert's opinion must be made known to counsel, of course, prior to the decision whether to call this person as a witness. Should this opinion be reduced to writing by the expert? In favor of a written report is its utility for the witness and counsel in preparing for trial and avoiding memory or transcription lapses. In opposition to the preparation of a written report is its potential use by opposing counsel on cross-examination.[27] The more detailed the report, the greater its use not only in refreshing recollection, but also as a source of potential inconsistencies between the report and testimony.

§6.11   —Evaluating the Expert

The decision to call a particular psychiatrist or psychologist who has given a favorable opinion entails several considerations. First, will the witness qualify as an expert in the field in which opinion is required? For example, although the witness is a psychologist, testimony may not be permitted as an expert on the effects of a particular antipsychotic medication. The qualifications for expert psychiatric and psychological testimony are discussed in Chapter 8, and pretrial questions to the expert on these subjects to ascertain qualification are obligatory.

If legally qualified, is this witness likely to be an effective communicator to the judge and jury? Does the witness speak clearly? Can the witness explain scientific concepts to people with no scientific training? Is the witness believable?

Does the witness fit for this case? Is the witness, for example, "too

---

[27] For a discussion of discovery of the expert's report, see §§6.17-6.19.

big city" for a "small town" jury? Is the witness too flamboyant or too somber given other considerations in the case? What experts will the opponent call; how will the jury compare this expert to the opponent's?

Finally, what is the alternative to calling this witness? Have all the sources of potential experts been systematically searched, and are there any other experts who might be better suited for this case? Does the case *require* an expert, or might lay opinion suffice in lieu of a questionable expert?

§6.12 —The Fee

Just as attorneys like to resolve the question of their fees at the preliminary stage of the attorney-client relationship, so do expert witnesses. Thus, it is prudent to discuss fees in the initial communications with the expert. A number of considerations should enter into the setting and structure of the fee.

The expert is entitled to a reasonable fee. The amount and structure of this fee may affect the expert's zealousness in preparation for testimony; however, it is also a legitimate subject for cross-examination.[28] Thus, it should be high enough to motivate the expert, but not so high as to offend the judge or jury. One method of establishing a reasonable fee initially or on cross-examination may be to consider the expert's regular pay or compensation when not testifying or suggested fee schedules of professional societies.[29]

The fee may be structured as a flat fee that includes all pretrial preparation and testimony, if necessary; separate flat fees for pretrial preparation and testimony; or an hourly fee. Contingent fees for testifying experts are ethically questionable[30] and tactically foolish.

From the attorney's perspective, it is beneficial that the contract with the expert be between the client and the expert so that the attorney does not get stuck for the fee if the client fails to pay. The expert's interest in being paid would work in favor of a contract between the client, the expert, and the attorney so that the expert has two potential sources of payment.

To illustrate the issues and their potential resolution, a sample form for a fee agreement is set forth:

---

[28] *See, e.g.*, Shaughnessey v Holt, 236 Ill 485, 86 NE 256 (1908); Commonwealth v Simmons, 361 Pa 391, 65 A2d 353, *cert denied*, 338 US 862 (1949).

[29] E. Imwinkelried, The Methods of Attacking Scientific Evidence 392 (1982).

[30] Graham, *Impeaching the Professional Witness by a Showing of Financial Interest*, 53 Ind LJ 35, 43 n 40 (1977-78.)

EXPERT PSYCHIATRIST/PSYCHOLOGIST ASSISTANCE AGREEMENT

1. This agreement between _____, attorney, and (_____psychiatrist/psychologist_____), expert, entered into on (__date__) in (__location__) shall constitute their entire agreement in the case of (__case name__).

2. The expert will render assistance to the attorney in this case by:

    ____a. Assisting in the case preparation, which assistance will include work on the following phases of the case:

      ____(1) pleading

      ____(2) discovery

      ____(3) witness preparation

      ____(4) jury selection (pretrial preparation)

      ____(5) jury selection (in court)

      ____(6) other (please specify)_____

    ____b. Preparation of an evaluation and a (__written/oral__) report on or before _____, the evaluation to be based upon:

      ____(1) information provided by the attorney

      ____(2) an examination by the expert

      ____(3) independent investigation by the expert

      ____(4) other (please specify) _____

    ____c. Testimony at the trial of this case which will occur in (____location,____) based upon the attorney's acceptance of the expert's evaluation and report. By this agreement the expert does not agree to testify to a particular conclusion. The expert does agree to prepare fully for testimony and to dress in appropriately business-like attire.

3. The expert shall be compensated in the following method:

    ____a. In the amount of $_____ for all services to be rendered in this case described in paragraph 2.

    ____b. At the rate of $_____ per hour for all services to be rendered in this case described in paragraph 2.

    ____c. In the amount of _____ percent of the plaintiff's total recovery; however, this paragraph may apply only if the services to be rendered are only those described in paragraph 2a.

    ____d. Other (please specify)_____

4. The expert's compensation shall be received as follows:

      ____a.   As a retainer, the amount of $_____ shall be paid prior to the rendition of any services.

      ____b.   Upon completion of the expert's services.

      ____c.   On or before _____.

      ____d.   Other (please specify)_____

5. The attorney (_does/does not_) guaranty payment of the expert's compensation by the client.

6. The expert shall not discuss this case with any person other than the attorney without prior written consent of the attorney or court order.

7. The attorney shall keep the expert advised on any cancellations or postponements in scheduled trial appearances or pretrial examinations.

8. This agreement may be terminated by the attorney or expert for any of the following grounds:

    a.   Failure to perform according to the terms of this agreement.

    b.   Misrepresentation of the facts of the case to the expert by the attorney.

    c.   A request by the attorney that the expert engage in unprofessional conduct.

Dated this _____ day of _____.

_____   _____

Expert   Attorney

                                        _____

                                        Client

§6.13   Trial Preparation—Substantive

Effective preparation of the expert witness for trial includes, at minimum, an explanation of the adversary system; courtroom logistics and the rules governing presentation of the expert's testimony; an overview of the evidence that will be presented, relevant issues in the case, and applicable law; the attorney's theory and structure of the case; what the attorney hopes to establish or achieve through the expert's testimony; what should be expected on cross-examination; and, a description of the judge and opposing counsel. Some of this preparation may be accomplished by a discussion with the expert and some of this can be achieved only with mock direct and cross-examination of the witness. The necessary extent of these activities will vary as a function of the expert's general trial experience, prior experience with this attorney, and the nature of the case.

One common problem experienced by psychiatrists and psychologists on the witness stand is the temptation to answer questions posed by counsel or the court on subjects which these professions have concluded is beyond their professional competence.[31] There is frequently an assumption by members of the legal profession, unjustified by the scientific literature, that because psychiatrists and psychologists are students of human behavior they should be able to tell us, for example, what someone was thinking about at any given point in the past or how someone will behave at any given point in the future. When there is no consensus within a scientific community that its members are capable of reaching accurate opinions on a particular question about past or future behavior, the expert who ventures an opinion beyond these accepted limits is open to a potentially devastating attack and fuels the argument for substantial limitations upon psychiatric and psychological expert testimony. Counsel must, therefore, explore with the expert not only the expert's own opinions, but the relevant professional community's acceptance of its ability to reach opinions on this subject with a reasonable degree of certainty and the appropriateness of the expert's responding to questions, "I don't know, that's outside my expertise."

The flow of information between attorney and expert is, thus, not just from attorney to expert. The attorney must achieve competence on the subject of the expert's testimony, learn from the expert or other sources the potential weak spots in the expert's testimony, and plan a response to objections, cross-examination, and other attacks on the witness.

§6.14 —Decorum

There is a substantial body of literature supporting the theory that the jury's perception or image of a witness is as or more important than the content of the witness's testimony in determining its effect on the jury.[32] It is particularly important to heed this lesson when using a psychiatrist or psychologist because of the wide-ranging public views about these professions and their utility in the courtroom. Moreover,

---

[31] *See, e.g.,* Dix, *Expert Prediction Testimony in Capital Sentencing: Evidentiary and Constitutional Considerations,* 19 Am Crim L Rev 1 (1981).

[32] A. Moenssens, R. Moses, & F. Inbau, Scientific Evidence in Criminal Cases 11-13 (2d ed 1978); D. Schwartz, The Proper Use of a Psychiatric Expert in Scientific and Expert Evidence in Criminal Advocacy (1975); Bank & Poythress, *The Elements of Persuasion in Expert Testimony,* 10 J Psychiatry & L 173 (1982).

the same attributes that may make an effective therapist may not make an effective expert witness.

Those factors often identified in the public stereotype of the empathetic male therapist—for example, no suit or tie and, instead, an open-necked shirt or turtleneck, a beard or long hair, and frequently expressed concern with feelings—may keep the therapist from being perceived as an authority figure by the patient, which may be important in therapy. The same effect in the courtroom, decreasing the expert's presence as an authority figure, is probably not desired by the proponent of the witness. Thus, in choosing between experts and in advising experts on courtroom decorum, responding to this perception should be an ongoing concern.

The language used by the psychiatrist or psychologist witness is another major concern. Unexplained psychiatric jargon at best will not help the proponent of the witness and at worst may offend the judge or jury. At the very least, the expert must explain all technical terms used in testifying. Ideally, the use of technical terms should be kept to a minimum. Instead, the use of common parlance with concrete explanations and examples from experiences likely to be within the jurors' background is optimal. For example, when describing a mental status examination and its purpose,[33] an example of an absence of orientation might be a senile grandparent. This is an occurrence likely to be familiar to most jurors and explains in concrete terms one of the objects of a mental status examination.

The standard expert witness admonitions apply to psychiatric and psychological witnesses.[34]

1. Listen to the question
2. Request a clarification of the question if you do not understand it
3. Answer the question truthfully and respectfully
4. Do not argue with the examiner or lose your cool
5. Do not be an advocate for a party (advocate *your* findings)
6. Do not volunteer information

---

[33] *See* §2.13.
[34] *See, e.g.,* T. Mauet, Fundamentals of Trial Techniques 137-38 (1980).

§6.15 —Logistics

Some psychiatrists and psychologists question whether it is ever appropriate for them to testify in judicial proceedings.[35] The frustration of many psychiatrists and psychologists with the judicial system's refusal to let them tell their story as they wish and with its casting them in ill-fitting roles can only be worsened when these witnesses are required to wait outside the courtroom, unable to enlighten the judge or jury and also unable to treat patients. The difficulty in predicting exactly when any witness will be called to the stand during a lengthy trial combined with the busy schedule of psychiatrist and psychologist witnesses creates a special logistical problem. If it is to be expected that these experts will, on an ongoing basis, be willing participants in the judicial system, attorneys must be particularly considerate of these logistical considerations. One obvious step would be not requiring the expert to arrive at the courthouse until shortly before the testimony is required and, instead, to have the expert keep the attorney's office apprised of the expert's location and availability.

Another potential consideration is the use of videotaped testimony by the expert, prepared at a convenient time for the expert and counsel.[36] This consideration must be balanced against the tactical aspects of this mode of presentation. Currently, there is not sufficient experience with the use of videotaped testimony to compare its effects on judges and jurors to that of live testimony.[37]

Included within the topic of logistics is the question of whether to have a subpoena issued to compel the appearance of a friendly witness. Although the psychiatrist or psychologist may initially be offended by service of a subpoena, a prior warning and explanation of its purpose may assuage any hurt feelings.

The fact that an expert has attended the proceedings and given testimony without the necessity of a subpoena is an appropriate subject for cross-examination and may cause the jury to find the expert witness less credible. If, even because of a bona fide psychiatric or psychological emergency, the psychiatrist or psychologist is unable to appear as requested and has not been served with a subpoena, the proponent of the witness will very likely regret nonservice. In the case of a deposition,

---

[35] *See* Symposium: *The Ethical Boundaries of Forensic Psychiatry,* 12 Bull Am Acad of Psychiatry & L 209 (1984).

[36] *See, e.g.,* Symposium: *The Use of Videotape in the Courtroom,* 1975 BYU L Rev 327.

[37] Berment & Jacoubovitch, *Fish Out of Water: A Brief Overview of Social and Psychological Concerns About Videotaped Trials,* 26 Hastings LJ 999 (1975).

if a nonsubpoenaed witness fails to attend, opponents appearing at the deposition may be entitled to receive reimbursement, including attorneys' fees from the party who noticed the deposition.[38] At trial, a continuance based on the failure of a witness to attend is addressed to the sound discretion of the trial judge. If the nonappearing witness was not subpoenaed, a denial of a continuance is not an abuse of discretion.[39]

§6.16 Compellability of Expert Testimony

Much of the preceding discussion has assumed that the attorney had a choice between more than one expert or between using an expert or not using any expert. In certain cases, however, expert testimony *must* be produced by the plaintiff or a directed verdict will be granted. For example, except in those psychiatric or psychological medical malpractice cases included within the res ipsa loquitur exception, the case will not be permitted to go to the jury without the appropriate expert medical testimony.[40] And, attorneys have frequently found that, while there are experts whose opinions are favorable to their case, for a variety of reasons, these experts refuse to testify voluntarily.

The judicial response to the compellability of expert testimony has tended to correspond to certain functional characterizations, specifically, the notion that the expert has a proprietary interest in the knowledge that serves as the basis for that expertise and, on the opposite side, the importance of receiving all probative evidence.[41] Most courts addressing this problem have held that an expert may be compelled to testify to previously formed opinions without special compensation, but may

---

[38] Fed R Civ P 30(b)(2):

> If the party giving the notice of the taking of a deposition of a witness fails to serve a subpoena upon him and the witness because of such failure does not attend, and if another party attends in person or by attorney because he expects the deposition of that witness to be taken, the court may order the party giving the notice to pay to such other party the reasonable expenses incurred by him and his attorney in attending, including reasonable attorney's fees.

See also Fino v McCollum Mining Co, 93 FRD 455 (ND Tex 1982).

[39] Royster v Lederle, 128 F2d 197, 200 (6th Cir 1972).

[40] W. Prosser, Handbook of the Law of Torts §39, at 226-27 (4th ed 1971).

[41] *See* Shuman, *Testimonial Compulsion: The Involuntary Medical Expert Witness,* 4 J Legal Med 419, 422-33 (1983).

not be compelled to conduct additional research.[42] These courts treat the experts' perceptions as inextricably interwoven with their substantive expertise. This position developed in cases involving experts who participated in the event itself,[43] for example, treating physicians in personal injury actions, and has been extended as a general rule to the case of all experts who may have reached an opinion prior to trial. However, if some additional study, testing, or evaluation is necessary, the majority would not compel it.

In a minority of jurisdictions—Indiana,[44] New Jersey,[45] New York,[46] and Pennsylvania[47]—an expert may be compelled to give fact testimony concerning matters perceived, but may not be compelled to draw opinions from these perceptions. Thus, an expert who witnessed the event may be compelled to describe it as would any lay witness, but not to utilize professional expertise in explaining it.

In yet another minority of jurisdictions, experts may be compelled to testify as experts and, if necessary, to engage in additional study, testing, or evaluation if compensated.[48]

§6.17   Pretrial Discovery of Experts

Pretrial discovery of an opponent's psychiatric and psychological experts or an opponent's attempt to discover one's own experts is a critical aspect of trial preparation. No attorney should plan to go to trial without discovery of an opponent's experts or expect that an opponent will do otherwise. This discovery may accomplish two different purposes: it may permit an effective challenge or response to an opponent's expert, and it may identify potential expert witnesses.

To permit an effective response to an opponent's psychiatric or psychological experts, it is necessary to discover whether an opponent

---

[42] *See, e.g.,* Carter-Wallace, Inc v Otte, 474 F2d 529 (2d Cir 1972), *cert denied,* 412 US 929 (1973); City & County of San Francisco v Superior Court, 37 Cal 2d 227, 231 P2d 26 (1951).

[43] Board of County Commrs v Lee, 3 Colo App 177, 32 P 841 (1893).

[44] Buchman v State, 59 Ind 1 (1877).

[45] Stanton v Rushmore, 112 NJL 113, 169 A 721 (1934). This rule only applies in civil cases in New Jersey. Tyree, *The Opinion Rule,* 10 Rutgers L Rev 601, 617 (1956).

[46] People *ex rel* Kraushaar Bros v Thorpe, 296 NY 223, 72 NE2d 165 (1947).

[47] Pennsylvania Co v Philadelphia, 262 Pa 439, 105 A 630 (1918). In Pennsylvania this rule applies only to private litigants. *Id.*

[48] *Ex parte* Dement, 53 Ala 389 (1875); Dixon v People, 168 Ill 179, 48 NE 108 (1897); Mason v Robinson, 340 NW2d 236 (Iowa 1983).

intends to call any experts and then to discover as much information about the witnesses' qualifications, bases for opinions, opinions, and compensation as is possible. The witness's qualifications[49] include professional education, training, employment, prior judicial testimony, professional association membership, academic posts, and publications. These must be learned to decide whether to challenge the witness's status as an expert and to determine methods of attacking credibility. The facts on which the psychiatrist or psychologist will base an opinion[50] and the method by which these facts come to be known by the expert, as well as the resulting opinion, are extremely important. The opinion can be no better than the facts on which it is based, and the opinion itself must flow from the application of some recognized scientific principles. The method for compensation of the expert is also significant. It describes the witness's allegiance and may reveal a bias.[51]

Discovery may also reveal potential witnesses for the case-in-chief. Psychiatrists and psychologists consulted by an opponent, but not chosen to testify because they would testify unfavorably for the opponent, if not thereby disqualified,[52] may be an excellent source of testimony. Therefore, discovery should seek the names of all experts consulted and not merely those whowill be called at trial.

Although the purposes of pretrial discovery of psychiatric and psychological experts will be the same in civil and criminal proceedings, the applicable rules vary and are, therefore, discussed separately. One limitation that exists in both civil and criminal proceedings is privilege. The physician, psychiatrist, psychologist, and psychotherapist-patient privileges are discussed in Chapter 10.

§6.18 —Civil

Rule 26(b)(4) of the Federal Rules of Civil Procedure[53] governs

---

[49] *See* **ch 8.**

[50] *See* **§9.01.**

[51] Graham, *Impeaching the Professional Witness by a Showing of Financial Interest,* 53 Ind LJ 35 (1977-78).

[52] *See* **§§10.06-10.08.**

[53] (4) Trial Preparation: Experts. Discovery of facts known and opinions held by experts, otherwise discoverable under the provisions of subdivision (b)(1) of this rule and acquired or developed in anticipation of litigation or for trial, may be obtained only as follows:

(A) (i)   A party may through interrogatories require any other party to identify each person whom the other party expects to call as a witness at trial, to state the subject matter on which the expert is

pretrial discovery of experts in civil actions in the federal courts and is the model for discovery of experts in 29 states.[54] It treats discovery of two categories of experts: those expected to be called as witnesses at

---

expected to testify, and to state the substance of the facts and opinions to which the expert is expected to testify and a summary of the grounds for each opinion. (ii) Upon motion, the court may order further discovery by other means, subject to such restrictions as to scope and such provisions, pursuant to subdivision (b)(4)(C) of this rule, concerning fees and expenses as the court may deem appropriate.

(B) A party may discover facts known or opinions held by an expert who has been retained or specially employed by another party in anticipation of litigation or preparation for trial and who is not expected to be called as a witness at trial, only as provided in Rule 35(b) or upon a showing of exceptional circumstances under which it is impracticable for the party seeking discovery to obtain facts or opinions on the same subject by other means.

(C) Unless manifest injustice would result, (i) the court shall require that the party seeking discovery pay the expert a reasonable fee for time spent in responding to discovery under subdivisions (b)(4)(A)(ii) and (b)(4)(B) of this rule; and (ii) with respect to discovery obtained under subdivision (b)(4)(A)(ii) of this rule the court may require, and with respect to discovery obtained under subdivision (b)(4)(B) of this rule the court shall require, the party seeking discovery to pay the other party a fair portion of the fees and expenses reasonably incurred by the latter party in obtaining facts and opinions from the expert.

[54] Simon, *Pretrial Discovery of Expert Information in Federal and State Courts: A Guide for the Expert,* 5 J Police Sci & Ad 247, 258 (1977). Seventeen states—Alaska, Arizona, Colorado, Delaware, Idaho, Kansas, Kentucky, Louisiana, Maine, Massachusetts, Minnesota, Nevada, North Dakota, Vermont, Virginia, Washington, and Wyoming—have adopted 26(b)(4) verbatim. *Id* 258.

Another group of states—Alabama, Florida, Georgia, Iowa, Mississippi, Missouri, New Jersey, North Carolina, and Wisconsin—has followed the basic pattern of Rule 26(b)(4), but included some local variations generally resulting in more liberal discovery. *Id.* A third group of states—Indiana, Ohio, and Utah—has adopted the proposed version of 26(b)(4) which would have permitted more liberal discovery of facts from experts, but more restrictive discovery of opinions. *Id* 259.

Another group of states—Arkansas, California, Hawaii, Michigan, Montana, Nebraska, New Mexico, Rhode Island, South Carolina, South Dakota, Tennessee, and West Virginia—has adopted a version of the pre-1970 Rule 26(b)(4) which generally limits discovery more than the current version. *Id.*

The remaining states—Connecticut, Illinois, Maryland, New Hampshire, New York, Oklahoma, Oregon, Pennsylvania, and Texas—follow no particular pattern. *Id* 260.

trial, and those retained in preparation for trial but not expected to be called as witnesses.

The idenity of experts intended to be called as witnesses, subject matter of testimony, facts and opinions upon which testimony is expected, and a summary of the grounds for opinion may be discovered by interrogatory.[55] The duty to supplement discovery applies to these answers,[56] and failure to respond may preclude the calling of the nonidentified expert.[57] Following the use of interrogatories a party may move for further discovery, typically by deposition or motion to produce. This motion is, minimally, subject to a requirement that the expert be compensated for time spent.[58] Although most courts impose no higher standard for granting this motion beyond the general scope of discovery,[59] a minority have imposed an additional burden cast in terms of good cause or substantial need.[60]

The discovery of experts retained, but not intended to be called at trial, is far more restricted. In the absence of a demonstration that the information in the possession of the expert is not reasonably available elsewhere or except as provided in Rule 35 which dictates reciprocal exchanges of the reports of physical or mental examinations,[61] the facts known or opinions held by these experts are not discoverable. Some courts permit an opponent to discover the names and addresses of these experts[62] and the rules do not forbid informal communications with

---

[55] Fed R Civ P 26(b)(4)(A)(ii).

[56] Fed R Civ P 26(e)(1)(B).

(e) *Supplementation of Responses.* A party who has responded to a request for discovery with a response that was complete when made is under no duty to supplement his response to include information thereafter acquired, except as follows:

(1) A party is under a duty seasonably to supplement his response with respect to any question directly addressed to . . . (B) the identity of each person expected to be called as an expert witness at trial, the subject matter on which he is expected to testify, and the substance of his testimony.

[57] Simonsen v Barlo Plastics Co, 551 F2d 469 (1st Cir 1977).

[58] Fed R Civ P 26(b)(4)(c).

[59] Herbst v International Tel & Tel Corp, 65 FRD 528 (D Conn 1975); United States v John R Piquette Corp, 52 FRD 370 (ED Mich 1971).

[60] Wilson v Resnick, 51 FRD 510 (ED Pa 1970).

[61] *See* **§10.03.**

[62] Baki v BF Diamond Constr Co, 71 FRD 179 (D Md 1976); Perry v WS Darley & Co, 54 FRD 278 (ED Wis 1971). *But see* Ager v James C Stormant Hosp & Training School for Nurses, 622 F2d 496 (10th Cir 1980).

them. Discovery of experts consulted but not retained has been held not to be compellable.[63]

A demonstration of "exceptional circumstances under which it is impracticable for the party seeking discovery to obtain facts or opinions on the same subject by other means"[64] imposes a substantial burden. It should apply when expertise on a particular subject is limited and one party has frustrated the other's discovery of this expertise by retaining the experts but not calling them at trial, or where tests have been performed by the experts and the evidence is not now available for tests by other experts.[65] The reported use of this exception for psychiatric and psychological experts has been rare. One reported instance, *Dixon v Cappellini*,[66] involved an action against a *deprogrammer* by a church member. The court permitted discovery by the defendant of reports of psychiatric and psychological treatment received by the plaintiff shortly after the deprogramming, but before suit, as unique and not otherwise obtainable, citing Rule 26(b)(4) of the Federal Rules of Civil Procedure. As noted by the court, it was highly questionable that these reports should have been protected in the first instance as they probably were not prepared in anticipation of litigation.

Experts whose knowledge of an event was not gained in anticipation of litigation or trial preparation are not protected from discovery by this subsection. Thus, for example, a defendant in a medical malpractice case is not immunized from discovery under Rule 26(b)(4).[67] Similarly, experts regularly employed by a party are not generally held to be exempt from discovery under this provision.[68]

The alternate provision for discovery of experts under the reciprocity provisions of Rule 35(b) of the Federal Rules of Civil Procedure governing physical and mental examinations is discussed in **§10.03.**

§6.19 —Criminal

Discovery in criminal cases, while sharing the same goals as discovery in civil cases, is far more limited.[69] Rule 16 of the Federal Rules of

---

[63] Baki v BF Diamond Constr Co, 71 FRD 179 (D Md 1976).

[64] Fed R Civ P 26(b)(4)(B).

[65] *Cf* Perry v WS Darley & Co, 54 FRD 278 (ED Wis 1971).

[66] 88 FRD 1 (MD Pa 1980).

[67] Rodriguez v Hrinda, 56 FRD 11 (WD Pa 1972).

[68] Grinnell Corp. v Hackett, 70 FRD 326 (D RI 1976).

[69] *See* Simon, *Pretrial Discovery of Expert Information in Federal and State Courts: A Guide for the Expert*, 5 J Police Sci & Ad 247, 262-70 (1977); A. Moenssens & F. Inbau, Scientific Evidence in Criminal Cases §§1.09-.15 (1978). A chart in

Criminal Procedure governs discovery in federal criminal cases. Its provisions pertaining to expert information are as follows:

(a)   Disclosure of Evidence by the Government.
   (1)   *Information Subject to Disclosure.* . . .
      (D)   Reports of Examinations and Tests. Upon request of a defendant the government shall permit the defendant to inspect and copy or photograph any results or reports of physical or mental examinations, and of scientific tests or experiments, or copies thereof, which are within the possession, custody, or control of the government, the existence of which is known, or by the exercise of due diligence may become known, to the attorney for the government, and which are material to the preparation of the defense or are intended for use by the government as evidence in chief at the trial.
(b)   Disclosure of Evidence by the Defendant.
   (1)   *Information Subject to Disclosure.* . . .
      (B)   Reports of Examinations and Tests. If the defendant requests disclosure under subdivision (a)(1)(C) or (D) of this rule, upon compliance with such request by the government, the defendant, on request of the government, shall permit the government to inspect and copy or photograph any result or reports of physical or mental examinations and of scientific tests or experiments made in connection with the particular case, or copies thereof, within the possession or control of the defendant, which the defendant intends to introduce as evidence in chief at the trial or which were prepared by a witness whom the defendant intends to call at the trial when the results or reports relate to his testimony.

Rule 16 utilizes a reciprocal approach to discovery. The defendant may, upon request, inspect and copy reports of any physical or mental examinations or tests possessed or controlled by the government that are material to the preparation of the defense or intended to be used by the government during its case-in-chief.[70] However, if the defendant

---

Moenssens & Inbau describes state criminal discovery provisions which govern discovery of experts. A. Moenssens & F. Inbau, *supra,* at 44.

[70] Certain reports such as examinations on competency to stand trial may be in the possession of the court, but not the government. 18 USC §4244. These reports are not governed by Rule 16. United States v Chaussee, 536 F2d 637 (7th Cir 1976).

makes this request and the government complies, the government is entitled to inspect and copy any of the defendant's similar reports.

Section (c) of Rule 16 imposes a continuing duty to disclose subsequently discovered material within the scope of an earlier request.[71] And, §(d)(2) of the rule permits the imposition of sanctions for failure to comply with the provisions of Rule 16, including a limitation on introduction at trial of the nondisclosed evidence.[72] Rule 16 does not, unlike the civil discovery provisions, contemplate an additional round of discovery by deposition or other means beyond inspection and copying. Therefore, discovery of the qualifications or compensation of the prospective witness, the author of the report, is not provided for by Rule 16.

Although there is no general obligation of disclosure imposed on the prosecution by the federal Constitution,[73] when the prosecution becomes aware of material information exculpating the defendant, it must be disclosed to the defendant.[74] Thus, apart from the requirements of Rule 16, if the government's psychiatrist has, for example, reported to the prosecution that the insanity defense raised by the defendant is well taken, this report must be disclosed.

An article by Paul G. Simon[75] has systematically reviewed and characterized rules governing discovery of expert information in state court criminal proceedings. The following survey is drawn from his work. Six states—Delaware (Superior Court),[76] Florida,[77] Kansas,[78]

---

[71]   (c) Continuing Duty to Disclose. If, prior to or during trial, a party discovers additional evidence or material previously requested or ordered, which is subject to discovery or inspection under this rule, he shall promptly notify the other party or his attorney or the court of the existence of the additional evidence or material.

[72]   (2) *Failure to Comply With a Request.* If at any time during the course of the proceedings it is brought to the attention of the court that a party has failed to comply with this rule, the court may order such party to permit the discovery or inspection, grant a continuance, or prohibit the party from introducing evidence not disclosed, or it may enter such other order as it deems just under the circumstances. The court may specify the time, place and manner of making the discovery and inspection and may prescribe such terms and conditions as are just.

[73] Moore v Illinois, 408 US 786, 795 (1972).

[74] United States v Agurs, 427 US 97 (1976); Miller v Pate, 386 US 1 (1967); Brady v Maryland, 373 US 83 (1963).

[75] Simon, *Pretrial Discovery of Expert Information in Federal and State Courts: A Guide for the Expert,* 5 J Police Sci & Ad 247 (1977).

[76] Del Sup Ct R Crim P 16.

[77] Fla R Crim P 3.220.

North Carolina,[79] Ohio,[80] and Rhode Island[81]—have extrajudicial reciprocal discovery provisions patterned after federal Rule 16. Five states—Iowa,[82] Kentucky,[83] Nebraska,[84] New York,[85] and Wyoming[86]—have adopted a version of the pre-1974 Rule 16 which requires reciprocal discovery, triggered by a motion to the court, and a demonstration by the prosecution that the defendant intends to introduce this evidence as a condition of discovery. Five other states— Arkansas,[87] Delaware (Common Pleas),[88] Nevada,[89] North Dakota,[90] and Virginia[91]—have similar reciprocal discovery provisions triggered by a motion, but impose no additional burden for discovery by the prosecution.

Other states have adopted criminal discovery provisions patterned after the American Bar Association standards which do not condition prosecution discovery upon reciprocity. Alaska,[92] Colorado,[93] Illinois,[94] New Mexico,[95] and Vermont[96] follow this nonreciprocal approach to discovery and require that the prosecution, but not the defense, obtain a prior court order for discovery. Idaho,[97] Tennessee,[98] and Wisconsin[99] follow this approach but require motions by the prosecution and

---

[78] Kansas Ct Crim P §22-3213 (1981).

[79] NC Gen Stat §§15A-903, 905 (1983).

[80] Ohio R Crim P 16 (1984).

[81] RI Sup Ct R Crim P 16.

[82] Iowa R Crim P 13.

[83] Ky R Crim P 7.24.

[84] Neb Rev Stat §§29-1912, 1916, 1917 (1979).

[85] NY Civ Prac Law §240.20 (McKinney 1982).

[86] Haight v Wyoming, 654 P2d 1232 (Wyo 1982).

[87] Ark Stat Ann §43-2011.2 (1985).

[88] Del Ct Common Pleas Crim R 16 (1981).

[89] Nev Rev Stat §§174.235, .255 (1979).

[90] ND R Crim P 16.

[91] Va R Ct 3A:11 (1985).

[92] Alaska R Crim P 16.

[93] Colo R Crim P 16.

[94] Ill Ann Stat §§114, 113 (Smith-Hurd 1985).

[95] NM R Crim P 30.

[96] Vt R Crim P 16.

[97] Idaho R Crim Prac & Proc 16.

[98] Smith v State, 205 Tenn 502, 327 SW2d 308 (1959).

[99] Wis Stat Ann §971.23 (West 1971).

the defense to institute discovery. Arizona,[100] Minnesota,[101] and Oregon[102] also reject reciprocity and do not require either side to obtain a court order for discovery.

Connecticut,[103] Maine,[104] Texas,[105] and West Virginia[106] permit discovery only by the defendant. Other states, such as California,[107] operate without court rules or statutes, but instead utilize a case-by-case approach, governed by case law, to regulate discovery.

Four states—Florida,[108] Iowa,[109] Indiana,[110] and Nebraska[111]— permit discovery of experts by depositions, a procedure not available under the Federal Rules of Criminal Procedure.

§6.20 Suggested Reading

Books

E. Imwinkelried, *The Methods of Attacking Scientific Evidence* (1982).

T. Mauet, *Fundamentals of Trial Techniques* (1980).

A. Moenssens & F. Inbau, *Scientific Evidence in Criminal Cases* (2d ed 1978).

W. Prosser, *Handbook of the Law of Torts* (4th ed 1971).

D. Schwartz, *The Proper Use of a Psychiatric Expert in Scientific and Expert Evidence in Criminal Advocacy* (1975).

J. Weinstein & M. Berger, *Weinstein's Evidence* (1982).

Articles

2 Am Jur *Trials* §§46, 47 (1964).

Annot, 2 Am Jur *Trials* 587 (1964).

---

[100] Ariz R Crim P 15.1 & .2.

[101] Minn R Crim P 9.01.

[102] Or Rev Stat §§135.815, .835 (1983).

[103] Conn Gen Stat §54-86a (1983).

[104] Me R Crim P 16.

[105] Tex Code Crim Proc Ann art 39.14 (Vernon 1979).

[106] W Va Code Ann §62-1B-2 (1977).

[107] Pitchess v Superior Court, 11 Cal 3d 531, 522 P2d 305, 113 Cal Rptr 897 (1974).

[108] Fla Stat Ann, Crim Rule 1.220(f).

[109] Iowa v Groscast, 355 NW2d 32 (Iowa 1984).

[110] Ind Stat Ann §35-37-4-3 (Burns 1985).

[111] Neb Rev Stat §29-1917 (1979).

Bank & Poythress, *The Elements of Persuasion in Expert Testimony*, 10 J Psychiatry & L 173 (1982).

Berment & Jacoubovitch, *Fish Out of Water: A Brief Overview of Social and Psychological Concerns About Videotaped Trials*, 26 Hastings LJ 999 (1975).

Diamond, *The Fallacy of the Impartial Expert*, 3 Archive Crim Psychodynamics 221 (1959).

Dix, *Expert Prediction Testimony in Capital Sentencing: Evidentiary and Constitutional Considerations*, 19 Am Crim L Rev 1 (1981).

Foster, *Expert Testimony—Prevalent Complaints and Proposed Remedies*, 11 Harv L Rev 169 (1897).

Gorman, *Are There Impartial Psychiatric Witnesses?*, 11 Bull Am Acad Psychiatry & L 379 (1983).

Graham, *Impeaching the Professional Witness by a Showing of Financial Interest*, 53 Ind LJ 35 (1977-78).

Note, *The Doctor in Court: Impartial Medical Testimony*, 40 S Cal L Rev 728 (1967).

Principle 5, *Ethical Principles of Psychologists*, 36 Am Psychologist 633 (1981).

The Principles of Medical Ethics, 24 JAMA 2187 (1981).

Report by Special Committee of the Association of the Bar of the City of New York: *Impartial Medical Testimony* (1956).

Shuman, *Testimonial Compulsion: The Involuntary Medical Expert Witness*, 4 J Legal Med 419 (1983).

Simon, *Pretrial Discovery of Expert Information in Federal and State Courts: A Guide for the Expert*, 5 J Police Sci & Ad 247 (1977).

Symposium: *The Ethical Boundaries of Forensic Psychiatry*, 12 Bull Am Acad of Psychiatry & L 209 (1984).

Symposium: *The Use of Videotape in the Courtroom*, 1975 BYU L Rev 327

Tyree, *The Opinion Rule*, 10 Rutgers L Rev 601 (1956).

Van Dusen, *A United States District Judge's View of the Impartial Medical Expert System*, 32 FRD 498 (1963).

Cases

Ager v James C Stormant Hospital & Training School for Nurses, 622 F2d 496 (10th Cir 1980).

Baki v BF Diamond Construction Co, 71 FRD 179 (D Md 1976).

Board of County Commissioners v Lee, 3 Colo App 177, 32 P 841 (1893).

Brady v Maryland, 373 US 83 (1963).

Buchman v State, 59 Ind 1 (1877).

Carter-Wallace, Inc v Otte, 474 F2d 529 (2d Cir 1972), *cert denied,* 412 US 929 (1973).

City & County of San Francisco v Superior Court, 37 Cal 2d 227, 231 P2d 26 (1951).

Commonwealth v Simmons, 361 Pa 391, 65 A2d 353, *cert denied,* 338 US 862 (1949).

Ex parte Dement, 53 Ala 389 (1875).

Dixon v Cappellini, 88 FRD 1 (MD Pa 1980).

Dixon v People, 168 Ill 179, 48 NE 108 (1897).

Fino v McCollum Mining Co, 93 FRD 455 (ND Tex 1982).

Grinnell Corp v Hackett, 70 FRD 326 (DRI 1976).

Haight v Wyoming, 654 P2d 1232 (Wyo 1982).

Herbst v International Telephone & Telegraph Corp, 65 FRD 528 (D Conn 1975).

Iowa v Groscost, 355 NW2d 32 (Iowa 1984).

Mason v Robinson, 340 NW2d (Iowa 1983).

Miller v Pate, 386 US 1 (1967).

Moore v Illinois, 408 US 786 (1972).

Pennsylvania Co v Philadelphia, 262 Pa 439, 105 A 630 (1918).

People ex rel Kraushaar Brothers v Thorpe, 296 NY 223, 72 NE2d 165 (1947).

Perry v WS Darley & Co, 54 FRD 278 (ED Wis 1971).

Pitchess v Superior Court, 11 Cal 3d 531, 522 P2d 305, 113 Cal Rptr 897 (1974).

Rodriguez v Hrinda, 56 FRD 11 (WD Pa 1972).

Royster v Lederle, 128 F2d 197 (6th Cir 1972).

Shaughnessey v Holt, 236 Ill 485, 86 NE 256 (1908).

Simonsen v Barlo Plastics Co, 551 F2d 469 (1st Cir 1977).

Smith v State, 205 Tenn 502, 327 SW2d 308 (1959).

Stanton v Rushmore, 112 NJL 113, 169 A 721 (1934).

United States v Agurs, 427 US 97 (1976).

United States v Chaussee, 536 F2d 637 (7th Cir 1976).

United States v John R Piquette Corp, 52 FRD 370 (ED Mich 1971).

Wilson v Resnick, 51 FRD 510 (ED Pa 1970).

Ziervogel v Royal Packing Co, 225 SW2d 798 (Mo 1949).

Rules and Statutes

Alaska R Crim P 16.

Ariz R Crim P 15.1 & .2.

Ark Stat Ann §43-2011.2 (1985).

Colo R Crim P 16.

Conn Gen Stat §54-86a (1983).

Del Ct Common Pleas Crim R 16 (1981).

Del Sup Ct R Crim P 16.

Fed R Civ P 26(b)(4)(B).

Fed R Civ P 30(b)(2).

Fla R Crim P 3.220.

Fla Stat Ann Crim R 1.220(f).

Idaho R Crim Prac & Proc 16.

Ill Ann Stat 38 §114-13 (Smith-Hurd 1985).

Ind Stat Ann §35-37-4-3 (Burns 1985).

Iowa R Crim P 13.

Kansas Ct Crim P §22-3213 (1981).

Ky R Crim P 7.24.

Me R Crim P 16.

Minn R Crim P 9.01.

NC Gen Stat §§15A-903, 905 (1983).

ND R Crim P 16.

Neb Rev Stat §§29-1912, 1916, 1917 (1979).

Nev Rev Stat §§174.235, 255 (1979).

NM R Crim P 30.

NY Civ Prac Law §240.20 (McKinney 1982).

Ohio R Crim P 16 (1984).

Or Rev Stat §§135.815, 835 (1983).

RI Sup Ct R Crim P 16.

Tex Code Crim P Ann art 39.14 (Vernon 1979).

18 USC §4244.

Va R Ct 3A:11 (1985).

Vt R Crim P 16.

W Va Code Ann §62-1B-2 (1977).

Wis Stat Ann §971.23 (West 1971).

§6.21   WESTLAW Search References

§6.01   *Introduction*
di expert witness

§6.02   *The Fallacy of the Impartial Expert*
evidence /s (rule +1 706) "court-appointed expert"

§6.03   *Sources of Experts*
text (psychiatry psychology) & "drug abuse"

§6.04   *—The Grapevine*
[no query]

§6.05   *—Professional Literature*
professional +1 publication literature /p witness testimony

§6.06   *—Academic Institutions*
professor faculty college university instructor /6 psychiatr**
psycholog!

§6.07   *—Professional Societies*
"american psych! association"

§6.08   *—Professional Witnesses*
"professional witness" /p reputation fee credib! ideolog! financial***

§6.09   *Getting the Expert to Court*
(expert +1 testimony witness) professional /p qualif! /p eva-
luat! /p psychiatr*** psycholog****

§6.10   *—The Initial Contact*
(expert +1 testimony witness) professional /p psychiatr***
psycholog**** /p cross-examin! /s opinion

§6.11   *—Evaluating the Expert*
157k535

§6.12   *—The Fee*
(expert +1 testimony witness) professional /5 fee & psychiatr*** psycholog****

§6.13   *Trial Preparation—Substantive*
expert +1 witness testimony /p hypothetical /p mental-state
psychiatr*** psycholog****

§6.14   *—Decorum.*
expert +1 witness testimony /p jury /s comprehen! incompre-

hen! underst**d! analys! language jargon /p psychiatr***
psycholog****

§6.15   *—Logistics*
        expert +1 witness testimony /s subpoena

§6.16   *Compellability of Expert Testimony*
        compel! /s expert +1 witness testimony

        carter-wallace /s 474 +5 529 /p expert +1 witness testimony

§6.17   *Pretrial Discovery of Experts*
        to (127) /p expert +1 witness testimony

§6.18   *—Civil Discovery*
        di,sy(civil /s discovery /s psychiatr! psycholog!) fi 88frdl

§6.19   *—Criminal Discovery*
        criminal /s discovery /s psychiatr! psycholog! /p reciproc****
        disclos*** inform

7

General Requirements for the Presentation of Expert Psychiatric and Psychological Evidence

§7.01   The Opinion Rule

Rules of evidence governing the presentation of expert evidence in common law jurisdictions are based on the assumption that a distinction exists between facts and opinions.[1] The significance of this distinction is its impact on the roles the judge and jury are expected to play in the resolution of disputes. Ordinarily, it is assumed, witnesses who have perceived some relevant event should describe their perceptions in factual terms and, if any inferences or opinions need be drawn, that is the exclusive function of the fact-finder, whether judge or jury.

This same theory recognizes that, since the judge and jury are not chosen because they possess any particular technical or scientific knowledge, in some instances they will be incapable of understanding or interpreting the facts presented without some specialized assistance. In these instances, witnesses possessing specialized knowledge that will

---

[1] E. Cleary, McCormick on Evidence §11 (3d ed 1984).

enable the judge or jury to understand the facts may present their opinions.[2] This is the basis for the rules of evidence limiting the testimony of ordinary or lay witnesses to facts and permitting expert witnesses to testify in the form of an opinion.

Regardless of the validity of this theory in the abstract, it has proved difficult to apply. Judges have understandably become mired in the semantic problem of distinguishing facts from opinions[3] and lay witnesses have found it difficult to describe their perceptions in factual terms without utilizing any conclusions, inferences, or opinions.[4] As a result of these difficulties, a relaxation of the opinion rule has occurred to avoid a substantial loss of probative evidence.

Relaxation of the rule has occurred in two ways. First, specific subjects have been found to be appropriate for lay opinion testimony. These are either subjects on which lay witnesses are thought capable of forming a rational opinion or subjects on which shorthand expressions are thought to communicate commonly understood concepts. Examples of these subjects include speed, size, and intoxication.[5] Second, more recently, a general relaxation of the limits on lay opinion testimony has occurred in Rule 701 of the Federal Rules of Evidence[6] and its state counterparts.[7] This approach attempts to avoid the loss of probative evidence through rigid limitations on the form of witnesses' testimony and leaves to the adversary system the potential problems with witnesses' opinions. Lay opinion testimony is permitted when the opinions are "rationally based on the perception of the witness and

---

[2] *Id* §13.

[3] 7 J. Wigmore, Evidence §1919 (Chadbourne rev 1978).

[4] Fed R Evid 701 advisory committee note, 56 FRD 183, 281 (1972).

[5] Vaughn v State, 493 SW2d 524 (Tex Crim App 1973); Littlefield v State, 167 Tex Crim R 443, 321 SW2d 79 (1959). *See* 7 J. Wigmore, *supra* note 3.

[6] If the witness is not testifying as an expert, his testimony in the form of opinions or inferences is limited to those opinions or inferences which are (a) rationally based on the perception of the witness and (b) helpful to a clear understanding of his testimony or the determination of a fact in issue.

[7] Alaska, Arizona, Arkansas, Colorado, Hawaii, Maine, Michigan, Minnesota, Montana, Nebraska, Nevada, New Mexico, North Dakota, Washington, Wisconsin, and Wyoming have adopted Federal Rule of Evidence 701 without change, while Florida and Delaware have adopted modified versions. J. Weinstein & M. Berger, 3 Weinstein's Evidence, ¶701 [03] (1984).

. . . helpful to a clear understanding of his testimony or the determination of a fact in issue."[8]

Under both the specific subject and the across-the-board approach to relaxation of the opinion rule discussed above, lay testimony about mental condition or capacity based on personal knowledge has been permitted as a convenient way of describing behavior.[9] Typically, this involves the testimony of a witness who has observed the behavior of one of the parties and is permitted, as an aspect of describing the behavior, to say the party was behaving in a crazy or bizarre manner.[10] For example, in *Stacy v Love,*[11] the cellmate of a defendant charged with murder who raised the insanity defense was allowed to describe the defendant's behavior. The defendant had the delusion that he was a member of the President's cabinet and had a habit of standing nude in the cell with toilet paper stuffed in his nostrils. The cellmate was then permitted to give his opinion of the defendant's sanity and did so "with a concision and clarity rarely associated with the interface of law and psychiatry . . . 'he ain't got good sense, he's crazy.' "[12]

To the extent that this lay testimony is simply a statement that the party did not behave the way most other people behave and is based on the personal knowledge and experience of the witness, this sort of testimony may provide valuable information for the judge or jury. Aberrance is often a consequential consideration when mental illness is an issue in the proceedings. To the extent that this lay testimony seeks to describe something more than aberrance and instead suggests lack of the requisite capacity to execute a document, for example, the limits of common knowledge are strained and the need for expert testimony arises.

§7.02   Required and Permitted Expert Psychiatric and Psychological Evidence

Consideration of the admissibility of expert psychiatric and psychological testimony requires that two categories be distinguished: evidence that *must* be presented and evidence that *may* be presented. As

---

[8] Fed R Evid 701.

[9] People v Teague, 108 Ill App 3d 891, 439 NE2d 1066 (1982); Taylor v State, 440 NE2d 1109 (Ind 1982). *See generally* 7 J. Wigmore, *supra* note 3, at §§1933-1938.

[10] Morse, *Crazy Behavior, Morals and Science: An Analysis of Mental Health Law,* 51 S Cal L Rev 527 (1978).

[11] 679 F2d 1209 (6th Cir 1982).

[12] *Id* 1214.

to the former, expert psychiatric and psychological evidence must be presented when psychiatric or psychological issues are material in a case and laypeople are incapable of reaching rationally based conclusions on these issues without specialized assistance.[13] Under these circumstances, if the party bearing the burden of production on this issue has not produced expert psychiatric or psychological testimony, a directed verdict is appropriate.

This issue frequently arises in malpractice actions.[14] Unless the act of the psychiatrist or psychologist in a malpractice case alleged to constitute negligence, standing alone, can be found by the jury to fall below the appropriate level of care, a situation governed by the doctrine of res ipsa loquitur, expert psychiatric or psychological evidence on the standard of care must be presented or a directed verdict will be granted against the plaintiff.[15] If, for example, the negligence alleged is a psychiatrist's failure to prescribe electroconvulsive therapy and a decision, instead, in favor of a low-level prescription and subsequent discontinuance of an antidepressant medication to a depressed patient who attempted suicide, it would not be expected that the jury would have the requisite understanding of psychopharmacology or choice of alternative treatments to decide this case without expert assistance.[16] Therefore, if the plaintiff's only evidence on causation is a description of the depression, the drug prescription, and the subsequent attempted suicide, a directed verdict is appropriate. Conversely, if the alleged act of negligence is placing a psychiatric patient, who recently attempted suicide, in a second-story room with a window that the patient could open and from which he then leapt, head first, to his death, expert psychiatric or psychological evidence might not be necessary to permit the plaintiff's case to reach the jury.[17] A jury does not need specialized

---

[13] See Stacy v Love, 679 F2d 1209 (6th Cir 1982); Meier v Ross Gen Hosp, 69 Cal 2d 420, 445 P2d 519, 71 Cal Rptr 903 (1968).

[14] Note, *The Application of Res Ipsa Loquitur in Medical Malpractice Cases*, 60 Nw L Rev 852 (1966).

[15] Cf Fritz v Parke Davis & Co, 277 Minn 210, 152 NW2d 129 (1967); Brandt v Grubin, 131 NJ Super 182, 329 A2d 82 (1974). For a general discussion of expert testimony in medical malpractice cases, see S. Pegalis & H. Wachsman, American Law of Medical Malpractice §11.2 (1980).

[16] Gowan v United States, 601 F Supp 1297 (D Or 1985).

[17] Meier v Ross Gen Hosp, 69 Cal 2d 420, 445 P2d 519, 71 Cal Rptr 903 (1968). See also Hammer v Rosen, 7 AD2d 216, 181 NYS2d 805 (1959), *modified*, 7 NY2d 376, 165 NE2d 756, 198 NYS2d 65 (1960), in which physical beatings of the patient were found to constitute negligence without the necessity of expert testimony.

assistance to determine whether the duty owed to a suicidal patient should include removal of the means to attempt suicide.

The circumstances under which expert psychiatric and psychological testimony, although not required, will be permitted are a function of the opinion rule discussed in §7.01. Because of the philosophy that it is the exclusive province of the jury to draw inferences or opinions from the facts presented, expert testimony was previously limited to instances in which juries were utterly incapable of reaching a rational decision without expert assistance.[18] This approach prevented the introduction of expert testimony in instances in which it would be helpful but not necessary. As the cost of this rigid application of the opinion rule has been recognized, a relaxation of the rule in most courts has evolved, illustrated by Rule 702 of the Federal Rules of Evidence that permits the introduction of expert testimony when "scientific, technical, or other specialized knowledge will assist the trier of fact to understand the evidence or to determine a fact in issue."[19] The crucial question under this rule is helpfulness; thus, even if the jury could decide the question without expert assistance, if such assistance would be helpful, it should be admitted.

Rule 702 has, however, not resulted in the receipt of all helpful psychiatric and psychological testimony. A vestige of the older approach, which feared intrusion on the jury, remains. In *United States v Webb*,[20] for example, the defendant charged with willfully shooting a passing helicopter was not permitted to introduce expert testimony, based on psychological tests, that the defendant was nonviolent and, therefore, not likely to have shot at the helicopter. The court of appeals affirmed the exclusion of the testimony on the grounds that this question was within the ken of lay jurors and, therefore, not a proper subject of expert testimony.[21] Similarly, in *United States v West*,[22] the court of appeals affirmed the exclusion of psychiatric testimony that the defendant's intelligence rendered it less likely that he understood he

---

[18] Ladd, *Expert Testimony*, 5 Vand L Rev 414 (1952).

[19] Fed R Evid 702. Alaska, Arizona, Arkansas, Colorado, Delaware, Maine, Minnesota, Montana, Nebraska, New Mexico, North Dakota, Ohio, Oklahoma, South Dakota, Washington, Wisconsin, and Wyoming have adopted a rule identical to Federal Rule of Evidence 702, while Florida, Hawaii, Michigan, and Nevada have adopted slightly modified versions of the rule. J. Weinstein & M. Berger, 3 Weinstein's Evidence, ¶702[06] (1984).

[20] 625 F2d 709 (5th Cir 1980).

[21] *Id* 711.

[22] 670 F2d 675 (7th Cir 1982).

was accepting a bribe, on the grounds that the issue was within the ability of the jury to determine without expert assistance.

Because of the rules permitting admission of expert testimony on issues as to which some degree of lay competence may exist and the rules permitting admission of lay testimony on questions of sanity, lay and expert testimony on sanity are frequently admitted on the same issue and may conflict. In these instances, courts usually permit the jury to reject the expert testimony and accept the conflicting lay testimony[23] based upon either the better perspective of the lay witness[24] or the expert's lack of credibility.[25]

§7.03   Validity of Psychiatric and Psychological Theory

The benefit of expert testimony is also the source of its major risk. Expert testimony is admitted because the judge or jury lacks specialized knowledge on an issue. The fact-finders are thus dependent on the expert; it is not their field. The extent to which the judge or jury ought reasonably to depend on the expert's opinion is a function, among other things,[26] of the validity of the theory that underlies the expert's specialized knowledge. If the expert's opinion, cloaked in professional jargon largely unintelligible to the lay public, is based on the assumption that one plus one equals three or that the sun rises in the west, the resulting opinion will be worthless and should not support a finding in the case. The fact-finder's lack of technical sophistication, it is often feared, either will not permit it to understand the flawed assumption or will require a substantial, and unjustified, lengthening of the trial and added costs to reveal the flawed assumption.

To respond to these fears courts have erected threshold tests of the validity of the underlying scientific theory. The threshold test most

---

[23] Bonnie & Slobogin, *The Role of Mental Health Professionals in the Criminal Process: The Case for Informed Speculation*, 66 Va L Rev 427, 463 n 118 (1980).

[24] De Mars v State, 352 NW2d 13 (Minn 1984); Commonwealth v Tyson, 485 Pa 344, 402 A2d 995 (1979).

[25] United States v Fortune, 513 F2d 883 (5th Cir), *cert denied*, 423 US 1020 (1975).

[26] The entire evaluation requires exploration of the validity of the underlying theory, a correct incorporation of that theory by the expert in an analysis of the facts, the accuracy of the facts to which the expert's theories are applied, and, as with all other witnesses, the sincerity of the witness.

commonly noted was articulated in a case involving the admissibility of polygraph evidence, *Frye v United States:*[27]

> Just when a scientific principle or discovery crosses the line between the experimental and demonstrable stages is difficult to define. Somewhere in this twilight zone the evidential force of the principle must be recognized, and while courts will go a long way in admitting expert testimony deduced from a well-recognized scientific principle or discovery, the thing from which the deduction is made must be sufficiently established to have gained general acceptance in the particular field in which it belongs.[28]

This test is essentially conservative and waits until members of the field to which the scientific theory belongs, this classification itself often a source of contention, have generally accepted the theory.[29] Although *Frye* may still be recognized as the standard governing the admissibility of scientific evidence in a majority of jurisdictions, it is not often rigidly or uniformly applied. Many courts have relaxed this general acceptance requirement and permit the jury to evaluate the validity of scientific evidence as it does all other evidence, viewing the issue simply as one of relevance.[30] Nonetheless, even under this seemingly more liberal test, the counterweights to mere relevance—unfair prejudice, confusion of the issues, and misleading the jury[31]—may still result in the exclusion of scientific evidence that rests on questionable theories. The time and expense necessary to explore the validity of an item of scientific evidence may not be justified in some cases.

Psychiatrists and psychologists testifying as expert witnesses have been subject to scrutiny under the *Frye* test and its variations.[32] Attacks on the underlying scientific basis of psychiatric and psychological testimony have proliferated and have tended to fall into one of three categories: scientific invalidity, diagnostic imprecision, and predictive limitations.

---

[27] 293 F 1013 (DC Cir 1923).

[28] *Id* 1014.

[29] Giannelli, *The Admissibility of Novel Scientific Evidence,* 80 Colum L Rev 1197 (1980).

[30] *See, e.g.,* Barefoot v Estelle, 463 US 880 (1983); State v Hall, 297 NW2d 80 (Iowa 1980); State v Williams, 388 A2d 500 (Me 1978); Watson v State, 64 Wis 2d 264, 219 NW2d 398 (1974).

[31] Fed R Evid 403.

[32] J. Ziskin, Coping with Psychiatric and Psychological Evidence (3d ed 1981).

§7.04   —Scientific Invalidity

It has been argued that psychiatry and psychology are merely pseudo sciences, for they do not involve the discovery and application of principles derived from the scientific method and are not, therefore, worthy of the weight accorded other branches of medicine whose principles are derived from the scientific method.[33] The scientific method, which is thought to distinguish real science from pseudo science, entails the formulation of a hypothesis and structured observation and testing of the hypothesis until it is validated or rejected. In psychiatry and psychology, it is argued, the scientific method has not been uniformly applied and these professions operate largely on unvalidated theories drawn from anecdotal evidence.[34] Moreover, resolution of the basic questions about the cause of mental disorder and its treatment fails to evoke even a professional consensus.[35] Thus, it is argued either that psychiatrists and psychologists are not scientists and should not be permitted to offer expert testimony masquerading as scientists or, minimally, that they have only unvalidated theories to offer that are not sufficiently probative to justify receipt into evidence and risk misleading the judge or jury. Psychiatry and psychology, it is argued, compared with other branches of medicine, are in their infancy, and the courts ought to wait until they have grown up before relying on information they provide.

Several responses to this attack are often made. The first response attempts, directly, to categorize psychiatry and psychology as a science to which the scientific method has been applied. The argument advanced is that Sigmund Freud and his successors have articulated theories that they tested through observation and other methods. Recognizing the absence of professional unanimity on this point, proponents of psychiatric and psychological testimony turn this in their favor, arguing that the lay public is aware of this diversity of opinion and thus likely to view this testimony critically, thereby avoiding the risk of unquestioned acceptance of this evidence.[36] In addition, criticism of the series of mental illness based on failure to apply the scientific method are most appropriately applied only to some psychological theories; organic, biological, and behavioral theories more clearly rest on

---

[33] *Id* 64.

[34] *Id* 96.

[35] *See* **ch 1.**

[36] Bonnie & Slobogin, *The Role of Mental Health Professionals in the Criminal Process: The Case for Informed Speculation,* 66 Va L Rev 427, 464-65 n 121 (1980).

research relying on the scientific method.[37]

Another response admits the diversity of professional opinions in the fields of psychiatry and psychology, but suggests that the same phenomenon exists in other fields of study recognized as sciences, such as physics.[38] Physics, as an example of a hard science, it is argued, consists of a multitude of theories currently unverified and perhaps unverifiable. Thus, the assumption that a science need consist of verified theories asks that psychiatry and psychology be put to a test not applied to other sciences. Moreover, even in other hard science branches of medicine, substantial disputes exist. The use of vitamin C to fight cancer[39] and the use of coronary bypass surgery versus drugs[40] to treat blockage of arteries to the heart find distinguished members of the medical profession in heated controversy. Yet, no claim is made that these branches of medicine are unscientific.

Finally, another response is that, even with the underlying uncertainties in psychiatric and psychological theory, by their education, training, and experience, psychiatrists and psychologists acquire a special ability to understand human behavior and treat aberrant behavior probably not possessed by the lay populace.[41] Thus, whatever flaws may exist in theories in these fields, the knowledge of psychiatrists and psychologists is likely to add to the knowledge of lay jurors on the subject of human behavior and for this reason should be received into evidence. This approach is often the bottom line response of courts to such criticisms.[42]

§7.05 —Diagnostic Imprecision

Even if the underlying psychiatric and psychological theory and resulting diagnostic labels have meanings that should be given legal effect, it is argued that the reliability of psychiatric diagnosis does not justify judicial reliance. There is evidence that in many instances a group

---

[37] *See* **ch 1.**

[38] Delman, *Participation by Psychologists in Insanity Defense Proceedings: An Advocacy,* 9 J Psychiatry & L 247, 295-50 (1981).

[39] Moertel, Fleming, Cregan, Rubin, O'Connell, & Mathews, *High-Dose Vitamin C Versus Placebo in the Treatment of Patients with Advanced Cancer Who Have Had No Prior Chemotherapy: A Randomized Double-Blind Comparison,* 312 New Eng J Med 137 (1985).

[40] VA Cooperative Group Study, *Eleven-Year Survival in the Veterans Administration Randomized Trial of Coronary Bypass Surgery for Stable Angina,* 311 New Eng J Med 1333 (1984).

[41] Bonnie & Slobogin, *supra* note 36, at 463-64 n 117.

[42] *See, e.g.,* Barefoot v Estelle, 463 US 880 (1983).

of psychiatrists diagnosing the same person disagree among themselves from 60 to 80 per cent over the diagnosis.[43] If the reliability of the diagnosis is no better than "flipping coins in the courtroom,"[44] arguably, juries should be protected from this evidence. Even the Chief Justice of the United States, Warren Burger, has acknowledged "the uncertainties of psychiatric diagnosis."[45]

At the outset, it is important to recognize that much of the literature challenging the reliability of psychiatric diagnosis is directed to diagnoses under DSM-I or II.[46] DSM-III, which became effective in 1979, sought to improve upon the reliability of its predecessors. Thus, even if the reliability of diagnosis for certain mental disorders was no better than random chance under earlier diagnostic criteria, current attacks must focus on DSM-III. Yet, it may be appropriate, given the serious problems of DSM-I and II, to presume that the same problems persist in DSM-III until a body of research comes into existence to rebut this presumption. Although some prepublication studies indicate good reliability for DSM-III diagnostic classifications,[47] considerable time will have to pass with clinicians utilizing DSM-III before any certainty exists.

One potential difficulty with DSM-III may be that in its attempt to increase reliability, it has sacrificed much in the way of validity.[48] Psychiatrists and psychologists may achieve greater agreement about the diagnosis of a patient under DSM-III, but that diagnosis may reveal less about the patient. All patients with the same diagnosis will not, for example, require the same treatment.

Notwithstanding these limitations, the relevant provisions of the criminal law, for example, continue to utilize a medical model of behavior in which diagnostic labels are of consequence in determining whether the relevant acts were the product of a mental disease or defect.[49] Until the substantive criminal law is revised no longer to require decisions on this basis, juries will be called upon to reach

---

[43] *See, e.g.*, Zubin, *Classification of the Behavior Disorders*, 18 Ann Rev Psychiatry 373 (1967).

[44] Ennis & Litwack, *Psychiatry and the Presumption of Expertise: Flipping Coins in the Courtroom*, 62 Cal L Rev 693 (1974).

[45] O'Connor v Donaldson, 422 US 563, 578 (1975) (Burger, CJ, concurring).

[46] Spritzer, Endicott and Robins, *Clinical Criteria for Psychiatric Diagnosis and DSM-III*, 132 Am J Psychiatry 1187 (1975).

[47] *See* §2.01.

[48] Valliant, *The Disadvantages of DSM-III*, 141 Am J Psychiatry 542, 595 (1984).

[49] Bonnie & Slobogin, *The Role of Mental Health Professionals in the Criminal Process: The Case for Informed Speculation*, 66 Va L Rev 427, 466 (1980).

diagnostic decisions and judges are likely to conclude that the assistance of psychiatrists and psychologists, however flawed, is preferable to an unguided lay diagnosis.

§7.06 —Predictive Limitations

Psychiatrists and psychologists testifying in court are frequently asked to predict the future dangerous behavior of an individual: if not executed will the defendant kill again,[50] if not civilly committed will this person commit a dangerous act,[51] if released will this insanity acquittee continue to pose a danger to society.[52] Only if psychiatrists or psychologists have some specialized knowledge not likely to be possessed by the judge or jury, it is argued, should predictions of future behavior by psychiatrists and psychologists be accepted. Increasingly, fueled by disclaimers of the professions themselves,[53] broad-based psychiatric and psychological expertise in predicting future behavior has been questioned.[54]

The techniques for prediction of future dangerous behavior are generally categorized as the *clinical* and *actuarial* methods. The clinical method of prediction, the one most commonly encountered in judicial proceedings, is based on a clinical examination of the patient, a history, psychological testing, and a variety of other *soft* variables. At the conclusion of the process the clinician arrives at an impression of the likelihood of the patient engaging in a particular behavior in the future. The majority of studies that have focused critically on predictions of dangerous behavior have examined clinical predictions. These studies have, with limited exception, revealed false positives, people erroneously identified as dangerous, of between 50 and 90 per cent.[55]

---

[50] Barefoot v Estelle, 463 US 880 (1983).

[51] Addington v Texas, 441 US 418 (1979).

[52] Jones v United States, 463 US 354 (1983).

[53] American Psychiatric Assn, *Clinical Aspects of the Violent Individual* (1974); *Report of the Task Force on the Role of Psychology in the Criminal Justice System,* 33 Am Psychologist 1099, 1110 (1978).

[54] J. Monohan, The Clinical Prediction of Violent Behavior (1981).

[55] *See* H. Steadman & J. Cocozza, Careers of the Criminally Insane (1974) (80%); T. Thornberry & J. Jacoby, The Criminally Insane: A Community Follow-up of Mentally Ill Offenders (1979) (80%); Kozol, Boucher, & Garofalo, *The Diagnosis and Treatment of Dangerousness,* 18 Crime & Delinq 371, 390 (1972) (65.3%); Steadman, *A New Look at Recidivism Among Patuxent Inmates,* 5 Bull Am Acad Psychiatry & L 200 (1977) (58.7%); Wenk & Emrich, *Assaultive Youth: An Exploratory Study of the Assaultive Experience and Assaultive Potential of California Youth Authority Wards,* 9 J Research Crime & Delinq 171 (1972) (92%).

The other principal method of prediction is actuarial. This method of prediction involves the application of statistics to prediction by assigning statistical probabilities to those variables that have been found to correlate with dangerous behavior and results in a numerical probability. Because crimes of violence are committed with greater frequency by males, for example, a patient who is male would be assigned a correlatively higher probability of engaging in dangerous behavior than a female. Other variables, including race, age, IQ, prior arrests, use of alcohol or drugs, and marital status are also considered in this type of prediction.[56] Studies of actuarial predictions reveal no greater accuracy than clinical predictions;[57] moreover, their aggregate quality fails to account for the possibility of individual choice.[58]

Although judges have expressed skepticism about the validity of psychiatric and psychological predictions of future dangerousness and have, occasionally, imposed limitations on this sort of testimony,[59] there has been an overall judicial reluctance to exclude this evidence.[60]

---

[56] J. Monohan, The Clinical Prediction of Violent Behavior 71-75 (1981).

[57] Wenk, Robison, & Smith, *Can Violence Be Predicted,* 18 Crime & Delinq 393 (1972) (86% false positives).

[58] In the context of the imposition of capital punishment, the United States Supreme Court has rejected the use of decision-making criteria that fail to take into account individual rather than aggregate behaviors. Lockett v Ohio, 438 US 586, 605 (1978) (plurality opinion of Burger, Stewart, Powell, & Stevens); Roberts v Louisiana, 428 US 325, 331-34 (1976) (plurality opinion of Stewart, Powell, & Stevens).

[59] *See, e.g.,* People v Murtishaw, 29 Cal 3d 733, 631 P2d 446, 175 Cal Rptr 738 (1981), *cert denied,* 455 US 922 (1982); *In re* Wilson, 33 Crim L Rptr 2115 (DC Super Ct Apr 14, 1983). *Cf* Smith v Estelle, 602 F2d 694 (5th Cir 1979), *affd on other grounds,* 451 US 454 (1981); White v Estelle, 554 F Supp 851 (SD Tex 1982).

[60] Barefoot v Estelle, 463 US 880 (1983).

The suggestion that no psychiatrist's testimony may be presented with respect to a defendant's future dangerousness is somewhat like asking us to disinvent the wheel. In the first place, it is contrary to our cases. If the likelihood of a defendant committing further crimes is a constitutionally acceptable criterion for imposing the death penalty, which it is, *Jurek v. Texas,* 428 U.S. 262 (1976), and if it is not impossible for even a lay person sensibly to arrive at that conclusion, it makes little sense, if any, to submit that psychiatrists, out of the entire universe of persons who might have an opinion on the issue, would know so little about the subject that they should not be permitted to testify. . . .

In the second place, the rules of evidence generally extant at the federal and state levels anticipate that relevant unprivileged evidence should be admitted and its weight left to the fact finder, who would have the benefit

Substantive legal criteria for capital punishment, civil commitment, and the release of insanity acquittees continue to require judges and juries to engage in predictions of future dangerousness. Even in the face of serious and substantial empirical challenges to expertise in this area, judges have been unwilling to deprive lay decision-makers of whatever guidance psychiatrists and psychologists may provide in this area, and have relegated challenges to the weight rather than the admissibility of this evidence. Thus, improvements are more likely to come in the careful presentation and challenge of this evidence.[61]

Because psychiatric and psychological education has not traditionally offered courses or training in prediction of future behavior,[62] the particular education, training, and experience of the purported expert witness should be examined to ascertain any basis for expertise. Any claim to expertise based upon experience should be examined to determine whether it provides a scientific basis for expertise. For example, the fact that a psychiatrist has made numerous predictions is not significant without a showing that systematic follow-up studies verified the accuracy of the earlier predictions or provided feedback on errors to improve future predictions.[63]

There is a body of literature that suggests some factors that do

---

of cross examination and contrary evidence by the opposing party. Psychiatric testimony predicting dangerousness may be countered not only as erroneous in a particular case but as generally so unreliable that it should be ignored. If the jury may make up its mind about future dangerousness unaided by psychiatric testimony, jurors should not be barred from hearing the views of the State's psychiatrists along with opposing views of the defendant's doctors. . . .

Third, petitioner's view mirrors the position expressed in the amicus brief of the American Psychiatric Association (APA). As indicated above, however, the same view was presented and rejected in *Estelle v. Smith*. We are no more convinced now that the view of the APA should be converted into a constitutional rule barring an entire category of expert testimony. We are not persuaded that such testimony is almost entirely unreliable and that the factfinder and the adversary system will not be competent to uncover, recognize, and take due account of its shortcomings.

Id 896-99.

[61] J. Monohan, *supra* note 56, at 91-100.

[62] *See* §§4.04, 4.10.

[63] Even this may pose problems for individuals confined based on the prediction of future dangerousness who do not act violently in the institution because of institutional constraints (medication, guards, etc.) or because the prediction was wrong. Individuals who are released based on a prediction of nondangerousness and not subsequently institutionalized may commit acts of violence not reported to the authorities.

increase predictive validity.[64] For example, if any predictions of future dangerousness are valid, it is short-term rather than long-term predictions. And, these predictions require a thorough gathering of background information about the patient and extensive examination of the patient.[65] Therefore, the familiarity of the witness with the literature on prediction and the comprehensiveness of the information providing the basis for the witness's opinion are important areas of inquiry.[66]

Increasingly, attorneys attempting to challenge predictions have utilized psychiatrists and psychologists familiar with the prediction literature who have not examined the patient. Instead, these witnesses are used to educate the judge and jury on the information that should form the basis for a prediction of future dangerous behavior or the limits on predictions of future dangerous behavior.

§7.07 Suggested Reading

Books

E. Cleary, *McCormick on Evidence* (3d ed 1984).

J. Monohan, *The Clinical Prediction of Violent Behavior* (1981).

S. Pegalis & H. Wachsman, *American Law of Medical Malpractice* (1980).

H. Steadman & J. Cocozza, *Careers of the Criminally Insane* (1974).

T. Thornberry & J. Jacoby, *The Criminally Insane: A Community Follow-up of Mentally Ill Offenders* (1979).

3 J. Weinstein & M. Berger, *Weinstein's Evidence* (1984).

7 J. Wigmore, *Evidence* (Chadbourne rev 1978).

J. Ziskin, *Coping with Psychiatric and Psychological Evidence* (3d ed 1981).

Articles

American Psychiatric Assn, *Clinical Aspects of the Violent Individual* (1974).

Bonnie & Slobogin, *The Role of Mental Health Professionals in the Criminal Process: The Case for Informed Speculation,* 66 Va L Rev 427 (1980).

Delman, *Participation by Psychologists in Insanity Defense Proceedings: An Advocacy,* 9 J Psychiatry & L 247 (1981).

---

[64] J. Monahan, *supra* note 56.

[65] Kozol, Boucher, & Garofalo, *The Diagnosis and Treatment of Dangerousness,* 18 Crime & Delinq 371, 383 (1972).

[66] Dix, *The Death Penalty, "Dangerousness," Psychiatric Testimony, and Professional Ethics,* 5 Am J Crim L 151, 175-77 (1977).

Dix, *The Death Penalty, "Dangerousness," Psychiatric Testimony, and Professional Ethics,* 5 Am J Crim L 151 (1977).

Ennis & Litwack, *Psychiatry and the Presumption of Expertise: Flipping Coins in the Courtroom,* 62 Cal L Rev 693 (1974).

Giannelli, *The Admissibility of Novel Scientific Evidence,* 80 Colum L Rev 1197 (1980).

Kozol, Boucher, & Garofalo, *The Diagnosis and Treatment of Dangerousness,* 18 Crime & Delinq 371 (1972).

Ladd, *Expert Testimony,* 5 Vand L Rev 414 (1952).

Moertel, *High Dose Vitamin C Versus Placebo in the Treatment of Patients with Advanced Cancer Who Have Had No Prior Chemotherapy: A Randomized Double-Blind Comparison,* 312 New Eng J Med 137 (1985).

Morse, *Crazy Behavior, Morals and Science: An Analysis of Mental Health Law,* 51 S Cal L Rev 527 (1978).

Note, *The Application of Res Ipsa Loquitur in Medical Malpractice Cases,* 60 Nw L Rev 852 (1966).

Report of the Task Force on the Role of Psychology in the Criminal Justice System, 33 Am Psychologist 1099 (1978).

Spritzer, Endicott, & Robins, Clinical Criteria for Psychiatric Diagnosis and DSM-III, 132 Am J Psychiatry 1187 (1975).

Steadman, *A New Look at Recidivism Among Patient Inmates,* 5 Bull Am Acad Psychiatry & Law 200 (1977).

VA Cooperative Group Study, *Eleven-Year Survival in the Veterans Administration Randomized Trial of Coronary Bypass Surgery for Stable Angina,* 311 New Eng J Med 1333 (1984).

Valliant, *The Disadvantages of DSM-III,* 141 Am J Psychiatry 542 (1984).

Wenk & Emrich, *Assaultive Youth: An Exploratory Study of the Assaultive Experience and Assaultive Potential of California Youth Authority Wards,* 9 J Research Crime & Delinq 171 (1972).

Wenk, Robison, & Smith, *Can Violence Be Predicted?,* 18 Crime & Delinq 393 (1972).

Zubin, *Classification of the Behavior Disorders,* 18 Ann Rev Psychiatry 373 (1967).

Cases

Addington v Texas, 441 US 418 (1979).

Barefoot v Estelle, 463 US 880 (1983).

Brandt v Grubin, 131 NJ Super 182, 329 A2d 82 (1974).

Commonwealth v Tyson, 485 Pa 344, 402 A2d 995 (1979).

De Mars v State, 352 NW2d 13 (Minn 1984)

Fritz v Parke Davis & Co, 277 Minn 210, 152 NW2d 129 (1967).

Hammer v Rosen, 7 AD2d 216, 181 NYS2d 805 (1959), *modified*, 7 NY2d 376, 165 NE2d 756, 198 NYS2d 65 (1960).

Jones v United States, 463 US 354 (1983).

Littlefield v State, 167 Tex Crim 443, 321 SW2d 79 (1959).

Lockett v Ohio, 438 US 586 (1978).

Meier v Ross Gen Hosp, 69 Cal 2d 420, 445 P2d 519, 71 Cal Rptr 903 (1968).

O'Connor v Donaldson, 422 US 563 (1975).

People v Murtishaw, 29 Cal 3d 733, 631 P2d 446, 175 Cal Rptr 738 (1981).

People v Teague, 108 Ill App 3d 891, 439 NE2d 1066 (1982).

Roberts v Louisiana, 428 US 325 (1976).

Smith v Estelle, 602 F2d 694 (5th Cir 1979).

Stacy v Love, 679 F2d 1209 (6th Cir 1982).

State v Hall, 297 NW2d 80 (Iowa 1980).

State v Williams, 388 A2d 500 (Me 1978).

Taylor v State, 440 NE2d 1109 (Ind 1982).

United States v Fortune, 513 F2d 883 (5th Cir), *cert denied*, 423 US 1020 (1975).

Vaughn v State, 493 SW2d 524 (Tex Crim App 1973).

Watson v State, 64 Wis 2d 264, 219 NW2d 398 (1974).

White v Estelle, 554 F Supp 851 (SD Tex 1982).

Wilson, In re, 33 Crim L Rptr 2115 (DC Super Ct Apr 14, 1983).

Rules

Fed R Evid 403.

Fed R Evid 701.

§7.08   WESTLAW Search References

§7.01   *The Opinion Rule*
 expert +1 testimony witness /s opinion /s fact /p psycholog! psychiatr!

§7.02   *Required and Permitted Psychiatric and Psychological Evidence*
expert +1 testimony /s admit**** admiss! /s psychiatr! psycholog!

§7.03   *Validity of Psychiatric and Psychological Theory*
evidence /s scientific! /p "sufficiently established" "general**
accept!"

frye /s 293 + 5 1013 /p "sufficiently established" "general**
accept!"

§7.04   —*Scientific Invalidity*
frye /s 293 +5 1013 /p psychiatr! psycholog!

§7.05   —*Diagnostic Imprecision*
dsm-iii

§7.06   —*Predictive Limitations*
psychiatr! psycholog! /p evidence /p future predict! /s behavior
conduct

8

Qualification of the Expert

§8.01 Introduction

Once the determination is reached that expert testimony may be received on a particular question and that a particular field of study or practice may include individuals who can provide that testimony, the next step is to identify the qualifications that satisfy the minimum threshold for admissibility and affect the weight given the testimony. On questions of mental disorder, expert testimony, as discussed in Chapter 7, is generally admissible and the universe of potential expert witnesses includes psychiatrists and psychologists.[1] Ideally, the admission of and

---

[1] Psychiatrists and psychologists are not the complete universe of potential experts on mental disorder. Other categories of potential expert witnesses on questions of mental disorder, not discussed here, include psychiatric social workers, Custody of a Minor, 377 Mass 876, 393 NE2d 379 (1979), and psychiatric nurses, State v Williams, 309 So 2d 303 (La 1975).

weight given this testimony should turn on the issue involved and the education, training, and experience of this witness on the particular question. The reported cases addressing expert testimony on questions of mental disorder often do not, unfortunately, correspond to this approach. Instead, the cases frequently recognize expertise on the basis of a degree, even when attainment of that degree does not necessarily entail education, training, or experience on the subject at issue.

Another facet of the case law that may appear conflicting is the rejection of a class of expert testimony on questions of mental disorder, typically psychological testimony, while accepting lay testimony on the same issue. The rationale for this dichotomy, not always convincing, is that this lay testimony is not received as *opinion* testimony; it describes the relevant perceptions of a lay witness in a form that may include conclusions or opinions, but its principal purpose is to describe firsthand perceptions. The rejected expert testimony has as its principal purpose the interpretation of firsthand perceptions provided by other sources, and courts therefore scrutinize the expertise necessary to engage in this interpretation in a fashion not applicable to lay testimony.

§8.02   Psychiatrist versus Psychologist

The cases addressing the minimum threshold qualifications for experts on questions of mental disorder frequently favor psychiatrists' testimony and disfavor psychologists' testimony.[2] This favoritism is manifested in some instances by rules forbidding the testimony of psychologists but permitting the testimony of psychiatrists, in other instances by rules permitting the testimony of psychologists but narrowly limiting the scope of their testimony, and in still other instances by rules presuming expertise of psychiatrists but requiring a demonstration of expertise by psychologists.

The disfavor of psychologists' testimony and preference for psychiatrists' testimony seems to be based, at least in part, on the medical or disease model of mental disorder.[3] The legal relevance of disordered behavior has, until recently, been stated almost exclusively in terms that

---

[2] Dix & Poythress, *Propriety of Medical Dominance of Forensic Mental Health Practice: The Empirical Evidence,* 23 Ariz L Rev 961 (1981); Comment, *The Psychologist as Expert Witness: Science in the Courtroom,* 38 Md L Rev 539 (1979).

[3] Odom v State, 174 Ala 4, 56 So 913 (1911); People v Hawthorne, 293 Mich 15, 291 NW 205 (1940).

assumed a medical disease as the root cause of the behavior.[4] If the cause of disordered behavior is a disease, like syphilis, then it follows that psychiatrists, who are medical doctors, should be recognized as experts on disordered behavior and psychologists, lacking medical training, should not. Although the disease model no longer occupies an exclusive position in explaining mental disorder[5] or in the testimony of psychiatrists in explaining relevant behavior in a legal setting, many limitations on the acceptance of psychologists' testimony still exist, apparently based upon this distinction. One example of this bias is found in those states that require a physician or psychiatrist to certify that a patient has met certain requirements for civil commitment but do not accept a psychologist's certification even in the absence of a local psychiatrist.[6]

In some jurisdictions, psychologists are permitted to testify to the results of psychological testing, but are limited in the conclusions they may draw from those tests.[7] Thus, for example, on the issue of the defendant's mental status at the time of the offense, a psychologist may offer the results of psychological tests administered, but may not be permitted to suggest whether the test results indicate that the defendant was sane at the time of the offense.[8] A psychiatrist, however, would be permitted to offer an opinion on this issue based upon this same evidence.

Other jurisdictions permit the testimony of psychiatrists and psychologists, but tend to assume that all psychiatrists are qualified to offer testimony on disordered behavior while requiring psychologists to demonstrate their expertise through experience and prior judicial testimony.[9]

There are several problems with these classwide presumptions. First, they are not responsive to the education received by the members of these two professions.[10] Most expert testimony about relevant disordered behavior in a legal setting does not turn on organic or biological explanations for behavior, for which a medical school education may be

---

[4] *See, e.g.,* People v Spigno, 156 Cal 2d 279, 319 P2d 458 (1957).

[5] *See* **ch 1.**

[6] NY Mental Hyg Law §9.27 (1978); Tex Const art 1, §15a.

[7] People v Nobble, 42 Ill 2d 425, 248 NE2d 96 (1969); State v Alexander, 252 La 564, 211 So 2d 650 (1968).

[8] Saul v State, 6 Md App 540, 252 A2d 282 (1969).

[9] People v Davis, 62 Cal 2d 791, 402 P2d 142, 44 Cal Rptr 454 (1965); Sandow v Weyerhaeuser Co, 252 Or 377, 449 P2d 426 (1969).

[10] *See* **ch 4.**

important. Instead, psychological and behavioral theories tend to underly these explanations, subjects on which psychologists have education and training at least equal to and perhaps superior to that of many psychiatrists.

Although many psychiatrists have completed extensive postgraduate training, it is not necessary to complete this training to hold oneself out as a non-board certified psychiatrist.[11] Since medical school provides most physicians with only an introductory course in psychiatry and a psychiatric clinical rotation,[12] a psychiatrist may have negligible education in psychological theories as compared with a Ph.D. or Psy.D. clinical psychologist who has received extensive education and training in these fields.[13] Moreover, the field of academic psychiatry has itself gradually begun to utilize its medical expertise to explore the organic and biological facets of mental disorder, leaving the psychological arena to psychologists.[14]

Another facet of the current classwide distinction is that it fails to test expertise in particular fields. Assuming that there are psychiatrists or psychologists who have expertise on the prediction of dangerous behavior, for example, it does not follow that any psychiatrist or psychologist should be considered an expert on this question. Has the witness conducted studies on this subject reported in the professional literature, or received postgraduate education that would result in expertise on this issue? Is the witness familiar with the existing literature on this subject? Licensure as a psychiatrist or psychologist does not speak to these questions.

In a growing number of courts these classwide distinctions play a lesser role in admissibility determinations. Instead of assuming expertise or its absence based merely on the possession of a particular degree, these courts have inquired further of the witness's own experience and training.[15] Given the judicial demand for evidence on questions often not addressed in the formal education of many psychiatrists and psychologists, scrutiny of the individual witness's background is a necessary correlate of the intelligent use of these witnesses.

---

[11] See §4.05.

[12] See §4.04.

[13] See §4.10.

[14] See ch 1.

[15] United States v Riggleman, 411 F2d 1190 (4th Cir 1969); Jenkins v United States, 307 F2d 637 (DC Cir 1962) (en banc); People v Crawford, 66 Mich App 581, 239 NW2d 670 (1976); Landreth v Reed, 570 SW2d 486 (Tex Civ App 1978) (no writ).

§8.03   Physician versus Psychiatrist

When expert medical testimony on mental disorders is admissible, it is reasonable to expect that the witness offered will be a psychiatrist, at least by title, if not by education, training, and experience. Yet, the case law reflects numerous instances in which nonpsychiatric physicians have been permitted to offer testimony on the subject of mental disorder.[16] This dilemma is more complex than might initially be thought.

Most mental health care provided by physicians in the United States is delivered by primary care physicians—internists, pediatricians, gynecologists, and family practitioners[17]—in connection with the treatment of physical complaints, not by psychiatrists. Thus, these nonpsychiatric physicians have more experience with mental disorders than might be expected and are likely, because of this exposure, to have patients whose mental disorders raise legal questions. Testamentary capacity, child abuse, and guardianship, for example, are likely to involve treatment by primary care physicians who, as the result of patient contact, gain valuable and in some instances unique knowledge of a case. Yet the psychiatric training received by the vast majority of these primary care physicians is an introductory course in medical school and a clinical rotation in psychiatry.[18] This training is hardly the ideal background for an expert witness on issues of mental disorder.

The response to this problem by the majority of courts is to recognize the discretion of the trial judge to consider the training and experience of the nonpsychiatric physician witness before qualifying the witness as an expert on the subject of mental disorder.[19] A relevant additional consideration may be the availability of other experts. If the closest psychiatrist or psychologist is several hundred miles away or the person whose mental status is at issue is now deceased, the results of an examination conducted by a primary care physician is preferable to no examination.

---

[16] *See, e.g.*, Cody v State, 259 Ind 570, 290 NE2d 38 (1973), *cert denied*, 416 US 960 (1974); Lux v Mental Health Bd, 202 Neb 106, 274 NW2d 141 (1979); Nelson v State, 35 Wis 2d 797, 151 NW2d 694 (1967).

[17] Orlean, *How Primary Care Physicians Treat Psychiatric Disorders: A National Survey of Family Practitioners*, 142 Am J Psychiatry 52 (1985).

[18] *See* §4.04.

[19] *See, e.g.*, Evans v Ohanesian, 39 Cal App 3d 121, 112 Cal Rptr 236 (1974); Commonwealth v Boyd, 367 Mass 169, 326 NE2d 320 (1975); State v Arpin, 410 A2d 1340 (RI 1980).

§8.04 The Qualifications

The proper qualifications of an expert witness are not an abstract proposition; the question must be asked in each instance—qualified to do what? The education and training necessary to interpret the Minnesota Multiphasic Personality Inventory[20] is quite different from the education and training necessary to interpret a computerized axial tomography scan.[21] Yet, both may be appropriate to diagnose a single patient. Similarly, the education and training necessary to treat a disorder diagnosed with the assistance of these techniques will be different from that necessary to reach the diagnosis in the first place.

To analyze these qualifications, one must understand the education and training generally available for psychiatrists and psychologists and available specialty programs. This is the substance of Chapter 4. The courses offered psychiatrists and psychologists, postgraduate education, specialty certification, and licensing requirements, considered in relation to the questions raised in the instant case, indicate the minimal qualifications to establish expertise and appropriate subjects for cross-examination.

§8.05 —Education and Training

The education of psychiatrists consists of undergraduate and graduate medical education.[22] Undergraduate medical education leading to the M.D. degree generally includes an introductory course in psychiatry and a clinical rotation in psychiatry designed to facilitate identification of psychiatric problems in practice for referral to a psychiatrist. Therefore, a physician who has received no additional education or training in psychiatry has very limited formal knowledge on this subject. When graduate medical education in psychiatry is combined with this undergraduate medical education, it provides important knowledge necessary to diagnose and treat interrelated medical problems. Thus, for example, the diagnosis and treatment of an organic mental disorder[23] caused by the ingestion of a toxic substance requires knowledge of physiology and biochemistry, subjects taught in medical school.

Graduate medical education, in the form of a four-year residency in

---

[20] *See* §2.17.

[21] *See* §2.13.

[22] This discussion relates to the more detailed discussion of the same subject in §§4.04, 4.10.

[23] *See* §2.08.

psychiatry, consists of the provision of supervised clinical psychiatric services and specialized seminars and colloquia. The first year, designated an internship, does not generally focus on psychiatry but includes a more general primary care focus. The latter portion of this residency, with work in psychopathology, diagnostic interviews, psychopharmacology, neurology, and the provision of clinical services to patients is the beginning of specialized psychiatric training. Because this graduate medical education is not necessary to hold oneself out as a psychiatrist, inquiry into this portion of any proposed psychiatric expert's education and training is obligatory. Acceptance into a particular prestigious residency program implies a favorable professional peer judgment, another subject appropriate for exploration with the witness.

Postgraduate medical education, one-to-three-year fellowships, permits an additional degree of specialized study. The presence or absence of this specialized study on the issues raised by the instant case may have a substantial bearing on the witness's expertise. Thus, for example, a fellowship involving research on depression may be relevant to the expertise necessary to understand the relationship between work-related injury and subsequent depression.

Another form of education and training beyond the undergraduate medical education is psychoanalytic training. This training at a psychoanalytic institute, which usually begins after completion of a psychiatric residency, consists of advanced study of the theories of Freud and his followers, lengthy psychoanalysis of the trainee, and supervised clinical work. When the attempt to explore relevant behavior involves the use of psychoanalytic theory, for example, in a case in which it is claimed that the defendant's acts on the victim were really an attempt to kill his father, who was not the actual victim,[24] psychoanalytic training would provide the witness with the relevant theoretical knowledge to explain this to the jury.

The education of psychologists also consists of undergraduate and graduate education. Unlike medicine, undergraduate education in psychology leads to the bachelor's degree. It consists of a broad range of courses in psychology encompassing one-third to one-quarter of the undergraduate curriculum, with the remainder including other social sciences. The Master's degree requires an additional 30 to 45 hours of psychology courses, and the doctoral degree another 30 to 45.

Unlike the medical doctorate, the doctorate in psychology entails a degree of specialization. Psychologists may choose among such fields

---

[24] *See, e.g.,* J. Bloom & J. Atkinson, Evidence of Love (1983).

as clinical psychology, experimental psychology, and school psychology. Although clinical psychology, which focuses on the evaluation and treatment of severe psychological difficulties, is the field most frequently thought relevant to legal behavioral issues in psychology, such broad generalizations as to qualifications are precarious. Research on eyewitness identification and the psychological aspects of perception and memory is likely to be carried out by experimental psychologists who could, thus, provide the relevant expertise in preference to clinical psychologists.[25] The impact of *mainstreaming*, placing handicapped children in nonspecialized schools and classrooms, in the education of both handicapped and nonhandicapped children is more likely to fit within the expertise of an educational or school psychologist than that of the clinical psychologist.

Within the field of clinical psychology there is another distinction. Recently, some graduate programs in clinical psychology have begun to grant a Doctor of Psychology degree (Psy.D.) rather than a Doctor of Philosophy (Ph.D.). The Ph.D. programs require completion of a dissertation involving research of a psychological issue, while the Psy.D. programs do not, but emphasize clinical training in its place. This clinical versus experimental orientation of the degree programs may be an important consideration in judging the witness's qualifications.

The fourth year of the clinical psychology program is generally a predoctoral internship consisting of supervised clinical practice. Postdoctoral fellowships are also available in specialized areas of psychology and may be a valuable service of expertise on a particular issue.

§8.06 —Licensing

Licensure of physicians,[26] a state function, generally requires graduation from an accredited medical school, passage of an examination demonstrating minimal medical competence, and evidence of good moral character. Physicians are licensed, like attorneys, to practice in any area of the profession. In addition to practicing in any specialized area of the profession, representation of oneself as a specialist in that area is permitted. Therefore, any licensed physician may utilize the label *psychiatrist* without having had a psychiatric residency, other specialized training, or board certification. Thus, in examining or cross-examining a psychiatrist, determining the presence or absence of this postgraduate education, training, and certification is extremely important.

---

[25] *See* §17.02.

[26] *See* §4.05, 4.11 for a more detailed discussion of this subject.

Licensing of psychologists is also a state function; however, it has somewhat different implications than licensing of physicians because of the degree of specialty it implies in the study of mental disorders. Licensure of doctoral-level psychologists entails two steps, certification and licensing. Certification permits the use of the title *psychologist* and supervised practice. It requires completion of an accredited doctoral program and passage of an examination testing psychological knowledge. Following certification, a psychologist is eligible for licensing, which entitles the psychologist to practice independently, after a period of supervised practice of at least one year.

Licensure is generally one of the minimal requirements for qualification as an expert in psychiatry or psychology; however, its implications are similar to those of licensure as an attorney. Although the inability to satisfy state licensing requirements is likely to indicate a serious professional deficiency, licensure is not itself a guarantee of competence or expertise.[27] Because most licensing laws are generic, licensure may communicate little about an expert's qualifications. For example, a social psychologist, licensed by the state, could be treating patients and yet not be trained as a clinician. Similarly, license suspension or revocation is indicative of a problem that may bear on professional competence, while uninterrupted licensure is not an affirmative determination of the absence of problems.

§8.07 —Specialty Certification

Although no special licensing governs physician specialization,[28] specialty certifications are available that permit representation of oneself as a board certified specialist in designated specialties. Specialty certification in psychiatry, neurology, and child psychiatry is provided by the American Board of Psychiatry and Neurology, founded by the American Psychiatric Association, the American Medical Association, and the American Neurological Association.

Eligibility for board certification in psychiatry requires state licensure and completion of an approved four-year residency program with at least two years of specialized training in psychiatry. In addition, the applicant must pass a written examination testing general knowledge in psychiatry and an oral examination testing clinical psychiatry, consisting of interviews and diagnosis of actual and hypothetical patients.

Specialty certification in neurology, the branch of medicine dealing

---

27 Gross, *The Myth of Professional Licensing*, 33 Am Psychologist 1009 (1978).
28 See §§**4.06, 4.12** for a more detailed discussion of this subject.

with diseases of the nervous system, is similar to certification in psychiatry. It requires state licensure, completion of an approved four-year residency program, and passage of a two-part examination. The first part of the examination is a written test of general knowledge of neurology and the second part is an oral examination testing clinical neurology, consisting of an examination and evaluation of actual and hypothetical patients.

Specialty certification in child psychiatry, which deals with the diagnosis and treatment of mental disorders in children and adolescents, requires satisfactory completion of the psychiatry examination plus licensure and completion of an approved residency program in addition to completion of a specialized examination testing basic competence in child psychiatry.

Specialty certification in a relevant specialty is not a prerequisite for qualification as an expert witness.[29] It is a test of knowledge and general competence, but not necessarily expertise. Yet it is clearly prestigious, and its presence or absence is relevant to the jury's evaluation of the witness. Two-thirds of all practicing psychiatrists are not board certified, and a substantial percentage of those seeking board certification fail the examination.

In addition to these certifications, the American Board of Forensic Psychiatry, formed in 1979 by the American Academy of Forensic Science, the Forensic Sciences Foundation, and the American Academy of Psychiatry and the Law, awards diplomate status in forensic psychiatry.[30] Applicants must be licensed psychiatrists who have completed five years of residency training and have had substantial experience in forensic psychiatry. Diplomate status is awarded after completion of an oral and written examination testing substantive legal knowledge and clinical skills. There are currently about 80 diplomates in the United States. Status as a diplomate is likely to increase the probability that the witness has a basic knowledge and competence in forensic psychiatry and will no doubt add to the witness's prestige, yet it is no assurance of expertise. Similarly, failure to seek diplomate status in forensic psychiatry is not necessarily evidence of the absence of expertise.

Massachusetts attempted in 1971 to institute its own program for limiting testimony on competence to stand trial and criminal responsibility to psychiatrists it found qualified in forensic psychiatry. The

---

[29] Christy v Salterman, 288 Minn 144, 179 NW2d 288 (1970).
[30] *See* §4.06.

program failed for reasons of budget and nonuniform judicial enforcement.[31]

Specialty certification of psychologists, in the form of diplomate status beyond the basic license, also exists on a voluntary basis. The American Board of Professional Psychology offers specialty certification in clinical psychology, industrial/organization psychology, school psychology, counseling psychology, and neuropsychology.[32] The requirements include completion of an approved education program, four years of postdoctoral experience, and successful completion of an examination including a review of a recording of a treatment session or psychological evaluation. Diplomate status, like board certification in psychiatry, is not a prerequisite for recognition as an expert. It is no more than a statement of peer recognition of professional competence, yet it clearly imparts prestige that may affect the weight given this witness's testimony.

As in the case of psychiatry, diplomate status in forensic psychology is offered by a different organization than the one that recognizes other specialty certifications.[33] The American Board of Forensic Psychology awards diplomate status to licensed psychologists who have four years of postdoctoral experience, provide documentation of their experience in forensic psychology, and submit a work sample demonstrating sensitivity to psychological, legal, and ethical issues. This status is not an assurance of expertise, nor is failure to seek this status necessarily indicative of the absence of expertise.

§8.08   —Professional Posts

The professional posts a psychiatrist or psychologist has held form an important component of professional qualifications. First, they may be an important source of experience. In a malpractice action for failure to seek psychiatric hospitalization of a patient who appeared in the emergency room, experience as the chief psychiatrist in the emergency room would clearly be a relevant consideration in the weight to give that witness's testimony. Second, the assignment of these posts is an important form of peer review.

Assignment to most professional posts, whether in psychiatry or

---

[31] McGarry, *Operational Aspects, Training, and Qualifications in Forensic Psychiatry*, in W. Curran, L. McGarry, & C. Petty, Modern Legal Medicine, Psychiatry, and Forensic Science 650 (1980).

[32] *See* §4.12.

[33] *Id.* This situation will probably change when the American Board of Forensic Psychology is acquired by the American Board of Professional Psychology, which awards diplomates in other psychological specialties.

psychology, is based, in part, on the initiative of the student. The student intern must apply for a professional post after reaching a given point in the professional educational process. Usually, in psychiatry, this post comes at the end of the student's educational career. The student traditionally then accepts or is accepted to a professional post at a hospital, treatment facility, or research center.

These professional posts are generally for at least one academic year (nine months), but may vary in length from a summer post of three months or less to an extensive working post of up to two years. However, the time length of the professional post may not be so important as the quality of the post as exemplified by the duties actually performed, the facility's reputation, the supervisory staff, and the level of responsibility and participation the student intern is allowed to assume.

Many internships involve more observation than participation. While observation may be beneficial when educational, it results in acquisition of only limited skills by the person while at the professional post. The shorter the internship or professional post, the more likely it is the intern may have less opportunity for actual involvement and participation because of time needed to gain acceptance and trust of supervisors. This may present less of a problem in public hospitals, Veterans' Administration hospitals, state mental hospitals, and other such treatment facilities in which the patient population may exceed the treatment staff's capabilities and the intern is thrust immediately into a work setting. The drawback here, however, is that the workload may leave little or no time for meaningful supervision. The attorney seeking to determine whether the professional post has further qualified the expert should question the duties performed, the level and quality of supervision, and skills actually acquired.

As previously stated, the professional post, under some degree plans, may be largely observational. While most doctoral-level degrees for the psychologist require an internship or professional post and programs are increasingly calling for a year-long, full-time post, there are many doctoral programs in psychology and Master's-level programs in psychology, social work, and guidance and counseling which merely require a *practicum*. The practicum may be full-time for a semester or a year or may merely be a part-time effort for a semester involving a couple of afternoons a week.

Because of this diversity in quality of post or practicum as determined by time, duties performed, supervision, and quality of the facility, it is important for the lawyer to inquire further into the post or practicum. The attempt should be made to determine whether the experience truly adds an extra degree of expertise, level of competence, or area of specialization in which the potential expert or proffered expert may testify.

§8.09   —Professional Associations

Membership or activity in professional associations may or may not be indicative of the level of skill, competence, or specialization of the potential or proffered expert. At the least, it may reveal that the psychiatrist or psychologist has met an educational and practice requirement to qualify for membership in a particular association at a particular level. At the most, it may be indicative of a level of involvement that puts the expert on the forefront of an area of treatment, research, or theory.

Professional associations may vary from the large and seemingly all-inclusive American Psychiatric Association and American Psychological Association to smaller, more specialized associations.[34] These large associations are nationwide, and include persons from all areas of specialization and general practice among their members. Members may vary in level of education and skill depending upon their level of association. For example, a student member may not have graduated from college, an associate member may be a graduate who is not yet certified or licensed, and a member may be a graduate who has been certified or licensed, but has no practical experience. Diplomate status theoretically indicates some higher level of skill or accomplishment, but it may be indicative merely of time spent in practice and the ability to play certain bureaucratic games.[35] While most reputable psychiatrists and psychologists belong to the relevant major professional associations on a national level and often on a state level, county level, and even city level in larger metropolitan areas, membership may not reveal much about the clinician's diagnostic skills or accuracy.

Nonmembership may indicate that the professional has chosen not to participate, is not eligible for membership, or has been expelled from the association. Expulsion would ordinarily indicate either nonpayment of dues or a finding of unethical conduct or practices. Membership or nonmembership may be determined by calling the local or national association. National associations such as the American Psychiatric Association and American Psychological Association publish a directory

---

[34] *See* §4.13.

[35] J. Ziskin, Coping with Psychiatric and Psychological Testimony 380 (3d ed 1981).

of members that can be purchased from the national association and is usually available in university or larger city libraries.[36]

Among the other associations to which an expert may belong are the American Orthopsychiatric Association, American Psychoanalytic Association, American Academy of Forensic Sciences, American Academy of Psychiatry and the Law, American Psychology-Law Society, American Psychosomatic Society, American Association of Mental Deficiency, Association for Research in Nervous and Mental Diseases, Academy of Psychoanalysis, and American Psychopathological Association.

These associations may require certain minimal professional qualifications. For example, to join the American Academy of Psychiatry and Law one must be a psychiatrist, and to join the American Psychoanalytic Association one must be a psychoanalyst. Beyond this, the only other qualification for membership is dues. Thus, a long listing of these organizational memberships may be initially impressive but can be revealed to express interests on the part of the psychiatrist or psychologist but not peer judgment recognizing professional excellence.

§8.10 Suggested Reading

Books

J. Ziskin, *Coping with Psychiatric and Psychological Testimony* (3d ed 1981).

Articles

Comment, *The Psychologist as Expert Witness: Science in the Courtroom,* 38 Md L Rev 539 (1979).

Dix & Poythress, *Propriety of Medical Dominance of Forensic Mental Health Practice: The Empirical Evidence,* 23 Ariz L Rev 961 (1981).

Gross, *The Myth of Professional Licensing,* 33 Am Psychologist 1009 (1978).

McGarry, *Operational Aspects, Training, and Qualifications in Forensic Psychiatry,* in W. Curran, L. McGarry, & C. Petty, Modern Legal Medicine, Psychiatry, and Forensic Science 650 (1980).

Orleans, George, Houpt, & Brodie *How Primary Care Physicians Treat Psychiatric Disorders: A National Survey of Family Practitioners,* 142 Am J Psychiatry 52 (1985).

Cases

Christy v Salterman, 288 Minn 144, 179 NW2d 288 (1970).

---

[36] *See* §4.13.

Cody v State, 259 Ind 570, 290 NE2d 38 (1973), *cert denied*, 416 US 860 (1974).

Commonwealth v Boyd, 367 Mass 169, 326 NE2d 320 (1975).

Custody of a Minor, 377 Mass 876, 393 NE2d 379 (1979).

Evans v Ohanesian, 39 Cal App 3d 121, 112 Cal Rptr 236 (1974).

Jenkins v United States, 307 F2d 637 (DC Cir 1962) (en banc).

Landreth v Reed, 570 SW2d 486 (Tex Civ App 1978) (no writ).

Lux v Mental Health Board, 202 Neb 106, 274 NW2d 141 (1979).

Nelson v State, 35 Wis 2d 797, 151 NW2d 694 (1967).

Odom v State, 174 Ala 4, 56 So 913 (1911).

People v Crawford, 66 Mich App 581, 239 NW2d 670 (1976).

People v Davis, 62 Cal 2d 791, 402 P2d 142, 44 Cal Rptr 454 (1965).

People v Hawthorne, 293 Mich 15, 291 NW 205 (1940).

People v Noble, 42 Ill 2d 425, 248 NE2d 96 (1969).

People v Spigno, 156 Cal 2d 279, 319 P2d 458 (1957).

Sandow v Weyerhaeuser Co, 252 Or 377, 449 P2d 426 (1969).

Saul v State, 6 Md App 540, 252 A2d 282 (1969).

State v Alexander, 252 La 564, 211 So 2d 650 (1968).

State v Arpin, 410 A2d 1340 (RI 1980).

State v Williams, 309 So 2d 303 (La 1975).

United States v Riggleman, 411 F2d 1190 (4th Cir 1969).

Statutes and Constitutions

NY Mental Hyg Law §9.27 (1978).

Tex Const art 1, §15a.

§8.11   WESTLAW Search References

§8.01   *Introduction*
opinion /s evidence /p psychiatr! psycholog! /s qualification expertise training experience education

§8.02   *Psychiatry versus Psychologist*
opinion /s evidence /p psychiatrist /p psychologist /p qualification expertise training experience education

§8.03   *Physician versus Psychiatrist*
opinion /s evidence /p psychiatrist /p physician intern nurse

pediatrician gynecologist general-practitioner /p qualification expertise training experience education

§8.04 *The Qualifications*
qualif! /s education training /p psychiatr! psycholog! /p expert +1 witness testimony

"minnesota multiphasic personality inventory" "computerized axial tomography scan" /p expert +1 witness testimony

§8.05 *—Education and Training*
opinion /s evidence /p clinical educational experimental +1 psycholog! psychiatr!

§8.06 *—Licensing*
psychiatrist psychologist /s licens*** /p expert +1 witness testimony

§8.07 *—Specialty Certification*
(opinion /s evidence) (expert +1 witness testimony) /p psychiatrist psychologist /s forensic neurolog! neuropsychology counseling industrial-organization child!

§8.08 *—Professional Posts*
psychiatrist psychologist /p post-graduate post-doctoral intern**** practicum /p hospital institution facility

§8.09 *—Professional Associations*
member**** diplomatic /s "american psychiatric association" "american psychological association"

9

Form and Mode of Presentation of Psychiatric and Psychological Evidence

§9.01   Introduction

Following the determination that expert psychiatric or psychological testimony will be accepted on an issue[1] and that a particular psychiatrist or psychologist is qualified to provide expert assistance to the judge or jury on that issue,[2] the testimony of the expert must be presented in an acceptable form and persuasive mode. In addition to those considerations that govern the presentation of all witnesses' testimony, two play a major role in the presentation of psychiatric and psychological testimony: the basis for these witnesses' opinions and the form of their testimony. It is these issues to which this chapter is addressed.

---

[1] *See* **ch 7.**

[2] *See* **ch 8.**

§9.02   Basis for Opinion

The conclusion that a psychiatrist or psychologist qualifies as an expert witness on an issue implies that the witness has acquired, through education, training, or experience, valuable knowledge of psychiatric or psychological principles that have a bearing on the instant case. Although it is conceivable that this witness could simply describe these relevant psychiatric or psychological principles to the judge or jury and permit the fact-finder to apply these principles to the facts of the case,[3] that is not the most common use of psychiatric and psychological witnesses. Instead, the psychiatrist or psychologist is most typically asked to apply these principles to the facts of the case and offer an opinion to the judge or jury. The expert is typically chosen because of a knowledge of the scientific principles and not because of knowledge of the event at issue gained as an eyewitness. How, then, is the expert to learn the facts which serve as the basis for an opinion?[4]

The basis for the psychiatrist's or psychologist's opinion presents two sets of related problems. The first set of problems is legal: on what information may the expert rely before offering an opinion in court; how may this information be made known to the expert; what amount or kinds of information must the expert rely upon before offering an opinion in court? The second set of problems are psychiatric and psychological: outside of the legal setting, when making diagnostic and treatment decisions, what sources of information are accepted as necessary and sufficient to reach an opinion? These two sets of problems are related because the legal requirements for the basis of the expert's opinion are, to some extent, dependent on the profession's standards and because the expert's profession's standards are relevant

---

[3] Fed R Evid 702 advisory committee note, 56 FRD 183, 282 (1972):

> Most of the literature assumes that experts testify only in the form of opinions. The assumption is logically unfounded. The rule accordingly recognizes that an expert on the stand may give a dissertation or exposition of scientific or other principles relevant to the case, leaving the trier of fact to apply them to the facts. Since much of the criticism of expert testimony has centered upon the hypothetical question, it seems wise to recognize that opinions are not indispensable and to encourage the use of expert testimony in nonopinion form when counsel believes the trier can itself draw the requisite inference. The use of opinions is not abolished by the rule, however. It will continue to be permissible for the expert to take the further step of suggesting the inference which should be drawn from applying the specialized knowledge to the facts. See Rules 703 to 705.

[4] Rheingold, *The Basis of Medical Testimony,* 15 Vand L Rev 473 (1962).

to the weight that should be accorded the basis of the expert's testimony.

§9.03 —Personal Knowledge

The basis for psychiatric or psychological opinion testimony generally thought to raise the fewest legal concerns is personal knowledge of the subject of the opinion gained through an examination or observation by the expert. An examination by a treating psychiatrist or psychologist is an example of this basis.[5] Because the expert has perceived the information on which the opinion is based, its reliability is frequently assumed. Yet this assumption cloaks a series of potential problems.

First, considerations unrelated to reliability may limit offering an opinion based upon an examination by the psychiatrist or psychologist. In the case of the treating psychiatrist or psychologist, for example, an applicable physician, psychiatrist, psychologist, or psychotherapist-patient privilege will prevent the witness from relying upon this information unless the privilege is waived or an exception applies.[6] If the psychiatrist or psychologist has performed a court-ordered examination of a defendant in a criminal case and the results of that examination are sought to be introduced at an inculpatory stage of the proceedings, the Fifth Amendment of the United States Constitution requires that the defendant have been warned prior to the examination of the possible inculpatory use of the examination and given the opportunity not to participate.[7] Therefore, the psychiatrist or psychologist may be prevented from offering an opinion based on a personal examination and may instead be required to utilize other sources of information.

Another potential legal limitation on the use of information gained in an examination is the hearsay rule.[8] Statements made by the subject of the examination while not on the witness stand, relied upon by the psychiatrist or psychologist for the truth of the matter asserted, raise hearsay problems.[9] If, however, the statements by the patient made

---

[5] Fed R Evid 703 advisory committee note, 56 FRD 183, 283 (1972).

[6] *See* **ch 10.**

[7] Estelle v Smith, 451 US 454 (1981).

[8] *See, e.g.,* Fed R Evid 801(C).

[9] Some argue that these statements are not proscribed by the hearsay rule because they are not admitted for their truth. Seidel & Gungrich, *Hearsay Objections to Expert Testimony and the Proposed Federal Rules of Evidence,* 39 UMKC

during an examination are sought to be used against the patient/party by an opponent, the admission exception/exclusion permits their admission directly into evidence[10] and provides no absolute limitation on their use as the basis for the expert's opinion. If these statements are sought to be used to support an opinion favorable to the patient, a different exception to the hearsay rule may apply when these statements are made for medical diagnosis or treatment.[11] If the statements were made in a setting in which the patient/party reasonably expected that therapeutic decisions would be based upon them and had no incentive to make self-serving statements in contemplation of litigation, the reliability of the patient's statements results in an exception to the hearsay rule permitting their admission directly into evidence and providing no absolute limitation on their use as the basis for the expert's opinion. If the statements sought to be utilized as the basis for the expert's opinion do not fit within these or other exceptions to the hearsay rule, an opinion may nonetheless be utilized in many jurisdictions if experts customarily and reasonably rely upon this source in reaching opinions.[12]

Reliability considerations often require greater scrutiny of what is meant by observation or examination of the subject or patient. First, was an examination conducted in a clinical setting or has the psychiatrist or psychologist merely observed the subject in another setting without the opportunity, for example, to conduct a mental status examination.[13] An example of this latter type of observation occurred in the trial of Alger Hiss when the defense offered a psychiatrist's opinion on the believability of the government's key witness, Whittaker Chambers, based solely upon an observation of him while testifying.[14] Although courts addressing this type of testimony have generally been more concerned with the risks of the expert's interfering with the jury's function than with the basis for the testimony,[15] the exclusive use of this basis for an opinion does not conform to good psychiatric or psychological practice. It fails

---

L Rev 141 144 (1970). Although some of the communications may not be evaluated for their truth, the psychiatrist's or psychologist's opinion is, in large measure, a translation of this out-of-court information that does turn on its veracity. Shuman, *The Road to Bedlam: Evidentiary Guideposts in Civil Commitment Proceedings,* 55 Notre Dame Law 53, 86 (1979).

[10] *See, e.g.,* Fed R Evid 801(d)(2).

[11] *See, e.g.,* Fed R Evid 803(4).

[12] *See* §9.05.

[13] *See* §2.14.

[14] United States v Hiss, 88 F Supp 559 (SDNY 1950).

[15] *See* §17.02.

to include a variety of information sources recognized as necessary for a psychiatric diagnosis—physical examination, complete history, mental status examination, and psychological tests.[16] In addition, the court-room setting is itself sufficiently stressful not to permit drawing of inferences about behavior without other data.

Even if the in-court opinion is based on a clinical examination, it may nonetheless provide an inadequate basis for an opinion on the issues raised in the case. The judicial phraseology asks whether the examination gave the witness adequate time and opportunity to observe the subject/patient.[17] For example, if standard psychiatric texts state that an adequate mental status exam should be conducted in private,[18] a diagnosis based on a mental status examination conducted in a corner of an open ward should not provide an adequate basis for an in-court opinion. More often than not, however, courts permit opinions to be offered in these circumstances and relegate the adequacy of the basis to the weight of the opinion.

A properly conducted clinical psychiatric interview may, nonetheless, pose problems due to the timing of the examination, the trial, and the event at issue. For example, a psychiatric examination of the testator a year prior to the date of the challenged will, standing alone, provides little basis for an opinion about the testator's mental status at the time of the execution of the will.[19] Similarly, an examination of a defendant to evaluate competence to stand trial conducted six months before the trial, standing alone, provides little basis for an opinion about the defendant's competence at the time of trial.[20] Thus, the examination must be timed to permit measurement of the mental status raised by the case.

§9.04   —Hypothetical Questions

A traditional method for providing the basis for the opinion of the expert witness who has inadequate personal knowledge of the subject/patient has been the hypothetical question.[21] The question asks the witness to assume the existence of certain facts that are supported by

---

[16] *See* §§2.12-2.18.

[17] Marshall v Sellers, 188 Md 508, 53 A2d 5 (1947).

[18] *See* §2.14.

[19] Harriford v Harriford, 336 SW2d 113 (Mo Ct App 1960).

[20] *See* §15.08.

[21] Guttmacher & Weihofen, *The Psychiatrist on the Witness Stand,* 32 BUL Rev 287, 300 (1952).

the evidence, to apply the witness's expertise to these facts, and to reach an opinion. In theory this provides the jury with a clear statement of the facts on which the opinion is based so that it may weigh the opinion as a function of its findings on these underlying facts. In practice, however, the hypothetical question has effected more confusion than clarification. Thus, the Federal Rules of Evidence[22] and many state rules[23] no longer require disclosure of the basis for the expert's opinion as a precondition of its admissibility. Although the hypothetical question is no longer required in these jurisdictions even when the expert has inadequate personal knowledge of the subject/patient, it remains available for use in these and other jurisdictions not following the approach of the Federal Rules of Evidence.

Courts have permitted psychiatrists and psychologists to offer opinions based on hypothetical questions.[24] In some instances, the hypothetical question may provide the only available basis for an opinion, as, for example, when the defendant has invoked the Fifth Amendment privilege against self-incrimination, refusing to talk with the government's psychiatrist or psychologist.[25] Yet, the offering of an opinion based in whole or in large part on a hypothetical question without a clinical examination of the patient poses serious problems.

Standard psychiatric and psychological diagnostic techniques include an examination of the patient, in part, because the clinical impressions of an experienced diagnostician are thought to play a major role in diagnostic decisions.[26] Although much of the thrust of DSM-III has been to minimize the impressionistic aspect of diagnosis,[27] the mental status examination remains an accepted component of a thorough

---

[22] Fed R Evid 705 provides:

> The expert may testify in terms of opinion or inference and give his reasons therefor without prior disclosure of the underlying facts or data, unless the court requires otherwise. The expert may in any event be required to disclose the underlying facts or data on cross-examination.

[23] Arkansas, Arizona, Colorado, Michigan, Minnesota, Montana, North Dakota, Oklahoma, Washington, and Wyoming have adopted rules identical to Federal Rule 705. J. Weinstein & M. Berger, Weinstein's Evidence ¶705[02] (1982). Florida, Nebraska, Nevada, New Mexico, and Wisconsin adopted substantially similar rules. *Id.*

[24] Barefoot v Estelle, 463 US 880 (1983). *See* I. Ray, Medical Jurisprudence of Insanity 635 (8th ed 1871).

[25] Estelle v Smith, 451 US 454 (1981).

[26] *See* §2.14.

[27] *See* §2.02.

diagnostic workup.[28] Thus, an in-court opinion not based on a personal examination of the patient violates accepted practice and that should bear on the weight given the resulting opinions.[29]

§9.05 —Extrajudicial Sources

Psychiatric diagnosis requires not only that the patient's current clinical status be assessed, but also that the patient's personal and family history, schooling, and any criminal record be learned by the diagnostician.[30] In addition, psychological and intelligence tests[31] plus physical and neurological examinations may be required.[32] Thus, outside of the legal context, in the treatment context, the diagnostician relies on a multitude of information in addition to a clinical examination of the patient.[33]

When an in-court opinion is offered relying on all of these sources, some of the sources may not have been independently offered as evidence because of logistical considerations and some may be inadmissible. Courts have evolved several rules for addressing this problem. Some limit any such opinion,[34] while others permit reliance on these extrajudicial sources if they play only a minor role in the opinion and are counterbalanced by a proper basis.[35] Another approach is taken in Rule 703 of the Federal Rules of Evidence[36] and the states that have adopted it.[37] This approach asks whether these extrajudicial sources are

---

[28] *See* §2.14.

[29] *See* Jiminez v O'Brien, 117 Utah 82, 213 P2d 337 (1949).

[30] *See* §2.14.

[31] *See* §§2.15-2.17.

[32] *See* §2.18.

[33] Guttmacher & Weihofen, *The Psychiatrist on the Witness Stand,* 32 BUL Rev 285, 298 (1952). The authors refer to this as a necessary "longitudinal study of behavior."

[34] Brackin v State, 417 So 2d 602 (Ala Crim App 1982).

[35] Moore v Grantham, 599 SW2d 287 (Tex 1980)

[36] Fed R Evid 703 provides:

The facts or data in the particular case upon which an expert bases an opinion or inference may be those perceived by or made known to him at or before the hearing. If of a type reasonably relied upon by experts in the particular field in forming opinions or inferences upon the subject, the facts or data need not be admissible in evidence.

[37] Arizona, Arkansas, Colorado, Delaware, Maine, Minnesota, Montana, Nebraska, Nevada, New Mexico, North Dakota, Oklahoma, South Dakota, Washington, Wisconsin, and Wyoming have adopted rules identical to Fed R

typically used by experts in the particular field and whether it is reasonable for them to do so; if so, the court is unconcerned with the extent to which this is counterbalanced by an admissible basis. For example, in *United States v Lawson*[38] a government psychiatrist who had spoken with the defendant informally, but had not interviewed him privately, was permitted to offer an opinion on the absence of mental illness based upon the reports of other physicians who had interviewed the defendant, tests administered the defendant, and information about the defendant acquired by other government agencies. Although these other reports and tests were admittedly hearsay, the court found them to be the sort of information upon which a reasonable psychiatrist would customarily rely.[39]

This approach has been lauded for bringing judicial testimony in line with the realities of medical practice[40] and criticized for failing to provide adequate scrutiny of the trustworthiness and reliability of the hearsay basis for psychiatric and psychological opinion testimony.[41] The laudatory comments point out that in medical practice input from many individuals, often *not* relayed firsthand to the physician, provides the basis for diagnoses based on which life and death decisions are made. The critical comments point out that Federal Rule of Evidence 703 contemplates not only customary use of this source of information, but also an independent determination by the court that use of this source is reasonable. In practice courts have often collapsed the two, assuming that if professionals customarily use this source it is reasonable for them to do so, thereby obviating scrutiny of information sources of questionable trustworthiness.[42]

Another problem raised by the use of these extrajudicial bases is whether the judge or jury may then consider the basis itself as evidence,

---

Evid 703. J. Weinstein & M. Berger, Weinstein's Evidence ¶703[05] (1982). Alaska, Hawaii, Florida, and Minnesota have adopted substantially similar rules. *Id.*

38 653 F2d 299 (7th Cir 1981), *cert denied,* 458 US 1150 (1982). *See also* United States v Sims, 514 F2d 147 (9th Cir), *cert denied,* 423 US 845 (1975); United States v Phillips, 515 F Supp 758 (ED Ky 1981).

39 653 F2d at 302 n 7.

40 Fed R Evid 703, advisory committee note, 56 FRD 183, 283 (1972).

41 Note, *Hearsay Bases of Psychiatric Opinion Testimony: A Critique of Federal Rule of Evidence 703,* 51 S Cal L Rev 129 (1977).

42 United States v Sims, 514 F2d 147, 149 (9th Cir), *cert denied,* 423 US 845 (1975).

independent of its use as the basis for an opinion.[43] Some courts have permitted independent admissibility of the extrajudicial basis.[44] However, this practice raises serious hearsay and confrontation problems.[45]

§9.06   Form of Testimony

The form of the psychiatrist's or psychologist's testimony raises legal and tactical considerations. The testimony must be admissible and it must be persuasive. Ultimately, these two goals need not be in conflict.

The limitations on the form of admissible expert testimony turn, as do many other limits on expert testimony, on fears of interference with jury function.[46] Conflicts between the need to depend on the expert in an area unfamiliar to the jury and the preservation of an autonomous jury that does not merely rubber-stamp the expert's conclusions yield a variety of rules on the form of the expert's testimony.

§9.07   —Degree of Certainty

A psychiatrist or psychologist who has examined a patient and considered other relevant sources of information may have formed an opinion about a relevant question in the case, but the degree of certainty about that opinion in an imperfect world with limited sources of information is likely to be less than 100 per cent. The inability of the witness to be "inside the head" of the defendant at the time of the murder or the testatrix at the time of the making of the will, the inherent uncertainties of psychiatric diagnosis,[47] and the many unresolved questions about human behavior[48] compel the conclusion that any psychiatrist's or psychologist's opinion can only be an assessment of probabilities. But, because of a fear that the jury may not fully realize these limits, courts have often required the medical expert to have reached a reasonable medical certainty before admitting this testimony.[49]

The meaning of the phrase *reasonable medical certainty* is not clear. In

---

[43] Carlson, *Collision Course on Expert Testimony: Limitations on Affirmative Introduction of Underlying Data*, 36 U Fla L Rev 234 (1984).

[44] *See, e.g.,* State v Davis, 269 NW2d 434 (Iowa 1978).

[45] State v Towne, 142 Vt 241, 453 A2d 1133 (1982).

[46] E. Cleary, McCormick on Evidence §12, at 30 (3d ed 1984).

[47] *See* **ch 2.**

[48] *See* **ch 1.**

[49] Loper v Andrews, 404 SW2d 300, 305 (Tex 1966).

some instances it appears to require that the opinion must, in the expert's opinion, be as probable as other medical experts in the field could hope to achieve and of the degree of certainty they would rely upon in making treatment decisions. In other instances it appears to correlate with the various standards of persuasion—preponderance, clear and convincing, beyond a reasonable doubt.[50] This reflects an apparent confusion of the standards for admissibility of evidence and sufficiency of the evidence to support a verdict.

The rule has a number of problems. It relies in large measure on the good faith of the testifying witness. If the witness is determined to present an opinion, the use of ambiguous language camouflaging its certainty can result in its admission. Conversely, the rule risks the exclusion of probative evidence offered by a witness who is *too* candid about its limitations. A candid psychiatrist or psychologist, describing all the potential limits on the accuracy of an opinion, would very likely cause exclusion of the opinion. Finally, the rule threatens to exclude much probative evidence rather than permitting the jury to consider these limitations on the weight of the testimony. Based on these problems, the trend has been to relegate these issues to the weight rather than the admissibility of this evidence.[51]

§9.08   —Conclusions

The extent to which the expert helps the jury to understand relevant scientific or technical knowledge, sort through the facts of the cases, and apply its independent judgment to these facts is a function of the kinds of information provided by the expert. If the expert only says, in effect, "I think you should find for the plaintiff in this case," the jury can only use this advice if it abrogates its function as an independent evaluator of the evidence. Thus, limits on the form of expert testimony have sought to encourage the expert's provision of information helpful to the jury in its function as independent evaluator of the evidence and to limit the expert's provision of information which merely asks the jury to affirm the expert's conclusions.

One vehicle thought to encourage expert testimony that aids but does interfere with the jury's functioning has been the rule limiting an

---

[50] Rappeport, *Reasonable Medical Certainty,* 13 Bull Am Acad Psychiatry & L 5, 6 (1985).

[51] Marco, *The Certainty of Expert Opinion* in Forensic Sciences (1984).

opinion on the ultimate issue in the case.[52] Under this rule, an expert witness may express an opinion, but not an opinion on the ultimate issue in the case, for that is the exclusive province of the jury. Psychiatrists or psychologists properly qualified as experts on criminal responsibility, for example, would be permitted to express an opinion on the defendant's sanity, but not the ability of the defendant to tell right from wrong, because that was the ultimate question for the jury.[53]

Although this rule still exists in many jurisdictions,[54] there is a trend represented by the original version of Federal Rule of Evidence 704[55] and in those states that have adopted it[56] to admit expert testimony embracing an ultimate issue that is otherwise helpful to the judge or jury.[57] Thus, a psychiatrist's opinion in a will contest that the testatrix understood the nature and extent of her property and objects of her bounty[58] should be admitted if it also provides the jury the reasoning used to reach this conclusion. Conversely, if that conclusion was all the psychologist said, it should be excluded as not helpful to the jury.

In the trial of Patty Hearst[59] for armed bank robbery, for example, the government's psychiatrists were permitted to respond to Ms. Hearst's claim of duress by the Symbionese Liberation Army with the conclusions that "she did not perform the bank robbery because she was in fear for her life" and "I think she entered the bank voluntarily in order to participate in the robbing of that bank. This was an act of her own

---

[52] E. Cleary, McCormick on Evidence §12 (3d ed 1984).

[53] Fed R Evid 704 advisory committee note, 56 FRD 183, 284 (1972). *See* Blocker v United States, 288 F2d 853, 863 (1961) (Burger, concurring); State v McCann, 329 Mo 748, 475 SW 95 (1932).

[54] Stoebuck, *Opinions on Ultimate Facts: Status, Trends, and a Note of Caution*, 41 Den L Center J 226 (1964).

[55] Fed R Evid 704, as enacted, provided: "Testimony in the form of an opinion or inference otherwise admissible is not objectionable because it embraces an ultimate issue to be decided by the trier of fact."

[56] Alaska, Arizona, Arkansas, Colorado, Hawaii, Maine, Michigan, Minnesota, Montana, Nebraska, Nevada, New Mexico, North Dakota, Oklahoma, Oregon, Texas, Utah, Vermont, Washington, Wisconsin, and Wyoming have adopted evidence rules identical to Fed R Evid 704. J. Weinstein & M. Berger, Weinstein's Evidence, ¶704[03] (1982). Delaware, Florida, and Ohio have adopted substantially similar rules. *Id.*

[57] Fed R Evid 701, 702.

[58] Fed R Evid 704 advisory committee note, 56 FRD 183, 285 (1972).

[59] United States v Hearst, 563 F2d 1331 (9th Cir 1977), *cert denied*, 435 US 1000 (1978).

free will.''[60] Positing that these conclusions would be understandable to the average lay person and, implicitly, of sufficient help to justify their admission, their admissibility was upheld.

In 1984, however, one response to the insanity acquittal of John Hinckley, President Reagan's would-be assassin, and the furor over the trial and resulting verdict, was an amendment to Federal Rule of Evidence 704 to limit the opinion of an expert witness testifying on criminal responsibility.[61] This limitation, similar to one recently enacted in California,[62] restricts expert testimony about mental status or conditions constituting an element of the crime charged in a criminal case, but leaves the original abrogation of the ultimate opinion rule unchanged in all other classes of cases.

The psychiatrist or psychologist governed by Rule 704(b) of the Federal Rules of Evidence may not express a conclusion about the defendant's mental status in the terms of the charge or available defense. Thus, for example, a psychiatrist's opinion, in a jurisdiction using *M'Naghten*,[63] that the defendant could tell the difference between right and wrong would not be admissible. An opinion in the same case that the defendant had been diagnosed as a paranoid schizophrenic would not be prohibited under the ultimate issue limitation. The

---

[60] 563 F2d at 1351.

[61] Fed R Evid 704 now provides:

 (*a*) *Except as provided in subdivision (b),* testimony in the form of an opinion or inference otherwise admissible is not objectionable because it embraces an ultimate issue to be decided by the trier of fact.

 (*b*) *No expert witness testifying with respect to the mental state or condition of a defendant in a criminal case may state an opinion or inference as to whether the defendant did or did not have the mental state or condition constituting an element of the crime charged or of a defense thereto. Such ultimate issues are matters for the trier of fact alone.*

[62]   In the guilt phase of a criminal action, any expert testifying about a defendant's mental illness, mental disorder, or mental defect shall not testify as to whether the defendant had or did not have the required mental states, which include, but are not limited to, purpose, intent, knowledge, or malice aforethought, for the crimes charged. The question as to whether the defendant had or did not have the required mental states shall be decided by the trier of fact.

Cal Penal Code §29 (West Supp 1985).

The California limitation addresses only testimony concerning a mental state relevant to the crime charged, while the federal limitation concerns both the crime charged or a defense. The consequence of this distinction had not yet been made clear in the case law.

[63] *See* **§12.02.**

possibility that the psychiatrist could then offer general psychiatric knowledge about the ability of paranoid schizophrenics to tell right from wrong, leaving the jury to apply this knowledge to this defendant, is not specifically prohibited, and points up the flaw in this approach.[64]

§9.09   —Psychobabble

Another aspect of the form of expert testimony that may also limit its usefulness to the judge or jury is psychiatric or psychological conclusions. At best, unexplained psychiatric jargon provides the judge or jury with no information to perform its function, and at worst, it may mislead or confuse the judge or jury. Thus, as a matter of admissibility and tactics, explanation of professional jargon is extremely important.

The admissibility of unexplained psychiatric jargon was pivotal in a series of decisions of the District of Columbia Circuit Court of Appeals that sought to establish rules that would render psychiatric and psychological testimony on the insanity defense more helpful to the jury.[65] One consequence of that court's adoption of an insanity defense in *Durham v United States,*[66] which excused acts that were the product of a mental disease or defect, was trial by label permitting expert witnesses to conclude that a defendant did or did not suffer from a mental disease or defect without articulating what definitions or standards governed their conclusions.[67] Although the court subsequently provided a definition of mental disease or defect,[68] and limited testimony on productivity of the acts alleged in relationship to the mental disease or defect,[69] testimony in the form of conclusory labels continued. Finally, in *United States v Brawner,*[70] the court changed its formulation of the insanity defense because of "undue dominance by the experts giving testimony"[71] in favor of the American Law Institute's test.[72]

---

64 *See* United States v Brawner, 471 F2d 969 (DC Cir 1972).

65 United States v Brawner, 471 F2d 969 (DC Cir 1972); Washington v United States, 390 F2d 444 (DC Cir 1967); Carter v United States, 252 F2d 608 (DC Cir 1957); Durham v United States, 214 F2d 862 (DC Cir 1954).

66 214 F2d 862 (DC Cir 1954).

67 United States v Brawner, 471 F2d 969, 978 (DC Cir 1972).

68 McDonald v United States, 312 F2d 847, 851 (DC Cir 1962) ("any abnormal condition of the mind which substantially affects mental or emotional processes and substantially impairs behavior controls").

69 Washington v United States, 390 F2d 444 (DC Cir 1967).

70 471 F2d 969 (DC Cir 1972).

71 *Id* 981.

72 *See* §**11.09.**

Tactically, unexplained psychiatric jargon may have negative effects.[73] It may confuse or mislead the judge or jury neutralizing the positive effects of the witness's testimony. It may also offend the judge or jury by creating the image of a witness with an air of superiority[74] not willing to speak the same language as the judge or jury. It should be avoided.

§9.10   Mode of Presentation

Although psychiatric and psychological evidence is often presented orally, this is not always the case. In many instances, written psychiatric and psychological evidence is presented. The presentation of this evidence in writing may be permitted because the rules of evidence are inapplicable in the particular proceedings in which the evidence is relevant or because an exception to the hearsay rule applies.

Psychiatric and psychological evidence is frequently relevant in proceedings in which traditional rules of evidence, including the hearsay rule, are not applicable. Included in those proceedings are hearings on bail,[75] competence to stand trial,[76] and disability determinations in the administrative setting—workers' compensation[77] and social security.[78] Therefore, psychiatric or psychological reports specifically prepared for these proceedings or records of treatment or testing prepared for other purposes may be admitted in these proceedings. Typically, the inapplicability of the rules of evidence is related, in whole or in part, to the absence of juries and, therefore, in those instances in some jurisdictions in which juries may determine these issues, the written psychiatric and pscyhological evidence is only permitted when it fits within an exception to the hearsay rule.

In those proceedings in which the rules of evidence are applicable, the hearsay rule imposes a limitation on psychiatric and psychological evidence not presented by live witnesses under oath. The exception to the hearsay rule most often at issue in determining the admissibility of psychiatric and psychological evidence, particularly in the case of

---

[73] Dietz, Cooke, Rapperpert, & Silvergleit, *Psychojargon in the Psychological Report: Ratings by Judges, Psychiatrists, and Psychologists,* 1(2) Behavioral Sci & L 77 (1983).

[74] Hilton, *Elements of Effective Expert Testimony,* 2 J Forensic Sci 73, 77 (1957).

[75] Fed R Evid 1101(d)(3).

[76] *Id.*

[77] *See, e.g.,* Sky Chefs, Inc v Rogers, 222 Va 800, 284 SE2d 605 (1985).

[78] 42 USC §405(9b)(1).

hospital records, is the business records exception.[79] Most jurisdictions have recognized that hospital records may fall within the requirements of the business records exception to the hearsay rule.[80] However, psychiatric and psychological opinions contained within these records have been singled out for additional scrutiny.[81]

Objective data contained within hospital records such as blood pressure or body temperature have not posed particular problems under the business records exception to the hearsay rule.[82] Similarly, diagnoses involving a relatively low-level inference in which little speculation is involved have not posed problems under this exception.[83] However, in the case of psychiatric and psychological diagnosis, many courts have considered that the degree of speculation and uncertainty involved in the diagnosis does not justify dispensing with cross-examination of the author of the opinion.[84] Thus, these courts exclude a psychiatric diagnosis of schizophrenia, for example, contained in hospital records otherwise excepted from the hearsay rule. Other jurisdictions have concluded that the costs of requiring the author's attendance in court would be too great a disruption in the delivery of health care to require it as a condition of the record's admissibility. These courts assume that if these opinions are of sufficient reliability to be used in treatment decisions they are sufficiently reliable for judicial use.[85]

---

[79] Fed R Evid 803(6).

[80] McDaniel v United States, 343 F2d 785 (5th Cir), *cert denied,* 382 US 826 (1965); State v Brierly, 109 Ariz 310, 509 P2d 203 (1973); People v Kirtdoll, 391 Mich 370, 217 NW2d 37 (1974); State v Finkley, 6 Wash App 228, 492 P2d 222 (1977); State v Olson, 75 Wis 2d 575, 250 NW2d 12 (1979).

[81] United States v Bohle, 445 F2d 54, 64-65 (7th Cir 1971); Birdsell v United States, 346 F2d 775, 779 (5th Cir), *cert denied,* 382 US 963 (1965); Otney v United States, 340 F2d 696, 699-700 (10th Cir 1965). *But see* Thomas v Hogan, 308 F2d 355, 361 (4th Cir 1962); Lyles v United States, 254 F2d 725, 738-39 (DC Cir 1957), *cert denied,* 356 US 961 (1958).

[82] D. Louisell & C. Mueller, Federal Evidence §451, at 697 (1980).

[83] *See, e.g.,* Thomas v Hogan, 308 F2d 355 (4th Cir 1962) (intoxication); Glawe v Rulon, 284 F2d 495 (8th Cir 1960) (protruded disk).

[84] Phillips v Neil, 452 F2d 337 (6th Cir 1971), *cert denied,* 409 US 884 (1972); United States v Bohle, 445 F2d 54 (7th Cir 1971); Birdsell v United States, 346 F2d 775 (8th Cir), *cert denied,* 382 US 963 (1965); Otney v United States, 340 F2d 696 (10th Cir 1965); New York Life Ins Co v Taylor, 147 F2d 297 (DC Cir 1945).

[85] *See, e.g.,* Thomas v Hogan, 308 F2d 355 (4th Cir 1960).

§9.11 Suggested Reading

Books

E. Cleary, *McCormick on Evidence* (3rd ed 1984).

D. Louisell & C. Mueller, *Federal Evidence* (1980).

I. Ray, *Medical Jurisprudence of Insanity* (8th ed 1871).

J. Weinstein & M. Berger, *Weinstein's Evidence* (1982).

Articles

Carlson, *Collision Course on Expert Testimony: Limitations on Affirmative Introduction of Underlying Data,* 36 U Fla L Rev 234 (1984).

Dietz, Cooke, Rapperpert, & Silvergleit, *Psychojargon in the Psychological Report: Ratings by Judges, Psychiatrists, and Psychologists,* 1(2) Behavioral Sci & Law 77 (1983).

Guttmacher & Weinhofen, *The Psychiatrist on the Witness Stand,* 32 BUL Rev 287 (1952).

Hilton, *Elements of Effective Expert Testimony,* 2 J Forensic Sci 73 (1957).

Marco, *The Certainty of Expert Opinion,* in Forensic Sciences (1984).

Note, *Hearsay Bases of Psychiatric Opinion Testimony: A Critique of Federal Rule of Evidence 703,* 51 S Cal L Rev 129 (1977).

Rappeport, *Reasonable Medical Certainty,* 13 Bull Am Acad Psychiatry & Law 5 (1985).

Rheingold, *The Basis of Medical Testimony,* 15 Vand L Rev 473 (1962).

Seidel & Gungrich, *Hearsay Objections to Expert Testimony and the Proposed Federal Rules of Evidence,* 39 UMKC L Rev 141 (1970).

Shuman, *The Road to Bedlam: Evidentiary Guideposts in Civil Commitment Proceedings,* 55 Notre Dame Law 53 (1979).

Stoebuck, *Opinions on Ultimate Facts: Status, Trends, and a Note of Caution,* 41 Denver L Center J 226 (1964).

Cases

Barefoot v Estelle, 463 US 880 (1983).

Blocker v United States, 288 F2d 853 (1961).

Birdsell v United States, 346 F2d 775 (5th Cir), *cert denied,* 382 US 963 (1965).

Brackin v State, 417 So 2d 602 (Ala Crim App 1982).

Carter v United States, 252 F2d 608 (DC Cir 1957).

Durham v United States, 214 F2d 862 (DC Cir 1954).

Estelle v Smith, 451 US 454 (1981).

Glawe v Rulon, 284 F2d 495 (8th Cir 1960).

Harriford v Harriford, 335 SW2d 113 (Mo Ct App 1960).

Jiminez v O'Brien, 117 Utah 82, 213 P2d 337 (1949).

Lopor v Andrews, 104 SW2d 300 (Tex 1966).

Lyles v United States, 254 F2d 725 (DC Cir 1957), *cert denied*, 356 US 961 (1958).

Marshall v Sellers, 188 Md 508, 53 A2d 5 (1947).

McDaniel v United States, 343 F2d 785 (5th Cir), *cert denied*, 382 US 826 (1965).

McDonald v United States, 312 F2d 847 (DC Cir 1962).

Moore v Grantham, 599 SW2d 287 (Tex 1980).

New York Life Ins Co v Taylor, 147 F2d 297 (DC Cir 1945).

Otney v United States, 340 F2d 696 (10th Cir 1965).

People v Kirtdoll, 391 Mich 370, 217 NW2d 37 (1974).

Phillips v Neil, 452 F2d 337 (6th Cir 1971), *cert denied*, 409 US 884 (1972).

Sky Chefs, Inc v Rogers, 222 Va 80, 284 SE2d 605 (1985).

State v Brierly, 109 Ariz 310, 509 P2d 203 (1973).

State v Davis, 269 NW2d 434 (Iowa 1978).

State v Finkley, 6 Wash App 228, 492 P2d 222 (1977).

State v McCann, 329 Mo 748, 475 SW 95 (1932).

State v Olson, 75 Wis 2d 575, 250 NW2d 12 (1977).

State v Towne, 142 Vt 241, 453 A2d 1133 (1982).

Steele v State, 97 Wis 2d 72, 294 NW2d 2 (1980).

Thomas v Hogan, 308 F2d 355 (4th Cir 1962).

United States v Brawner, 471 F2d 969 (DC Cir 1972).

United States v Hearst, 563 F2d 1331 (9th Cir 1977), *cert denied*, 435 US 1000 (1979).

United States v Hiss, 88 F Supp 559 (SDNY 1950).

United States v Phillips, 515 F Supp 758 (Ed Ky 1981).

United States v Sims, 514 F2d 147 (9th Cir 1975).

Washington v United States, 390 F2d 444 (DC Cir 1967).

Statutes and Rules

Cal Penal Code §29 (West Supp 1985).

Fed R Evid 701.

Fed R Evid 702 advisory committee note, 56 FRD 183, 282 (1972).

Fed R Evid 703 advisory committee note, 56 FRD 183, 283 (1972).

Fed R Evid 704 advisory committee note, 56 FRD 183, 284 (1972).

Fed R Evid 705.

Fed R Evid 801(c), (d)(2).

Fed R Evid 803(4), (6).

Fed R Evid 1101(d)(3).

42 USC §405(b)(1).

§9.12 WESTLAW Search References

§9.01 *Introduction*
di testimony

§9.02 *Basis for Opinion*
expert /s witness testimony /p psychiatr! psycholog! /p bas**
/s opinion /s fact!

§9.03 *—Personal Knowledge*
expert /s witness testimony /p psychiatr! psycholog! /p hearsay

§9.04 *—Hypothetical Questions*
expert /s witness testimony psychiatr! psycholog! /p hypothetical

§9.05 *—Extrajudicial Sources*
expert /s witness testimony /p psychiatr! psycholog! /p trustworthiness reliab! /p record report examination source

§9.06 *Form of Testimony*
di(expert /s testimony /s admit! admiss! /s psychiatr! psycholog!)

§9.07 *—Degree of Certainty*
reasonabl! /4 certain! /p psychiatr! psycholog!

§9.08 *—Conclusions*
psychiatr! psycholog! /p testimony /p "ultimate issue" (mental
/s element)

§9.09 *—Psychobabble*
(psycholog! psychiatr! /5 jargon language terminology mumbo-
jumbo gibberish) psycho-babble

brawner /s 471 +5 969 /p "american law institute" a.l.i.

§9.10   *Mode of Presentation*
         to(157) /p psychiatr! psycholog! /p report record writ***

10

General Limitations on Psychiatric and Psychological Evidence

§10.01 Introduction

Most of the rules of evidence that bear on psychiatric and psychological evidence concern its probative value. For example, when a psychiatrist is required to describe a mental status examination of a patient or when a psychologist is asked to explain the validity of certain psychological tests as a condition of their admissibility, the primary concern is whether this evidence meets a minimum threshold of probative value. Is a mental status examination an accurate vehicle to gauge the mental capacity of a patient and was it administered in a manner likely to maximize its accuracy? Is a particular psychological test a valid diagnostic technique and was it properly administered? A negative answer to any of these questions reflects on the probative value of the potential evidence. One set of evidence rules, however, considers exclusion of psychiatric and psychological evidence for reasons unrelated to its probative value. Rules of relational privilege are concerned with preserving the sanctity of a relationship notwithstanding the probative value of the evidence that might be obtained from the relationship.

The professions themselves have adopted codes that address these same concerns, and describe the circumstances under which members of the profession should keep professional secrets as well as circumstances which may justify disclosure.[1] These codes describe the professional's duty of confidentiality and limit gratuitous disclosures of patient communications to a narrowly described set of circumstances that involve a risk to the patient or the public.[2] The codes may have legal significance in actions for professional discipline[3] or breach of privacy following an unjustified disclosure of confidential information by a psychiatrist or psychologist.[4] However, these codes do not purport to govern, and arguably as privately imposed professional norms could not govern, judicially compelled disclosure. That is the province of the rules of evidence and related constitutional considerations grouped under the heading of *privilege*.

Medical privileges are, in the first instance, largely a matter of statutory law because the common law did not recognize a physician-patient privilege.[5] Thus, any privilege applicable to psychiatrists or psychologists will, with limited exception,[6] be a legislative creation. These legislative creations have a common pattern; they describe the prerequisites for recognition of a privilege, the consequences of its recognition, and exceptions to the privilege. The specifics of these patterns are described in §§10.02-10.04.

Because psychiatrists as physicians are included within physician-patient privilege statutes, in those jurisdictions with no privilege statute exclusively applicable to psychiatrists, it is necessary to resort to the general physician-patient privilege discussed in §10.02. Many jurisdic-

---

[1] Americal Medical Assn, *The Principles of Medical Ethics*, 246 JAMA 2187 (1981); American Psychological Assn, *Principle 5, Ethical Standards of Psychologists*, 36 Am Psychologist 633 (1981).

[2] "A physician shall respect the rights of patients, of colleagues, and of other health professionals, and shall safeguard patient confidences within the constraints of the law." American Medical Assn, *The Principles of Medical Ethics*, 246 JAMA 2187-88 (1981).

[3] *See, e.g.*, Cal Bus & Prof Code §2263 (West Supp 1984).

[4] Doe v Roe, 93 Misc 2d 201, 400 NYS2d 668 (Sup Ct 1977).

[5] Whalen v Roe, 429 US 589, 602 n 28 (1977); Duchess of Kingston's Case, 20 How St Trials 355, 573 (1776).

[6] Allred v State, 554 P2d 411 (Alaska 1976).

tions have adopted specialized psychiatrist, psychologist, and psychotherapist-patient privileges. These specialized privileges may exist in lieu of a general physician-patient privilege or in addition to it, but with different effect. These specialized privileges are examined in §10.05.

The traditional concept of practitioners of the healing arts and their relationship to litigation has changed substantially over the years. Physicians, psychiatrists, and psychologists now may play many roles in the litigation process. They may have a therapeutic relationship with a patient-litigant entered into prior to the onset of litigation that is now of consequence in the litigation; they may have a nontherapeutic relationship with the patient-litigant and see the patient-litigant only to assist in testifying at trial; or they may not have a therapeutic relation, nor examine, nor testify at trial about the patient-litigant, and instead function exclusively as the attorney's assistant in preparing the case.

The first situation, the therapeutic relationship, raises problems of medical privilege—physician, psychiatrist, psychologist, or psychotherapist-patient privilege. The latter two situations, both nontherapeutic, raise questions of privilege not of therapist and patient, but of the attorney and client and of the attorney's assistants. These questions are addressed in §§10.06-10.08.

§10.02 The Physician-Patient Privilege—General Rule

Although the common law did not recognize a physician-patient privilege, most state legislatures have now modified the common law in their states and enacted a physician-patient privilege.[7] The rationale for these privileges is that they permit the patient to disclose a condition fully and truthfully to a physician in order to be effectively treated.[8] Notwithstanding suggestions that these privileges actually play a negligible role in physician–patient relationships and frustrate factual inquiries in the trial process,[9] the number of physician–patient privileges has grown substantially over the years. The response to criticisms of these privileges has been, instead, strictly to interpret the require-

---

[7] See Shuman & Weiner, *The Privilege Study: An Empirical Examination of the Psychotherapist-Patient Privilege*, 60 NCL Rev 893, 907 n 100 (1982) for a chart describing the pattern of medical privileges in the states.

[8] *See, e.g.,* State v White, 169 Conn 223, 363 A2d 143, *cert denied,* 423 US 1025 (1975); Jones v State, 610 SW2d 535 (Tex Civ App 1980), writ refd nre.

[9] Chafee, *Privileged Communications: Is Justice Served or Obstructed by Closing the Doctor's Mouth on the Witness Stand?*, 52 Yale LJ 607 (1943); Ladd, *A Modern Code of Evidence,* 27 Iowa L Rev 213 (1942).

ments for recognition of a privilege and to find a waiver or exception rather liberally.[10]

The physician-patient privilege statutes from state to state have certain common requirements for recognition of a privilege. There must be a patient, an individual who seeks out a physician for the purpose of obtaining medical treatment.[11] The person the patient seeks out for treatment must be a licensed physician or there must be a reasonable basis for the patient to assume that the individual is a physician who is licensed to practice medicine.[12] If it later appears that the individual sought out by the patient was not a physician or was not then licensed to practice medicine, the inquiry will focus on the reasonableness of the belief that the patient had consulted a licensed physician. Thus, for example, contacting an individual listed under the physician listing in the phone book would be the basis for a reasonable belief that the individual was a licensed physician.

Physician is generally defined to include allopathic and osteopathic physicians without reference to specialty; thus, psychiatrists are included within the definition of physician. Generally not included within the statutory definition of physician are other practitioners of the healing arts such as psychologists, nurses, chiropractors, or pharmacists.[13] Therefore, in the absence of a specialized privilege applicable to these practitioners or inclusion under an existing privilege,[14] no bar exists to the judicial compulsion of disclosure of their confidential communications with patients. There is a split of authority concerning whether interns not yet licensed to practice medicine qualify as physicians for purposes of the privilege.[15]

The communication between physician and patient sought to be protected by the privilege must be related to medical treatment and occur during the course of treatment.[16] Thus, for example, a discussion with one's physician during an office visit about investment opportunities or a gratuitous remark about one's condition after termination of

---

[10] J. Weinstein & M. Berger, Weinstein's Evidence §504[01], at 504-09 (1982).

[11] State v Sweet, 142 Vt 238, 453 A2d 1131 (1982); State v Jenkins, 80 Wis 2d 426, 259 NW2d 109 (1977).

[12] *See, e.g.,* Ill Rev Stat ch 51, §5.2 (1966).

[13] E. Cleary, McCormick on Evidence §99, at 246 n 1 (3d ed 1984).

[14] *See* **§10.05.**

[15] *See, e.g.,* Eureka-Maryland Assurance Co v Gray, 121 F2d 104 (DC Cir 1941) (intern included); Frederick v Federal Life Ins Co, 57 P2d 235 (Cal 1936) (intern excluded).

[16] San Francisco v Superior Court, 37 Cal 2d 227, 231 P2d 26 (1951).

the relationship would not qualify for protection under the privilege. Although some states limit the privilege's protection to oral communications or substitutes for oral communications such as pointing gestures, rather than all information learned from the patient including communications as well as the physician's observations of matters the patient may not have intended to communicate, most states now cloak both categories in the privilege.[17]

The communication between physician and patient sought to be protected must have been intended by the patient to be confidential. It is not necessary, in order to conclude that the communication was intended to be confidential, that it have taken place in the physician's office, and the fact that it occurred in the physician's office is not a guarantee that it will be found to have been confidential. A communication in a private setting outside the physician's office suggests that confidentiality was intended while a communication in the physician's waiting room in the presence and hearing of other patients does not suggest that confidentiality was intended.

The presence of someone other than the physician and patient during the communication was, at one time, generally thought to be inconsistent with confidentiality. At present, a more functional approach is usually used, inquiring about the necessity for the third party's presence. For example, the presence of a parent during the examination of a child[18] or of a nurse who is needed to assist the physician should not destroy confidentiality.[19]

Inclusion of privileged information within a medical record does not result in a loss of its privileged status.[20] Although many people have access to this information, the courts have assumed that this recording is a practical necessity and everyone with access to the medical record is part of the treatment team with a medical need for this information.

The consequence of the recognition of a physician-patient privilege is that the patient may refuse to permit the physician's testimony about confidential communications between them. The physician is not rendered incompetent as a witness generally, and thus even in the absence of an exception or waiver the physician may testify to nonprivileged information, such as discussions with the patient before

---

[17] D. Louisell & C. Meuller, Federal Evidence §215, at 599 (1978).

[18] Grosslight v Superior Court, 72 Cal App 2d 50, 140 Cal Rptr 228 (1977).

[19] Ostrowski v Mockridge, 242 Minn 265, 65 NW2d 185 (1954); State v Scott, 491 SW2d 514 (Mo 1973).

[20] Rudnick v Superior Court, 11 Cal 3d 924, 523 P2d 643, 114 Cal Rptr 603 (1974).

the onset of the physician-patient relationship or after its termination and nontherapeutic or nonconfidential communications during the relationship. Most jurisdictions do not regard the existence of the physician-patient relationship itself as privileged; thus, the physician may be asked whether and when someone was a patient.[21]

§10.03　—Waiver

Because the physician–patient privilege is not a rule rendering the physician incompetent as a witness, but rather a right of the patient to prevent the physician from testifying as to certain confidential communications, it may be waived. However, unless waived or excepted, its effect on the physician's testimony is generally held to continue beyond the termination of the physician-patient relationship and even after the death of the patient.[22] When the physician's testimony is sought and the patient is not present, it should be assumed, in the absence of clear evidence to the contrary, that the patient did not wish the privilege waived.[23]

A waiver of the privilege by the patient may be express or implied. An express waiver could occur in court, for example, when the patient notifies the court of a wish to waive the privilege, or it may occur out of court in an application for health insurance.[24] As with other waivers of rights, so long as it is knowing, intelligent, and voluntary, the waiver will be effective.[25] Conversely, evidence that the patient did not understand the waiver language in the insurance application because it was written in legalese or did not understand the significance of submitting a death certificate to an insurance company in support of a claim for life insurance benefits without another method of substantiating a claim and without knowledge of its waiver effect will defeat the waiver.[26]

---

[21] *In re* Zuniga, 714 F2d 632, 640 (6th Cir), *cert denied,* 104 S Ct 426 (1983). *But see Ex parte* Abell, 613 SW2d 255 (Tex 1981).

[22] Bassil v Ford Motor Co, 278 Mich 173, 270 NW 258 (1936); Prink v Rockefeller Center, Inc, 48 NY2d 309, 398 NE2d 517, 422 NYS2d 911 (1979).

[23] *In re* Grand Jury Investigation, 59 NY2d 130, 450 NE2d 678, 463 NYS2d 758 (1983).

[24] United States v Radetsky, 535 F2d 556, 569 n 14 (10th Cir), *cert denied,* 429 US 820 (1976); Leach v Millers Life Ins Co, 400 F2d 179, 182 (5th Cir 1968).

[25] *In re* Pebsworth, 705 F2d 261, 262 (7th Cir 1983); Gaynier v Johnson, 673 SW2d 899, 905 (Tex Civ App 1984).

[26] Kelly v Allegan County Circuit Judge, 382 Mich 425, 169 NW2d 916 (1969).

When a patient acts in a manner inconsistent with an intention to maintain the confidentiality of communications, a waiver of the privilege will be implied. This will occur when the patient publicly discloses communications with the physician in testimony or elsewhere[27] or calls the physician as a witness and examines the physician as to the communications.[28] In some jurisdictions, the filing of a lawsuit in which the condition for which the patient was treated by the particular physician is at issue will effect an implied waiver of the privilege.[29]

Another implied waiver is addressed by Rule 35 of the Federal Rules of Civil Procedure. Rule 35 permits the court to order a mental or physical examination of a party or a person in the custody or legal control of a party when that person's mental or physical condition is in controversy, and good cause for the examination exists.[30] The person

---

[27] *Id.*

[28] State v Carter, 641 SW2d 54 (Mo 1982); People v Smith, 59 NY2d 156, 451 NE2d 157, 464 NYS2d 399 (1983).

[29] *See, e.g.,* San Francisco v Superior Court, 37 Cal 2d 227, 231 P2d 26 (1951); Tex R Evid 510(d)(5).

[30] Fed R Civ P 35. The full text of the rule provides:

PHYSICAL AND MENTAL EXAMINATION OF PERSONS

(a) Order for examination. When the mental or physical condition (including the blood group) of a party, or of a person in the custody or under the legal control of a party, is in controversy, the court in which the action is pending may order the party to submit to a physical or mental examination by a physician or to produce for examination the person in his custody or legal control. The order may be made only on motion for good cause shown and upon notice to the person to be examined and to all parties and shall specify the time, place, manner, conditions, and scope of the examination and the person or persons by whom it is to be made.

(b) Report of Examining Physician.

(1) If requested by the party against whom an order is made under Rule 35(a) or the person examined, the party causing the examination to be made shall deliver to him a copy of a detailed written report of the examining physician setting out his findings, including results of all tests made, diagnoses and conclusions, together with like reports of all earlier examinations of the same condition. After delivery the party causing the examination shall be entitled upon request to receive from the party against whom the order is made a like report of any examination, previously or thereafter made, of the same condition, unless, in the case of a report of examination of a person not a party, the party shows that he is unable to obtain it. The court on motion may make an order against a party requiring delivery of a report on such terms as are just, and if a physician fails or refuses to make a report the court may exclude his testimony if offered at the trial.

examined may request a copy of the report of the examination, but the request "waives any privilege he may have in that action or any other involving the same controversy, regarding the testimony of every other person who has examined or may thereafter examine him in respect of the same mental or physical condition."[31] Thus, even if the filing of the action does not constitute an implied waiver of the privilege, a waiver will occur if there is a request made for copies of the report resulting from a court-ordered examination.

As suggested by these liberal provisions for implied waiver, another question that arises in the case of both implied and express waivers is the effect of the waiver beyond a particular communication with a particular physician. Just as some courts find a waiver without much difficulty, so these same courts also give a broad effect to the waiver. The latter group of courts would permit inquiry not only into all other relevant communications with the particular physician not discussed on direct examination, but also into all relevant communications with other physicians. Conversely, those same courts that are not liberal about finding a waiver limit the effect of a waiver to the particular physician in a case where the implied waiver consists in calling the physician as a witness,[32] and these courts narrowly construe the conditions or treatment they will find related to the present condition where the implied waiver consists in instituting litigation related to a particular condition.[33]

---

(2) By requesting and obtaining a report of the examination so ordered or by taking the deposition of the examiner, the party examined waives any privilege he may have in that action or any other involving the same controversy, regarding the testimony of every other person who has examined or may thereafter examine him in respect to the same mental or physical condition.

(3) This subdivision applies to examinations made by agreement of the parties, unless the agreement expressly provides otherwise. This subdivision does not preclude discovery of a report of an examining physician or the taking of a deposition of the physician in accordance with the provisions of any other rule.

[31] *Id.*

[32] State v Olsen, 271 Or 369, 532 P2d 230 (1975); Gaynier v Johnson, 673 SW2d 899, 905 (Tex Civ App 1984).

[33] Roberts v Superior Court, 9 Cal 3d 330, 508 P2d 309, 107 Cal Rptr 309 (1973); State *ex rel* Floyd v Court of Common Pleas, 55 Ohio St 2d 27, 377 NE2d 794 (1978).

§10.04 —Exceptions

There are certain physician-patient relationships which, because of their purpose, do not satisfy the requirements of the physician-patient privilege. This category includes court-ordered examinations,[34] employment examinations by the employer's physician,[35] and insurance examinations by the insurer's physician.[36] In these instances, the purpose of the relationship is not treatment; thus, the privilege's concern with full disclosure for effective treatment is not served and disclosure to a third person, the court, employer, or insurer, is necessary to satisfy the purpose of the relationship. Regardless of the absence of the privilege's protection, the physician may nonetheless be legally[37] and/or ethically[38] bound to explain the purpose of the examination and its nonprivileged nature to the patient prior to commencing the examination.

Because balancing the sanctity of a physician-patient relationship against obtaining the information it may cloak does not yield universally accepted conclusions, but rather conclusions varying from state to state, the physician-patient privilege is inapplicable in certain categories of cases. Not all states except the privilege's application as to the same categories; some recognize very few exceptions, while others recognize many. However, all states recognize some exceptions. The categories of cases in which the physician-patient privilege may not apply include criminal,[39] civil commitment,[40] workers' compensation,[41] will contests,[42] and child abuse[43] or custody.[44]

---

[34] *See, e.g.,* State v Cole, 295 NW2d 29 (Iowa 1980); Jones v State, 610 SW2d 535 (Tex Civ App 1980), writ refd nre.

[35] McCormick v Caterpillar Tractor Co, 85 Ill 2d 352, 423 NE2d 876 (1981).

[36] Grey v Los Angeles Superior Court, 62 Cal App 3d 698, 133 Cal Rptr 318 (1976).

[37] Estelle v Smith, 451 US 454 (1981), discussed more fully in **§11.06.** *See also* Salas v State, 592 SW2d 653 (Tex Civ App 1979) (no writ).

[38] S. Halleck, Psychiatry and the Dilemma of Crime 329 (1967); American Psychological Assn *Report of the Task Force on the Role of Psychology in the Criminal Justice System,* 33 Am Psychologist 1099, 1102 (1978).

[39] People v Arcega, 32 Cal 3d 504, 651 P2d 338, 186 Cal Rptr 94 (1982); State v Soney, 177 NJ Super 47, 424 A2d 1182 (1980).

[40] *In re* Alvarez, 342 So 2d 492 (Fla 1977).

[41] McCormick v Caterpillar Tractor Co, 85 Ill 2d 352, 423 NE2d 876 (1981); State *ex rel* Holman v Dayton Press, 11 Ohio St 3d 66, 463 NE2d 1243 (1984).

[42] Gaynier v Johnson, 673 SW2d 899 (Tex Civ App 1984).

[43] People v Stritzinger, 34 Cal 3d 505, 668 P2d 738, 194 Cal Rptr 431 (1983); *In re* Courtney S, 130 Cal App 3d 567, 181 Cal Rptr 843 (1982); NC Gen Stat §8-53.1 (1981).

Similarly, there are certain activities thought sufficiently injurious to public health and safety to require that application of the privilege be excepted and that reporting to an appropriate public official be required. Included in this category are instances of venereal disease,[45] gunshot wounds,[46] and fetal death.[47] In other jurisdictions, in addition to these specified exceptions, the trial judge is granted broad authority not to apply the privilege when it would not serve the interests of justice.[48] This provision permits the trial court to recognize and balance exceptions based on the exigencies of a particular case.

§10.05   The Psychiatrist, Psychologist, and Psychotherapist-Patient Privileges

Although the physician-patient privilege has been much criticized as an insignificant factor in physician-patient relationships where physical problems are the subject of treatment and a significant factor in the exclusion of probative evidence at trial,[49] this same criticism has not generally been applied to the treatment of mental or emotional problems.[50] Because of the inherently sensitive and embarrassing nature of mental and emotional problems and the information that must be disclosed if treatment is to be effective, it is thought that a privilege is particularly appropriate for treatment of these types of problems. This reasoning has led to the adoption of specialized psychiatrist, psychologist and psychotherapist–patient privileges. The Federal Rules of Evidence, for example, as originally proposed did not contain a

---

[44] People v Florendo, 95 Ill 2d 155, 447 NE2d 282 (1983); Perry v Fiumano, 61 AD2d 512, 403 NYS2d 57 (1978).

[45] State v Efrid, 309 NC 802, 309 SE2d 228 (1983).

[46] *In re* Grand Jury Investigation, 59 NY2d 130, 450 NE2d 678, 463 NYS2d 758, (1983).

[47] Schulman v New York City Health & Hosp Corp, 44 AD2d 482, 355 NYS2d 781 (1974).

[48] *See, e.g.,* NC Gen Stat §8-53 (1981).

[49] Chafee, *Privileged Communications: Is Justice Served or Obstructed by Closing the Doctor's Mouth on the Witness Stand?,* 52 Yale LJ 607 (1943); Ladd, *A Modern Code of Evidence,* 27 Iowa L Rev 213 (1942).

[50] Guttmacher & Weihofen, *Privileged Communications Between Psychiatrist and Patient: Reflections on the Law of Privileged Communications,* 28 Ind LJ 32 (1952); Slovenko, *Psychiatry and a Second Look at the Medical Privilege,* 6 Wayne L Rev 175 (1960).

physician–patient privilege but did contain a psychotherapist-patient privilege.[51]

These specialized privilege statutes generally follow the same pattern as the physician-patient privilege statutes, but substitute a different sort of therapist who must be seen by the patient to trigger the privilege. Psychiatrist-patient privileges apply to care rendered by a psychiatrist. Nonpsychiatric physicians frequently provide counseling for the mental and emotional aspects of their patients' problems.[52] However, this care is not included within the scope of the specialized psychiatrist-patient privilege.[53] Only when the physician is a psychiatrist or devotes a substantial portion of practice to psychiatry will this privilege apply. Although some states, for example, California, recognize a psychiatrist-patient privilege in addition to a physician-patient privilege,[54] most states that recognize a psychiatrist-patient privilege do not recognize a general physician-patient privilege.[55]

Psychologist-patient privilege statutes, unlike psychiatrist–patient privilege statutes, do not overlap with physician-patient privilege statutes. They exist in states that do not recognize a physician-patient privilege[56] and also in states that do recognize a physician-patient privilege.[57] The psychologist-patient privileges require that the patient consult a licensed psychologist for treatment of a mental or emotional problem. Sometimes explicit[58] but at other times implicit is the requirement that the psychologist be a clinical psychologist rather than, for example, an industrial or educational psychologist.[59]

Psychotherapist-patient privileges generally combine a psychiatrist and psychologist-patient privilege; however, they are broader in some instances. While specialized psychiatrist-patient privileges include only treatment by a psychiatric physician, psychotherapist-patient privileges

---

[51] Prop Fed R Evid 504, 56 FRD 183, 242 (1972).

[52] Orleans, George, Houpt, & Brodie, *How Primary Care Physicians Treat Psychiatric Disorders: A National Survey of Family Practitioners*, 142 Am J Psychiatry 52 (1985).

[53] *See, e.g.*, Ala Code §34-36-2 (Supp 1984); Conn Gen Stat §52-146d (1983).

[54] Cal Evid Code §§990-1007, 1010-1026 (West 1966, Supp 1984).

[55] *See, e.g.*, Conn Gen Stat Ann §52-146(c) (West 1983); Fla Stat Ann §90.503 (West 1979); Md Cts & Jud Proc Code Ann §9-109 (1984).

[56] Ala Code §34-26-2 (Supp 1984); Conn Gen Stat Ann §52-146(c) (West Supp 1983).

[57] Ill Ann Stat ch 111, §5306 (Smith-Hurd 1978, Supp 1984-85); Mo Ann Stat §337.055 (Vernon Supp 1984).

[58] Conn Gen Stat Ann §52-146(c)(a) (West Supp 1983).

[59] *See* D. Louisell & C. Mueller, Federal Evidence §126, at 607 (1978).

may include the treatment of a mental or emotional problem by a nonpsychiatric physician.[60]

One question raised by the psychotherapist-patient privilege is whether to include a host of nonpsychiatric or psychological therapists who may nonetheless provide helpful psychotherapy.[61] This potential ambit includes marriage counselors, drug and alcohol counselors, psychiatric social workers, and various lay therapists. A more broadly drawn provision could also include friends and relatives who provide sage advice or a sympathetic shoulder.[62] Most psychotherapist-patient privileges do not include nonphysician or nonpsychologist therapists because of a fear either of the quality of therapy rendered by this other class of therapists or of excluding too much probative evidence. Some states, however, include some of these other therapists within the psychotherapist-patient privilege[63] or in special privileges for these other therapists.[64]

The requirements for recognition of a psychiatrist, psychologist, or psychotherapist-patient privilege are the same as for the physician-patient privilege. Someone seeking treatment must consult the appropriate type of therapist and communicate in a confidential fashion on a topic necessarily related to treatment. Similarly, the same pattern of waiver and exclusion or exception exists. There are certain problems, however, which are unique to these privileges.

As noted above, the identity of the patient is not generally protected from disclosure under the physician-patient privilege.[65] Because being identified as the patient of a psychiatrist or psychologist is, unlike the general physician-patient relationship, thought to be a source of embarrassment and stigma,[66] the argument is that these privileges

---

[60] Fla Stat Ann §90.503 (West 1979); NM R Evid 504 (1978); Prop Fed R Evid 504, 56 FRD 183, 242 (1973).

[61] Comment, *Underprivileged Communications: Extension of the Pyschotherapist-Patient Privilege*, 61 Cal L Rev 1050 (1973); Note, *The Social Worker–Client Relationship and Privileged Communications*, 1965 Wash ULQ 362.

[62] Krattemacker, *Testimonial Privileges in Federal Court - An Alternative to the Proposed Federal Rules of Evidence*, 62 Geo LJ 61 (1973).

[63] Nev Rev Stat §49.215.2 (1979) (includes psychiatric social worker in the definition of physician).

[64] Mich Comp Laws Ann §338.1043 (West 1976) (marriage counselors).

[65] *In re* Zuniga, 714 F2d 632, 640 (6th Cir 1982), *cert denied*, 104 S Ct 423 (1983). *But see Ex parte* Abell, 613 SW2d 255 (Tex 1981). *See* §10.02.

[66] *See* Shuman & Weiner, *The Privilege Study: An Empirical Examination of the Psychotherapist–Patient Privilege*, 60 NCL Rev 893 (1982).

should cloak the identity of the patient as well as the substance of the communications.[67] Most jurisdictions have yet to accept this argument.[68]

Group therapy, a form of treatment used by some psychiatrists, psychologists, and other psychotherapists,[69] presents another unique problem. Because the presence of someone other than the therapist and the patient is thought to imply an absence of confidentiality, most privilege statutes would not include within their protection communications between patient and therapist or patient and patient during group therapy. Based on the argument that group therapy is an effective and comparatively inexpensive form of therapy in which patients become each others' therapists, it has been argued that group therapy should be included within these privileges.[70] Acceptance of this argument exists but is limited,[71] perhaps because even if the privilege applies to the psychiatrist's or psychologist's testimony, the mouths of the other patients are not necessarily shut.

§10.06   The Attorney-Client Privilege and the Work Product Rule

Physician, psychiatrist, psychologist, and psychotherapist-patient privileges apply only when the relationship has as at least one of its purposes treatment of the patient or diagnosis in contemplation of treatment. Thus, when the purpose of the relationship is not treatment at all but exclusively preparation for expert testimony or assistance in preparation of the case, an attempt to cloak these communications under the physician, psychiatrist, psychologist, or psychotherapist-patient privilege will fail. However, in many instances, viewing these communications from the perspective of the attorney-client relationship, its privilege, and related rules may yield a different result.

§10.07   —Civil Proceedings

The attorney-client privilege, which was recognized at common law, has traditionally been thought to apply to confidential communications

---

[67] J. Weinstein & M. Berger, Weinstein's Evidence §504[05], at 504-23 (1981).

[68] *But see Ex parte* Abell, 613 SW2d 255 (Tex 1981).

[69] *See* **§3.09.**

[70] Cross, *Privileged Communications Between Participants in Group Psychotherapy,* 1970 Law & Soc Ord 191.

[71] State v Andrig, 342 NW2d 128 (Minn 1984).

between attorney and client on the subject of legal services. Communications between the attorney and the attorney's assistant or potential witness have not been included within the traditional contemplation of this privilege, yet have nonetheless been found deserving of protection. The work product doctrine, which received recognition in the United States Supreme Court's decision in *Hickman v Taylor* [72] and has been amplified by rules of procedure incorporating this concept,[73] has been an additional source of protection. *Hickman* limited discovery by the defendant of the written statements of prospective witnesses and memoranda of oral statements obtained by the plaintiff's attorney to restricted circumstances, to prevent disclosure of the attorney's thought processes and to limit disclosure of written statements of witnesses to circumstances of necessity.

One question not addressed in *Hickman v Taylor* was the discovery of expert witnesses retained by an adverse party in preparation for trial. This question has now been addressed in civil actions in the federal courts by the 1970 amendments to Rule 26(b)(4) of the Federal Rules of Civil Procedure, which is more cautious in its approach than many states.[74] The rule provides:

> (4) Trial Preparation: Experts. Discovery of facts known and opinions held by experts, otherwise discoverable under the provisions of subdivision (b)(1) of this rule and acquired or developed in anticipation of litigation or for trial, may be obtained as follows:
>
> (A) (i) A party may through interrogatories require any other party to identify each person whom the other party expects to call as an expert witness at trial, to state the subject matter on which the expert is expected to testify, and to state the substance of the facts and opinions to which the expert is expected to testify and a summary of the grounds for each opinion. (ii) Upon motion, the court may order further discovery by other means, subject to such restrictions as to scope and such provisions, pursuant to subdivision (b)(4)(C) of this rule, concerning fees and expenses as the court may deem appropriate.
>
> (B) A party may discover facts known or opinions held by an expert

---

[72] 329 US 497 (1947).

[73] Fed R Civ P 26(b)(3), (4).

[74] C. Wright & A. Miller, Federal Practice and Procedure §2029, at 241 (1970).

who has been retained or specially employed by another party in anticipation of litigation or preparation for trial and who is not expected to be called as a witness at trial, only as provided in Rule 35(b) or upon a showing of exceptional circumstances under which it is impracticable for the party seeking discovery to obtain facts or opinions on the same subject by other means.

(C) Unless manifest injustice would result, (i) the court shall require that the party seeking discovery pay the expert a reasonable fee for time spent in responding to discovery under subdivisions (b)(4)(A)(ii) and (b)(4)(B) of this rule; and (ii) with respect to discovery obtained under subdivision (b)(4)(A)(ii) of this rule the court may require, and with respect to discovery obtained under subdivision (b)(4)(B) of this rule the court shall require, the party seeking discovery to pay the other party a fair portion of the fees and expenses reasonably incurred by the latter party in obtaining facts and opinions from the expert.[75]

This rule addresses the discovery of two categories of experts: those expected to be called as a witness at trial and those utilized in case preparation and not expected to be called as a witness at trial.

Regarding those individuals whom the opposing party may call as a witness at trial, a chronology for discovery is prescribed. First, Rule 26(b)(4)(A)(i) permits a demand of the opposing party by interrogatory for the identity of each proposed expert expected to be called, the subject matter of the expert's testimony and the substance of the facts and opinions as to which the expert will testify, and a summary of the grounds for each opinion. Some courts have interpreted the identity requirement to include sufficient information to identify and locate the particular individual.[76] The duty to supplement responses in Rule 26(e) of the Federal Rules of Civil Procedure applies here, making insufficient the response at trial that there was a decision to use the expert only after responding to the interrogatory.[77] Failure to list an expert in answer to the interrogatory may result in a restriction of that expert's testimony.[78]

Following this interrogatory stage of discovery under Rule 26(b)(4)(A)(ii), a party may move for further discovery of this expert, typically by deposition; however, the court may also order the produc-

---

[75] Fed R Civ P 26(b)(4).

[76] Mann v Newport Tankers Corp, 96 FRD 31 (SDNY 1982).

[77] Fed R Civ P 26(e).

[78] Simonsen v Barlo Plastics Co, 551 F2d 469 (1st Cir 1977).

tion of documents.[79] The court's order permitting this additional discovery should provide for reasonable compensation of the expert by the party seeking discovery and may restrict the scope or sequence.[80] However, most courts require no showing of substantial need or good cause for this subsequent stage of discovery.[81]

Discovery under Rule 26(b)(4)(B) of experts retained by an opponent, but not intended to be called at trial, is severely limited. An opposing party may in most courts discover the names and addresses of these experts,[82] but the party may discover relevant facts and opinions in the possession of these individuals only if this information is not reasonably available elsewhere or as provided in Rule 35(b) of the Federal Rules of Civil Procedure. This limitation applies to formal discovery only. Thus, to the extent that the expert retained by a party is willing to talk informally with the opposing party, the discovery rules have no application. If the expert is consulted, but not retained or not expected to be called as a witness, no disclosure even of the expert's identity need occur.[83]

Rule 35(b) of the Federal Rules of Civil Procedure deals with a request for the report of a court-ordered examination by the examined party that triggers a corresponding obligation by the requesting party to turn over any reports of examinations performed before or after the court-ordered examination for the same condition. Thus, for example, even if the plaintiff did not intend to call as a witness a psychologist who examined the plaintiff and prepared a report to help prepare for trial, if the plaintiff is examined under Rule 35 by the defendant's psychiatrist and the plaintiff requests and receives a copy of that report, the plaintiff is obligated to deliver to the defendant, upon request, a copy of the psychologist's report. If the psychologist provides assistance to the plaintiff's attorney without conducting an examination of the plaintiff, for example, by suggesting topics for cross-examining the defendant's

---

[79] *In re* IBM Peripheral EDP Devices Antitrust Litig, 77 FRD 39 (ND Cal 1977).

[80] Fed R Civ P 26(b)(4)(C).

[81] Herbst v International Tel & Tel Corp, 65 FRD 528 (D Conn 1975); United States v John R Piquette Corp, 52 FRD 370 (ED Mich 1971). *But see* Wilson v Resnick, 51 FRD 510 (ED Pa 1970).

[82] Baki v BF Diamond Constr Co, 71 FRD 179 (D Md 1976). *But see* Ager v James C Stormant Hosp & Training School for Nurses, 622 F2d 496 (10th Cir 1980).

[83] Baki v BF Diamond Constr Co, 71 FRD 179 (D Md 1976).

expert, the reciprocity provisions of Rule 35(b) are not triggered.[84]

The other circumstance under which experts not intended to be called are discoverable is "upon a showing of exceptional circumstances under which it is impracticable for the party seeking discovery to obtain facts or opinions on the same subject by other means."[85] This provision applies to the situation in which expertise on the subject of the litigation is severely limited and one party has prevented the opponent from utilizing an expert by retaining that expert for trial preparation but not for testimony. For example, in *Dixon v Cappellini,* [86] an action against a deprogrammer by a member of an alleged church, psychiatric and psychological reports of treatment received by the plaintiff shortly after the deprogramming were found to be unique and to contain relevant information not otherwise obtainable by the defendants following institution of the lawsuit eight months later. The court questioned inclusion of the reports within Rule 26(b)(4) as trial preparation materials, but explained the treatment that should be given these reports if governed by Rule 26(b)(4).

Witnesses who may qualify as experts but whose knowledge was not gained in anticipation of the instant litigation are not addressed by Rule 26(b)(4).[87] For example, the defendant psychiatrist or psychologist in an action for malpractice may be sent interrogatories or be subjected to depositions in the same manner as any other defendant.[88]

§10.08 —Criminal Proceedings

Most courts recognize that communications between the defendant in a criminal proceeding and a psychiatrist or psychologist not treating the defendant but retained to assist in preparation for trial should be privileged, if at all, under the attorney-client privilege and not a medical privilege. The extension of the attorney-client privilege in criminal cases to communications between a defendant and a psychiatrist or psychologist retained to assist in case preparation is governed largely by case law. Frequently, these cases involve a psychiatrist or psychologist consulted by the defense on the viability of an insanity defense, who

---

[84] Nemetz v Aye, 63 FRD 66 (WD Pa 1974).

[85] Fed R Civ P 26(b)(4)(B).

[86] 88 FRD 1 (MD Pa 1980).

[87] Rodriguez v Hrinda, 56 FRD 11 (WD Pa 1972).

[88] Keith v Van Dorn Plastic Mach Co, 86 FRD 458 (ED Pa 1980); Rodriguez v Hrinda, 56 FRD 11 (WD Pa 1972).

renders an opinion unfavorable to the defendant which the prosecution discovers and seeks to introduce into evidence.

Most courts have had little problem concluding that in criminal cases, the attorney-client privilege extends to communications made to a psychiatrist or psychologist retained to assist in preparation of the case.[89] The difficulty arises in determining whether, by raising the insanity defense, the privilege is impliedly waived as to the nontestifying psychiatrist or psychologist who rendered the unfavorable opinion.

The majority of courts addressing this problem reject the notion that raising the insanity defense waives the attorney-client privilege as to the retained nontestifying expert.[90] The rationale for this approach is that recognizing a waiver under these circumstances would chill the defendant's willingness to confide in these experts and thereby restrict the attorney's ability to prepare the case for trial and investigate viable defenses. Thus, in the majority of American jurisdictions, the defense may prevent compelled judicial disclosure of unfavorable pretrial psychiatric and psychological examinations prepared at the request of defense counsel.

The minority rule rests on the conclusion that raising the insanity defense is inconsistent with the retention of confidentiality in all relevant psychiatrist or psychologist–patient communications sought to be protected by either a medical privilege[91] or the attorney-client privilege,[92] and results in a waiver of any applicable privilege. Under this rule, a privilege generally applies until the insanity defense is raised; thus, a decision not to raise this or related defenses prevents the prosecution from discovering pretrial psychiatric or psychological examinations prepared at the request of defense counsel. Of course, even under the majority rule, once the defendant calls a psychiatrist or psychologist to the witness stand, regardless of the previous attorney-client or medical privilege, a waiver occurs as to communications with that psychiatrist or psychologist.[93]

---

[89] United States v Alvarez, 519 F2d 1036 (3d Cir 1975), People v Lines, 13 Cal 2d 500, 531 P2d 793, 119 Cal Rptr 225 (1975).

[90] United States v Alvarez, 519 F2d 1036 (3d Cir 1979); People v Lines, 13 Cal 3d 500, 531 P2d 793, 119 Cal Rptr 225 (1975); State v Pratt, 284 Md 516, 398 A2d 421 (1979); People v Hilliker, 29 Mich App 543, 185 NW2d 831 (1971); State v Kociolek, 23 NJ 400, 129 A2d 417 (1957).

[91] People v Al-Kanani, 33 NY2d 260, 307 NE2d 43, 351 NYS2d 969 (1973).

[92] State v Carter, 641 SW2d 54 (Mo 1982); People v Edny, 39 NY2d 620, 350 NE2d 400 (1976).

[93] Ballew v State, 640 SW2d 237 (Tex Crim App 1982).

§10.09   Constitutional Support for the Psychotherapist-Patient Privilege

In the absence of a statutory privilege protecting confidential communications between a psychiatrist or psychologist and patient, an argument may be advanced in favor of a constitutional right to privacy that cloaks confidential psychotherapist-patient communications. This argument relies on such Supreme Court decisions as *Roe v Wade* [94] and *Griswold v Connecticut* [95] to support the conclusion that a constitutional zone of privacy may be found relying upon various provisions in the Bill of Rights sufficient to protect against compelled disclosure of intimate personal details and to protect autonomy in personal decision making, specifically, the decision to consult a psychotherapist.[96]

The Supreme Court has not yet clearly accepted or rejected this contention. In *Whalen v Roe,* [97] a challenge to a New York computerized storage scheme for certain prescriptions, the Court concluded only that the New York scheme did not, "on its face, pose a sufficiently grievous threat to either interest to establish a constitutional violation."[98] Whether this conclusion should be read to support an implicit recognition of a zone of privacy cloaking physician-patient relations generally has yet to be clarified. There are, however, a number of lower federal court and state court decisions before and after *Whalen* that address this issue.

The decisions can be grouped into three categories. The first category includes cases that reject the existence of a constitutional right of privacy cloaking psychotherapist-patient relationships; the second category includes cases that recognize the existence of the right, but find it should not apply in the instant case; and the third category includes cases that recognize the existence of the right and find it should apply in the instant case.

The rejection of a constitutional right of privacy cloaking psychiatrist-patient relationships is illustrated by *Felber v Foote,* [99] a challenge by a psychiatrist to a Connecticut statutory scheme requiring disclosure of names and other information about drug-dependent people to the state commissioner of health. The federal district court summarily rejected this challenge with the admonition that there is no general constitution-

---

[94] 410 US 113 (1973).

[95] 381 US 479 (1965).

[96] Lora v Board of Educ, 74 FRD 565, 570 (EDNY 1977).

[97] 429 US 589 (1977).

[98] *Id* 600.

[99] 321 F Supp 85 (D Conn 1970).

al right of privacy and that specific recognitions of this right have not included the physician-patient relationship. It is significant that this case was decided before *Roe v Wade,* [100] which extended the right of privacy to a particular physician-patient relationship, that of a pregnant woman and her physician, and *Whalen v Roe.* [101]

The cases recognizing a constitutional right of privacy cloaking the psychotherapist-patient relationship are subsequent to *Roe v Wade,* have involved a patient who entered therapy prior to the litigation, and have not involved a plaintiff-patient. *In re B,* [102] for example, had to do with an attempt to compel disclosure, regarding treatment of a juvenile's mother some years earlier, in the dispositional phase of a delinquency proceeding. Relying on the state and federal constitutions, the Supreme Court of Pennsylvania concluded that a right of privacy existed as to these past treatments, but the same protection would not apply to current voluntary evaluation by a court-appointed psychiatrist.

Hawaii Psychiatric Society v Anyoshu [103] involved an attempt to enjoin an investigation of fraud in the Hawaii Medicaid program that entailed a search of the records of a clinical psychologist. The district court held that a constitutional right of privacy cloaks the psychotherapist-patient relationship and that, in the absence of a compelling state interest, judicially compelled disclosure should not occur. Because nothing had yet suggested that this psychologist had engaged in fraud or that a search of this sort of record was necessary to prevent fraud on a programmatic level, the court enjoined the record search.

In the next category of cases, the court recognized the existence of a right of privacy but concluded that its protections had been waived by the patient or that a compelling state interest in favor of disclosure existed. *In re Lifshultz* [104] was the case of a patient who initiated a personal injury action and who had received psychiatric care 10 years earlier. The Supreme Court of California recognized the existence of a right of privacy for psychotherapist-patient relationships, but found that this protection was waived by the patient as to those conditions disclosed in bringing the action.

Another illustration of this position is found in *Lora v Board of*

---

[100] 410 US 113 (1973).

[101] 429 US 589 (1977).

[102] 394 A2d 419 (Pa 1978).

[103] 481 F Supp 1028 (D Hawaii 1979).

[104] 2 Cal 3d 415, 467 P2d 557, 85 Cal Rptr 829 (1970). *See also* Ceaser v Mountanos, 542 F2d 1064 (9th Cir 1976).

Education, [105] a suit challenging the placement of emotionally hand-icapped children. There, the plaintiffs sought to have their experts inspect randomly selected student diagnostic and referral files without student names or identifying information. In response to the school board's assertion of these students' right to privacy, the court recognized the existence of the right but found that the need for the information in the litigation to protect the interest of this class of students, and the protection against disclosure of the identity of individual students, justified limited disclosure.

§10.10   Federal Program Limitations

The federal government provides services and funding for a number of programs designed to treat mental or emotional disorders. Specific limitations on the disclosure of confidences made within treatment programs operated or funded by the federal government apply to drug[106] and alcohol treatment programs.[107] These limitations, although set forth in separate sections, create identical limitations. The drug treatment statute, representative of both, provides:

§290ee-3. Confidentiality of patient records
(a) Disclosure authorization
Records of the identity, diagnosis, prognosis, or treatment of any patient which are maintained in connection with the performance of any drug abuse prevention function conducted, regulated, or directly or indirectly assisted by any department or agency of the United States shall, except as provided in subsection (e) of this section, be confidential and be disclosed only for the purposes and under the circumstances expressly authorized under subsection (b) of this section.
(b) Purposes and circumstances of disclosure affecting consenting patient and patient regardless of consent
(1)   The content of any record referred to in subsection (a) of this section may be disclosed in accordance with the prior written consent of the patient with respect to whom such record is maintained, but only to such extent, under such circumstances and for such purposes as may be allowed under regulations prescribed pursuant to subsection (g) of this section.

---

[105] 74 FRD 565 (EDNY 1977).
[106] 42 USC §290ee-3.
[107] *Id* §290dd-3.

Whether or not the patient, with respect to whom any given record referred to in subsection (a) of this section is maintained, gives his written consent, the content of such record may be disclosed as follows:

(A)   To medical personnel to the extent necessary to meet a bona fide medical emergency.

(B)   To qualified personnel for the purpose of conducting scientific research, management audits, financial audits, or program evaluation, but such personnel may not identify, directly or indirectly, any individual patient in any report of such research, audit, or evaluation, or otherwise disclose patient identities in any manner.

(C)   If authorized by an appropriate order of a court of competent jurisdiction granted after application showing good cause therefor. In assessing good cause the court shall weigh the public interest and the need for disclosure against the injury to the patient, to the physician-patient relationship, and to the treatment services. Upon the granting of such order, the court, in determining the extent to which any disclosure of all or any part of any record is necessary, shall impose appropriate safeguards against unauthorized disclosure.

(c) Prohibition against use of record in making criminal charges or investigation of patient

Except as authorized by a court order granted under subsection (b)(2)(C) of this section, no record referred to in subsection (a) of this section may be used to initiate or substantiate any criminal charges against a patient or to conduct any investigation of a patient.

(d) Continuing prohibition against disclosure irrespective of status as patient

The prohibitions of this section continue to apply to records concerning any individual who has been a patient, irrespective of whether or when he ceases to be a patient.

(e) Armed Forces and Veterans' Administration: interchange of records

The prohibitions of this section do not apply to any interchange of records –

(1)   within the Armed Forces or within those components of the Veterans' Administration furnishing health care to veterans, or

(2)   between such components and the Armed Forces.

(f) Penalty for first and subsequent offenses

Any person who violates any provision of this section or any regulation issued pursuant to this section shall be fined not more than $500 in the case of a first offense, and not more than $5,000 in the case of each subsequent offense.

(g) Regulations; interagency consultations; definitions, safeguards, and procedures, including procedures and criteria for issuance and scope of orders

Except as provided in subsection (h) of this section, the Secretary, after consultation with the Administrator of Veterans' Affairs and the heads of other Federal departments and agencies substantially affected thereby, shall prescribe regulations to carry out the purposes of this section. These regulations may contain such definitions, and may provide for such safeguards and procedures, including procedures and criteria for the issuance and scope of orders under subsection (b)(2)(C) of this section, as in the judgment of the Secretary are necessary or proper to effectuate the purposes of this section, to prevent circumvention or evasion thereof, or to facilitate compliance therewith.[108]

Both sections operate much like a relational privilege to limit compelled judicial disclosure of records of a patient's identity, diagnosis, prognosis, or treatment in a drug or alcohol program conducted, regulated, or assisted by the federal government. Two exceptions apply in the context of judicial disclosure: written consent by the patient and a court order based on a showing of good cause. The statute directs a court in gauging good cause to weigh the public interest in favor of disclosure against its consequence to this and other patients' treatment.

A number of decisions, particularly in the field of drug treatment, have addressed the court-ordered disclosure exception. Disclosure under this section should be extremely limited, and where other sources of similar evidence exist, disclosure should not occur.[109] When no other similar evidence is available and the public interest in the outcome is substantial, as, for example, in cases of child abuse or neglect, disclosure may be ordered.[110]

Frequently, this issue arises in prosecution for drug-related offenses when the government's case against a participant in the drug treatment

---

[108] *Id* §290ee-3.

[109] United States v Graham, 548 F2d 1302, 1314 (8th Cir 1977).

[110] *In re* Baby X, 97 Mich App 111, 293 NW2d 736 (1980).

program has been assisted by a fellow patient.[111] Although regulations have been promulgated formally prohibiting the employment or enrollment of undercover agents in these programs,[112] the problem continues. The cases seek to draw fine distinctions by concluding that the informant was not there to ferret out drug offenses[113] or that the statute limits disclosure of records but not an informant's testimony not based upon these records.[114]

---

[111] United States v Coffman, 567 F2d 960 (10th Cir 1977); Armenta v Superior Court, 61 Cal App 3d 584, 132 Cal Rptr 586 (1976); State v Keleher, 5 Kan App 2d 400, 617 P2d 1265 (1980).

[112] 42 CFR

§ 2.19 Undercover agents and informants—Rules.

(a) *Definitions.* As used in this section, § 2.19-1, and §§ 2.67 and 2.67-1,—

(1) The term "undercover agent" means a member of any Federal, State, or local law enforcement or investigative agency whose identity as such is concealed from either the patients or personnel of a program in which he enrolls or attempts to enroll.

(2) The term "informant" means a person who, at the request of a Federal, State, or local law enforcement or investigative agency or officer, carries on observation of one or more persons enrolled in or employed by a program in which he is enrolled or employed, for the purpose of reporting to such agency or officer information concerning such persons which he obtains as a result of such observation subsequent to such request.

(b) *General prohibition.* Except as otherwise provided in paragraph (c) of this section, or as specifically authorized by a court order granted under § 2.67 –

(1) No undercover agent or informant may be employed by or enrolled in any alcohol or drug abuse treatment program;

(2) No supervisor or other person having authority over an undercover agent may knowingly permit such agent to be or remain employed by or enrolled in any such program; and

(3) No law enforcement or investigative officer may recruit or retain an informant with respect to such a program.

(c) *Exceptions.* The enrollment of a law enforcement officer in a treatment program shall not be deemed a violation of this section if (1) such enrollment is solely for the purpose of enabling the officer to obtain treatment for his own abuse of alcohol or drugs, and (2) his status as a law enforcement officer is known to the program director.

[113] United States v Coffman, 567 F2d 960 (10th Cir 1977).

[114] Armenta v Superior Court, 61 Cal App 3d 584, 132 Cal Rptr 586 (1976); State v Keleher, 5 Kan App 2d 400, 617 P2d 1265 (1980); State v Bethea, 35 NC App 512, 241 SE2d 869 (1978).

§10.11 Suggested Reading

Books

E. Cleary, *McCormick on Evidence* (3d ed 1984).

S. Halleck, *Psychiatry and the Dilemma of Crime* (1967).

D. Louisell & C. Mueller, *Federal Evidence* (1978).

J. Weinstein & M. Berger, *Weinstein's Evidence* (1982).

C. Wright & A. Miller, *Federal Practice and Procedure* (1970).

Articles

Chafee, *Privileged Communications: Is Justice Served or Obstructed by Closing the Doctor's Mouth on the Witness Stand*, 52 Yale LJ 607 (1943).

Comment, *Underprivileged Communications: Extension of the Pyschotherapist-Patient Privilege*, 61 Cal L Rev 1050 (1973).

Cross, *Privileged Communications Between Participants in Group Psychotherapy*, 1970 Law & Soc Ord 191.

Guttmacher & Weihofen, *Privileged Communications Between Psychiatrist and Patient: Reflections on the Law of Privileged Communications*, 28 Ind LJ 32 (1952).

Krattemacker, *Testimonial Privileges in Federal Court- An Alternative to the Proposed Federal Rules of Evidence*, 62 Geo LJ 61 (1973).

Ladd, *A Modern Code of Evidence*, 27 Iowa L Rev 213 (1942).

Note, *The Social Worker-Client Relationship and Privileged Communications*, 1965 Wash ULQ 362.

Orleans, George, Houpt, & Brodie, *How Primary Care Physicians Treat Psychiatric Disorders: A National Survey of Family Practitioners*, 142 Am J Psychiatry 52 (1985).

American Medical Assn, *The Principles of Medical Ethics*, 24 JAMA 2187 (1981).

American Psychological Assn, *Principle 5, Ethical Standards of Psychologists*, 36 Am Psychologist 633 (1981).

American Psychological Assn, *Report of the Task Force on the Role of Psychology in the Criminal Justice System*, 33 Am Psychologist 1099 (1978).

Shuman & Weiner, *The Privilege Study: An Empirical Examination of the Psychotherapist-Patient Privilege*, 60 NC L Rev 893 (1982).

Slovenko, *Psychiatry and a Second Look at the Medical Privilege*, 6 Wayne L Rev 175 (1960).

Cases

Abell, Ex parte, 613 SW2d 255 (Tex 1981).

Ager v James C Stormant Hosp & Training School for Nurses, 622 F2d 496 (10th Cir 1980).

Allred v State, 554 P2d 411 (Alaska 1976).

Alvarez, In re, 342 So 2d 492 (Fla 1977).

Armenta v Superior Court, 61 Cal App 3d 584, 132 Cal Rptr 586 (1976).

B, In re, 482 Pa 471, 394 A2d 419 (Pa 1978).

Baby X, In re, 97 Mich App 111, 293 NW2d 736 (1980).

Baki v BF Diamond Construction Co, 71 FRD 179 (D Md 1976).

Ballew v State, 640 SW2d 237 (Tex Crim App 1982).

Ceaser v Mountanos, 542 F2d 1064 (9th Cir 1976).

Courtney S, In re, 130 Cal App 3d 567, 181 Cal Rptr 843 (1982).

Dixon v Cappellini, 88 FRD 1 (MD Pa 1980).

Doe v Roe, 93 Misc 2d 201, 400 NYS2d 668 (1977).

Duchess of Kingston's Case, 20 How St Trials 355 (1776).

Estelle v Smith, 451 US 454 (1981).

Eureka-Maryland Assurance Co v Gray, 121 F2d 104 (DC Cir 1941).

Felber v Foote, 321 F Supp 85 (D Conn 1970).

Frederick v Federal Life Insurance Co, 57 P2d 235 (1935).

Gaynier v Johnson, 673 SW2d 899 (Tex Civ App 1984).

Grand Jury Investigation of Onondaga Co, In re, 59 NY2d 130, 450 NE2d 678, 463 NYS2d 758 (1983).

Grey v Los Angeles Superior Court, 62 Cal App 3d 698, 133 Cal Rptr 318 (1976).

Griswold v Connecticut, 381 US 479 (1965).

Grosslight v Superior Court, 72 Cal App 2d 50, 140 Cal Rptr 228 (1977).

Hawaii Psychiatric Society v Anyoshu, 481 F Supp 1028 (D Hawaii 1070).

Herbst v International Telephone & Telegraph Corp, 65 FRD 528 (D Conn 1975).

Hickman v Taylor, 329 US 497 (1947).

IBM Peripheral EDP Devices Antitrust Litigation, In re, 77 FRD 39 (ND Cal 1977).

Jones v State, 610 SW2d 535 (Tex Civ App 1980) (writ refd nre).

Keith v Van Dorn Plastic Machinery Co, 86 FRD 458 (ED Pa 1980).

Kelly v Allegan County Circuit Judge, 382 Mich 425, 169 NW2d 916 (1969).

Leach v Millers Life Insurance Co, 400 F2d 179 (5th Cir 1968).

Lifshultz, In re, 467 P2d 557, 85 Cal Rptr 829 (1970).

Lora v Board of Education, 74 FRD 565 (EDNY 1977).

Mann v Newport Tankers Corp, 96 FRD 31 (SDNY 1982).

McCormick v Caterpillar Tractor Co, 85 Ill 2d 352, 423 NE2d 876 (1981).

Nemetz v Aye, 63 FRD 66 (WD Pa 1974).

Ostrowski v Mockridge, 242 Minn 265, 65 NW2d 185 (1954).

Pebsworth, In re, 705 F2d 261 (7th Cir 1983).

People v Al-Kanani, 33 NY2d 260, 307 NE2d 43, 351 NYS2d 969 (1973).

People v Arcega, 32 Cal 3d 504, 651 P2d 338, 186 Cal Rptr 94 (1982).

People v Edny, 39 NY2d 620, 350 NE2d 400, 385 NYS2d 23 (1976).

People v Florendo, 95 Ill 2d 155, 447 NE2d 282 (1983).

People v Hilliker, 29 Mich App 543, 185 NW2d 831 (1971).

People v Lines, 13 Cal 2d 500, 531 P2d 793, 119 Cal Rptr 225 (1975).

People v Smith, 59 NY2d 156, 451 NE2d 157, 464 NYS2d 399 (1983).

People v Stritzinger, 34 Cal 3d 505, 668 P2d 738, 194 Cal Rptr 431 (1983).

Perry v Fiumano, 61 AD2d 512, 403 NYS2d 57 (1978).

Roberts v Superior Court, 9 Cal 3d 330, 508 P2d 309, 107 Cal Rptr 309 (1973).

Rudnick v Superior Court, 11 Cal 3d 924, 523 P2d 643, 114 Cal Rptr 603 (1974).

Rodriguez v Hrinda, 56 FRD 11 (WD Pa 1972).

Roe v Wade, 410 US 113 (1973).

Salas v State, 592 SW2d 653 (Tex Civ App 1979) (no writ).

San Francisco v Superior Court, 37 Cal 2d 227, 231 P2d 26 (1951).

Schulman v New York Health & Hosp Corp, 44 AD2d 482, 35 NYS2d 781 (1974).

Simonsen v Barlo Plastics Co, 551 F2d 469 (1st Cir 1977).

State ex rel Floyd v Court of Common Pleas, 55 Ohio St 2d 27, 377 NE2d 794 (1978).

State ex rel Holman v Dayton Press, 11 Ohio St 3d 66, 463 NE2d 1243 (1984).

State v Andrig, 342 NW2d 128 (Minn 1984).

State v Bethea, 35 NC App 512, 241 SE2d 869 (1978).

State v Carter, 641 SW2d 54 (Mo 1982).

State v Cole, 295 NW2d 29 (Iowa 1980).

State v Efrid, 309 NC 802, 309 SE2d 228 (1983).

State v Jenkins, 80 Wis 2d 411, 259 NW2d 109 (1977).

State v Keleher, 5 Kan App 2d 400, 617 P2d 1265 (1980).

State v Kociolek, 23 NJ 400, 129 A2d 417 (1957).

State v Olsen, 271 Or 369, 532 P2d 230 (1975).

State v Pratt, 284 Md 516, 398 A2d 421 (1979).

State v Scott, 491 SW2d 514 (Mo 1973).

State v Soney, 177 NJ Super 47, 424 A2d 1182 (1980).

State v Sweet, 142 Vt 241, 453 A2d 1131 (1982).

State v White, 169 Conn 223, 363 A2d 143, *cert denied*, 423 US 1025 (1975).

United States v Alvarez, 519 F2d 1036 (3d Cir 1975).

United States v Coffman, 567 F2d 960 (10th Cir 1977).

United States v Graham, 548 F2d 1302 (8th Cir 1977).

United States v John R Piquette Corp, 52 FRD 370 (ED Mich 1971).

United States v Radetsky, 535 F2d 556 (10th Cir), *cert denied*, 429 US 820 (1976).

Whalen v Roe, 429 US 589 (1977).

Wilson v Resnick, 51 FRD 510 (ED Pa 1970).

Zuniga, In re, 714 F2d 632 (6th Cir), *cert denied*, 104 S Ct 426 (1983).

Statutes and Rules

Fed R Civ P 26.

Fed R Civ P 35.

Prop Fed R Evid 504, 56 FRD 183, 242 (1972).

42 USC §§290dd-3, 290ee-3.

Ala Code §34-26-2 (Supp 1984).

Cal Bus and Prof Code §2263 (West Supp 1984).

Cal Evid Code §§990-1007, 1010-1026 (West 1966 & Supp 1984).

Conn Gen Stat Ann §52-146(c) (West Supp 1983).

Conn Gen Stat §52-146d (1983).

Fla Stat Ann §90.503 (West 1979).

Ill Ann Stat ch 111, §5306 (Smith-Hurd 1978 & Supp 1984-85).

Ill Rev Stat ch 51, §5.2 (1966).

Md Cts & Judic Proc Ann §9-109 (1984).

Mich Comp Laws Ann §338.1043 (West 1976).

Mo Ann Stat §337.055 (Vernon Supp 1984).

NC Gen Stat §8-53, 53.1 (1981).

NM R Evid 504 (1978).

Nev Rev Stat §49.215.2 (1979).

Tex R Evid 510.

Regulations

42 CFR §2.19.

§10.12 WESTLAW Search References

§10.01 *Introduction*
    sy(psychiatr! psycholog! /s patient /s privilege*)

§10.02 *The Physician-Patient Privilege—General Rule*
    di(physician-patient /s privilege* /s statut***)

§10.03 *—Waiver*
    410k219 /p physician-patient /s privilege*

§10.04 *—Exceptions*
    physician-patient /s privilege* /s exception

§10.05 *The Psychiatrist, Psychologist, and Psychotherapist—Patient Privileges*
    psychotherapist psychiatrist psychologist +1 patient /s privilege* /p statut***

§10.06 *The Attorney-Client Privilege and the Work Product Rule*
    psychotherap psychiatr! psycholog! /s record report examin! /p privilege* /p attorney-client work-product (preparation /5 case trial testimony)

§10.07 *—Civil Proceedings*
    discovery deposition interrogatory /p (expert +1 witness testimony) psychiatr! psycholog! psychotherap! /p preparation /5 case trial

§10.08 *—Criminal Proceedings*
    insan*** /p psychiatr! psycholog! psychotherap! /p (attorney-client /s privilege*) work-product (preparation /5 case trial)

§10.09 *Constitutional Support for the Psychotherapist-Patient Privilege*
    psychiatrist psychologist psychotherapist /s patient /p constitu-
    tion! /s privacy

§10.10 *Federal Program Limitations*
    confiden /p patient /p record report file /p federal government
    statut! /s treatment program

Part Three

Particular Applications of Psychiatric and Psychological Evidence

11 Criminal Proceedings: Pretrial

§11.01 Bail—The Legal Standard

The use of pretrial detention not merely to assure the accused's attendance at trial, but to prevent the commission of crimes by the accused pending trial, has been a subject of much recent concern.[1] Commission of crimes by defendants on bail is a major societal problem. From 10 to 15 per cent of all crime in major urban areas may be committed by defendants released on bail for other offenses.[2] Conversely, pretrial preventive detention, confinement of persons who have not yet been tried and convicted of an offense based upon a prediction

---

[1] M. Moore, S. Estrich, D. McGillis, & W. Spelman, Dangerous Offenders 118 (1984).
[2] Id 126.

that they might commit a crime in the future, raises the problems of the prediction of future dangerousness in yet another setting.[3]

A preliminary problem raised by the denial or revocation of bail based on the determination that the defendant poses a danger to society is whether the federal or state constitutions are violated by a legislative or judicial public safety exception to bail.[4] Although some states have rejected denial of bail for noncapital crimes for reasons unrelated to attendance at trial as a violation of constitutional bail provisions,[5] the trend is to the contrary. Arizona,[6] California,[7] Florida,[8] Michigan,[9] Nebraska,[10] Texas,[11] and Utah[12] have specifically amended their constitutions to permit the denial or revocation of bail in noncapital cases for reasons unrelated to attendance at trial. In *Schall v Martin* [13] the United States Supreme Court upheld the constitutionality of a New York statute which authorizes pretrial detention of a juvenile when "there is a serious risk that he may before the return date commit an act which if committed by an adult would constitute a crime."[14] And, finally, the Federal Comprehensive Crime Control Act of 1984 permits

---

[3] *See* §7.06.

[4] *See, e.g., In re* Humphrey, 601 P2d 103, 106-07 (Okla Crim App 1979).

[5] *In re* Underwood, 9 Cal 3d 345, 508 P2d 721, 107 Cal Rptr 401 (1973); *but see* Cal Const art 1, §12 (amended 1982); *In re* Humphrey, 601 P2d 103 (Okla Crim App 1979); State v Pray, 133 Vt 537, 346 A2d 227 (1975).

[6] Ariz Const art 2, §22.

[7] Cal Const art 1, §12. Beyond the amendment to the California constitution permitting the denial of bail for felonies involving violence based upon a finding by "clear and convincing evidence that there is a substantial likelihood that the person's release would result in great bodily harm to others," the Victims' Bill of Rights makes public safety a primary consideration in bail determinations. Art 1, §28. *In re* Nordin, 143 Cal App 3d 542, 192 Cal Rptr 38 (1983).

[8] Fla Const art 1, §14 permits pretrial detention "[i]f no conditions of release can reasonably protect the community from risk of physical harm to persons. . . ."

[9] Mich Const art 1, §15.

[10] Tex Const art 1, §§11, 11a.

[11] Neb Const art 1, §9.

[12] Utah Const art 1, §8.

[13] 104 S Ct 2403 (1984). *See also* Atkins v Michigan, 644 F2d 543, 549 (6th Cir), *cert denied*, 452 US 964 (1981), authorizing pretrial detention based upon the defendant's dangerousness.

[14] NY Fam Ct Act §320.5(3)(b) (Consol 1984).

the denial of bail for a person who "will endanger the community."[15] Thus, trial courts will increasingly face the problem of predicting future criminal behavior and risks to the safety of the community prior to trial in bail applications.

§11.02   —The Role of the Expert

As trial courts are called on to make predictions of pretrial criminal conduct, it is likely, as in questions of sentencing for a capital offense[16] and civil commitment,[17] that psychiatrists and psychologists will be called on to provide prediction testimony. This testimony may be offered by the prosecution to make its case for bail denial, by the defense to respond to the prosecution psychiatrists or psychologists opposing bail, or by the defense to respond to rebuttable statutory presumptions of dangerousness recognized in case of commission of certain felonies while on bail.[18] These presumptions ease the case for the prosecution by avoiding the need to rely on *expert* prediction testimony that has been the subject of substantial criticism.[19] Instead, the necessity for use of this testimony to rebut the presumption is shifted to the defense, which is more accustomed to seeking its exclusion in capital sentencing or civil commitment determinations.

Although these presumptions appear to avoid prediction problems, they raise those same problems covered by a different veneer. These presumptions of dangerousness are actuarial predictions based on unarticulated probabilities.[20] For example, a presumption that a defendant on bail charged with the commission of a subsequent offense will be dangerous is based on a specific probability that one who is charged with the commission of a particular class of crime will commit another, bolstered by allegations of the commission of a subsequent offense. These specific probabilities and the research that supports them are not divulged. There is no reason to expect that these predictions are exempt from the problems that plague predictions in other settings. Moreover, they avoid individual decision making, since a presumption based on any probability less than 100 per cent

---

[15] 38 USC §3142(b)(c). *See* Serr, *The Federal Bail Reform Act of 1984: The First Wave of Case Law,* 39 Ark L Rev 169 (1985).

[16] *See* **§12.07.**

[17] *See* **§16.01.**

[18] 38 USC §3142(e), (f).

[19] *See* **§7.07.**

[20] M. Moore, S. Estrich, D. McGillis, & W. Spelman, Dangerous Offenders 37 (1984).

erroneously labels some individuals as dangerous who are not.[21] Psychiatrists and psychologists might be used to reveal on an aggregate basis the problems with this sort of probabilistic analysis of behavior and its degree of error.[22] Psychiatrists and psychologists may also provide reasons why this probabilistic analysis may not be appropriate in the case of a particular defendant.

The defendant's use of psychiatric or psychological testimony on this question presupposes access to this sort of evidence. When the defendant lacks the financial ability to retain a psychiatrist or psychologist, the existence of the right to a court-appointed psychiatrist or psychologist to assist the defense is raised. The United States Supreme Court recognized in *Ake v Oklahoma*[23] that an indigent criminal defendant who has made an initial showing that his sanity at the time of the offense is likely to be a significant consideration at trial is entitled to a psychiatrist at state expense. Although the case expressly deals only with expert assistance at trial, its reasoning may support a broader application. The *Ake* decision rests in large measure on "the belief that justice cannot be equal where, simply as a result of his poverty, a defendant is denied the opportunity to participate meaningfully in a judicial proceeding in which his liberty is at stake."[24] If the defendant's interest in pretrial release is a cognizable liberty interest and a meaningful opportunity to participate in the bail hearing requires a psychiatrist or psychologist to respond to the state's psychiatrist's prediction or a presumption based upon an actuarial prediction, a cogent argument for court-appointed or compensated defense psychiatrists at bail hearings exists. The Court's own statements strongly support this conclusion:

---

[21] Assume that one person out of a thousand will kill. Assume also that an exceptionally accurate test is created which differentiates with ninety-five percent effectiveness those who will kill from those who will not. If 100,000 people were tested, out of the 100 who would kill, 95 would be isolated. Unfortunately, out of the 99,900 who would not kill, 4,995 people would also be isolated as potential killers. In these circumstances, it is clear that we could not justify incarcerating all 5,000 people. If, in the criminal law, it is better that ten guilty men go free than that one innocent man suffer, how can we say in the civil commitment area that it is better that fifty-four harmless people be incarcerated lest one dangerous man be free?

Livermore, Malmquist, & Meehl, *On the Justifications for Civil Commitment*, 117 U Pa L Rev 75, 84 (1968).

[22] Dangerous Offenders, *supra* note 20, at 131.

[23] 105 S Ct 1087 (1985).

[24] *Id* 1093.

This Court has upheld the practice in many States of placing before the jury psychiatric testimony on the question of future dangerousness, see *Barefoot v. Estelle*, 463 U.S. 800, 896-905 (1983), at least where the defendant has had access to an expert of his own, *id.*, at 899, n. 5. In so holding, the Court relied, in part, on the assumption that the factfinder would have before it both the views of the prosecutor's psychiatrists and the "opposing views of the defendant's doctors" and would therefore be competent to "uncover, recognize, and take due account of . . . shortcomings" in predictions on this point. *Id.*, at 899. Without a psychiatrist's assistance, the defendant cannot offer a well-informed expert's opposing view, and thereby loses a significant opportunity to raise in the jurors' minds questions about the State's proof of an aggravating factor. In such a circumstance, where the consequence of error is so great, the relevance of responsive psychiatric testimony so evident, and the burden on the State so slim, due process requires access to a psychiatric examination on relevant issues, to the testimony of the psychiatrist, and to assistance in preparation at the sentencing phase.[25]

§11.03   —Basis

At this preliminary stage of the proceedings the available information on which a psychiatrist or psychologist might base a prediction of future criminal conduct is limited. The crime charged will not have been proven and the presentation of all the available evidence of the accused's guilt must await trial. The initial bail hearing occurs shortly after arrest, further limiting gathering of background information on the accused. Thus, any prediction decision is likely to be based, in large measure, on the yet unproven allegations which the psychiatrist or psychologist is unlikely to be able to verify or on actuarial data—age, sex, offense alleged, length of time in the community, employment, and criminal record.[26] Given the inherent limitations on predictions of future dangerousness and the importance of a clinical examination and a complete history in cases where something close to an acceptable

---

[25] *Id* 1097.

[26] See Center for Government Research, *Final Report: An Empirical Study and Policy Examination of the Future of Pretrial Release Services in New York* (1983), in which the number of arrests for violent felonies and nonfelonies within the preceding five years, longevity of current employment, and education were found to correlate with rearrest while on bail.

clinical prediction of dangerousness might be ventured,[27] the setting of these decisions renders them inherently suspect. Actuarial predictions, however, are not similarly affected, as much of the information on which they rely is easily obtained and verified.

§11.04 —Limitations

There is authority for the proposition that a federal court must make a bail decision on the basis of the information available at the bail hearing and is not authorized to order a psychiatric examination on the issue of dangerousness.[28] However, in jurisdictions permitting court-ordered examinations on this issue, the privilege against self-incrimination[29] limits the use of the information gained in the examination. The privilege against self-incrimination applies to information used at an inculpatory stage of the proceedings. Thus, a defendant apparently does not enjoy a Fifth Amendment right to refuse to discuss questions relating to bail with the state's psychiatrists or psychologists because bail does not entail a determination of culpability.[30] However, unless the defendant is properly warned of possible use of this evidence at an inculpatory stage of the proceedings and given an opportunity to refuse to speak, information learned by these psychiatrists or psychologists may not be used at the guilt or sentencing phase of the proceeding.[31]

The physician–patient privilege, and its related psychiatrist, psychologist, and psychotherapist versions,[32] does not prevent a court-appointed psychiatrist or psychologist from testifying about the results of an interview with the defendant as the purpose of the examination is a report to the court and not therapy.[33] It would, however, limit compelled testimony of a psychiatrist or psychologist who had treated the defendant.[34] Except for those exceptions generally applicable in criminal cases,[35] no specific exceptions apply to bail proceedings.

The rules of evidence are generally inapplicable in bail application

---

[27] *See* **§7.06.**

[28] United States v Martin-Trigona, 767 F2d 35 (2d Cir 1985).

[29] US Const amend V.

[30] *Cf* Estelle v Smith, 451 US 454 (1981).

[31] *Id.*

[32] *See* **ch 10.**

[33] *See* **§10.04.**

[34] *See* **§10.02.**

[35] People v Arcega, 32 Cal 3d 504, 651 P2d 338, 186 Cal Rptr 94 (1982); State v Soney, 177 NJ Super 47, 424 A2d 1182 (1980).

proceedings;[36] thus, the hearsay rule is no bar to the use of court information by a psychiatrist or psychologist in these proceedings. Although privilege rules are also a part of the rules of evidence, their purpose is not, like the hearsay rule, to protect the jury form unreliable evidence. Thus, even though the other rules of evidence are not applicable, the rules on privilege still apply.[37]

§11.05 —Testimony

The use of psychiatric or psychological testimony in bail proceedings is, for the present, rarer than its use regarding other issues in the criminal justice system such as competence to stand trial, the insanity defense, and capital sentencing. Nonetheless, its use in particular cases may be significant in convincing the court of the dangerousness, pending trial, of the defendant. As with other uses of psychiatric and psychological testimony in the criminal justice system, there are risks posed by unexplained conclusory testimony embracing the ultimate issue before the court and by psychiatric jargon. It is as important, if not more important in this setting, that these witnesses explain their education, training, or experience in predictions of dangerousness, the basis for an opinion in the particular case, the methodology used to predict, and the limits of that methodology, using language comprehensible to laypersons.

§11.06 Competence to Stand Trial—The Legal Standard

The guarantees of the Sixth Amendment of the United States Constitution that a criminal defendant is entitled to confront opposing witnesses and have the assistance of counsel[38] are of little benefit if the defendant's mental condition does not permit recognition of the witnesses or communication with counsel. The defendant's opportunity

---

36 *See, e.g.,* Fed R Evid 1101(d)(3).

37 *See, e.g.,* Fed R Evid 1101(c).

38 In all criminal prosecutions, the accused shall enjoy the right to a speedy and public trial, by an impartial jury of the State and district wherein the crime shall have been committed, which district shall have been previously ascertained by law, and to be informed of the nature and cause of the accusation; to be confronted with the witnesses against him; to have compulsory process for obtaining witnesses in his favor, and to have the Assistance of Counsel for his defence.

US Const amend VI.

to exercise this right to meaningful participation in a defense turns, in part, on the defendant's mental condition. Thus, the basic concepts of procedural fairness in criminal proceedings explicit in the Sixth Amendment and implicit in the due process clause frequently require an evaluation of the defendant's competence to stand trial.[39]

The test articulated by the United States Supreme Court in *Dusky v United States* [40] to guide courts in the determination of the defendant's competence to stand trial asks whether the defendant "has sufficient present ability to consult with his lawyer with a reasonable degree of rational understanding—and whether he has a rational as well as factual understanding of the proceedings against him."[41] This test, while embellished in some states,[42] is the same one generally followed by most states.[43]

The test involves two interrelated components—the abilities to consult with counsel and to understand the proceedings. Effective consultation with counsel requires the capacity to work on a cooperative basis with counsel, to communicate relevant information to counsel, to understand counsel's communications, to evaluate counsel's advice, and to make decisions regarding the exercise of legal rights.[44] A rational and factual understanding of the proceedings requires the capacity to reach an understanding of the specific charges, the procedures that will be used to resolve those charges, the roles of the principal participants in the trial—judge, jury, prosecutor, defender, and witnesses—and the consequences of a conviction.[45]

Competence to stand trial under this test requires a functional analysis of the defendant's capacities. It is not given to resolution through a simplistic resort to diagnostic categories. Thus, persons diagnosed as psychotic have nonetheless been found competent to stand trial.[46]

The question of the defendant's competence to stand trial may be raised by motion of the defense counsel, the prosecutor, or sua sponte

---

[39] Drope v Missouri, 420 US 162 (1975).

[40] 362 US 402 (1960).

[41] *Id.*

[42] *See, e.g.,* Ill Ann Stat ch 38, §104-16(b) (Smith-Hurd 1980).

[43] R. Reisner, Law and the Mental Health System 541 (1985).

[44] Martin v Estelle, 546 F2d 177, 180 (5th Cir 1977).

[45] *Id.*

[46] Feguer v United States, 302 F2d 214 (8th Cir 1962); State v Stevens, 18 Kan 213, 336 P2d 447 (1959).

by the judge.[47] Defense counsel's interest in raising this question may be to protect the defendant's right to a fair trial, or, with less altruism, to protect counsel from a subsequent claim of ineffective assistance of counsel. Although some defense counsel have raised the question of competence to stand trial to obtain an opinion on the viability of an insanity defense, the Supreme Court's decision in *Ake v Oklahoma* [48] granting indigent defendants whose sanity is likely to be a significant issue at trial the right to access to an independent psychiatrist at state expense may limit the necessity for this practice.

The prosecutor's interest in raising the question of the defendant's competence to stand trial may result from an interest in protecting the defendant's right to a fair trial or protecting the record in the event of a conviction and appeal. Although a finding of incompetence to stand trial and commitment pending restoration to competence once had unlimited potential as a weapon allowing prosecutors to confine defendants for lengthy periods without proof of guilt, constitutional[49] and statutory[50] limits have been imposed on the period of confinement for incompetence to stand trial.

The conviction of an incompetent defendant violates due process.[51] An incompetent defendant, by virtue of that incompetence, lacks the capacity to waive the question of competence to stand trial. Therefore, when "the evidence raises a *'bona fide* doubt' as to the defendant's competence to stand trial, the judge on his own motion must . . . conduct a sanity hearing. . . ."[52] This requirement has been codified in the

---

[47] *See, e.g.,* 18 USC §4241(a):

Motion to determine competency of defendant.—At any time after the commencement of a prosecution for an offense and prior to the sentencing of the defendant, the defendant or the attorney for the Government may file a motion for a hearing to determine the mental competency of the defendant. The court shall grant the motion, or shall order such a hearing on its own motion, if there is reasonable cause to believe that the defendant may presently be suffering from a mental disease or defect rendering him mentally incompetent to the extent that he is unable to understand the nature and consequences of the proceedings against him or to assist properly in his defense.

[48] 105 S Ct 1087 (1985).

[49] Jackson v Indiana, 406 US 715 (1972).

[50] Ill Ann Stat ch 38, §104-16(d) (Smith-Hurd 1980) (1 year); Tex Code Crim Proc Ann art 46.02, §5(e) (Vernon 1979) (18 months).

[51] Bishop v United States, 350 US 961 (1956).

[52] Pate v Robinson, 383 US 375, 385 (1966).

federal courts to require a hearing on the court's own motion, or counsel's,

> if there is a reasonable cause to believe that the defendant may presently be suffering from a mental disease or defect rendering him mentally incompetent to the extent that he is unable to understand the nature and consequences of the proceedings against him or to assist properly in his defense.[53]

§11.07   —The Role of the Expert

Trial courts are generally authorized to order a psychiatric or psychological examination of the defendant on the issue of competence to stand trial and presentation of a report to the court.[54] Alternatively, counsel may present reports of privately performed psychiatric or psychological examinations regarding the defendant's competence to stand trial. Nonetheless, it has been argued that psychiatric or psychological evidence is particularly intrusive and unnecessary on the question of competence to stand trial and need not be received for courts to resolve this question. Testimony by defense counsel is admissible on this issue and defense counsel should have the experience to know what is required of a defendant to prepare and present a defense and is best situated, after consultation with the defendant, to determine whether this capacity is present. In clear cases, this observation may be correct; however, in marginal cases the expertise of a psychiatrist or psychologist to identify malingering, for example, may be necessary.[55] Minimally, the use of psychiatric or psychological evidence on this question protects the record. Moreover, it may assuage the judge that the issue is not raised to delay the trial.

Ideally, an expert reporting on the issue of competence to stand trial should address the existence of any mental disorder and its effect on the capacity of the defendant to perceive external events, remember them, and communicate with others about them. In addition, the expert should address the available treatments for any mental disorder from

---

[53] 18 USC §4241(a).

[54] 18 USC §4241. Although some of these statutes refer to psychiatric examiners, courts have, in some instances, expanded this category to include psychologists. People v Lewis, 75 Ill App 3d 560, 393 NE2d 1380 (1979).

[55] Of course, even the experts may be fooled, as Rudolf Hess's claims of amnesia during the Nuremberg Trials, verified by a battery of psychiatrists and subsequently admitted by Hess to be false, indicate. R. Slovenko, Psychiatry and Law 94-95 (1973).

which the defendant suffers, its likely effect on the defendant's capacity to remember and discuss relevant events, and the timetable within which these treatments might occur.

§11.08   —Basis

The weight that should be given a psychiatric or psychological opinion bearing on the defendant's competence to stand trial is a function of the information used in forming the opinion. The more complete the information, the greater the weight to be accorded any resulting opinion. The possible sources of information include the defendant and the defendant's family and friends, counsel, jail personnel, other psychiatrists or psychologists who have diagnosed or treated the defendant, physical or neurological examinations of the defendant, and the results of psychological or intelligence testing.

A number of instruments have been developed to assist examiners in reaching more accurate and formalized decisions on competence to stand trial.[56] One commonly used written competence examination, the Competency Screening Test,[57] is designed to identify defendants who require more thorough evaluations. It asks the defendant to complete 22 sentences. These sentences address the defendant's understanding of the proceedings and ability to consult with counsel by asking the defendant, for example: "When I go to court the lawyer will_____"; "When the evidence in George's case was presented to the jury _____"; and, "When the lawyer questioned his client in court, the client said_____."[58] The defendant's completion of these sentences is then compared with sample responses of a normal population, graded for appropriateness, and again compared to the scores of the normal population.

§11.09   —Limitations

The physician, psychiatrist, psychologist, and psychotherapist–patient privilege and the Fifth Amendment privilege against self-incrimination provide potential limitations on the bases for a psychiatric or psychological opinion on the question of competence to stand trial.

---

[56] T. Grisso, *Evaluating Competencies: Forensic Assessments and Instruments* 62-112 (1986).

[57] Lipsitt, Lelos, & McGarry, *Competency for Trial: A Screening Instrument,* 128 Am J Psychiatry 105 (1971).

[58] *Id* 106.

Limits imposed by the physician, psychiatrist, psychologist, or psycho-therapist–patient privilege turn on the nature of the therapist–patient relationship.[59] If the relationship is entered into exclusively pursuant to a court-ordered examination on the question of competence to stand trial, a privilege will not come into existence because the purpose of the relationship is not treatment and a public disclosure is contemplated.[60]

An attempt to compel testimony on the question of competence to stand trial of a psychiatrist or psychologist who has treated the defendant, in a jurisdiction that recognizes an applicable privilege, does raise privilege problems. If the defendant refuses to waive the privilege, and its application is not otherwise excepted, the testimony of the treating psychiatrist or psychologist typically may not be compelled.[61] In some jurisdictions a general exception to the privilege exists for criminal proceedings.[62] Specific exceptions for competence proceedings do not exist. The defendant may, of course, call the treating psychiatrist or psychologist and waive any applicable privilege.[63]

The limitations imposed at a competence hearing by the Fifth Amendment's privilege against self-incrimination depend upon the exposure such testimony invites in the determination of guilt.[64] Although a finding of incompetence to stand trial may result in commitment to a psychiatric hospital, a deprivation of liberty, the Supreme Court has not found this to be an inculpatory determination.[65] This conclusion appears reasonable in that the ability of the defendant to recall and communicate the substance of the act charged must necessarily be inquired into by the court and experts on the question of competence to stand trial. Moreover, the court's finding on the competence question implies no judgment on the question of guilt. And, finally, the Fifth Amendment does not permit any statement of the defendant to an expert on the question of competence to stand trial to be introduced, over the defendant's objection, at the guilt or penalty

---

[59] *See generally* **ch 10.**

[60] Taylor v United States, 222 F2d 398 (DC Cir 1955). *See generally* **§10.04**

[61] *See* **§10.02.**

[62] People v Arcega, 32 Cal 3d 504, 651 P2d 338, 186 Cal Rptr 94 (1982); State v Soney, 177 NJ Super 47, 424 A2d 1182 (1980).

[63] *See* **§10.03.**

[64] *In re* Gault, 387 US 1, 49 (1967).

[65] Estelle v Smith, 451 US 454 (1981).

phase of the trial unless the defendant was properly warned of this risk and given the opportunity not to speak to the expert.[66]

The defendant's competence to stand trial is not, in most jurisdictions, a jury question.[67] Thus, the hearsay rule is generally not applicable and extrajudicial sources of information may be relied upon by the expert as the basis for an opinion on competence to stand trial without the same limitations applicable at trial. Even in the absence of the rules of evidence, however, the rules on privilege, whose application is unrelated to the presence of the jury, still apply.[68]

§11.10   —Testimony

The requisite expertise to examine a defendant on the question of competence to stand trial and report to the court is frequently prescribed by statute. In federal court[69] and many state courts,[70] both psychiatrists and clinical psychologists are recognized as expert witnesses on the question of competence to stand trial. Although no additional requirements beyond basic education and licensure are generally imposed on psychiatrists or clinical psychologists, the weight that should be given their opinions is a function of their knowledge of the criminal justice system, interviewing skills, and knowledge of the legal criteria for competence to stand trial.[71] Research on this issue has revealed that purported experts often use legally irrelevant criteria, such as the criteria for criminal responsibility, to evaluate competence to stand trial.[72] Thus, paper credentials are not alone adequate assurances of expertise.

Although competence to stand trial is determined by a jury in some jurisdictions,[73] it is more typically decided by the judge alone.[74] The absence of the jury results in a relaxation of the rules of evidence and permits receipt of the psychiatrist's or psychologist's written report by

---

66 *Id.*

67 *See, e.g.,* United States v Maret, 433 F2d 1064, 1067 (8th Cir 1970), *cert denied,* 402 US 989 (1971).

68 Fed R Evid 1101(c).

69 18 USC §§4241(b), 4247(b) & (c).

70 *See, e.g.,* Ill Ann Stat ch 38, §104-13(a) (Smith-Hurd 1980).

71 Rosenberg & McGarry, *Competency for Trial: The Making of an Expert,* 128 Am J Psychiatry 1092, 1095 (1972).

72 McGarry, *Demonstration and Research in Competency for Trial and Mental Illness: Review and Preview,* 49 BUL Rev 46 (1969).

73 Tex Code Crim Proc Ann art 46.02, §4 (Vernon 1979).

74 18 USC §4241(c), (d).

the court without the limitations of the hearsay rule.[75] Either party or the court is, however, at liberty to call the preparer of the report.[76]

Most jurisdictions provide only general guidance to the examining psychiatrist or psychologist asking for history, symptoms, test results, findings and opinions with regard to the test for competence to stand trial.[77] Because experts may be confused as to the meaning of the applicable legal tests[78] and psychiatric diagnostic categories are not necessarily helpful in this inquiry, better directions for these experts are appropriate. One proposal suggests that experts divide their inquiry into three categories—comprehension of court proceedings, ability to advise counsel, and the potential for decompensation during court proceedings.[79]

Comprehension of court proceedings, the second prong of the *Dusky* [80] test, would require the expert to consider the defendant's understanding of the charges, the actors in the trial process (judge, prosecutor, defendant, witnesses, and jury), possible penalties, rights of the defendant, and applicable procedures.[81] The ability to advise counsel, the first prong of the *Dusky* test, would require the expert to consider the defendant's ability to maintain a meaningful relationship with counsel, recall relevant events, assist in planning or deciding strategy, and testify.[82] The third consideration overlaps both prongs of the *Dusky* test and asks the expert to evaluate the possibility that the defendant will decompensate or become violent while at trial.[83] This checklist identifies in a practical way the considerations of consequence to the court in a determination of competence to stand trial and provides realistic guidance to the experts.

---

[75] 18 USC §4247(c). *See* E. Cleary, McCormick in Evidence §60 (3d ed 1984).

[76] The defendant's right to call a witness does not necessarily entail a right to do so at government expense. Feguer v United States, 302 F2d 214, 241 (8th Cir), *cert denied,* 371 US 872 (1962).

[77] *See, e g,* 18 USC §4247(c); Tex Code Crim Proc Ann art 46.02, §3(d) (Vernon 1979).

[78] McGarry, *supra* note 71.

[79] Robey, *Criteria for Competency to Stand Trial: A Checklist for Psychiatrists,* 122 Am J Psychiatry 616 (1965).

[80] 362 US 402 (1960).

[81] Robey, *supra* note 77, at 618.

[82] *Id.*

[83] *Id.*

§11.11   Suggested Reading

Books

E. Cleary, *McCormick on Evidence* (3d ed 1984).

T. Grisso, *Evaluating Competencies: Forensic Assessments and Instruments* (1986).

M. Moore, S. Estrich, D. McGillis, & W. Spelman, *Dangerous Offenders* (1984).

R. Reisner, *Law and the Mental Health System* (1985).

R. Slovenko, *Psychiatry and Law* (1973).

Articles

Center for Government Research, *Final Report: An Empirical Study and Policy Examination of the Future of Pretrial Release Services in New York* (1983).

Lipsitt, Lelos, & McGarry, *Competency for Trial: A Screening Instrument*, 128 Am J Psychiatry 105 (1971).

Livermore, Malmquist, & Meehl, *On the Justifications for Civil Commitments*, 117 U Pa L Rev 75 (1968).

McGarry, *Demonstration and Research in Competency for Trial and Mental Illness: Review and Preview*, 49 BUL Rev 46 (1969).

Robey, *Criteria for Competency to Stand Trial: A Checklist for Psychiatrists*, 122 Am J Psychiatry 616 (1965).

Rosenberg & McGarry, *Competency for Trial: The Making of an Expert*, 128 Am J Psychiatry 1092 (1972).

Serr, *The Federal Bail Reform Act of 1984: The First wave of Case Law*, 34 Ark L Rev 169 (1985).

Cases

Ake v Oklahoma, 105 S Ct 1087 (1985).

Atkins v Michigan, 644 F2d 543 (6th Cir), *cert denied*, 452 US 964 (1981).

Bishop v United States, 350 US 961 (1956).

Drope v Missouri, 420 US 162 (1975).

Dusky v United States, 362 US 402 (1960).

Estelle v Smith, 451 US 454 (1981).

Feguer v United States, 302 F2d 214 (8th Cir), *cert denied*, 371 US 872 (1962).

Gault, In re, 387 US 1 (1967).

Humphrey, In re, 601 P2d 103 (Okla Crim App 1979).

Jackson v Indiana, 406 US 715 (1972).

Martin v Estelle, 546 F2d 177 (5th Cir 1977).

Nordin, In re, 143 Cal App 3d 542, 192 Cal Rptr 38 (1983).

Pate v Robinson, 383 US 375 (1966).

People v Arcoga, 32 Cal 3d 504, 651 P2d 338, 186 Cal Rptr 94 (1982).

People v Lewis, 75 Ill App 3d 560, 393 NE2d 1380 (1979).

Schall v Martin, 104 S Ct 2403 (1984).

State v Pray, 133 Vt 537, 346 A2d 227 (1975).

State v Soney, 177 NJ Super 47, 424 A2d 1182 (1980).

State v Stevens, 18 Kan 213, 336 P2d 447 (1959).

Taylor v United States, 222 F2d 398 (DC Cir 1955).

Underwood, In re, 9 Cal 3d 345, 508 P2d 721, 107 Cal Rptr 401 (1973).

United States v Maret, 433 F2d 1064 (8th Cir 1970), cert denied, 402 US 989 (1971).

United States v Martin-Trigona, 767 F2d 35 (2d Cir 1985).

Constitutions, Statutes and Rules

Ariz Const art 2, §22.

Cal Const art 1, §12 (amended 1982).

Fed R Evid 104(a), 1101(c) & (d)(3).

Fla Const art 1, §14.

Ill Ann Stat ch 38 §104-16(b) (Smith-Hurd 1980).

Mich Const art 1, §15.

Neb Const art 1, §9.

NY Fam Ct Act §320.5(3)(b) (Consol 1984).

Tex Code Crim Proc Ann art 46.02, §§3, 4, 5 (Vernon 1979).

Tex Const art 1, §§11, 11a.

18 USC §§4241, 4247.

38 USC §3142.

US Const amend V.

US Const amend VI.

Utah Const art 1, §8.

§11.12 WESTLAW Search References

§11.01 *Bail—The Legal Standard*

topic(49) /p deny deni** revok*** revocation /s danger! harm threat! menace

sellers /s 89 +4 36 /p bail /p danger! harm threat! menace

topic(49) /p deny deni** /s non-capital

§11.02 —*The Role of the Expert*
bail /p predict! /s behavior conduct

§11.03 —*Basis*
[no queries]

§11.04 —*Limitations*
bail /s self-incrimination

bail /s appl*** application hearing proceeding /s rule /3 evidence

§11.05 —*Testimony*
bail /5 appl*** application /s testi!

§11.06 *Competence to Stand Trial—The Legal Standard*
dusky /s 80 +4 788 /p competen** /5 trial /s standard test

test standard /s competen** /5 trial /s comprehen! underst**d*** /4 proceeding

test standard /s competen** /5 trial /s consult /3 counsel attorney lawyer

topic(92) /p incompeten** competen** /5 trial /s convict*** /s "due process"

§11.07 —*The Role of the Expert*
topic(110) /p competen** incompeten** /5 trial /s psychiatri** psychologi*** /4 exam!

topic(410) /p competen** incompeten** /5 trial /s psychiatri** psychologi*** /4 exam! % 410k77

§11.08 —*Basis*
competen** incompeten** /5 trial /s screen***

§11.09 —*Limitations*
Competen** incompeten** /5 trial /s self-incrimination

competen** incompeten** /5 trial /s physician psychologist psychiatrist doctor /4 privilege*

§11.10 —*Testimony*
incompeten** competen** /5 "stand trial" /s decision decide
discretion*** /4 judge jur**

12 Criminal Proceedings: Trial

§12.01   Insanity and Related Defenses

The insanity defense does not challenge the defendant's commission of the wrongful act alleged, but instead looks to the accompanying mental state. It attempts to distinguish performance of a prescribed act and responsibility for that act. Some theorize that the insanity defense is an affirmative defense beyond a negation of the intent requirement, while others are of the opinion that the existence of insanity, to a

273

sufficient degree, negates mens rea and, therefore, should not require a separate defense.[1]

One feature that distinguishes the insanity defense from other defenses is the consequence of its successful invocation. When other defenses yield an acquittal, they result in the release of the defendant. Insanity acquittees are subject to commitment to a mental institution for a period of time not necessarily related to the maximum sentence that might have been imposed if they had been found guilty.[2]

A number of novel defenses have been attempted recently, with varying degrees of success, that rely in whole or in part upon psychiatric and psychological testimony to challenge the mental status necessary to convict. These defenses may be provable under an insanity defense or they may negate specific intent. Thus, the consequence of their successful invocation may be an insanity acquittal, an unrestricted acquittal, or reduction of the degree of the offense.

Premenstrual syndrome (PMS) is a new term used to describe the cyclical psychological and somatic effects some women experience from their menstrual cycle.[3] The gist of the PMS defense is that the effect of the premenstrual tension and emotional disturbance results in diminished capacity to form the specific intent required for certain offenses. When the defense has been allowed, it has required that the defendant not anticipate the onset of PMS[4] and that PMS and its effect be proved by medical and psychiatric testimony.[5]

Vietnam veterans' post-traumatic stress disorder is a term used to describe the psychological stress experienced by some Vietnam combat veterans.[6] Like other post-traumatic stress disorders, it involves reexperiencing a traumatic event, in this instance combat in Vietnam, in a manner outside the range of usual human experiences.[7] The theory of

---

[1] N. Morris, Madness and the Criminal Law (1982).

[2] *See* §16.01. The Supreme Court has held that the procedures for commitment of insanity acquittees need not be identical to those applicable to other civil committees. Jones v United States, 463 US 354 (1983).

[3] *See* Wallach, *The Premenstrual Syndrome and Criminal Responsibility*, 10 UCLA L Rev 209 (1971); Note *Criminal Law: Premenstrual Syndrome in the Courts*, 24 Washburn LJ 54 (1984).

[4] Wallach, *supra* note 3, at 285.

[5] *See* Reid v Florida Real Estate Commn, 188 So 2d 846 (Fla Dist Ct App 1966).

[6] Erlinder, *Paying the Price for Vietman: Post-Traumatic Stress Disorder and Criminal Behavior*, 25 BCL Rev 305 (1984).

[7] Diagnostic and Statistical Manual of Mental Disorders 308.30 & 308.81 (3d ed 1980).

this disorder as applied to Vietnam combat veterans is that their current instances of violence may be caused by a *flashback* or reexperiencing of combat in which the veteran believes he is back in Vietnam and assults an individual he believes to be an enemy. Providing some support for this theory is a higher arrest rate for Vietnam heavy combat veterans than for those with minimal combat experience or for nonveterans.[8] The consequence of a successful invocation of this defense may be to support an insanity defense or to negate the specific intent requirement of certain offenses.[9]

The *battered wife syndrome*[10] is another new defense that has found some degree of success in criminal law.[11] It seeks to explain the violence of battered wives directed at their husbands as self-defense in response to prior batterings.[12] The reaction of the battered wife to her battering is often delayed and occurs at an uncommonly serene moment. Thus, it may be explained that the husband's seemingly innocuous behavior created a belief of imminent danger on the part of the wife, justifying the use of deadly force.[13] Expert testimony may assist the jury to understand the wife's emotions and behavior in the years preceding the homicide, corroborating the marital history of violence. Expert testimony may also be useful to explain that women may remain in abusive relationships because they are terrified of leaving and believe they cannot survive on their own, and not necessarily because the abuse is only minimal.[14]

§12.02   Insanity Defense—The Legal Standard

An understanding of the legal standard for the insanity defense today requires an historical overview. The oldest standard typically associated with the insanity defense in common law jurisdictions was articulated in the *M'Naghten* case.[15] An accused is not responsible for criminal conduct, according to the test articulated in that case, if "labouring

---

[8] Milstein & Snyder, *PTSD: The War Is Over, The Battle Goes On,* 19(1) Trial 86 (1983).

[9] *See, e.g.,* People v Lisnow, 80 Cal App 3d 21, 151 Cal Rptr 621 (1978).

[10] L. Walker, The Battered Woman (1976).

[11] *See, e.g.,* Hawthorne v State, 408 So 2d 801 (Fla Dist Ct App 1982); Smith v State, 247 Ga 612, 277 SE2d 678 (1981); Ibn-Tamas v United States, 407 A2d 626 (DC 1979); State v Allery, 101 Wash 2d 591, 682 P2d 312 (1984).

[12] R. Langley & R. Levy, Wife Beating: The Silent Crisis (1979).

[13] *See, e.g.,* State v Kelly, 97 NJ 178, 478 A2d 364 (1984).

[14] People v Powell, 442 NYS2d 645, 83 AD2d 719 (1981).

[15] 2 Eng Rep 718 (1843)

under such a defect of reason, from disease of mind as not to know the nature and quality of the act he was doing: or if he did 'know' it, that he did not know he was doing what was wrong."[16] Although the *M'Naghten* test was adopted in most American jurisdictions,[17] it has had many critics.[18] One facet of criticism focused on the significant aspect of the word *know*, not separately defined. Does the word *know* refer only to knowledge of specific legal rules or to some more general societal norms? Does the word *know* merely contemplate cognition of proscriptions, whether formal or normative, or some higher-level appreciation by the defendant of the impact of conduct?[19] And, if the test only exculpates cognitive defects, does it assume an unduly restrictive view of human behavior?

Gradually, in an effort to expand the cognitive component of *M'Naghten,* the insanity test was expanded to include instances in which the defendant could distinguish right from wrong, but lacked a minimal ability to control behavior.[20] This expanded test, labeled *irresistible impulse,* became the insanity test followed in a majority of American jurisdictions in the first half of the twentieth century.[21] Yet, this test also came under attack for failing to include lack of impulse control resulting from chronic rather than acute conditions,[22] failing to delimit its ambits with clarity,[23] and failing to reflect contemporary views about insanity and criminal responsibility.[24]

A consequence of this dissatisfaction with the irresistible impulse test was a new test articulated by the United States Court of Appeals for the District of Columbia in *Durham v United States.*[25] That test provides that "an accused is not criminally responsible if his unlawful act was the product of mental disease or defect."[26] Because of the relationship between the unlawful act and a mental disease or defect contemplated

---

[16] *Id.*

[17] H. Weihofen, Insanity as a Defense in Criminal Law (1933).

[18] M. Guttmacher & H. Weihofen, Psychiatry and the Law 403-08 (1952); Glueck, *Psychiatry and the Criminal Law,* 12 Mental Hygiene 557, 580 (1928).

[19] A. Goldstein, The Insanity Defense 49 (1967).

[20] Davis v United States, 17 S Ct 360 (1897); Parsons v State, 2 So 854 (Ala 1887).

[21] Goldstein, *supra* note 19, at 236 n 13.

[22] *Id* 70-71.

[23] United States v Brawner, 471 F2d 969, 976 (DC Cir 1962) (en banc).

[24] *Id* 976.

[25] 214 F2d 862 (DC Cir 1954).

[26] *Id* 874-75.

by the *Durham* test, however, psychiatric and psychological dominance of juries became a significant problem with this test.[27]

During the late 1960s and early 1970s, many states turned to the insanity defense standard formulated by the American Law Institute (ALI) in its Model Penal Code: "A person is not responsible for criminal conduct if at the time of such conduct as a result of mental disease or defect he lacks substantial capacity to appreciate the criminal responsibility [wrongfulness] of his conduct or to conform this conduct to the law."[28] This test had the advantage of a definition of the mental disease or defect included, often a source of controversy with other tests. The mental disease or defects included in the ALI test include any abnormal mental condition that substantially affects the mental or emotional process and impairs behavior controls but excludes personality or character disorders.[29] The test itself contemplates a more sophisticated cognitive element than *M'Naghten*, with a volitional component along the lines of the irresistible impulse test.

A version of the ALI test was adopted by the Fifth Circuit Court of Appeals, but failed to include the volitional prong.[30] Subsequently, in the wave of changes in the insanity defense proposed after John Hinckley's insanity acquittal, the Congress adopted a similar test for use in all federal prosecutions.

> It is an affirmative defense to a prosecution under any Federal statute that, at the time of the commission of the acts constituting the offense, the defendant, as a result of a severe mental disease or defect, was unable to appreciate the nature and quality or the wrongfulness of his acts. Mental disease or defect does not otherwise constitute a defense.[31]

Like the Fifth Circuit test, this new test does not include a volitional or

---

[27] Washington v United States, 390 F2d 444 (DC Cir 1967). *See Symposium: Insanity and the Criminal Law - A Critique of Durham v United States*, 22 U Chi L Rev 317 (1955).

[28] Model Penal Code §401(1) (proposed official draft 1962).

[29] *Id* §401(2).

[30] United States v Lyons, 731 F2d 243, 248, 5th Cir, *cert denied*, 105 S Ct 323 (1984). ("[A] person is not responsible for criminal conduct on the grounds of insanity only if at the time of that conduct, as a result of mental disease or defect, he is unable to appreciate the wrongfulness of that conduct.") This substitutes *is unable to appreciate* for *lacks substantial capacity to appreciate* as proposed by the ALI.

[31] 18 USC §20(a).

irresistible impulse component. Instead, it exculpates only impairments affecting cognition.

The ALI test, with a volitional component, is used in approximately half the states,[32] including Illinois,[33] Indiana,[34] New York,[35] Oregon,[36] and Texas.[37]

The *M'Naghten* test is currently employed in the other half of the states, including Arizona,[38] California,[39] Maryland,[40] Ohio,[41] Pennsylvania,[42] and Virginia.[43]

§12.03 —The Role of the Expert

Although both lay and expert testimony bearing on the insanity defense may be considered by the factfinder,[44] much of the debate over the various tests for the insanity defense has turned on the role of psychiatrists and psychologists in applying these tests. The cognitive limits of the *M'Naghten*[45] test have been criticized as unduly restricting

---

[32] *See The Insanity Defense ABA and APA Proposals for Change,* 7 Mental Disability L Rep 136, 140 (1983).

[33] Ill Rev Stat ch 38 §6-2 (1985).

[34] Ind Code Ann §35-41-3-6 (Burns 1985).

[35] NY Penal Law §30.05 (McKinney 1985). New York's version of the ALI test eliminates the language regarding the inability "to conform one's conduct to the requirements of the law."

[36] Or Rev Stat Ann §161.295 (1983).

[37] Tex Penal Code Ann §8.01 (Vernon 1984): It is an affirmative defense to prosecution that, at the time of the conduct charged, the actor, as a result of mental disease or defect, either did not know that his conduct was wrong or was incapable of conforming his conduct to the requirements of the law he allegedly violated.

[38] Ariz Rev Stat Ann §13-502 (West 1985).

[39] Cal Penal Code §25(b) (West 1985). Although California did utilize the ALI test, it has since returned to a test that exculpates a defendant who is "incapable of knowing or understanding the nature and quality of his or her act and of distinguishing right from wrong at the time of the commission of the offense." *Id.*

[40] Raithel v Maryland, 280 Md 291, 372 A2d 1069 (1977).

[41] State v Staten, 18 Ohio St 2d 13, 247 NE2d 293 (1969).

[42] Commonwealth v Oblek, 496 Pa 521, 437 A2d 1162 (1981).

[43] Price v Commonwealth, 228 Va 452, 323 SE2d 106 (1984).

[44] Mims v United States, 375 F2d 135, 143 (5th Cir 1967).

[45] 2 Eng Rep 718 (1843).

the opportunity for expert testimony,[46] while the product requirement of the *Durham*[47] test has been criticized as inviting the dominance of expert testimony.[48] Yet, throughout, it remains clear that psychiatric and psychological testimony plays a major role in the insanity defense.

The major role played by psychiatric and psychological testimony in the insanity defense is further complicated by many conceptual differences between law and the behavioral sciences of psychiatry and psychology. The criminal law rests on the assumption that free will exists and that it is therefore generally legally and morally appropriate to punish violations of the criminal laws. Psychiatric and psychological explanations for aberrant behavior focus on various biochemical, genetic, organic, behavioral, and psychological considerations.[49] The extent to which psychiatrists and psychologists view these considerations as a sufficient limitation on human conduct to exculpate responsibility for criminal behavior and the extent to which the legal system, through the insanity defense, views these considerations as a sufficient limitation on free will to exculpate responsibility for criminal behavior are often at odds. In addition, the legal system's usage of the terms *mental disease* or *defect* does not correspond to standard psychiatric diagnostic nomenclature.[50]

Expert testimony on the insanity defense is heavily influenced by personal—not just professional—values. For example, a psychiatrist who believes that capital punishment is immoral would be less likely to testify in opposition to a defendant who raises an insanity defense in a murder prosecution than a psychiatrist who does not find capital punishment immoral.

The role the psychiatrist or psychologist plays in the proceedings will be a function of who invites the participation in the proceeding—the court, the prosecution, or the defense. The court may order an examination of the defendant on its own motion or the motion of either party.[51] The defense may utilize its own expert, and if the defendant is indigent and has made an initial showing that sanity at the time of the offense is likely to be a significant consideration at trial, the defendant

---

[46] T. Gutheil & P. Appelbaum, Clinical Handbook of Psychiatry and the Law 281 (1982).

[47] 214 F2d 862 (DC Cir 1954).

[48] United States v Brawner, 471 F2d 969, 977 (DC Cir 1972) (en banc).

[49] *See* **ch 1.**

[50] McDonald v United States, 312 F2d 847, 851 (DC Cir 1962).

[51] Fed R Crim P 12.2(c).

is entitled to a court-appointed psychiatrist to assist the defense.[52] And, the prosecution may request an examination to respond to an insanity defense.

Because of the phrasing of the various insanity tests in language using terms such as *disease*, thought to be within the exclusive province of persons medically trained, a preference for psychiatric over psychological testimony has often occurred.[53] This preference has manifested itself at times in wholesale exclusion of psychological testimony and at other times in imposition of greater limitations on psychological testimony.[54] Standards currently articulated, however, have tended to reduce these classwide presumptions, and examine the qualifications of the individual psychologist.[55] The considerations articulated by courts in evaluating minimum qualifications of a psychologist to testify on the insanity defense include a Ph.D. or Psy.D., postgraduate training, internship in a psychiatric hospital, forensic training, and prior forensic experience.[56] Similar scrutiny of the minimum qualifications of psychiatrists has not tended to occur in these proceedings.

§12.04   —Basis

The insanity defense requires an assessment of the defendant's mental status at the time of the offense. Because the psychiatrist or psychologist whose opinion is sought on the defendant's mental status is unlikely to have been present at the offense, this witness faces an extremely difficult task. If an acceptable opinion is to be given, it must be based upon a thorough reconstruction of the event and the time surrounding it. The potential sources of information that may assist in this reconstruction include the defendant, the victim and any witnesses, the arresting officer and jail personnel, and the defendant's family and friends.

An examination of the defendant to reconstruct behavior and mental status at the time of the offense is an extremely important component of an opinion about the defendant's sanity at the time of the offense. However, its availability to the prosecution will be affected by the

---

[52] Ake v Oklahoma, 105 S Ct 1087 (1985).

[53] *See* **§8.02.**

[54] *See, e.g.*, Saul v State, 6 Md App 540, 242 A2d 282 (1969).

[55] State v Portis, 542 F2d 414 (7th Cir 1976); United States v Riggleman, 411 F2d 1190 (4th Cir 1969); Jenkins v United States, 307 F2d 637 (DC Cir 1962) (en banc).

[56] *See* **§§4.08-4.12.**

availability to the defendant of the privilege against self-incrimination.[57] And, even in the case of the defendant's expert whose examination of the defendant is not limited by the privilege against self-incrimination, the passage of time or the affects of a mental disorder may complicate the expert's task of reconstructing the defendant's mental status at the time of the offense. Thus, some courts have required the state to make available to the defendant's psychiatrist or psychologist, in timely fashion, copies of any confessions or statements made by the defendant.[58]

Others present at the offense, victim or witnesses, may be able to describe the defendant's behavior both to provide independent evidence for the jury and as the basis for an expert's opinion of the mental status at the time of the offense. Family and friends may be able to describe the defendant's behavior before and after the event and other events occurring in the defendant's life that may be relevant to behavior at the time of the offense. The arresting officers and jail personnel may be able to describe the defendant's actions shortly after the event, upon arrest and confinement. The extent to which police and correctional authorities may cooperate with the expert may depend on whether they have a perception that the expert is trying to "get a defendant off." Psychological testing may provide evidence of the defendant's current level of functioning suggesting the existence of chronic conditions that may have existed at the time of the offense.

Several efforts have been made to provide a structured approach for examinations of criminal responsibility.[59] The benefit of these structured examinations is that they guide the examiner through an inquiry into the principal relevant sources of information about criminal responsibility. On representative approach is the Time of the Offense Screening Evaluation which is a structured evaluation designed to be administered within one hour and to identify defendants who require more extensive evaluations.[60] It has three sections that address information relevant to past history, the offense, and current mental status. Each section contains specific information that should be obtained, but does not prescribe specific questions that should be asked to obtain that information. Based on the information obtained, the

---

[57] See §12.05.

[58] Blake v Kemp, 750 F2d 523 (11th Cir 1985).

[59] T. Grisso, Evaluating Competencies: Forensic Assessments and Instruments 172-82 (1986).

[60] Slobogin, Melton, & Showalter, *The Feasibility of a Brief Evaluation of Mental State at the Time of the Offense*, 8 Law & Hum Behav 305 (1984).

examiner is asked whether it is sufficiently likely that the defendant had a significant mental abnormality affecting his actions at the time of the offense such that a more extensive evaluation is warranted.

§12.05 —Limitations

Three sets of limitations exist on the basis for a psychiatrist's or psychologist's opinion of the defendant's sanity at the time of the offense—the privilege against self-incrimination, the physician-patient privilege and its variants, and the hearsay rule. The Fifth Amendment privilege against self-incrimination[61] permits the defendant to refrain from assisting the prosecution in proving its case by volunteering incriminating information. Thus, the defendant may seek the protection of the privilege against self-incrimination and refuse to participate in a court-ordered examination of the defendant's sanity at the time of the offense.[62] The consequence of permitting this refusal is that the government's psychiatrists and psychologists will not enjoy an important element of the necessary basis for their opinion.[63] This potential consequence has led most courts to limit the Fifth Amendment's application in sanity examinations triggered by a defendant's plea of not guilty by reason of insanity.[64] The government or court-appointed psychiatrist or psychologist may utilize all that the defendant has revealed as the basis for an opinion on sanity at the time of the offense. Specific statements of the defendant to the examiner, however, are excludable under the Fifth Amendment on the issue of the occurrence of the act.[65] If, notwithstanding denial of the shelter of the Fifth Amendment, the defendant blatantly refuses to cooperate with the prosecution or court-appointed psychiatrist or psychologist in an examination, the defendant's right to present psychiatric or psychological evidence supporting an insanity defense may be restricted.[66]

The physician-patient privilege and its variants, the psychiatrist, psychologist and psychotherapist–patient privilege, are another poten-

---

[61] US Const amend V.

[62] Estelle v Smith, 451 US 454 (1980).

[63] *See* §2.14.

[64] *See, e.g.,* United States v Byers, 740 F2d 1104 (DC Cir 1984); United States v Cohen, 530 F2d 43 (8th Cir), *cert denied,* 429 US 855 (1976); Karstetter v Cardwell, 526 F2d 1144 (9th Cir 1975); Parker v State, 649 SW2d 46 (Tex Crim App), *cert denied,* 104 S Ct 496 (1983).

[65] Watters v Hubbard, 725 F2d 381 (6th Cir), *cert denied,* 105 S Ct 133 (1984).

[66] Lee v County Court, 27 NY2d 431, 267 NE2d 252, 318 NYS2d 705 (1971).

tial limitation on the basis for an opinion regarding the defendant's sanity at the time of the offense. These privileges apply, if they exist in the jurisdiction, when an attempt is made to compel the testimony of a psychiatrist or psychologist who has treated the defendant.[67] They are waivable; thus, the defendant may choose to present the testimony of a treating psychiatrist or psychologist without a limitation imposed by privilege. And, in some jurisdictions, these privileges are not applicable in criminal cases[68] or are impliedly waived by raising the insanity defense.[69]

These medical privileges do not apply when the purpose of the relationship is not treatment. Thus, a court-ordered examination or an examination by an expert retained by the defense exclusively to evaluate an insanity plea is not covered by a medical privilege.[70] If the expert is functioning as the attorney's assistant, however, communications between the expert and the defendant may be covered by the attorney-client or work product privilege.[71]

The critical question typically is not the existence of the attorney-client or work product privilege as to the nontestifying psychiatrist or psychologist, but its waiver by raising the insanity defense. This question most often arises when the defendant retains a psychiatrist or psychologist who examines the defendant and renders an unfavorable opinion about the likely success of an insanity defense. When the defendant nonetheless raises an insanity defense and does not call the psychiatrist or psychologist who rendered the unfavorable opinion, the prosecution may seek to call this individual, whose identity may be discovered through a source such as jail visitor logs. In the majority of jurisdictions, raising the insanity defense does not waive the attorney-client or work product privilege as to the retained nontestifying psychiatrist or psychologist.[72] A minority of jurisdictions conclude, however, that raising the insanity defense is inconsistent with the retention of confidentiality in psychiatrist or psychologist communica-

---

[67] See §10.02.

[68] People v Arcega, 32 Cal 3d 504, 651 P2d 338, 186 Cal Rptr 94 (1982); State v Soney, 177 NJ Super 47, 424 A2d 1182 (1980).

[69] People v Al-Kanani, 33 NY2d 260, 307 NE2d 43, 351 NYS2d 969 (1973), cert denied, 417 US 916 (1974).

[70] See §10.04.

[71] See §10.08.

[72] United States v Alvarez, 519 F2d 1036 (3d Cir 1975); People v Lines, 13 Cal 3d 500, 531 P2d 793, 119 Cal Rptr 225 (1975); State v Pratt, 284 Md 516, 398 A2d 421 (1979); People v Hilliker, 29 Mich App 543, 185 NW2d 831 (1971); State v Kociolek, 23 NJ 400, 129 A2d 417 (1957).

tions governed by the attorney-client privilege.[73] Thus, under the minority rule, the privilege comes into existence, but is waived when the insanity defense is raised. Under both rules, once the defendant calls the psychiatrist or psychologist as a witness, any existing privilege as to that expert is waived.[74]

The hearsay rule, on its face, limits the admissibility of out-of-court statements used for their truth as the basis for the expert's in-court opinion. However, several exceptions limit the impact of the hearsay bar in this context. If the testifying psychiatrist or psychologist utilizes statements made by the defendant while treating the defendant which are reasonably pertinent to treatment, these statements are excepted from the hearsay rule under the *statements for purposes of medical diagnosis or treatment* exception to the hearsay rule.[75] If the testifying psychiatrist or psychologist is called by the government, the defendant's statements are admissions viewed as an exception to the hearsay rule in some jurisdictions and as not hearsay in others.[76]

Even if the out-of-court statements relied on by the psychiatrist or psychologist do not come within a specific exception to the hearsay rule, a relaxation of the bar of the hearsay rule exists as a basis for expert testimony.[77] If the expert's basis is not independently admissible, it may nonetheless be permitted if customarily and reasonably relied upon by other experts in the field in forming opinions on this subject.[78] Thus, for example, as psychiatrists and psychologists regularly take a history during a clinical interview,[79] reliance on historical data related by the defendant out of court may be a permissible basis for an opinion.[80]

§12.06 —Testimony

Once the insanity defense has been raised and a psychiatrist or psychologist is determined by the judge to be qualified to offer opinion

---

73 State v Carter, 641 SW2d 54 (Mo 1982), *cert denied*, 461 US 932 (1983); People v Edny, 39 NY2d 620, 350 NE2d 400 (1976).

74 Ballew v State, 640 SW2d 237 (Tex Crim App 1982).

75 Fed R Evid 803(4).

76 Fed R Evid 801(d)(2).

77 *See* §9.05.

78 Fed R Evid 703.

79 *See* §2.14

80 *See, e.g.,* United States v Lawson, 653 F2d 299 (7th Cir 1981), *cert denied*, 459 US 893 (1982).

testimony[81] on the defendant's sanity at the time of the offense and has an appropriate basis for that opinion,[82] the issues most often raised concern the form of that testimony. One concern is the witness's use of the language of the ultimate issue before the jury, and has at its core a fear of expert usurpation of the jury's function. Another concern is the use of unexplained psychiatric jargon, and has at its core a fear that the testimony will not benefit and may confuse the jury.

Expert witnesses may testify in the form of an opinion interpreting facts provided by other witnesses rather than simply describing facts they have perceived.[83] One limitation imposed on expert opinion testimony has involved the ultimate issue in the case.[84] Experts have often been prohibited from expressing opinions in terms embracing the ultimate issue in the case based on a fear that the jury might accept this uncritically and not review the evidence independently. Although this ultimate issue limitation still exists in some jurisdictions, the trend, represented by the original version of Federal Rule of Evidence 704, has been to admit expert testimony embracing an issue that is otherwise helpful to the factfinder.[85] Under this rule, if the expert's testimony helps to explain evidence to the jury, it will not be excluded merely because it also includes an opinion embracing the ultimate issue in the case.[86]

A reversal of this trend has occurred, however, for expert testimony in criminal cases on the effect of a mental illness on criminal responsibility. In response to public concerns with the insanity defense precipitated by the John Hinckley insanity acquittal, Federal Rule of Evidence 704 was amended to add a subpart (b):

> (b)   No expert witness testifying with respect to the mental state

---

[81] *See* **ch 8.**

[82] *See* **§11.13.**

[83] *See* **§7.01.**

[84] *See* **§9.08.**

[85] Fed R Evid 704, as enacted, provided: "Testimony in the form of an opinion or inference otherwise admissible is not objectionable because it embraces an ultimate issue to be decided by the trier of fact." Alaska, Arizona, Arkansas, Colorado, Hawaii, Maine, Michigan, Minnesota, Montana, Nebraska, Nevada, New Mexico, North Dakota, Oklahoma, Oregon, Texas, Utah, Vermont, Washington, Wisconsin, and Wyoming have adopted evidence rules identical to Fed R Evid 704. J. Weinstein & M. Berger, Weinstein's Evidence ¶704[03] (1982). Delaware, Florida, and Ohio have adopted substantially similar rules. *Id.*

[86] United States v Hearst, 563 F2d 1331 (9th Cir 1977), *cert denied*, 435 US 1000 (1978).

or condition of a defendant in a criminal case may state an opinion or inference as to whether the defendant did or did not have the mental state or condition constituting an element of the crime charged or of a defense thereto. Such ultimate issues are matters for the trier of fact alone.[87]

A similar limitation has been enacted in California.[88]

The effect of these new ultimate issue rules is that a psychiatrist or psychologist may not utilize the language of the applicable insanity defense to state, for example, that the defendant could not tell right from wrong or lacked the capacity to conform conduct to the requirements of the law. Instead, the expert may only assist the jury by providing information to enable it to reach this conclusion itself. The expert may describe the behavior of the defendant observed during an interview, responses to questions, and results of personality or intelligence tests. How much further the expert may go in providing information to assist the jury in reaching this conclusion itself is unclear. The psychiatrist or psychologist may, in all likelihood, express an opinion as to the defendant's diagnosis at relevant times. And, these new ultimate issue rules do not expressly prohibit the witness from telling the jury about the profession's current understanding of the ability of persons with this diagnosis to distinguish right from wrong or conform their conduct to the requirements of the law. Whether this is a violation of the spirit of these new rules is unclear.

The other issue concerned with conclusory psychiatric and psychological testimony involves the use of unexplained psychiatric jargon.[89] The use of *psychobabble*, words having meaning known only to mental health professionals, without adequate explanation, leaves the jury unenlightened, confused, or offended. Presentation of unexplained

---

[87] Fed R Evid 704(b).

[88]   In the guilt phase of a criminal action, any expert testifying about a defendant's mental illness, mental disorder, or mental defect shall not testify as to whether the defendant had or did not have the required mental states, which include, but are not limited to, purpose, intent, knowledge, or malice aforethought, for the crimes charged. The question as to whether the defendant had or did not have the required mental states shall be decided by the trier of fact.

Cal Penal Code §29 (West Supp 1985).

Although the addition to the federal rule addresses testimony about the elements of the Crime or a defense thereto, the California statute appears limited to "required mental states". The consequence of this difference has not been made clear in reported cases.

[89] *See* §9.09.

psychiatric jargon is bad strategy and may be a basis for excluding psychiatrist or psychological testimony as not helping the jury,[90] or worse, confusing the jury.[91]

§12.07 Sentencing and Disposition—Legal Relevance of Psychiatric and Psychological Testimony

The imposition of criminal punishment is thought to further one or more of four goals—restraint, rehabilitation, retribution, or deterrence.[92] Psychiatric and psychological testimony may be relevant to the furtherance of these four goals in any given case.[93] The need to restrain the defendant from engaging in future criminal conduct may be better understood by the court if psychiatric or psychological testimony can help to explain why the defendant committed the crime charged and whether that conduct is likely to be repeated by the defendant. The amenability of the defendant to rehabilitation may be clarified for the court if psychiatric and psychological testimony can identify the existence of any mental illness and the viability and availability of treatment. The utility of deterring this defendant by the imposition of criminal sanctions can be better understood if psychiatric and psychological testimony can explain the effect on the conduct of the defendant's actions of any mental illness from which the defendant may suffer. And, the appropriateness of retribution is amplified if psychiatrists and psychologists can explain the defendant's mental status at the time of the offense.

Although the criminal justice system once manifested great faith in the ability of psychiatrists and psychologists to provide answers to these questions, that faith has subsided.[94] The apparent failure of rehabilitation within the criminal justice system has resulted in cynicism about rehabilitation as a valid goal of punishment.[95] The failure of rehabilitation has had additional costs as well. The rehabilitative goal was sought to be achieved with substantial sentencing discretion to address the

---

[90] Fed R Evid 702.

[91] Fed R Evid 403.

[92] Gardiner, *The Purposes of Criminal Punishment*, 21 Mod L Rev 117 (1958).

[93] American Psychiatric Assn, *Psychiatry in the Sentencing Process: A Report of the Task Force on the Role of Psychiatry in the Sentencing Process* (1984).

[94] Dershowitz, *The Role of Psychiatry in the Sentencing Process*, 1 Intl J L & Psychiatry 63 (1978).

[95] The Rehabilitation of Criminal Offenders (1979).

unique problems of each individual defendant. A perception that that discretion has been abused and that defendants have not been treated equally now permeates the system. The consequence of this disenchantment has been a movement toward determinate and presumptive sentences in noncapital cases within which sentencing discretion is far more limited. Yet, within these limits, much opportunity for psychiatric and psychological input remains.[96] And, the role of psychiatrists and psychologists in sentencing in capital cases has expanded for reasons unrelated to renewed faith in these professions.

§12.08 —Capital Offenses

The United States Supreme Court's decisions in 1972 finding various state procedures for imposition of the death penalty unconstitutional[97] spawned a new wave of capital punishment legislation. These new schemes sought to respond to the Court's requirements, inter alia, by requiring decisions in individual cases, following the determination of guilt, about the future likelihood of the defendant's commission of violent criminal acts if the death penalty were not applied.[98] Not surprisingly, psychiatric and psychological testimony has often been sought on this issue and has generated heated debate.[99]

The principal issue in this debate is whether psychiatrists and psychologists as a class or individually have some degree of expertise in the prediction of future dangerous behavior. The position of the psychiatric and psychological establishment has been that the available research does not demonstrate that they possess any special abilities to predict future dangerous behavior.[100] These professional groups claim

---

[96] Monohan & Ruggiero, *Psychological and Psychiatric Aspects of Determinate Criminal Sentencing*, 3 Intl J L & Psychiatry 143 (1980).

[97] *See, e.g.,* Furman v Georgia, 408 US 238 (1972).

[98] Idaho Code §19-2515(g)(8) (Supp 1984); Okla Stat Ann tit 21, §701.12 (West 1983); Tex Code Crim Proc Ann art 37.071(b)(2) (Vernon 1981); Va Code §19.2-264.4c (1983); Wash Rev Code Ann §10.95.070(8) (Supp 1984). The Texas statute, representative of the others, provides that the court shall submit as an issue to the jury "whether there is a probability that the defendant would commit criminal acts of violence that would constitute a continuing threat to society."

[99] *See, e.g.,* Bonnie, *Psychiatry and the Death Penalty: Emerging Problems in Virginia,* 66 Va L Rev 167 (1980); Dix, *The Death Penalty, "Dangerousness," Psychiatric Testimony and Professional Ethics,* 5 Am J Crim L 151 (1977).

[100] American Psychiatric Assn, *Clinical Aspects of the Violent Individual* (1974); *Report of the Task Force on the Role of Psychology in the Criminal Justice System,* 33 Am Psychologist 1099, 1110 (1978).

that they have little, if anything, to offer in the determination of future dangerousness, except in limited circumstances and then only regarding the immediate future. It has been claimed that psychiatrists and psychologists who hold out expertise in prediction of future dangerousness misrepresent their abilities. Behavior, including violent behavior, is a product of individual personality factors, environmental factors, and the interaction of personality and environment. An evaluation of the defendant examines only one of the three determinates of behavior.

Because courts are concerned about thrusting jurors into complex scientific disputes about which they have no common knowledge, they have generally waited for scientific communities to reach some resolution of their disputes before utilizing the questioned scientific procedures.[101] Based on this approach, it might be expected that, until a respectable component of the psychiatric and psychological communities concluded that reasonably accurate predictions of dangerousness could be made, no expert testimony on this issue would be admitted. The United States Supreme Court has, notwithstanding the professions' disclaimers, specifically permitted psychiatric and psychological testimony on future dangerousness in capital punishment sentencing determinations, relegating prediction problems to the weight of the testimony.[102] Thus, wholesale exclusion of this testimony as a matter

---

[101] *See, e.g.,* Frye v United States, 293 F 1013 (DC Cir 1923).

[102] Barefoot v Estelle, 463 US 880, 896-99 (1983):

The suggestion that no psychiatrist's testimony may be presented with respect to a defendant's future dangerousness is somewhat like asking us to disinvent the wheel. In the first place, it is contrary to our cases. If the likelihood of a defendant committing further crimes is a constitutionally acceptable criterion for imposing the death penalty, which it is, *Jurek v. Texas,* 428 U.S. 262 (1976), and if it is not impossible for even a lay person sensibly to arrive at that conclusion, it makes little sense, if any, to submit that psychiatrists, out of the entire universe of persons who might have an opinion on the issue, would know so little about the subject that they should not be permitted to testify. . . .

In the second place, the rules of evidence generally extant at the federal and state levels anticipate that relevant unprivileged evidence should be admitted and its weight left to the factfinder, who would have the benefit of cross examination and contrary evidence by the opposing party. Psychiatric testimony predicting dangerousness may be countered not only as erroneous in a particular case but as generally so unreliable that it should be ignored. If the jury may make up its mind about future dangerousness unaided by psychiatric testimony, jurors should not be barred from hearing the views of the State's psychiatrists along with opposing views of the defendant's doctors. . . .

Third, petitioner's view mirrors the position expressed in the amicus

of federal constitutional law is not required. Rather, attacks on the admissibility and weight of this testimony must now be directed to the qualifications of the expert, the basis for the opinion, and the specific prediction methodology utilized.[103]

Beyond statutory schemes raising the issue of prediction of future dangerousness as a prerequisite to capital punishment and related mental health expertise, the Supreme Court has opened another avenue to psychiatric and psychological input in capital sentencing by requiring an opportunity for the defendant to introduce evidence mitigating imposition of a death sentence.[104] This opens the door for introduction of psychiatric and psychological evidence falling short of that required to exculpate under the applicable insanity defense, but nonetheless relevant to imposition of the ultimate punishment.

§12.09 —Noncapital Offenses

In contrast with the movement toward individualized sentencing in capital punishment cases, sentencing in noncapital punishment cases has become less individualized. The failure of rehabilitation within the criminal justice system and perceived abuses of sentencing discretion have resulted in a reduction of discretion in sentencing determinations through determinate and presumptive sentences. There remain, however, specific areas for psychiatric and psychological input in these determinations rebutting statutory presumptive sentences or fixing the high or low end of a determinate sentence.[105]

Psychiatric and psychological testimony may help explain the defendant's likely reaction to incarceration. Specifically, this may include the risk of suicide or escape and response to homosexuality or gangs in prison. This information may be useful in sentencing if there is a choice whether or where to incarcerate. Psychiatric and psychological testimony may reveal the existence of alternatives to incarceration that respond

---

brief of the American Psychiatric Association (APA). As indicated above, however, the same view was presented and rejected in *Estelle v. Smith.* We are no more convinced now that the view of the APA should be converted into a constitutional rule barring an entire category of expert testimony. We are not persuaded that such testimony is almost entirely unreliable and that the factfinder and the adversary system will not be competent to uncover, recognize, and take due account of its shortcomings.

[103] *See* J. Monahan, The Clinical Prediction of Violent Behavior (1981).

[104] Lockett v Ohio, 438 US 586 (1978).

[105] Monohan & Ruggiero, *Psychological and Psychiatric Aspects of Determinate Criminal Sentencing,* 3 Intl J L & Psychiatry 143 (1980).

to the goals of restraint, rehabilitation, or deterrence. This may include the availability of psychiatric treatments on an inpatient or outpatient basis and the defendant's amenability to these treatments. Included in this may be information about the defendant's dangerousness as manifested by the offense for which a conviction occurred. This information may be useful in sentencing if discretion exists whether to incarcerate.

Formal articulations of the rules applicable in sentencing proceedings recognize that psychiatric or psychological testimony bearing on relevant issues is admissible.[106] Nevertheless, there is often a coolness to this testimony, particularly when the jury sentences.[107] Underlying this coolness is the fear that this testimony will be too persuasive and preempt independent analysis by the jury.

§12.10 —The Role of the Expert

Participation of psychiatrists and psychologists in sentencing determinations involves two ethical issues that have legal implications. The first issue is a potential conflict between the duties owed by the psychiatrist or psychologist to the individual and to society.[108] The assumption that psychiatrists and psychologists are and should be concerned primarily with individual rather than societal welfare is widely held. This may create a conflict of interest for the psychiatrist or psychologist trained to address individual patient concerns and now asked by the court to respond to societal concerns in the sentencing decision. In addition, this assumption may lead the defendant to conclude that the psychiatrist or psychologist is primarily concerned with the defendant's own welfare rather than society's. Minimally, this potential conflict requires that the defendant be informed of the purpose of any psychiatric or psychological examination and the actual role of the psychiatrist or psychologist.[109]

The second ethical dilemma involves the psychiatrist or psychologist presenting prediction testimony unsupported by the available research

---

[106] *See, e.g.,* Hopkins v State, 480 SW2d 212 (Tex Crim App 1972).

[107] *See, e.g.,* Clemons v State, 638 SW2d 657 (Tex Ct App 1982) (no writ).

[108] American Psychiatric, Assn, *Psychiatry in the Sentencing Process: A Report of the Task Force on the Role of Psychiatry in the Sentencing Process* (1984).

[109] *Id. Report of the Task Force on the Role of Psychology in the Criminal Justice System,* 33 Am Psychologist 1099, 1102 (1978).

and the professions.[110] One concept that has typified the traditional definition of a profession is that of a unique fund of knowledge not possessed by the lay populace.[111] The risk that members of the lay populace will assume the truth of anything within that professional sphere told to them by members of the profession, particularly in sentencing determinations, imposes an obligation on members of the profession to guard against disclosure of unsubstantiated theories.[112] Thus, in the absence of empirical studies demonstrating expertise in prediction, psychiatric and psychological prediction testimony has been called unethical.[113]

If a psychiatrist or psychologist is to offer prediction testimony, certain minimal qualifications should be present. First, the witness's qualifications should include training and substantial experience in forensic psychiatry or psychology as well as a thorough familiarity with the literature on prediction. Second, the basis for any opinion on future dangerousness should include an extensive history and examination of the patient. Third, the admissibility of an opinion should be preceded by a description of the methodology used so that the judge or jury will be permitted to scrutinize it. Finally, extensive cross-examination and rebuttal should be permitted so that the judge or jury may truly understand the utility and limits of this testimony.

The minimum qualifications for psychiatric or psychological testimony in sentencing on issues other than future dangerousness have been less controversial. Yet, it is nonetheless important to inquire into more than basic education and licensure of these witnesses. Testimony, for example, that administration of Depo-Provera in a community setting to a sex offender[114] will be a viable alternative to incarceration requires a special fund of knowledge about the theories seeking to explain the behavior of sexual offenders and the efficacy research on Depo-Provera treatment. The majority of psychiatrists and psychologists will not necessarily have extensive knowledge of these theories and existing research on this topic.

---

110 *Id.*

111 Wasserstom, *Lawyers as Professionals: Some Moral Issues,* 5 Human Rights 1-2 n 1 (1975).

112 Dix, *The Death Penalty, "Dangerousness," Psychiatric Testimony, and Professional Ethics,* 5 Am J of Crim L 151 (1977).

113 *See* A. Stone, Law, Psychiatry and Morality 59-73 (1984).

114 Comment, *The Use of Depo-Provera for Treating Male Sex Offenders: A Review of the Constitutional and Medical Issues,* 16 Toledo L Rev 181 (1984).

§12.11 —Basis

As with all psychiatric diagnoses, a clinical examination of the defendant including a mental status examination and history is an important basis for an opinion on sentencing.[115] For reasons discussed in **§12.12,** however, this may not be available to the prosecution's expert. In the absence of this basis the use of a hypothetical question to supply this information has been permitted,[116] although as a basis for a diagnostic opinion or prediction it is highly suspect.[117]

Other information relevant to an opinion on sentencing may include the commission of other crimes by the defendant for which a conviction may or may not have been obtained. Statements by victims and witnesses to the crime may help to reveal the defendant's mental status at the time of the offense. Family and social history of the defendant as well as standard psychological and intelligence tests are also important.

A nonclinical, actuarial prediction of the defendant's future conduct, involving the application of statistical probabilities to variables that have been found to correlate with dangerous behavior—age, sex, race, prior arrests, use of alcohol or drugs—may also be considered. In the context of capital sentencing, however, the United States Supreme Court has rejected the use of aggregate criteria that fail to take into account individual variables.[118] Although the Court has not yet addressed the use of expert psychiatric or psychological prediction testimony based on actuarial data, its failure to take into account individual variance poses serious problems. A prudent use of these data would involve a meshing of the actuarial and clinical techniques.

§12.12 —Limitations

The privilege against self-incrimination of the Fifth Amendment provides a substantial limitation on the state or court-appointed psychiatrist's ability to examine the defendant as a prerequisite to offering an opinion about future dangerousness in sentencing. In *Estelle*

---

[115] *See* §§2.12-2.14.

[116] Barefoot v Estelle, 463 US 880 (1983).

[117] American Psychiatric Assn, *Psychiatry in the Sentencing Process: A Report of the Task Force on the Role of Psychiatry in the Sentencing Process* (1984).

[118] Lockett v Ohio, 438 US 586, 605 (1978) (plurality opinion of Burger, Stewart, Powell, & Stevens); Roberts v Louisiana, 428 US 325, 333-34 (1976) (plurality opinion of Stewart, Powell, & Stevens).

v Smith, [119] the United States Supreme Court held that a court-appointed psychiatrist who examined a defendant on the issue of competence to stand trial could not utilize the defendant's statements obtained in that examination on the issue of capital punishment, unless the defendant was first properly warned of his privilege against self-incrimination. The consequence of *Estelle* is that court-appointed and government psychiatrists or psychologists are now frequently limited to such sources as hypothetical questions and interviews with others present at the offense as the basis for an opinion on capital punishment. Although this is a highly suspect basis, the Court has sanctioned its use.[120]

The physician-patient privilege and its variants are applicable in sentencing determinations unless specifically excepted[121] or waived by the defendant's introduction of psychiatric or psychological testimony.[122] Thus, the government may not compel the disclosure of confidential communications by the defendant's treating therapist in the absence of a general exception to the privilege applicable in criminal proceedings or a waiver of the privilege.

The Federal Rules of Evidence, and other evidence codes in jurisdictions in which sentencing determinations are made by the judge, provide that the rules of evidence, with the exception of the rules on privilege, are not applicable to sentencing determinations.[123] Thus, hearsay may be received and relied on directly by the court[124] and, implicitly, by an expert in reaching an opinion on an issue relevant to sentencing. Evidence of other crimes and convictions, not generally admissible at trial, may also be heard by the court in sentencing[125] and,

---

[119] 451 US 454 (1980).

[120] Barefoot v Estelle, 463 US 880 (1983).

[121] *See, e.g.,* People v Arcega, 32 Cal 3d 504, 651 P2d 338, 186 Cal Rptr 94 (1982) specifically excepting the privilege in criminal cases, and implicitly, therefore, in sentencing determinations. *See also* Fed R Evid 1101 (c).

[122] *See* §10.03.

[123] Fed R Evid 1102 (d)(3); 18 USC §3577. A similar provision providing for inapplicability of the rules of evidence in sentencing exists in Arkansas, Colorado, Delaware, Hawaii, Maine, Minnesota, Montana, Nevada, New Mexico, North Dakota, Ohio, Oklahoma, Oregon, South Dakota, Vermont, Washington, Wisconsin, and Wyoming. J. Weinstein & M. Berger, Weinstein's Evidence ¶1101[05] (1983).

[124] United States v Jarrett, 705 F2d 198, 208 (7th Cir 1983), *cert denied,* 104 S Ct 995 (1984); United States v Rosner, 549 F2d 259, 263 n 5 (2d Cir), *cert denied,* 434 US 826 (1977).

[125] Fed R Crim P 32(c); United States v Benton, 637 F2d 1052, 1060 (5th Cir 1981).

implicitly, relied on by an expert in forming an opinion. In sentencing decisions made by the jury, the rules of evidence apply; however, they do not exclude evidence bearing on character or prior convictions.[126]

§12.13   —Testimony

The utility of psychiatric or psychological testimony for the judge or jury on sentencing will be in shedding light on how restraint, rehabilitation, retribution, and deterrence may be served by the various punishments imposable in a given case. Conclusory testimony, unexplained psychiatric jargon, or testimony in the language of the ultimate issue before the judge or jury do little to assist them.

§12.14   Suggested Reading

Books

American Psychiatric Assn, *Diagnostic and Statistical Manual of Mental Disorders* (3d ed 1980) (DSM-III).

A. Goldstein, *The Insanity Defense* (1967).

T. Grisso, *Evaluating Competencies: Forensic Assessments and Instruments* (1986).

T. Gutheil & P. Appelbaum, *Clinical Handbook of Psychiatry and the Law* (1982).

M. Guttmacher & H. Weihofen, *Psychiatry and the Law* (1952).

R. Langley & R. Levy, *Wife Beating: The Silent Crisis* (1979).

J. Monahan, *The Clinical Prediction of Violent Behavior* (1981).

N. Morris, *Madness and the Criminal Law* (1982).

The Rehabilitation of Criminal Offenders (Sechrest, White, & Brown eds 1979).

A. Stone, *Law, Psychiatry and Morality* (1984).

H. Weihofen, *Insanity as a Defense in Criminal Law* (1933).

J. Weinstein & M. Berger, *Weinstein's Evidence* (1982).

Articles

American Psychiatric Assn, *Psychiatry in the Sentencing Process: A Report of the Task Force on the Role of Psychiatry in the Sentencing Process* (1984).

---

[126] *See, e.g.,* Tex Code Crim Proc art 37.07.3 (Vernon 1981).

American Psychiatric Assn, *Clinical Aspects of the Violent Individual* (1974).

Bonnie, *Psychiatry and the Death Penalty: Emerging Problems in Virginia*, 66 Va L Rev 167 (1980).

Comment, *The Use of Depo-Provera for Treating Male Sex Offenders: A Review of the Constitutional and Medical Issues*, 16 Toledo L Rev 181 (1984).

Dershowitz, *The Role of Psychiatry in the Sentencing Process*, 1 Intl J L & Psychiatry 63 (1978).

Dix, *The Death Penalty, "Dangerousness," Psychiatric Testimony and Professional Ethics*, 5 Am J Crim L 151 (1977).

Erlinder, *Paying the Price for Vietnam Veterans: Post-Traumatic Stress Disorder and Criminal Behavior*, 25 BCL Rev 305 (1984).

Gardiner, *The Purposes of Criminal Punishment*, 21 Mod L Rev 117 (1958).

Glueck, *Psychiatry and the Criminal Law*, 12 Mental Hygiene 557 (1928).

The Insanity Defense ABA and APA Proposals for Change, 7 Mental Disability L Rep 136 (1983).

Milstein & Snyder, *PTSD: The War is Over, the Battle Goes On*, 19(1) Trial 86 (1983).

Monohan & Ruggiero, *Psychological and Psychiatric Aspects of Determinate Criminal Sentencing*, 3 Intl J L & Psychiatry 143 (1980).

Note, *Criminal Law: Premenstrual Syndrome in the Courts*, 24 Washburn LJ 54 (1984).

Report of the Task Force on the Role of Psychology in the Criminal Justice System, 33 Am Psychologist 1099 (1978).

Slobogin, Melton, & Showalter, *The Feasibility of a Brief Evaluation of Mental State at the Time of the Offense*, 8 Law & Hum Behav 305 (1984).

Symposium: Insanity and the Criminal Law—A Critique of Durham v United States, 22 U Chi L Rev 317 (1955).

Wallach, *The Premenstrual Syndrome and Criminal Responsibility*, 19 UCLA L Rev 209 (1971).

Cases

Ake v Oklahoma, 105 S Ct 1087 (1985).

Ballew v State, 640 SW2d 237 (Tex Crim App 1982).

Barefoot v Estelle, 463 US 880 (1983).

Clemons v State, 638 SW2d 657 (Tex Ct App 1982), no writ.

Commonwealth v Oblek, 496 Pa 521, 437 A2d 1162 (1981).

Davis v United States, 17 S Ct 360 (1897).

Durham v United States, 214 F2d 862 (DC Cir 1954).

Estelle v Smith, 451 US 454 (1980).

Frye v United States, 293 F 1013 (DC Cir 1923).

Furman v Georgia, 408 US 238 (1972).

Hawthorne v State, 408 So 2d 801 (Fla Dist Ct App 1982).

Hopkins v State, 480 SW2d 212 (Tex Crim App 1972).

Ibn-Tamas v United States, 407 A2d 626 (DC 1979).

Jenkins v United States, 307 F2d 637 (DC Cir 1962) (en banc).

Jones v United States, 463 US 354 (1983).

Karstetter v Cardwell, 526 F2d 1144 (9th Cir 1975).

Lee v County Court, 27 NY2d 431, 267 NE2d 252, 318 NYS2d 705 (1971).

Lockett v Ohio, 438 US 586 (1978).

McDonald v United States, 312 F2d 847 (DC Cir 1962).

M'Naghten, 2 Eng Rep 718 (1843).

Mims v United States, 375 F2d 135 (5th Cir 1967).

Parker v State, 649 SW2d 46 (Tex Crim App), *cert denied,* 104 S Ct 496 (1983).

Parsons v State, 2 So 854 (Ala 1887).

People v Al-Kanani, 33 NY2d 260, 307 NE2d 43, 351 NYS2d 969 (1973), *cert denied,* 417 US 916 (1974).

People v Arcega, 32 Cal 3d 504, 651 P2d 338, 186 Cal Rptr 94 (1982).

People v Edny, 39 NY2d 620, 350 NE2d 400 (1976).

People v Hilliker, 29 Mich App 543, 185 NW2d 831 (1971).

People v Lines, 13 Cal 3d 500, 531 P2d 793, 119 Cal Rptr 225 (1975).

People v Lisnow, 80 Cal App 3d 21, 151 Cal Rptr 621 (1978).

People v Powell, 442 NYS2d 645, 83 AD2d 719 (1981).

Price v Commonwealth, 228 Va 452, 323 SE2d 106 (1984).

Raithel v Maryland, 280 Md 291, 372 A2d 1069 (1977).

Reid v Florida Real Estate Comm, 188 So 2d 846 (Fla Dist Ct App 1966).

Roberts v Louisiana, 428 US 325 (1976).

Saul v State, 6 Md App 540, 242 A2d 282 (1969).

Smith v State, 247 Ga 612, 277 SE2d 678 (1981).

State v Allery, 101 Wash 2d 591, 682 P2d 312 (1984).

State v Carter, 641 SW2d 54 (Mo 1982), *cert denied,* 461 US 932 (1983).

State v Kelly, 97 NJ 178, 478 A2d 364 (1984).

State v Kociolek, 23 NJ 400, 129 A2d 417 (1957).

State v Portis, 542 F2d 414 (7th Cir 1976).

State v Pratt, 284 Md 516, 398 A2d 421 (1979).

State v Soney, 177 NJ Super 47, 424 A2d 1182 (1980).

State v Staten, 18 Ohio St 2d 13, 247 NE2d 293 (1969).

Steele v State, 97 Wis 2d 72, 294 NW2d 2 (1980).

United States v Alvarez, 519 F2d 1036 (3d Cir 1975).

United States v Brawner, 471 F2d 969 (DC Cir 1962) (en banc).

United States v Byers, 740 F2d 1104 (DC Cir 1984).

United States v Cohen, 530 F2d 43 (8th Cir), *cert denied*, 429 US 855 (1976).

United States v Hearst, 563 F2d 1331 (9th Cir 1977), *cert denied*, 435 US 1000 (1978).

United States v Lawson, 653 F2d 299 (7th Cir 1981), *cert denied*, 459 US 893 (1982).

United States v Lyons, 731 F2d 243, (5th Cir) *cert denied*, 105 S Ct 323 (1984).

United States v Riggleman, 411 F2d 1190 (4th Cir 1969).

United States v Washington, 390 F2d 444 (DC Cir 1967).

Watters v Hubbard, 725 F2d 831 (6th Cir), *cert denied*, 105 S Ct 133 (1984).

Constitutions, Statutes, and Rules

Ariz Rev Stat Ann §13-502 (West 1985).

Cal Penal Code §25(b) (West 1985).

Cal Penal Code §29 (West Supp 1985).

Fed R Crim P 12.2(c).

Fed R Evid 403.

Fed R Evid 404(a) and (b).

Fed R Evid 702.

Fed R Evid 703.

Fed R Evid 704.

Fed R Evid 801(d)(2).

Fed R Evid 803(4).

Idaho Code §19-2515(g)(8) (Supp 1984).

Ill Rev Stat ch 38, §6-2 (1985).

Ind Code Ann §35-41-3-6 (Burns 1985).

Model Penal Code §401(1) (proposed official draft 1962).

NY Penal Law §30.05 (McKinney 1985).

Okla Stat Ann tit 21, §701.12 (West 1983).

Or Rev Stat Ann §161.295 (1983).

Tex Code Crim Proc Ann art 37.071(b)(2) (Vernon 1981).

Tex Penal Code Ann §8.02 (Vernon 1984).

US Const amend V.

Va Code §19.2-264.4c (1983).

Wash Rev Code Ann §10.95.070(8) (Supp 1984).

§12.15   WESTLAW Search References

§12.01 *Insanity Defense and Related Defenses*
    vietnam /p stress disorder trauma*** /p insan*** (mental** /3
    ill**** defect*** disease*)

    battered /3 wife woman /3 syndrome

§12.02 *Insanity Defense—The Legal Standard*
    rule standard test /s m*naghten /s critic!

    durham /s test standard rule /s mental** /3 ill! disease*
    defect***

    "model penal code" /s insan*** /s test standard rule

§12.03 —*The Role of the Expert*
    di(expert /3 testimony witness opinion /p insan*** (mental**
    /3 disease defect ill****))

    mcdonald /s 312 +4 847 /p expert /3 testimony witness opinion
    /p insan*** (mental /3 disease defect)

§12.04 —*Basis*
    synopsis,digest(expert /3 testimony opinion /5 bas** founda-
    tion /p insan*** (mental /3 defect disease))

§12.05 —*Limitations*
    expert /3 testimony witness opinion /p insan*** /s defense /p
    self-incrimination

    expert /3 testimony opinion /5 hearsay /p insan*** (mental /3
    defect disease)

§12.06 —*Testimony*
    expert /3 testimony opinion witness /s jury /5 confus***
    mislead*** /p insan***

§12.07 *Sentencing and Disposition—Legal Relevance of Psychiatric and Psychological Testimony*
punishment /3 goal purpose /p insan*** (mental /3 ill illness disorder** disease* defect***) /p psychiatr*** psycholog!

§12.08 —*Capital Offenses*
predict*** /s danger! /p (capital /3 crime punishment offense) (death /3 sentence penalty)

§12.09 —*Noncapital Offenses*
[no queries]

§12.10 —*Role of the Expert*
psychiatrist psychologist /s qualif! /s expert*** /s predict!

§12.11 —*Basis*
di(psycholog! psychiatr! /p "hypothetical question")

barefoot /p "hypothetical question"

§12.12 —*Limitations*
state court-appointed government /5 psychiatr! psycholog! /p self-incriminat!

§12.13 —*Testimony*
psychiatr*** psycholog! /3 testimony opinion /5 utility purpose

13 Legal Issues Involving Children

§13.01 Child Custody and Visitation—The Legal Standard

The placement, custody, and control of children can be an issue in a variety of legal contexts. The first half of this chapter addresses psychiatric and psychological input into these issues in the civil context—the granting of a divorce decree, its subsequent modification, and proceedings for the termination of parental rights. Discussion of these and related issues in the criminal context of prosecutions for child abuse follows.[1]

The movement of the law regarding the legal standards for child

---

[1]*See* **§13.06.**

custody and visitation has been relatively uniform nationwide.[2] By statute[3] or case law,[4] the articulated standard for custody and visitation decisions has become *the best interests of the child.* The simplicity and flexibility of this standard also prevents generalizations about its meaning or content. It requires case-by-case application and is not, like its predecessor that provided that fathers would always be given custody[5] or the tender years doctrine, that erected a presumption in favor of custody for mothers of young children,[6] necessarily given to predictable results.

Actions to change or modify a custody or visitation order apply the same *best interests* standard and set an additional requirement, a showing that since the granting of the order to be modified there has been a substantial change in circumstances.[7] This is necessary to avoid preclusion under the doctrines of res judicata and collateral estoppel. In operation the required changes in circumstances vary from case to case but contemplate some substantial change that the court issuing the order to be modified did not and could not have considered.

The legal standard for the termination of parental rights presumes that the best interests of the child will ordinarily be served by the continuation of the rights of the biological parents. This presumption is rebutted when parental abandonment, neglect, or unfitness is shown by clear and convincing evidence.[8] These showings may be made in the context of an adjudication of neglect in an action in juvenile court instituted by the welfare department or in a separate adoption or termination proceeding.

The impact of two books by Goldstein, Freud and Solnit, the first in 1973 and the second in 1979, on the content of this *best interests* test has

---

[2] *See* Mnookin, *Child Custody Adjudication: Judicial Functions in the Face of Indeterminacy,* 39 Law & Contemp Probs 226, 236 (1975).

[3] *See* Ill Ann Stat ch 40, §602 (Smith-Hurd 1980); NY Dom Rel Law §240 (McKinney Supp 1983-84); Tex Fam Code §§3.55, 14.01 (Vernon 1975).

[4] Fitzgibbon v Fitzgibbon, 197 NJ Super 63, 484 A2d 46 (1984); Baker v Baker, 411 Mich 567, 309 NW2d 532 (1981).

[5] Roth, *The Tender Years Presumption in Child Custody Disputes,* 15 J Fam L 423, 425-48 (1976-77).

[6] *Id* 432-38.

[7] *See, e.g.,* Cal Civ Code §4608 (West 1985); NY Dom Rel Law §240 *et seq* (McKinney 1985); Tex Fam Code §14.08 (Vernon Supp 1985).

[8] Santosky v Kramer, 455 US 745 (1982); Tex Fam Code §15.02 (Vernon Supp 1985). Mental illness may constitute a separate ground for termination. Ariz Rev Stat Ann §8-533(B)(3) (1974-84 Supp).

been substantial.[9] *Beyond the Best Interests of the Child*[10] and *Before the Best Interests of the Child*[11] argue that the child's best interests are served by awarding custody to the person who fills the role of psychological parent, even if that person is not the biological parent. Disruption of the bond between the child and psychological parent is thought to have untoward consequences for the child's development and to justify denial of custody to biological parents in favor of continuity with the psychological parent. The effect of these books is that much custody litigation now seeks to ascertain and turns upon the identity of the psychological parent.[12]

§13.02 —The Role of the Expert

The *best interests* standard for child custody and visitation litigation is not expressly a standard that, on its face, calls for the receipt of psychiatric or psychological evidence.[13] Unlike the legal standards for civil commitment[14] or the insanity defense,[15] for example, that are frequently cast in terms that center on the existence of a mental illness and, therefore, implicitly call for expert psychiatric or psychological testimony, the *best interests* standard in custody or visitation litigation does not, on its face, suggest a special need for expert testimony. It is a functional standard that contemplates utilization of community norms, parental experience, and common sense that does not, in the abstract, require the expertise of psychiatrists or psychologists.

Although psychiatric and psychological testimony is not required in custody and visitation proceedings, this is probably the proceeding in which such evidence is most frequently used.[16] As with many other uses of psychiatric and psychological evidence, however, its use in custody

---

[9] Symposium, *The Impact of Psychological Parenting on Child Welfare Decision-Making*, 12 NYU Rev L & Soc Change 485 (1983-84).

[10] J. Goldstein, A. Freud, & A. Solnit, Beyond the Best Interests of the Child (1973).

[11] J. Goldstein, A. Freud, & A. Solnit, Before the Best Interests of the Child (1979).

[12] Guggenheim, *The Political and Legal Implications of the Psychological Parenting Theory*, 12 NYU Rev L & Soc Change 549, 551 (1983-84).

[13] *In re* Davis, 465 A2d 614 (Pa 1983).

[14] *See* §16.01.

[15] *See* §11.10.

[16] Shuman & Weiner, *The Privilege Study: An Empirical Examination of the Psychotherapist-Patient Privilege*, 60 NC L Rev 893, 922-24 (1982).

and related determinations has been criticized.[17] The thrust of this criticism is that no empirical data exist to demonstrate that the application of psychological theory is useful in child custody determinations, that ambiguous psychological theories are often used as excuses for bad legal decisions, and that, at best, testimony based on psychological theory is simply common sense and a superfluous use of experts.[18]

In response to this criticism, it has been suggested that while there are misuses of this type of evidence in child custody, visitation, and termination proceedings, psychiatry and psychology may perform a useful function by providing courts with various information they would not otherwise receive.[19] Included in this category are the feelings, attitudes, and personality traits of the relevant parties;[20] the communication of emotions the parties are themselves unable to communicate to the court directly;[21] and the highlighting of significant portions of the evidence that might otherwise go unnoticed or unappreciated.[22]

One unique aspect of child custody and visitation litigation is that there is a broader range of categories of witnesses courts will recognize as behavioral experts than in many other types of cases. Courts that are reluctant to accept psychological testimony in criminal cases, for example, are not troubled by the admission of psychological testimony in custody and visitation cases.[23] There is little concern about experience or certification as a child or family therapist in the judicial articulation of the minimum qualifications of experts.[24] Instead, these considerations seem to have a bearing only on the weight of the evidence. The explanation for this relaxation of minimum qualifications may be that less fear exists that the jury will be inclined to follow the expert blindly on these issues on which the jury may have some experience or that the wealth of professional expertise is not limited to certain specialties. An alternate explanation may be that juries are used

---

[17] Okpaku, *Psychology: Impediment or Aid in Child Custody Cases?*, 29 Rutgers L Rev 1117 (1976).

[18] *Id.*

[19] Litwack, Gerbert, & Fenster, *The Proper Role of Psychology in Child Custody Disputes*, 18 J Fam L 269, 283 (1980).

[20] *Id.*

[21] *Id* 288.

[22] *Id* 289.

[23] Baker v Baker, 411 Mich 567, 309 NW2d 532 (1981); Richard P v Wendy P, 47 NY2d 943, 393 NE2d 1022, 419 NYS2d 949 (1979).

[24] *See, e.g., In re* Jamie M, 134 Cal App 3d 805, 184 Cal Rptr 778 (1982); Brantmeier v Brazoria Protective Serv Unit, 661 SW2d 234 (Tex Civ App 1983), (no writ).

less frequently in custody litigation than in other civil and criminal litigation.

The expert may become involved in these cases either as a court-ordered examiner or as an expert privately retained by one of the parties. When the examination occurs pursuant to a court order, the authority for which typically exists by statute,[25] the charge to the expert is clear. The expert is to conduct an examination and present a report to the court. The expert is not retained separately by either party, but instead owes a duty to remain neutral.[26]

The privately retained expert has a different role and a different set of loyalties. The privately retained expert owes a duty to the retaining party that does not exist in the case of the court-appointed expert. While the court-appointed expert is charged with making findings known to the court, the privately retained expert may not be asked in all instances to divulge findings to the court and opposing party. The privately retained expert may be utilized only to assist the attorney in preparation of the case,[27] only to treat the patient, or, following a negative report, not at all. This distinction is of consequence on the question of a testimonial privilege[28] and discovery.[29]

The use of a privately retained expert may be important in fairly traditional custody and visitation proceedings; however, it has particular appeal in those cases in which the court is being asked to reach a decision outside the community norm. Thus, for example, when the court is being asked to award custody to a homosexual parent or to a grandparent rather than a parent, psychiatric or psychological testimony may be helpful in assuaging the judge's or jury's likely adverse reaction to a nontraditional result.[30]

§13.03 —Basis

The findings of the expert should address three major areas to be helpful to the court in determining the best interests of the child—the

---

[25] Collins v Superior Court, 74 Cal App 3d 47, 141 Cal Rptr 273 (1977); DeRusse v State, 579 SW2d 224 (Tex Crim App 1979).

[26] *But see* Diamond, *The Fallacy of the Impartial Expert,* 3 Archives Crim Psychodynamics 221 (1959).

[27] *See* §18.01.

[28] *See* §13.04.

[29] *See* §10.06.

[30] *See* Painter v Bannister, 258 Iowa 1390, 140 NW2d 152, *cert denied,* 385 US 949 (1966).

reciprocal attachment between parent and child, the child's needs and the adults' parenting capacities, and relevant family dynamics.[31] The basis for an opinion addressing these areas requires the receipt of information from the parents, the child, and a variety of third parties. Failure to utilize these appropriate sources reduces the value of any resulting opinion and is a fertile ground for cross-examination.

Most determinations of custody involve a comparison of the child's biological parents and their relative abilities as custodial parents to serve the best interests of the child. To compare the two parents it is necessary that the expert have complete and comparable interviews with both parents.[32] This will happen infrequently unless the examination is court-ordered. Thus, privately retained experts will often be less likely to have an adequate basis for their opinion than court-appointed experts.

The individual parent interviews with the expert should include a mental status examination and a psychiatric history. The information gathered in this setting may reveal any gross psychopathy,[33] ulterior reasons for seeking custody such as punishing the other parent or resolving unmet needs from some unrelated situation,[34] or unrealistic expectations about parenting.[35]

A separate interview of each parent conducted with the child provides an opportunity to observe the interaction between parent and child. During this interview the child's attachment to the parents can be observed, in addition to communications between parent and child, affection, and empathy. Some experts have the parent and child perform specific tasks to facilitate this interraction.[36]

A separate interview with the child is necessary to identify the child's needs for affection, protection, and guidance. Psychological tests such as the MMPI, Rorschach, and TAT are frequently utilized as tools in this

---

[31] American Psychiatric Assn, *A Report of the Task Force on Clinical Assessment in Child Custody Cases* (1981).

[32] T. Gutheil & A. Appelbaum, Clinical Handbook of Psychiatry and the Law 274 (1982).

[33] *Id.*

[34] American Psychiatric Assn, *supra* note 31.

[35] *Id.*

[36] *Id.* There are a number of testing instruments, not designed for forensic evaluations, that address parenting abilities. T. Grisso, Evaluating Competencies: Forensic Assessments and Instruments 207-67 (1986). They may be useful structural aids to the evaluation.

evaluation.[37] There is some debate about the wisdom of asking a child for a parental preference directly, but the use of family drawings and a recently developed projective psychological test, the Bricklin Perceptual Scale, are helpful in determining the person the child considers to be the psychological parent.

The expert or social service agency should gather information from a variety of additional sources. The child's school records are an important indicator of adjustment in the environment in which most of the child's waking hours are spent. Grade fluctuations, truancy, and fighting are important sources of information about the child's adjustment to life conditions. A social service study of the home environment may reveal important information about the ability to meet the child's physical and emotional needs. Included within this category is adequate food, sleeping arrangements, clothing, play area, and privacy. Medical records, including psychiatric or psychological treatment, and law enforcement records are also relevant to provide a more complete picture of the parent and child.

§13.04   —Limitations

The principal limitation on the availability of information that may provide the basis for an expert opinion is the physician–patient privilege and its variants, the psychiatrist-patient privilege, the psychologist–patient privilege, and the psychotherapist-patient privilege.[38] Treatment of this issue is simplified by distinguishing court-ordered examinations from private examinations. Court-ordered examinations are not privileged because their purpose is not the provision of treatment to be facilitated through a confidential relationship, but, instead, the provision of a report to the court.[39] The relationship was never intended to be confidential, and, subject to this fact being made clear to the interviewee through an appropriate warning or disclosure, no obligation of nondisclosure accrues in the judicial setting.

Privately retained psychiatrists and psychologists may be divided, loosely, into those retained to treat and those retained to assist in presentation of the case. In those jurisdictions in which an applicable medical privilege exists, a privilege comes into existence initially in the case of confidential communications to a treating psychiatrist or

---

[37] *See* §2.17.

[38] *See generally* **ch 10.**

[39] **§10.02.**

psychologist.[40] This privilege may be waived and, therefore, the patient may choose to present the testimony of the treating psychiatrist or psychologist.[41] When the patient is the child and the parents are locked in a custody battle, the question of which parent may decide whether the privilege should be waived is often unclear. One approach to this question has been to appoint a guardian to determine and act upon the child's best interests in the waiver decision.[42]

The privilege may also be excepted, and statutory exceptions to the privilege are often found in child custody cases.[43] Even in those instances in which exceptions are not expressly recognized by statute for custody or visitation cases, courts often stretch other exceptions to fit this context.[44] Given the interests at stake, courts are less concerned with the parents' privacy interests here than in many other contexts. The difficulty, however, is not really whether an exception should exist, but what is relevant to the issue in the case. For example, a disclosure by the wife to her psychologist about an extramarital affair, conducted after the parties separated and while the children were otherwise properly cared for, may be within an exception to the privilege, but probably is not relevant to the best interests of the child in a custody determination. Thus, inquiry into this subject with the psychologist should be excluded on the basis of its irrelevance rather than privilege.

The psychiatrist or psychologist who is retained not to treat but to assist in preparation of the case is not covered by the physician–patient privilege or its variants, but, instead, by the attorney–client or work product privilege.[45] If the expert is not intended to be called as a witness, the information disclosed by the client to the expert in preparation for trial is protected from disclosure to the same extent as attorney–client communications.[46] If the expert is intended to be called

---

[40] *Id.*

[41] *See* §**10.03.**

[42] Nagle v Hooks, 296 Md 123, 460 A2d 49 (Ct Spec App 1983); Reames v Reames, 604 SW2d 335 (Tex Civ App 1980).

[43] *See* §**10.04.** *See also* Guernsey, *The Psychotherapist–Patient Privilege in Child Custody Placement: A Relevancy Analysis,* 26 Vill L Rev 955 (1981).

[44] *In re* Fred J, 89 Cal App 3d 168, 152 Cal Rptr 327 (1979) (expansive interpretation of waiver); Atwood v Atwood, 550 SW2d 465 (Ky 1976) (patient-litigant exception found applicable in child custody proceedings); Perry v Fiumano, 61 AD2d 512, 403 NYS2d 382 (1978) (importance of custody determination requires judicially created exception to privilege).

[45] *See* §**10.06.**

[46] Field v State, 379 So 2d 408 (Fla 1980). *See* People v Strinzger 34 Cal 3d 505, 668 P2d 738, 194 Cal Rptr 431 (1983).

at trial, the privilege will be deemed waived as to this expert.[47]

§13.05 —Testimony

The decision to accept expert testimony in custody and visitation proceedings is generally within the discretion of the trial judge. The discretion extends to the qualification of experts, the number of experts, and the admissibility of testimony of privately retained experts.[48]

The *best interests* standard applicable in custody and visitation proceedings is sufficiently vague to pose a major risk that experts will testify in unexplained conclusory fashion, masking a transformation of the applicable legal standard into a psychiatric best interests test.[49] Thus, some writers question whether experts ought even to offer a conclusion in these proceedings.[50] Although an absolute ban on psychiatric and psychological testimony utilizing the language of the ultimate issue in the case may not be directly proscribed,[51] the testimony must be helpful. This cautions against conclusory testimony or the use of unexplained psychiatric jargon.[52]

The utility of psychiatric and psychological testimony in these proceedings is in the provision of information that would be otherwise unavailable in a form that is understandable. The expert's testimony can best assist the judge or jury in determining the best interests of the child if it addresses three major areas—the reciprocal attachment between parent and child, the child's needs and the adult's parenting capacities, and relevant family dynamics.[53] The reciprocal attachment between parent and child involves an assessment of the strength and quality of the ties between each parent and the child and the child and each parent. Included in this category are such things as trust, love, and realistic relationship expectations.

Children require affection, protection, and guidance; however, the

---

[47] Fitzgibbon v Fitzgibbon, 197 NJ Super 63, 484 A2d 46 (1984); DeRusse v State, 579 SW2d 224 (Tex Crim App 1979).

[48] *In re* Department of Pub Welfare, 376 Mass 252, 381 NE2d 565 (1978); *In re* Davis, 502 Pa 110, 465 A2d 614 (1983).

[49] *See* Slovenko, *Psychological Testimony and Presumptions in Child Custody Cases,* in Law and Ethics in the Practice of Psychiatry (1981).

[50] T. Gutheil & P. Appelbaum, Clinical Handbook of Psychiatry and the Law 277 (1982).

[51] *See* §9.08.

[52] *See* §9.09.

[53] American Psychiatric Assn, *A Report of the Task Force on Clinical Assessment in Child Custody Cases* (1981).

nature and intensity of each of these requirements varies from child to child and from year to year. Similarly, the ability of each parent to provide affection, protection, and guidance varies. The expert can provide valuable assistance to the judge or jury by evaluating the child's current needs for affection, protection, and guidance, and the ability of each parent to satisfy the child's needs.

The expert may also provide useful information to the court by providing insight into family dynamics. This might include, for example, reasons the parent is seeking custody unrelated to a desire to further the welfare of the child or the effect of other relationships on the custody determination.

§13.06   Child Abuse—The Legal Standard

Criminal prosecutions for child abuse, the subject of this section, may arise out of the death or serious physical or emotional injury of a child. Accordingly, the prosecution may take the form of a charge of murder, assault, sexual assault, or rape. The ultimate legal standard for prosecution of these cases will be set by the statutory definition of the offense charged. Although the same underlying acts may give rise to civil proceedings to modify custody or visitation or to terminate parental rights, the consequences of a criminal conviction may include death or imprisonment and, therefore, invoke certain procedural protections reserved to the criminal law.

§13.07   —The Role of the Expert

In the absence of the raising of the insanity defense by the defendant charged with an act of child abuse, the receipt of psychiatric or psychological testimony is not expressly called for by the terms of the statutes in defining proceedings. Charges of murder, assault, and rape can be prosecuted or defended, at least on the face of the statute, without the necessity for psychiatric or psychological testimony. However, the nature of the victims in this class of crime—children—and the frequent absence of other witnesses raises a host of special problems. Prosecution for acts against an infant involves a victim physically unable to testify. Prosecution for acts against a young child involves a victim who may be legally disqualified from testifying[54] or whose testimony

---

[54] A child is usually presumed competent to testify at an age between 10 and 14. Below that age the child is not absolutely disqualified from testifying; instead, the judge must evaluate the "capacity and intelligence of the child, his

may be suspect because of age.[55] Moreover, the child victim may be subject to coercion by an adult—defendant, parent, police, or prosecutor. Accordingly, both the prosecution and the defense may seek to use psychiatric or psychological testimony to explain, clarify, or question evidence in these proceedings.

Because criminal proceedings reach the court after the commission of the specific act charged, the appointment of an independent examiner, as used in custody or visitation proceedings, who attempts to assess an ongoing situation, is not generally feasible. And, the ability of an expert to interview the family in a criminal proceeding will be limited by the privilege against self-incrimination. Instead, the psychologists and psychiatrists presented will largely be those chosen by the parties. Their role is not the neutral assessment of the ongoing *best interests of the child*, but to assist in the discovery of information concerning the commission of a past act.

§13.08 —Basis

One potential source of information about the injuries suffered by an allegedly abused child is the individual who provided treatment for these injuries. This may be the family physician or emergency room physician who, on one or more occasion, has seen the child and has personal knowledge of the child's physical or mental condition at a relevant time. Medical records, x-rays, and photographs of previous incidents may also be useful in establishing a history of unexplained injuries. This source of information is highly probative but may be limited by an applicable privilege, a problem discussed in §13.09.

The parents and, in some instances, the child may have received mental health care for related or unrelated problems in which acts of abuse were discussed. While these communications may provide highly relevant information about instances of abuse, their use raises the problem of privilege discussed in §13.09.

Certain circumstantial evidence, unrelated to the direct provision of medical care, is important to utilize recognized syndromes present in many instances of abuse. The information important to this analysis includes family patterns of behavior both current and historical, the

---

appreciation of the difference between truth and falsehood as well as the duty to tell the former.'' Wheeler v United States, 159 US 523, 524-25 (1895). Children as young as 5 or 6 have in some instances been found qualified to testify, but courts have been reluctant to permit younger children to testify.

[55] Cohen & Harnick, *The Susceptibility of Child Witnesses to Suggestion*, 4 Law & Hum Behav 201 (1980).

existence of other judicial proceedings for abuse, and use of alcohol or drugs.

§13.09 —Limitations

The limitation on disclosure of psychiatrist and psychologist–patient communications imposed by the physician–patient privilege and its variants is often excepted in prosecutions for child abuse.[56] In addition, many states have enacted mandatory reporting laws requiring health care professionals who witness suspected cases of child abuse to report these cases to child welfare authorities.[57] Moreover, if the patient is the child and not the parent, waiver by a court-appointed guardian avoids the privilege's limitations.[58] Thus, the scope of otherwise applicable relational privileges is substantially restricted in child abuse proceedings.

Because of the criminal consequences of these proceedings, the Fifth Amendment's privilege against self-incrimination applies to limit the admissibility of communications made to psychiatrists and psychologists conducting court-ordered examinations[59] or those permanently employed by the government. Therefore, a suspected abuser would have the right to refuse to speak with a court-appointed or government-employed psychiatrist or psychologist following the institution of charges or after the investigation reached a critical stage. Communications in the treatment context with a psychiatrist or psychologist in an emergency room, even of a public hospital, concerning the cause of the child's injuries before the commencement of an investigation, however, would not be governed by the privilege against self-incrimination.

The use of medical records of past injuries and other similar evidence raises a number of evidentiary problems. These records are hearsay, although they may be excepted from the bar of the hearsay rule under the business records exception to the hearsay rule.[60] However, to the extent that these records contain psychiatric or psychological opinions about the cause of the injuries which require a high level of inference,

---

[56] *See, e.g.*, Cal Penal Code §11171(b) (West 1982).

[57] Smith & Meyer, *Child Abuse Reporting Laws and Psychotherapy: A Time for Reconsideration*, 7 Intl J L & Psychiatry 351 (1984); Comment, *Vanishing Exception to the Psychotherapist–Patient Privilege: The Child Abuse Reporting Act*, 16 Pac LJ 335 (1984).

[58] *Cf* Nagle v Hooks, 296 Md 123, 460 A2d 49 (Ct Spec App 1983); Reames v Reames, 604 SW2d 335 (Tex Civ App 1980), (no writ).

[59] Estelle v Smith, 451 US 454 (1981).

[60] Fed R Evid 803(6).

courts may be disinclined to dispense with cross-examination.[61] The indirect introduction of these records as the basis for an in-court expert opinion is likely to have greater success than admission under the exception to the hearsay rule,[62] but may nonetheless run afoul of the rule prohibiting evidence of other crimes or wrongs to suggest that it is more likely that the accused committed the offense charged.[63]

§13.10 —Testimony

Psychiatric and psychological testimony in child abuse proceedings is often directed to one of two ends—the likelihood that a particular adult has committed an act of child abuse and the likelihood that a particular child has been abused. The likelihood that a particular adult has committed an act of child abuse is thought to be made more or less probable by the adult's conformance to a cluster of traits common in parents who are known to have abused children. This cluster of traits is often referred to as the *battering parent syndrome*.[64] Testimony on the battering parent syndrome may be useful when evidence of abuse is clear, but more than one adult had the opportunity to abuse and the identity of the abuser is not clear. Similarly, when the defendant claims that the child's injuries were accidental, testimony on the battering parent syndrome may be relevant.

The particular traits of a parent thought to make up the battering parent syndrome include low self-esteem, a short fuse, high blood pressure, strict authoritarian orientation, social isolation, and lack of trust.[65] Although there is a relatively high degree of agreement about the existence of this syndrome, not all adults who conform to it abuse

---

[61] New York Life Ins Co v Taylor, 147 F2d 297, 304 (DC Cir 1945).

[62] Fed R Evid 703.

[63] Fed R Evid 404(b) provides:

> Evidence of other crimes, wrongs, or acts is not admissible to prove the character of a person in order to show that he acted in conformity therewith. It may however be admissible for other purposes, such as proof of motive, opportunity, intent, preparation, plan, knowledge, identity, or absence of mistake or accident.

But see State v Schlak, 253 Iowa 113, 111 NW2d 289 (1961).

[64] Kempe, *Pediatric Implications of the Battered Baby Syndrome*, 46 Archives Disease in Childhood 28 (1971). *See also* B. Justice & R. Justice, The Abusing Family (1976).

[65] *Child Abuse and Neglect: Issues on Innovation and Implementation*, II Proceedings of the Second Annual National Conference on Child Abuse and Neglect 319 (1977).

children and not all child abusers conform to the syndrome. Thus, its application may be deceptive to the judge or jury.[66]

The probative value of the battering parent syndrome is the identification of a character trait that may be applied to a particular defendant to suggest behavior in conformity with that trait at the time of the act charged. The rules of evidence in most jurisdictions, however, prohibit the introduction of character evidence to show conformity.[67] An exception exists in criminal cases where the defendant may open the door to evidence of a relevant character trait, either the defendant's own or the victim's. The rationale for the rejection of character evidence to show conformity is that it is generally of low probative value and tends to distract the jury from the crime charged.[68] Therefore, evidence of the battering parent syndrome introduced by the prosecution, in the absence of the defendant's prior introduction of personal character evidence, has been rejected as a violation of the rule prohibiting the introduction of character evidence to show conformity.[69] However, because these rules are principally concerned with fairness to the defendant, evidence of the battering parent syndrome to suggest that

---

[66] Schneider, Hoffmeister, & Helfer, *A Predictive Screening Questionnaire for Potential Problems in Mother-Child Interactions,* in Child Abuse and Neglect (1976). *See In re* Cheryl, 153 Cal App 3d 1098, 200 Cal Rptr 789, 805 n 28 (1984)

[67] Fed R Evid 404(a) provides:

(a)　Character evidence generally. Evidence of a person's character or a trait of his character is not admissible for the purpose of proving that he acted in conformity therewith on a particular occasion, except:

(1)　Character of accused. Evidence of a pertinent trait of his character by an accused, or by the prosecution to rebut the same;

(2)　Character of victim. Evidence of a pertinent trait of character of the victim of the crime offered by an accused, or by the prosecution to rebut the same, or evidence of a character trait of peacefulness of the victim offered by the prosecution in a homicide case to rebut evidence that the victim was the first aggressor;

(3)　Character of witness. Evidence of the character of a witness, as provided in rules 607, 608, and 609

Arkansas, Arizona, Colorado, Nebraska, New Mexico, South Dakota, and Wyoming have adopted identical versions of Fed R Evid 404(a). J. Weinstein & M. Berger, Weinstein's Evidence ¶404(21) (1982). Alaska, Florida, Maine, Michigan, Minnesota, Montana, Nevada, North Dakota, Oklahoma, Washington, and Wisconsin have adopted substantially similar versions of the federal rule. *Id. But see* Mendez, *California's New Law on Character Evidence: Evidence Code § 352 and the Impact of Recent Psychological Studies,* 31 UCLA L Rev 1003 (1984).

[68] Fed R Evid 404 advisory committee notes, 56 FRD 183, 219-21 (1972).

[69] *In re* Cheryl, 153 Cal App 3d 1098, 200 Cal Rptr 789 (1984); State v Loebach, 310 NW2d 58 (Minn 1981).

a person other than the defendant is the abuser has been permitted.[70]

In some jurisdictions the prohibition on the use of character evidence to show conformity has been relaxed in cases involving sex crimes.[71] The rationale, often unclear, may be that conformity is thought greater for this character trait or that the rules require relaxation to prevent acquittal of this class of offenders. In these jurisdictions, evidence of the battering parent syndrome may be admissible in cases of sexual abuse.

Evidence that injuries suffered by a child were the result of abuse and not an accident is thought to be helped by testimony describing the *battered child syndrome*.[72] This cluster of symptoms, including a series of unexplained physical injuries, a wariness of contacts with adults including parents, and extremely aggressive or withdrawn behavior, describes patterns found to be common in children who have been abused. By comparing the syndrome with the facts of the instant case, issues of accident or mistake are thought to be clarified. In contrast with the battering parent syndrome, courts seem willing to admit testimony on the battered child syndrome in cases of both child beating and sexual molestation.[73] This seems to result from a characterization of this evidence as the equivalent of forensic pathology describing the cause of injuries and not character evidence of the defendant. In other instances, courts may view it as the diagnosis of a treating physician.[74] The limitation imposed, however, is that testimony concerning the person who probably committed the abuse is not permitted as an aspect of this syndrome.[75]

Another related form of testimony often sought in these cases involves an expert who, based upon conversations and play therapy with the child, opines that a child has been abused. This opinion is based on an interpretation of conversations with the child or the display of inappropriate sexual knowledge not likely to be possessed by a child who had not been subjected to sexual activities. One difficulty with this testimony is the use of the child's out-of-court assertions as the basis

---

[70] State v Conlogue, 474 A2d 167 (Me 1984).

[71] State v Huey, 145 Ariz 59, 699 P2d 1290 (1985); State v Schlak, 253 Iowa 113, 111 NW2d 289 (1961).

[72] R. Helfer & C. Kempe, The Battered Child (2d ed 1975).

[73] *In re* Cheryl, 153 Cal App 3d 1098, 200 Cal Rptr 789 (1984); State v Conlogue, 474 A2d 167 (Me 1984); State v Loebach, 310 NW2d 58 (Minn 1981); State v Wilkerson, 295 NC 559, 247 SE2d 905 (1978).

[74] Goldade v State, 674 P2d 721 (Wyo 1983).

[75] United States v Nick, 604 F2d 1199 (9th Cir 1979); *In re* Cheryl, 153 Cal App 3d 1089, 200 Cal Rptr 789 (1984); State v Durfee, 322 NW2d 778, 783 (Minn 1983). *But see* Goldade v State, 674 P2d 721 (Wyo 1983).

for the expert's in-court opinion. Some courts have flatly rejected this practice as a violation of the hearsay rule,[76] while others have viewed activities such as play with dolls as nonassertive conduct and, therefore, not hearsay.[77]

Although the child's out-of-court activities are used for the truth of the assertions implied therein and are, therefore, hearsay in many jurisdictions, they may nonetheless constitute an acceptable basis for an expert opinion. First, if the expert has treated the child and the statements were made for purposes of treatment, the child's out-of-court assertions may be expected from the hearsay rule as statements made for medical diagnosis or treatment.[78] Second, even if not excepted from the bar of the hearsay rule, an expert may base an opinion on hearsay if other experts in the field reasonably do so.[79] This would not, of course, resolve the constitutional question raised under the confrontation clause.

A related issue is the independent admission of the child's out-of-court statement as a special exception to the hearsay rule.[80] In response to concerns about sexual abuse of young children, several states have recently enacted exceptions to the hearsay rule permitting admission of the out-of-court statement of a victim of sexual abuse.[81] These statutes require that the child testify or that the child be unavailable to testify and that there be a judicial finding that the out-of-court statement is reliable. Although the constitutionality of these exceptions under the confrontation clause has yet to be resolved, they provide another potential basis for the opinion of an expert.

---

[76] Iowa v Mueller, 344 NW2d 262 (Iowa Ct App 1983).

[77] *In re* Cheryl, 153 Cal App 3d 1089, 200 Cal Rptr 789 (1984).

[78] Fed R Evid 803(4). Although the child's description of the cause of the injury to the treating physician is admissible under this exception, the identity of the assailant is thought not pertinent to treatment and, thus, not excepted. United States v Nick, 604 F2d 1199 (9th Cir 1979); State v Hankins, 612 SW2d 438(Mo Ct App 1981).

[79] Fed R Evid 703 permits an expert to base an opinion on hearsay if "of a type reasonably relied upon by experts in the particular field in forming opinions or inferences upon the subject." *Id. See* Note, *A Comprehensive Approach to Child Hearsay Statements in Sex Abuse Cases,* 83 Colum L Rev 1745 (1983).

[80] Bulkley, *Evidentiary and Procedural Trends in State Legislation and Other Emerging Legal Issues in Child Sexual Abuse Cases,* 89 Dick L Rev 645, 650 (1985); Note, *The Sexually Abused Infant Hearsay Exception: A Constitutional Analysis,* 8 J Juv L 59 (1984).

[81] Colo Rev Stat §13-25-129 (1984 Supp); Kan Stat Ann §60-460(dd) (1982 Supp); Utah Code Ann §76-5-411 (1985); Wash Rev Code Ann §9A44.120 (1985).

Still another form of evidence sought to be introduced in these proceedings is testimony regarding the credibility of the child witness. Typically, but not always, this testimony is presented by the defense to impeach. This testimony may address claims that the child's testimony is pure fantasy, an attempt at retaliation, for example, against a teacher for a low grade or a stepparent for reasons of jealousy, or the result of coercion by the police or prosecution. In addition to the general problems of intruding on the function of the jury raised by this evidence,[82] the absence of other eyewitnesses to most instances of child abuse and the fear that the child witness in these cases may be subject to a variety of influences not present in the case of adults presents a unique problem. Therefore, courts have been more willing to admit expert testimony describing typical behavior of child victims of sexual abuse to explain inconsistencies in the victim's statements than in other judicial proceedings.[83] In a majority of jurisdictions, the trial judge has the authority to order a psychiatric examination of the complaining witness in a case involving sexual abuse where corroboration is lacking and the issue of the effect of the victim's mental condition on veracity is raised.[84]

§13.11   Suggested Reading

Books

Child Abuse and Neglect: Issues on Innovation and Implementation, in II Proceedings of the Second Annual National Conference on Child Abuse and Neglect (1977).

J. Goldstein, A. Freud, & A. Solnit, *Before the Best Interests of the Child* (1979).

J. Goldstein, A. Freud, & A. Solnit, *Beyond the Best Interests of the Child* (1973).

T. Grisso, *Evaluating Competencies: Forensic Assessments and Instruments* (1986).

---

[82] *See* **ch 17.**

[83] State v Middleton, 294 Or 427, 657 P2d 1215 (1983).

[84] *See, e.g.,* State v Wahrlich, 105 Ariz 102, 459 P2d 727 (1969); Ballard v Superior Court, 64 Cal 2d 159, 410 P2d 838, 49 Cal Rptr 302 (1966); State v Gregg, 226 Kan 481, 602 P2d 85 (1979); State v Maestas, 190 Neb 312, 207 NW2d 699 (1973); Washington v State, 96 Nev 305, 608 P2d 1101 (1980). *But see* Commonwealth v Widrick, 392 Mass 884, 467 NE2d 1353 (1984); People v Souvenir, 83 Misc 2d 1038, 373 NYS2d 824 (Crim Ct 1975).

T. Gutheil & P. Appelbaum, *Clinical Handbook of Psychiatry and the Law* (1982).

R. Helfer & C. Kempe, *The Battered Child* (2d ed 1975).

B. Justice & R. Justice, *The Abusing Family* (1976).

J. Weinstein & M. Berger, *Weinstein's Evidence* (1982).

Articles

American Psychiatric Assn, *A Report of the Task Force on Clinical Assessment in Child Custody Cases* (1981).

Bulkley, *Evidentiary and Procedural Trends in State Legislation and Other Emerging Legal Issues in Child Sexual Abuse Cases*, 89 Dick L Rev 645 (1985).

Cohen & Harnick, *The Susceptibility of Child Witnesses to Suggestion*, 4 Law & Hum Behav 201 (1980).

Comment, *Vanishing Exception to the Psychotherapist-Patient Privilege: The Child Abuse Reporting Act*, 16 Pac LJ 335 (1984).

Diamond, *The Fallacy of the Impartial Expert*, 3 Archives Crim Psychodynamics 221 (1959).

Guernsey, *The Psychotherapist-Patient Privilege in Child Custody Placement: A Relevancy Analysis*, 26 Vill L Rev 955 (1981).

Guggenheim, *The Political and Legal Implications of the Psychological Parenting Theory*, 12 NYU Rev of L & Soc Change 549 (1983-84).

Kempe, *Pediatric Implications of the Battered Baby Syndrome*, 46 Archives Disease in Childhood 28 (1971).

Litwack, Gerbert, & Fenster, *The Proper Role of Psychology in Child Custody Disputes*, 18 J Fam L 269 (1980).

Mendez, *California's New Law on Character Evidence: Evidence Code § 352 and the Impact of Recent Psychological Studies*, 31 UCLA L Rev 1003 (1984).

Mnookin, *Child Custody Adjudication: Judicial Functions in the Face of Indeterminancy*, 39 L & Contemp Probs 226 (1975).

Note, *A Comprehensive Approach to Child Hearsay Statements in Sex Abuse Cases*, 83 Colum L Rev 1745 (1983).

Note, *The Sexually Abused Infant Hearsay Exception: A Constitutional Analysis*, 8 J Juv L 59 (1984).

Okpaku, *Psychology: Impediment or Aid in Child Custody Cases?*, 29 Rutgers L Rev 1117 (1976).

Roth, *The Tender Years Presumption in Child Custody Disputes*, 15 J Fam L 423 (1976-77).

Schneider, Hoffmeister, & Helfer, *A Predictive Screening Questionnaire for*

Potential Problems in Mother-Child Interactions, in Child Abuse and Neglect (1976).

Shuman & Weiner, *The Privilege Study: An Empirical Examination of the Psychotherapist-Patient Privilege,* 60 NC L Rev 893 (1982).

Slovenko, *Psychological Testimony and Presumptions in Child Custody Cases,* in Law and Ethics in the Practice of Psychiatry (1981).

Smith & Meyer, *Child Abuse Reporting Laws and Psychotherapy: A Time for Reconsideration,* 7 Intl J L & Psychiatry 351 (1984).

Symposium, *The Impact of Psychological Parenting on Child Welfare Decision-Making,* 12 NYU Rev of L & Soc Change, 485 (1983-84).

Cases

Atwood v Atwood, 550 SW2d 465 (Ky 1976).

Baker v Baker, 411 Mich 567, 309 NW2d 532 (1981).

Ballard v Superior Court, 64 Cal 2d 159, 410 P2d 838, 49 Cal Rptr 302 (1966).

Brantmeier v Brazoria Protective Service Unit, 661 SW2d 234 (Tex Civ App 1983) (no writ).

Cheryl, In re, 153 Cal App 3d 1098, 200 Cal Rptr 789 (1984).

Collins v Superior Court, 74 Cal App 3d 47, 141 Cal Rptr 273 (1977).

Commonwealth v Widrick, 392 Mass 884, 467 NE2d 1353 (1984).

Davis, In re, 502 Pa 110, 465 A2d 614 (1983).

Department of Public Welfare, In re, 376 Mass 252, 381 NE2d 565 (1978).

DeRusse v State, 579 SW2d 224 (Tex Crim App 1979).

Estelle v Smith, 451 US 454 (1981).

Field v State, 379 So 2d 408 (Fla 1980).

Fitzgibbon v Fitzgibbon, 197 NJ Super 63, 484 A2d 46 (1984).

Fred J, In re, 89 Cal App 3d 168, 152 Cal Rptr 327 (1979).

Goldade v State, 674 P2d 721 (Wyo 1983).

Iowa v Mueller, 344 NW2d 262 (Iowa Ct App 1983).

Jamie M, In re, 134 Cal App 3d 805, 184 Cal Rptr 778 (1982).

Mault v Elliot, 329 Mich 544, 46 NW2d 373 (1951).

Nagle v Hooks, 296 Md 123, 460 A2d 49 (Ct Spec App 1983).

New York Life Insurance Co v Taylor, 147 F2d 297 (DC Cir 1945).

People v Souvenir, 83 Misc 2d 1038, 373 NYS2d 824 (1975).

Richard P v Wendy P, 47 NY2d 943, 393 NE2d 1022, 419 NYS2d 949 (1979).

Painter v Bannister, 258 Iowa 1390, 140 NW2d 152, *cert denied,* 385 US 949 (1966).

People v Strinzger, 34 Cal 3d 505, 668 P2d 738, 194 Cal Rptr 431 (1983).

Perry v Fiumano, 61 AD2d 512, 403 NYS2d 382 (1978).

Reames v Reames, 604 SW2d 335 (Tex Civ App 1980), (no writ)

Santosky v Kramer, 455 US 745 (1982).

State v Conlogue, 474 A2d 167 (Me 1984).

State v Durfee, 322 NW2d 778 (Minn 1983).

State v Gregg, 226 Kan 481, 602 P2d 85 (1979).

State v Hankins, 612 SW2d 438 (Mo Ct App 1981).

State v Huey, 145 Ariz 59, 699 P2d 1290 (1985).

State v Loebach, 310 NW2d 58 (Minn 1981).

State v Maestas, 190 Neb 312, 207 NW2d 699 (1973).

State v Middleton, 294 Or 427, 657 P2d 1215 (1983).

State v Schlak, 253 Iowa 113, 111 NW2d 289 (1961).

State v Wahrlich, 105 Ariz 102, 459 P2d 727 (1969).

State v Wilkerson, 295 NC 559, 247 SE2d 905 (1978).

United States v Nick, 604 F2d 1199 (9th Cir 1979).

Washington v State, 96 Nev 305, 608 P2d 1101 (1980).

Wheeler v United States, 159 US 523 (1895).

Statutes and Rules

Ariz Rev Stat §8-533(B)(3) (1974-84 Supp).

Cal Civ Code §4608 (West 1985).

Cal Penal Code §11171(b) (West 1982).

Colo Rev Stat §13-25-129 (1984 Supp).

Fed R Evid 404.

Fed R Evid 703.

Fed R Evid 803(4) & (6).

Ill Ann Stat ch 40, §602 (Smith-Hurd 1980).

Kan Stat Ann §60-460(dd) (1982 Supp).

NY Dom Rel Laws §240 *et seq* (McKinney 1985).

Tex Fam Code §§3.55, 14.01 (Vernon 1975).

Tex Fam Code §§14.08, 15.02 (Vernon Supp 1985).

Utah Code Ann §76-5-411 (1985).

Wash Rev Code Ann §9A44.120 (1985).

§13.12   WESTLAW Search References

§13.01 *Child Custody and Visitation—The Legal Standard*
　　　"best interest" /s child! /s standard

§13.02 *—The Role of the Expert*
　　　custody visitation /s psycholog! psychiatr*** /3 testimony
　　　evidence % topic(110)

§13.03 *—Basis*
　　　custody visitation /p psycholog! psychiatr*** expert /3 opinion
　　　testimony /5 foundation % topic(110)

§13.04 *—Limitations*
　　　custody visitation /p psycholog! psychiatr*** /s privilege* %
　　　topic(110)

§13.05 *—Testimony*
　　　custody visitation /p psycholog! psychiatr*** /s testi! /s judge
　　　jury % topic(110)

§13.06 *Child Abuse—The Legal Standard*
　　　topic(134) & custody visitation /s "child abuse"

§13.07 *—The Role of the Expert*
　　　custody visitation /p psycholog! psychiatr*** expert /3 testimo-
　　　ny evidence /p "child abuse"

§13.08 *—Basis*
　　　[no queries]

§13.09 *—Limitations*
　　　custody visitation /p child /3 abuse /p self-incrimination
　　　physician doctor psychiatr*** psycholog! /5 privilege*

§13.10 *—Testimony*
　　　child /3 abus! /p "battering parent"

　　　child /3 abus! /p "character trait"

　　　"child abuse" /p victim witness /s credib!

14

Personal Injury Litigation

Personal Injuries in the Judicial Setting

§14.01   Personal Injury Litigation

Sections 14.01 through **14.08** deal with actions in which the state and federal courts have original jurisdiction to try claims for which damages are sought for mental or emotional injuries. This class of actions is to be distinguished from actions in which damages are sought for mental or emotional injuries where original jurisdiction exists in an administrative tribunal. The latter class of administrative determinations includes social security disability and workers' compensation claims, which are treated in §§**14.09** through **14.19.**

One of the critical distinctions between judicial and administrative determinations is that, unlike judicial determinations, administrative determinations do not typically involve juries or traditional rules of evidence. In addition, the reasons underlying the creation of the administrative systems give rise to awards varying in structure and size from those given in judicial proceedings. Therefore, the judicial and administrative systems are examined separately to consider the differences they portend for the use of psychiatric and psychological evidence. The treatment of judicial proceedings seeking recovery for mental or emotional injuries is itself divided, according to the distinction made in the substantive law, between actions seeking damages for mental or emotional injuries that are a consequence of physical injuries and mental or emotional injuries that are not a consequence of physical impact or injury. A separate discussion of the legal standard and role of the expert is provided for each; however, the sections on basis, limitations, and testimony are treated jointly.

§14.02   Mental and Emotional Consequences of Physical Injuries—The Legal Standard

The common law has long been wary of permitting recovery for mental or emotional injuries because of the fear that an absence of demonstrably verifiable injuries posed a risk of fraud to which the courts could not effectively respond. One aspect of a gradual diminution of that fear is that a plaintiff may now recover damages for mental or emotional injuries, in all jurisdictions, if these are proximately related to compensable physical injuries.[1] The presence of related physical

---

[1] Oziokonshi v Babineau, 375 Mass 555, 380 NE2d 1295 (1978); Tobin v Grossman, 24 NY2d 609, 249 NE2d 419 (1969); Sinn v Byrd, 486 Pa 146, 404 A2d 672 (1979); Hughes v Moore, 214 Va 27, 197 SE2d 214 (1973).

injuries serves two purposes. First, the physical injuries are thought to provide some safeguard against fraud by demanding some demonstrable evidence that the plaintiff has actually been injured. Second, courts have come to accept that physical trauma may have an emotional consequence and are, therefore, more willing to permit recovery in these instances.[2]

A common illustration of this rule is recovery for pain resulting from a physical injury proximately caused by the defendant's negligence.[3] Another example would be recovery for a seizure disorder resulting in blackouts caused by physical injuries suffered in an automobile collision resulting from the defendant's negligence.[4]

§14.03 —The Role of the Expert

The necessity for presenting expert psychiatric or psychological testimony to support a claim for mental or emotional injuries depends on the nature of the relationship between the accident and the injuries. If the relationship of the mental or emotional injuries to the accident or the physical trauma is not a matter of common knowledge likely to be possessed by the average judge or juror, expert testimony is required to avoid a directed verdict on this item of damages.[5] For example, expert psychiatric or psychological testimony has been required to establish a relationship between a fall and schizophrenia[6] or electric shock and *psychoneurosis.*[7] These injuries are not likely to be understood by a typical judge or juror as following from physical trauma. Conversely, pain and suffering have been explainable without the necessity of expert testimony.[8] A typical judge or juror is thought likely to understand that pain and suffering may follow from physical trauma.

Two frequent uses of psychiatric and psychological evidence on the mental or emotional consequences of physical injuries are testimony regarding organic brain injury and psychological adjustment to physical injury.[9] Organic brain injury resulting from a physical trauma may

---

[2] Murphy v Penn Fruit Co, 274 Pa Super 427, 418 A2d 480 (1980).

[3] Tramutola v Bortine, 63 NJ 9, 304 A2d 197 (1973).

[4] Galovich v Hertz Corp, 513 SW2d 325 (Mo 1974).

[5] Foley v Kibrick, 12 Mass App Ct 382, 425 NE2d 376 (1981).

[6] Pagan v Dewitt P Henry Co, 27 Pa Commw 495, 365 A2d 463 (1976).

[7] Hess v Philadelphia Transp Co, 358 Pa 144, 56 A2d 89 (1948).

[8] Jones v Miller, 290 A2d 587 (DC 1972).

[9] Hyath v Sierra Boat Co, 79 Cal App 3d 325, 145 Cal Rptr 47 (1978).

include nerve and spinal cord damage[10] or paralysis.[11] Generally, the central issue in these cases is the degree of relation between the physical injury and the organic brain injury. The cases typically turn on the requirement of reasonable medical certainty.[12] If the expert expresses uncertainty about the relationship between the physical injury and the organic brain injury, exclusion of the testimony and a directed verdict on this issue may result.[13]

Psychological testimony about adjustment to physical injuries frequently entails testimony about pain. Although expert testimony is not generally necessary to support a claim for pain resulting from physical injuries,[14] expert testimony on this issue is admissible.[15] Frequently, such testimony raises a question of the scope of psychological expertise. Some courts are hesitant to permit psychologists, who lack a medical education,[16] to suggest that pain is likely to occur in the future,[17] apparently because that entails a prediction of the course of the physical injury. However, other courts have permitted psychologists to opine that the cause of pain was organic because no evidence of malingering was found.[18]

Other testimony about psychological adjustment to physical injury relates to post-traumatic stress disorder.[19] This disorder, formally recognized in DSM-III, involves reexperiencing a traumatic event in a manner that has psychological consequences beyond the range of common human experience.[20] The consequences may include anxiety, muscular tension, irritability, impaired memory, repetitive nightmares, sexual inhibitions, or social withdrawal.[21] The explanation often given for this disorder is that it entails a psychological transformation of

---

[10] Lindsay v Baltimore & Ohio Ry Co, 98 Ohio App 63, 128 NE2d 242 (1954).

[11] Buckler v Sinclair Ref Co, 68 Ill App 2d 283, 216 NE2d 14 (1966).

[12] Bell v New York City Health & Hosp Corp, 104 NE2d 872, 456 NYS2d 787 (1982). See §9.07.

[13] Hussey v May Dept Stores, Inc, 238 Pa Super 431, 357 A2d 635 (1976).

[14] Jones v Miller, 290 A2d 587 (DC 1972).

[15] Riddle v Dickens, 241 Md 579, 217 A2d 304 (1966).

[16] See §4.10.

[17] Casimere v Herman, 28 Wis 2d 437, 137 NW2d 73 (1975).

[18] Buckler v Sinclair Ref Co, 68 Ill App 2d 283, 216 NE2d 14 (1966).

[19] See H. Davidson, Post Traumatic Psychoses (1972).

[20] American Psychiatric Assn, Diagnostic and Statistical Manual of Mental Disorders 308.30 & 308.81 (3d ed 1980) (DSM-III).

[21] Modlin, The Post Accident Anxiety Syndrome: Psychosocial Aspects, 123 Am J Psychiatry 1008 (1967).

excessive stress and tension involved in the injury from an unacceptable form, such as poor performance at work, to an acceptable form of disability, such as paralysis of a limb.[22] Post-traumatic stress disorder is distinguished from malingering, the voluntary production of false or exaggerated symptoms to achieve a particular goal such as compensation.[23]

§14.04   Emotional Assaults—The Legal Standard

The initial response of American courts to attempts to recover for mental or emotional injuries sustained in the absence of physical impact was to deny recovery.[24] Without some objective event, a physical impact, to verify that the defendant's conduct caused harm to the plaintiff, courts found that the risk of fraud and the absence of an adequate measure of damages prevented judicial control of these actions and denied recovery. Although a minority of jurisdictions still cling to this limitation,[25] the majority have relaxed this limitation in one fashion or another. The first form of relaxation of the limitation on recovery for mental or emotional injuries in the absence of physical impact was in cases involving intentional rather than negligent infliction of emotional distress.[26] Subsequently, in varying degrees in most jurisdictions, the limitation has been relaxed in cases of negligent infliction of emotional harm.

One approach has been to permit recovery for emotional harm in the absence of a physical impact when the emotional consequences are accompanied by some physical or objective evidence corroborating the emotional disorder.[27] For example, in *Landreth v Reed*,[28] a behavioral psychologist was permitted to testify to a child's emotional injuries in a case in which the child observed the drowning of a sibling and these injuries were accompanied by hyperactivity, loss of weight, nervousness, and difficulty sleeping.

---

[22] Weinstein, *The Concept of the Disability Process,* 19 Psychomatics 94 (1978).

[23] DSM III, *supra note 20, at VG5 20.*

[24] Magruder, *Mental and Emotional Disturbances in the Law of Torts,* 49 Harv L Rev 1033 (1936).

[25] Butchikas v Travelers Indem Co, 343 So 2d 816 (Fla 1976); Howard v Bloodworth, 137 Ga App 478, 224 SE2d 122 (1976); Kroger v Beck, 175 Ind App 202, 375 NE2d 640 (1978).

[26] Nickerson v Hodges, 146 La 735, 84 So 37 (1920).

[27] Sutton Motor Co v Crysel, 289 SW2d 631 (Tex Civ App 1956) (no writ); Hunsley v Giard, 87 Wash 2d 424, 553 P2d 1096 (1976).

[28] 570 SW2d 486 (Tex Civ App 1976), (no writ).

Other jurisdictions have abandoned the requirement of physical impact or objective consequences and have focused instead on proximate causation as a limitation on the range of liability-producing events. The question in these jurisdictions is whether the injured party was in the zone of risk.[29] More recently, that question has been reformulated to ask whether the injuries to that person were foreseeable.[30] For example, in *Molien v Kaiser Foundation Hospital*,[31] a physician negligently misdiagnosed and informed Mrs. Molien that she had tested positively for syphilis. She informed her husband, accused him of extramarital sexual relations, and initiated proceedings for divorce. The court found the wife's disclosure to the husband foreseeable, and the physician's duty therefore extended to the husband even in the absence of physical injuries suffered by him.

§14.05   —The Role of the Expert

The recognition of the right to recover for emotional injuries without accompanying physical impact or consequence relies heavily on the assumption that psychiatrists and psychologists can verify the legitimacy of such claims. Judges and juries expect psychiatric and psychological testimony in support of the claims and may be extremely skeptical of claimants who do not present this testimony. However, as a matter of law, psychiatric and psychological testimony may not be required to support all claims for emotional injuries. Laypersons may testify to their perception of pain, for example, and friends or neighbors may testify to changes observed in the claimant's behavior.[32]

A major issue in the use of psychiatrists and psychologists to verify mental or emotional injuries in cases without accompanying physical impact or injury is whether psychiatrists and psychologists are capable of detecting malingering,[33] the voluntary falsification or fabrication of physical or psychological symptoms.[34] Three approaches have been

---

[29] Tobin v Grossman, 24 NY2d 609, 249 NE2d 419, 301 NYS2d 554 (1969).

[30] Dillon v Legg, 68 Cal 2d 728, 441 P2d 912, 69 Cal Rptr 72 (1968); Rodrigues v State, 52 Hawaii 156, 472 P2d 509 (1970); Sinn v Byrd, 486 Pa 146, 404 A2d 672 (1979); Sanchez v Schindler, 651 SW2d 249 (Tex 1983).

[31] 27 Cal 3d 916, 616 P2d 813, 167 Cal Rptr 831 (1980).

[32] Jones v Miller, 290 A2d 587 (DC 1972). *But see* Fischer v Famous—Barr Co, 618 SW2d 446 (Mo Ct App 1981).

[33] Rogers & Cavanaugh, *"Nothing but the Truth"* . . . *A Reexamination of Malingering,* 11 J Psychiatry & L 443 (1983).

[34] American Psychiatric Assn, Diagnostic and Statistical Manual of Mental Disorders V65.20 (3d ed 1980) (DSM-III).

utilized by psychiatrists and psychologists to detect malingering—psychometric measurements, clinical interviews and observations, and psychophysiological measurements. Psychometric detection of malingering involves the use of psychological tests to provide an indirect measurement of malingering. The MMPI has been found to be the most helpful psychological test in identifying exaggeration and minimization of symptoms, although it will not identify all malingering and erroneously identifies malingering in other instances.[35] The WAIS and Rorschach tests have been found less helpful in identifying malingering than the MMPI. Clinical observation and interviewing, while often relied on in judicial proceedings, have not yet been proven in the scientific literature to be effective in the detection of malingering.[36] Psychophysiological measurement of malingering, by use of the polygraph, is mired in the controversy surrounding its use in general, and its utility in the detection of malingering is not clear.[37]

§14.06   —Basis

The psychiatrist or psychologist whose testimony is offered may have become familiar with the patient-litigant during treatment or solely for purposes of the trial. This distinction is consequential on the subject of privilege discussed in §14.07 and, as discussed in this section, on the permissible bases to support an opinion at trial. The psychiatrist or psychologist who has treated the patient is permitted to utilize an examination of the patient and relevant history related by the patient as the basis for an opinion without the bar of the hearsay rule. The examination is not hearsay, for it is not an oral assertion or necessarily assertive conduct, but, instead, an observation. The patient's rendition of a history is an out-of-court assertion utilized for its truth and may, therefore, constitute hearsay; however, an applicable exception to the hearsay rule exists. Statements of medical history, made for purposes of medical diagnosis or treatment, are excepted from the hearsay rule because it is assumed that a patient has an incentive to be truthful when medical treatment turns on the accuracy of the information provided.[38] Thus, a treating psychiatrist or psychologist may use statements made

---

[35] Rogers & Cavanaugh, *supra* note 33, at 450.

[36] *Id* 452.

[37] *Id* 453.

[38] Fed R Evid 803(4) excepts "[s]tatements made for purposes of medical diagnosis or treatment and describing medical history, or past or present symptoms, pain, or sensations, or the inception or general character of the

by the patient in treatment that were pertinent to treatment as the basis for an in-court opinion. The time that is of consequence in determining whether the expert is a treating psychiatrist or psychologist is the time the statement was made by the patient. Even if the expert is not treating the patient at the time of trial, if the expert was when the statement was made, it falls within the exception.

Statements made by the patient to a nontreating expert are not assumed to be made with the same incentive to be truthful and, therefore, do not qualify as an exception to the hearsay rule under the statements made for medical diagnosis or treatment exception.[39] Thus, they constitute hearsay, and, without more, may not be used as the basis for an expert's opinion. Although a general relaxation of the use of hearsay as the basis for an expert's opinion has been permitted in those instances in which the out-of-court basis is typically and reasonably used by experts in the field, this relaxation has been more favored in the case of treating physicians.[40] If the patient's statements are sought to be relied upon by an opponent, they fall within the admission exception to the hearsay rule.[41]

§14.07   —Limitations

In addition to the hearsay rule discussed in §14.06, privilege and work product provide another potential limitation on the testimony of psychiatrists and psychologists in these proceedings.[42] The initial distinction of consequence in application of a privilege is that of the treating versus the examining expert. A privilege comes into existence initially in the case of the treating psychiatrist or psychologist; however, the patient-litigant may waive the privilege by calling the therapist as

---

cause or external source thereof insofar as reasonably pertinent to diagnosis or treatment."

Identical versions of this rule have been adopted in the following states: Alaska, Arizona, Colorado, Delaware, Hawaii, Iowa, Maine, Montana, Nebraska, North Carolina, North Dakota, Ohio, Oregon, South Dakota, Texas, Utah, Washington, and Wyoming. J. Weinstein & M. Berger, Weinstein's Evidence ¶803(4) [02] (1984). Florida, Michigan, Oklahoma, and Vermont have adopted substantially similar rules. *Id.*

[39] Marshall v Papineau, 132 So 2d 786 (Fla Dist Ct App 1961); Preveden v Metropolitan Life Ins Co, 200 Minn 524, 274 NW 685 (1937); Texas Employers Assoc v Wallace, 70 SW2d 832 (Tex Civ App 1934) (no writ).

[40] *See* §9.05.

[41] Fed R Evid 801(d)(2).

[42] *See generally* ch 10.

a witness. Even in the absence of an express waiver, in virtually all jurisdictions the patient-litigant exception to the privilege excepts the application of the privilege to communications made in the context of treatment for injuries for which damages are sought.[43] The major question that arises in these instances is the extent of the waiver as to more remote treatments for the same condition and treatments for other conditions. This issue arises frequently when the defendant claims, for example, the existence of an earlier injury as the entire or partial cause of the plaintiff's injuries. The resolution of this question does not turn on a privilege analysis so much as it does on a relevance analysis.[44]

Statements to a nontreating psychiatrist or psychologist are not cloaked with any protection by the physician–patient privilege or its variants. Instead, any protection enjoyed derives from the attorney–client or work product privilege.[45] If the expert is called as a witness by the retaining party, any protection is waived and introduction of statements made by the patient-litigant may be obtained without the bar of the hearsay rule under the admissions exception.[46] If the expert is

---

[43] *See, e.g., In re* Lifshultz, 2 Cal 3d 415, 467 P2d 557, 85 Cal Rptr 829 (1970). In addition, a request to receive copies of reports prepared following a court-ordered examination, under Rule 35 of the Federal Rules of Civil Procedure, operates as a waiver of any applicable privilege for examinations of the same condition. *See* §**10.03.**

[44] Drake v Goodman, 386 Mass 88, 434 NE2d 1211 (1982) (medical malpractice and psychiatry); Walsh v Snyder, 295 Pa Super 94, 441 A2d 365 (1981) (heart condition and stress leading to a heart attack).

[45] *See* §**10.07.**

[46] Fed R Evid 801:

> (d) Statements which are not hearsay. A statement is not hearsay if—
> . . .
> (2) Admission by party-opponent. The statement is offered against a party and is (A) his own statement, in either his individual or a representative capacity or (B) a statement of which he has manifested his adoption or belief in its truth, or (C) a statement by a person authorized by him to make a statement concerning the subject, or (D) a statement by his agent or servant concerning a matter within the scope of his agency or employment, made during the existence of the relationship, or (E) a statement by a coconspirator of a party during the course and in furtherance of the conspiracy.

Alaska, Arizona, Colorado, Iowa, Minnesota, Montana, Nebraska, New Mexico, North Dakota, South Dakota, Utah, Vermont, Wisconsin, and Wyoming have adopted identical versions of the federal rule. J. Weinstein & M. Berger, Weinstein's Evidence, ¶801(d)(2)[02] (1984). Arkansas, Delaware, Florida, Ohio, Oklahoma, Oregon, North Carolina, and Texas adopted substantially similar versions of the federal rule. *Id.*

intended to be called as a witness, the expert's identity is subject to discovery and so, in all likelihood, is the basis for the opinion.[47] Only if the expert is used exclusively to prepare for trial but is not called or intended to be called as a witness can disclosures to a nontreating expert be protected from compelled disclosure.

§14.08   —Testimony

Courts generally accept that psychiatric and psychological testimony may be valuable in explaining psychological stress and mental disease.[48] The difficulties encountered with psychiatric and psychological testimony instead concern the relatedness of the accident and the psychological injury and the degree of the certainty expressed by the witness concerning this relationship. Courts have often expressed skepticism as experts have sought to relate seeming unrelated emotional injury to an accident. Courts may resolve these disputes by permitting the jury to evaluate the expert's testimony or by concluding that the limits of believability have been exceeded. The vehicle for accomplishing this latter result is often the manner in which the expert expresses the degree of confidence in the nexus between the accident and emotional injury. If the expert states that the relationship is merely possible, but does not utilize the language of reasonable medical certainty,[49] the court may conclude that the requisite degree of certainty is not present and exclude the opinion.

Personal Injuries in the Administrative Setting

§14.09   Disability Claims in the Administrative Setting

Variations in state law may result in a claim for a particular injury being determined by an administrative tribunal in one state and a court in another state. The difference in the setting for the adjudication greatly affects the use of psychiatric and psychological evidence. Administrative mechanisms for adjudication of claims like workers' compensation were created to dispose of claims more efficiently than the courts were able to do and with greater certainty. One aspect of

---

[47] *See* §**10.07.**
[48] Casimere v Herman, 28 Wis 2d 437, 137 NW2d 73 (1965).
[49] *See* §**9.07.**

greater efficiency has been the elimination of jury trials. And, with the elimination of jury trials, the rules of evidence, a product of the jury system, have also largely been eliminated leaving relevance as the principal limitation on the admissibility of evidence. Thus, the hearsay rule is not typically applicable, with the result that expert evidence in these proceedings is frequently not presented orally. This may increase the availability of expert evidence while at the same time decreasing its effect.

The specialized decision-makers in these administrative proceedings also gain a familiarity with the types of injuries compensable under these schemes—their cause, treatment, and prognosis. This familiarity affects the use of experts by reducing the possibility that the decision-maker will be in awe of the expert and blindly rubber-stamp the expert's conclusions. In addition, it creates the risk that the expert's opinion may be given too little weight when it appears inconsistent with evidence given in similar cases.

§14.10 Workers' Compensation—The Legal Standard

The workers' compensation system is a state-created statutory scheme created to compensate workers who are unable to perform or obtain work suitable to their qualifications as the result of an injury that has a substantial causal nexus to an accident that occurred while the worker was employed. Physical injury or trauma causing mental or emotional injury is compensable in workers' compensation systems in virtually all jurisdictions.[50] For example, a waitress struck in the face by a customer was permitted to recover for resulting numbness, dizziness, and forgetfulness.[51] In another case of recovery for mental or emotional consequences of a physical injury, a miner injured in the neck and shoulders by falling debris was permitted to recover for the paralysis of his arm without apparent physiological cause.[52]

Controversy arises when the mental or emotional injuries are not caused by physical injury or trauma, but instead by a psychological stress alone. The majority of courts addressing this issue have interpreted the applicable state statutes not to distinguish between physical and mental

---

[50] A. Larson, The Law of Workman's Compensation §42.22 (1982).

[51] Mitchell v White Castle Sys, 290 NW2d 753 (Minn 1980).

[52] American Smelting & Ref Co v Industrial Commn, 59 Ariz 87, 123 P2d 163 (1942).

injuries if the consequence is to disable the worker.[53] Thus, for example, in *Bailey v American General Insurance Co*,[54] a worker who witnessed a coworker's eight-story fatal fall, but who suffered no physical injury himself, was permitted to recover for a fear of disaster. And, in *Wolfe v Sibley, Lindsay & Curr & Co*,[55] a worker was permitted to recover for emotional strain after discovering the body of a supervisor who committed suicide.

Some courts that permit recovery for mental or emotional injuries suffered in the workplace without a precipitating physical cause require something more than the stress of the day-to-day workplace to cause the mental or emotional injury.[56] Thus, for example, the daily strain of work on an assembly line or the ongoing strain of a busy newspaper production manager will not justify compensation.[57] Instead, some stressful event beyond that encountered in an average workday is required.

A minority of jurisdictions do not permit recovery for mental or emotional injury unless caused by a physical injury or trauma.[58] Even in the face of an extremely stressful event to the claimant in this minority of jurisdictions, no recovery is permitted in the absence of a physical injury. Thus, for example, in *Followill v Emerson Electric Co*,[59] a worker who saw a friend and coworker's head crushed in a die cast press was denied recovery for consequential emotional injuries.

Although malingering, the voluntary falsification or exaggeration of physical or psychological symptoms,[60] is not compensable,[61] post-

---

[53] Carter v GM Corp, 361 Mich 577, 106 NW2d 105 (1960); *In re* Compensation of McGarrah, 59 Or App 448, 651 P2d 153, (1982); Wolfe v Sibley, Lindsay & Curr & Co, 36 NY 505, 330 NE2d 603, 369 NYS2d 637 (1975); Bailey v American Gen Ins Co, 154 Tex 430, 279 SW2d 315 (1955).

[54] 154 Tex 430, 279 SW2d 315 (1955).

[55] 36 NY 505, 330 NE2d 603, 369 NYS2d 637 (1975).

[56] Transportation Ins Co v Maksyn, 580 SW2d 334 (Tex 1979); School Dist No 1 v Department of Indus, Labor & Human Relations, 62 Wis 2d 370, 215 NW2d 373 (1974); Consolidated Freightways v Drake, 678 P2d 874 (Wyo 1984).

[57] Transportation Ins Co v Maksyn, 580 SW2d 334 (Tex 1979).

[58] Brady v Royal Mfg Co, 117 Ga App 312, 160 SE2d 424 (1968); Followill v Emerson Elec Co, 234 Kan 791, 674 P2d 1050 (1984).

[59] 234 Kan 791, 674 P2d 1050 (1984).

[60] American Psychiatric Assn, Diagnostic and Statistical Manual of Mental Disorders V65.20 (3d ed 1980) (DSM-III).

[61] Swift & Co v Ware, 53 Ga App 500, 186 SE 452 (1936).

traumatic stress disorder[62] is generally compensable if sufficiently related to a requisite accident or injury.[63]

§14.11 —The Role of the Expert

Although expert testimony is not generally necessary to tie the accident to the injury claimed, where lay knowledge is not adequate to link the two, expert testimony will be required to substantiate a claim.[64] This requirement is frequently invoked when claims for nervous injuries or traumatic neurosis are made.[65] Thus, for example, in the case of a high school teacher who claimed to have suffered mental stress and emotional trauma after an assault by a student, but who presented no expert psychiatric or psychological testimony to substantiate his injury and its relation to the assault, recovery was denied.[66]

Frequently, a distinction is drawn between the needs for psychiatric and for psychological evidence to support an award. For example, in *Bilbrey v Industrial Commission,*[67] psychological testimony was not sufficient to support a causal relationship between the initial physical injury, caused when the claimant fell and struck his head on an iron structure, and the claimed emotional disability. The court reasoned, without apparent statutory basis, that the claim could only be determined by expert medical testimony.

§14.12 —Basis

The psychiatrist or psychologist whose opinion is sought to be introduced at the hearing may be treating the claimant or examining the claimant for the insurance carrier or the commission. In virtually all jurisdictions, the opinion must, at minimum, be based on an examina-

---

[62] DSM-III, *supra* note 60, at 308.30 & 308.81.

[63] Detjen v Workman's Compensation Appeals Bd, 422 Cal App 3d 470, 116 Cal Rptr 860 (1974); Allis Chalmers Mfg Co v Industrial Commn, 57 Ill 2d 257, 312 NE2d 280 (1974); Gallagher v Industrial Commn, 9 Wis 2d 361, 101 NW2d 72 (1960).

[64] Bilbrey v Industrial Commn, 27 Ariz App 473, 556 P2d 27 (1976).

[65] Andrus v Rimmer & Garrett, Inc, 316 So 2d 433 (La Ct App 1975); Bates v Merchants Co, 161 So 2d 652 (Miss 1964); Marston v Compensation Dept, 252 Or 640, 452 P2d 311 (1969).

[66] Deadwyler v Industrial Commn, 86 Ill 106, 427 NE2d 560 (1981).

[67] 126 Ariz App 473, 556 P2d 27 (1976). *But see* Sandow v Weyerhaeuser Co, 252 Or 377, 449 P2d 426 (1969).

tion of the patient.[68] Reliance on the reports of others as the exclusive basis for an opinion is generally unacceptable. However, a review of relevant medical records is an important supplement to the examination. Psychological tests may also be an important basis for an opinion. A psychiatrist or psychologist treating the patient may rely on the statements of the patient made for purposes of medical diagnosis or treatment.[69] These should include the patient's work history and ability to relate to fellow workers.[70]

§14.13   —Limitations

A potential limitation on the information that may be relied on by a psychiatrist or psychologist in workers' compensation proceedings is the physician-patient privilege and its variants. The privilege's application is substantially limited in these proceedings, however. In the case of an examination of a claimant by a psychiatrist or psychologist retained by the employer, insurer, or commission, no privilege comes into existence because the purpose of the examination is not treatment but the rendition of a report to a third party.[71] In the case of the claimant's treating psychiatrist or psychologist, if the claimant presents the testimony of this expert, the privilege is waived as to all related communications.[72] Even in the absence of the claimant's presentation of this witness, most states provide an exception to medical privilege in workers' compensation cases for all treatments related to the injury claimed.[73]

These proceedings are not generally tried to a jury. Accordingly, the rules of evidence, including the hearsay rule but excluding privilege rules, are not generally applicable.[74] Instead, the reliability of the informational sources bears upon the weight given to the evidence rather than its admissibility.

---

[68] *See, e.g.,* Texas Employers Assn v Thames, 236 SW2d 203 (Tex Civ App-Ft Worth 1951)(writ ref).

[69] Greenfarb v Arre, 62 NJ Super 420, 163 A2d 173 (1960); Cody v SKF Indus, 447 Pa 558, 291 A2d 772 (1972).

[70] American Medical Assn, Guides to the Evaluation of Permanent Impairment 216 (2d ed 1984).

[71] *See* **§10.02.**

[72] *See* **§10.03.**

[73] *See, e.g.,* Sewell v Roosevelt Hotel, 58 AD2d 924, 396 NYS2d 726 (1977).

[74] Thom v Callahan, 97 Idaho 151, 540 P2d 1330 (1975); Carroll v Knickerbocker Ice Co, 218 NY 435, 113 NE 507 (1916); Sky Chefs, Inc v Rogers, 222 Va 800, 284 SE2d 605 (1985).

§14.14   —Testimony

The rules of evidence governing judicial proceedings are not generally applicable in workers' compensation proceedings on questions of admissibility of evidence.[75] Thus, the hearsay rule is not generally applicable and medical reports[76] as well as hospital records[77] may be received into evidence if probative. However, the majority of jurisdictions require that the award ultimately be supported by a residuum of competent evidence.[78] Thus, in the majority of jurisdictions, there must be sufficient evidence that would be admissible under the traditional rules of evidence to support the award. Two minority rules exist. One permits an award to rest entirely on evidence that would not be admissible under traditional rules of evidence and the other will not permit an award that does not rest on evidence admissible under the traditional rules.[79]

The requirement of reasonable medical certainty,[80] requiring a high degree of certainty on the part of the medical witness before permitting an opinion to be accepted, appears relaxed in workers' compensation proceedings. Instead of limiting speculative testimony that links the injury and the accident, the admission of opinions that are expressed in terms of probability is acceptable.[81]

§14.15   Social Security Disability Benefits—The Legal Standard

A number of federal disability programs provide benefits to disabled persons and their dependants.[82] Included among these programs are

---

[75] Thom v Callahan, 97 Idaho 151, 540 P2d 1330 (1975); Carroll v Knickerbocker Ice Co, 218 NY 435, 113 NE 507 (1916); Sky Chefs, Inc v Rogers, 222 Va 800, 284 SE2d 605 (1985).

[76] Forrest v Industrial Commn, 77 Ill2d 86, 395 NE2d 576 (1979); Cook v State Ind Ct, 518 P2d 311 (Okla 1974). *But see* Georgia Pac Corp v McLaurin, 370 So 2d 1359 (Miss 1979).

[77] Hedrick v Southland Corp, 41 NC App 431, 255 SE2d 198, *cert denied*, 298 NC 296 (1979).

[78] 3 A. Larson, The Law of Workman's Compensation §79.22 (1983).

[79] *Id.*

[80] *See* **§9.07.**

[81] Schope v Red Owl Stores, Inc, 323 NW2d 801 (Minn 1982).

[82] *See generally* F. Bloch, Federal Disability Law and Practice (1984).

Social Security Disability Insurance Benefits[83] and Supplemental Security Income,[84] Veterans' Disability Benefits,[85] Civil Service Disability Retirement Benefits,[86] Black Lung Disability Benefits,[87] and the Railroad Retirement Act.[88] Each of these programs affects a large number of claimants and beneficiaries and separate treatment of each merits a treatise on this topic itself.[89] However, the Social Security programs have the broadest scope and guide the criteria for the Railroad Retirement disability determinations.[90] Thus, they will be the vehicle to survey psychiatric and psychological evidence in federal disability programs.

The Social Security Disability Insurance Benefits program provides benefits to disabled wage earners on whose behalf Social Security taxes have been paid for the requisite quarters of coverage.[91] The Supplemental Security Income program is a federalized public assistance program to disabled persons who meet certain income and asset limitations, but lack the required quarters of coverage.[92] Both programs, however, are governed by the same disability standard. This standard requires that the claimant demonstrate an "inability to engage in any substantial gainful activity by reason of any medically determined physical or mental impairment which can be expected to result in death or which has lasted or can be expected to last for a continuous period of not less than 12 months."[93] If the claimant is not currently engaged in substantial gainful activity, consideration of the nature of the disability entails a review of the Administration's Listing of Impairments that presumptively satisfy the impairment requirement, if found to exist with the requisite degree of severity, limiting the claimant's capacity to work. The listing is set forth in regulations issued by the Social Security Administration.[94] Included in §12 of this listing are those mental disorders that qualify as mental impairments in the determination of the

---

[83] 42 USC §423.

[84] 42 USC §1381 *et seq.*

[85] 38 USC §1506 *et seq.*

[86] 5 USC §8337.

[87] 30 USC §901 *et seq.*

[88] 45 USC §231.

[89] *See* Bloch, *supra* note 82.

[90] Duncan v Railroad Retirement Bd, 375 F2d 915 (4th Cir 1967).

[91] 42 USC §§416(i), 423.

[92] 20 CFR §1110 *et seq.*

[93] 42 USC §423(d)(1)(A).

[94] 20 CFR §404, subt P, App 1.

Administration.[95] They include chronic brain syndromes, psychotic disorders, functional nonpsychotic disorders, and mental retardation.[96] The list of mental impairments does not specifically correspond to

---

[95] *See generally* ABA Commission on the Mentally Disabled, *Social Security Benefits: Legal Issues for the Mentally Disabled,* 4 Mental Disability L Rep 356 (1980).

[96] 12.01 CATEGORY OF IMPAIRMENTS, MENTAL

12.02 *Chronic brain syndromes* (organic brain syndromes). With both A and B:

A. Demonstrated deterioration in intellectual functioning, manifested by persistence of one or more of the following clinical signs:

1. Marked memory defect for recent events; or
2. Impoverished, slowed, perseverative thinking, with confusion or disorientation; or
3. Labile, shallow, or coarse affect;

B. Resulting persistence of marked restriction of daily activities and constriction of interests and deterioration in personal habits and seriously impaired ability to relate to other people.

12.03 *Functional psychotic disorders* (mood disorders, schizophrenias, paranoid states). With both A and B:

A. Manifested persistence of one or more of the following clinical signs:

1. Depression (or elation); or
2. Agitation; or
3. Psychomotor disturbances; or
4. Hallucinations or delusions; or
5. Autistic or other regressive behavior; or
6. Inappropriateness of affect; or
7. Illogical association of ideas;

B. Resulting persistence of marked restriction of daily activities and constriction of interests and seriously impaired ability to relate to other people.

12.04 *Functional nonpsychotic disorders* (psychophysiologic, neurotic, and personality disorders; addictive dependence on alcohol or drugs). With both A and B:

A. Manifested persistence of one or more of the following clinical signs:

1. Demonstrable and persistent structural changes mediated through psychophysiological channels (e.g., duodenal ulcer); or
2. Recurrent and persistent periods of anxiety, with tension, apprehension, and interference with concentration and memory; or
3. Persistent depressive affect with insomnia, loss of weight, and suicidal preoccupation; or
4. Persistant phobic or obsessive ruminations with inappropriate, bizarre, or disruptive behavior; or
5. Persistent compulsive, ritualistic behavior; or
6. Persistent functional disturbance of vision, speech, hearing, or use of a limb with demonstrable structural or trophic changes; or

DSM-III;[97] however, it is designed to measure the severity of the impairment even in the absence of diagnostic agreement.[98]

The effect of this Listing of Impairments as an exclusive enumeration of impairments resulting in compensable disabilities has been sharply questioned. Judicial construction of the listing has curtailed its exclusivity and permitted claimants to demonstrate an impairment not listed.[99] Ultimately, the listing may be helpful, but the appropriate test for the impairment is whether it results in the claimant's inability to engage in substantial gainful activity.[100]

§14.16 —The Role of the Expert

The standard for disability benefits set forth in the Social Security Act requires the existence of a "medically determined physical or mental impairment."[101] This is elaborated to make clear that the impairment must result from an anatomical, physiological, or psychological abnormality that is "demonstrable by medically acceptable clinical and

---

7. Persistent, deeply ingrained, maladaptive patterns of behavior manifested by either:
   a. Seclusiveness or autistic thinking; or
   b. Pathologically inappropriate suspiciousness or hostility;
   B. Resulting persistence of marked restriction of daily activities and constriction of interests and deterioration in personal habits and seriously impaired ability to relate to other people.
   12.05 *Mental retardation.* As manifested by:
   A. Severe mental and social incapacity as evidenced by marked dependence upon others for personal needs (e.g., bathing, washing, dressing, etc.) and inability to understand the spoken word and inability to avoid physical danger (fire, cars, etc.) and inability to follow simple directions and inability to read, write, and perform simple calculations; or
   B. IQ of 59 of less (*see* 12.00B4); or
   C. IQ of 60 to 69 inclusive (*see* 12.00B4) and a physical or other mental impairment imposing additional and significant work-related limitation of function.
20 CFR §404, sub P, app 1, §12.

[97] American Psychiatric Assn, Diagnostic and Statistical Manual of Mental Disorders (3d ed 1980) (DSM-III).

[98] 20 CFR §404, sub P, app I, §12.00A.

[99] Martin v Secretary of Health, Educ, & Welfare, 492 F2d 905 (4th Cir 1974); Mental Health Assn v Schweiker, 554 F Supp 157 (D Minn 1982), *affd in part, modified in part,* 720 F2d 965 (8th Cir 1983).

[100] Lewis v Weinberger, 541 F2d 417, 420 (4th Cir 1976).

[101] 42 USC §423(d)(1)(A).

laboratory techniques."[102] Thus, while the claimant's statements or other lay testimony may be valuable, they are not themselves sufficient to support a disability determination. Objective[103] medical evidence is necessary.[104] Courts have recognized, however, that objective medical evidence of mental disorders exists infrequently.[105]

The medical evidence requirement contemplates psychiatric and psychological reports to support an impairment based upon a mental disorder[106] and the use of standardized psychological tests such as the Wechsler Adult Intelligence Scale (WAIS) and the Minnesota Multi-phasic Personality Inventory (MMPI).[107] Neither the act nor the regulations discriminate against psychological in favor of psychiatric input.

There is often a distinction drawn between the opinions of psychiatrists and psychologists who have treated the claimant and those who have examined the claimant only for purposes of a disability determination. The latter class largely consists of local practitioners acting as consultants for the Social Security Administration.[108] The former class consists of practitioners who have treated the patient and incidentally write to support a disability claim. While no regulation expressing a formal rule of preference exists, given equally qualified experts, judicial review of administrative determinations has manifested a preference in favor of the opinion of the treating therapist who, although perhaps biased in the claimant's favor, frequently has more information on which to base an opinion.[109] The weight given an opinion of a treating psychologist or psychiatrist is shown in the judicial response that if the report contains sufficient findings that the disability standard has been met, it satisfies the claimant's burden of production and requires substantial evidence in opposition to deny the claim.[110]

---

[102] 42 USC §423(d)(3).

[103] Underwood v Ribicoff, 298 F2d 850, 851 (4th Cir 1962).

[104] 20 CFR §§404.1508, 416.908.

[105] Branham v Gardner, 383 F2d 614 (6th Cir 1967).

[106] 20 CFR §404, sub P, app 1, §12.00A (1989) ("The severity and duration of the impairment(s) should be evaluated on the basis of reports from psychiatrists, psychologists, and hospitals, in conjunction with adequate descriptions of daily activities from these or other services").

[107] Id.

[108] 20 CFR §404.1517.

[109] Wiggins v Schweiker, 679 F2d 1387 (11th Cir 1982); Bailey v Califano, 614 F2d 146 (8th Cir 1980).

[110] Aubeuf v Schweiker, 649 F2d 107 (2d Cir 1981); Smith v Schweiker, 646 F2d 1075 (5th Cir 1981).

§14.17 —Basis

The Social Security Act's disability criteria's requirement of a "medically determined physical or mental impairment"[111] demonstrated by "medically acceptable clinical and laboratory techniques"[112] does not contemplate the receipt of conclusory medical findings or opinions. The weight accorded any medical finding or opinion will be a function of the information on which it demonstrates it is based.[113] The more thorough the diagnostic evaluations, the greater the weight of the resulting report. A conclusory opinion lacking a description of its basis will not be of consequence to a determination.

The appropriate bases include all that is proper to reach a diagnosis outside of disability determinations[114]—medical examinations, clinical psychiatric interviews, and psychological tests, with special emphasis on particular data relevant to this disability standard. Because a disability is measured in the context of employability, for example, an employment history of the patient is important information for the psychiatrist or psychologist in evaluating the extent of an impairment.[115] Similarly, a description of the claimant's daily activities is also valuable to gauge an ability to work, as are psychological tests describing the claimant's functional capacities.[116]

§14.18 —Limitations

The physician–patient privilege and its variants[117] have limited effect in Social Security disability proceedings. Consulting examinations[118] conducted at the request of the Social Security Administration are not privileged, as their purpose is not treatment but the preparation of a report to the Social Security Administration.[119] The existence of a privilege between the claimant and a treating psychiatrist or psychologist is waived if the claimant requests that person to submit a report or

---

[111] 42 USC §423(d)(1)(A).

[112] 42 USC §423(d)(3).

[113] Richardson v Perales, 402 US 389, 407 (1971).

[114] *See* §§2.12-2.19.

[115] Rayborn v Weinberger, 398 F Supp 1303 (ND Ind 1975).

[116] 20 CFR §404, sub P, App I, §12.00A.

[117] *See* ch 10.

[118] 20 CFR §404.1517.

[119] *See* §10.02.

records to the Social Security Administration in support of a claim.[120] Moreover, as to other treating psychiatrists and psychologists who have provided treatment related to the disability alleged but who are not requested by the claimant to provide information to the Social Security Administration, waiver may be implied in the filing of a claim.[121] However, the Administration tends to rely on consulting exams in an attempt to assess the claimant's current condition only, thereby avoiding this issue.

§14.19 —Testimony

The determination of an application for Social Security disability benefits involves an initial set of administrative determinations based almost exclusively upon written reports.[122] If the initial administrative and reconsideration determinations are adverse to the claimant, and administrative hearing may be demanded, presided over by an administrative law judge. At the administrative hearing the claimant may appear with a representative and present additional evidence. The hearing is not truly adversarial, however, as the Social Security Administration is not represented at the hearing.[123]

The claimant is entitled to present relevant oral or documentary evidence at the hearing and the administrative law judge is required to consider all relevant evidence supplied by the claimant.[124] The rules of evidence do not apply at the hearing[125] and, therefore, the hearsay rule does not prohibit the introduction of written medical reports.[126] Thus, the consulting examiners' reports will be admitted without the necessity of their attendance. A claimant who wishes to cross-examine the author of a report may, however, have a subpoena issued for the author's appearance at the hearing.[127]

The claimant may present live psychiatric and psychological testimony at the hearing; however, cost considerations frequently result, instead, in the presentation of written reports. Although a psychiatrist's or psychologist's written report may be accepted in lieu of live

---

[120] See §10.03.

[121] Id.

[122] F. Bloch, Federal Disability Law and Practice §4.4 (1984).

[123] Ware v Schweiker, 651 F2d 408 (5th Cir 1981), cert denied, 455 US 912 (1982).

[124] Kozaczka v Schweiker, 520 F Supp 1189 (WDNY 1981).

[125] 42 USC §405(b)(1).

[126] Richardson v Perales, 402 US 389 (1971).

[127] Id 404.

testimony, acceptance of a report into evidence does not guarantee that it will be given substantial weight. First, the report must demonstrate an adequate basis.[128] The facts on which the report is based including laboratory findings, psychological tests, dates of treatment, examinations, or interviews should be explicitly set forth. Second, the report should reach a medical finding in the terms contemplated by the List of Impairments or its equivalent.[129] Third, the report should address the specific limits imposed by the impairment on the claimant's ability to work as it affects daily activities and interests, personal care for personal needs, and relations with others.[130] Specifically, the disability's effect on the claimant's ability to follow instructions and to respond to supervisors and coworkers as well as changes in work routines should be elaborated on in the report.[131] Conclusory findings without this analysis are entitled to little weight.[132] If the psychiatrist or psychologist's opinion is presented only in a written report, the qualifications of the author should be provided, as this will also affect the consideration given the report.[133]

Research Aids

§14.20   Suggested Reading

Books

American Medical Assn, *Guides to the Evaluation of Permanent Impairment* (2d ed 1984).

American Psychiatric Assn, *Diagnostic and Statistical Manual of Mental Disorders* (3d ed 1980) (DSM-III).

F. Bloch, *Federal Disability Law and Practice* (1984).

H. Davidson, *Post Traumatic Psychoses* (1972).

---

[128] Vasquez v Schweiker, 701 F2d 733 (8th Cir 1983).

[129] 20 CFR §404, sub P, app I.

[130] *Id.*

[131] Legal Counsel for the Elderly, Disability Practice Manual for Social Security and SSI Programs 2.3.2 (1984).

[132] Laffoon v Califano, 558 F2d 253 (5th Cir 1973); Reyes v Harris, 482 F Supp 638 (SDNY 1979).

[133] Alvaredo v Weinberger, 511 F2d 1046 (1st Cir 1975); Bryant v Schweiker, 537 F Supp 1 (ED Pa 1982).

3 A. Larson, *The Law of Workman's Compensation* (1983).

J. Weinstein & M. Berger, *Weinstein's Evidence* (1984)

Articles

ABA Commission on the Mentally Disabled, *Social Security Benefits: Legal Issues for the Mentally Disabled*, 4 Mental Disability L Rep 356 (1980).

Legal Counsel for the Elderly, *Disability Practice Manual for Social Security and SSI Programs* (1984).

Magruder, *Mental and Emotional Disturbances in the Law of Torts*, 49 Harv L Rev 1033 (1936).

Modlin, *The Post Accident Anxiety Syndrome: Psychosocial Aspects*, 123 Am J Psychiatry 1008 (1967).

Rogers & Cavanaugh, *"Nothing but the Truth" . . . A Reexamination of Malingering*, 11 J Psychiatry & Law 443 (1983).

Weinstein, *The Concept of the Disability Process*, 19 Psychomatics 94 (1978).

Cases

Allis Chalmers Manufacturing Co v Industrial Commission, 57 Ill 2d 257, 312 NE2d 280 (1974).

Alvaredo v Weinberger, 511 F2d 1046 (1st Cir 1975).

American Smelting & Refining Co v Industrial Commission, 59 Ariz 87, 123 P2d 163 (1942).

Andrus v Rimmer & Garrett, Inc, 316 So 2d 433 (La Ct App 1975).

Aubeuf v Schweiker, 649 F2d 107 (2d Cir 1981).

Bailey v American General Insurance Co, 154 Tex 430, 279 SW2d 315 (1955).

Bailey v Califano, 614 F2d 146 (8th Cir 1980).

Bates v Merchants Co, 161 So 2d 652 (Miss 1964).

Bell v New York City Health & Hospital Corp, 104 NE2d 872, 456 NYS2d 787 (1982).

Bilbrey v Industrial Commission, 126 Ariz App 473, 556 P2d 27 (1976).

Brady v Royal Manufacturing Co, 117 Ga App 312, 160 SE2d 424 (1968).

Branham v Gardner, 383 F2d 614 (6th Cir 1967).

Bryant v Schweiker, 537 F Supp 1 (ED Pa 1982).

Buckler v Sinclair Refining Co, 68 Ill App 2d 283, 216 NE2d 14 (1966).

Butchikas v Travelers Indemnity Co, 343 So 2d 816 (Fla 1976).

Carroll v Knickerbocker Ice Co, 218 NY 435, 113 NE 507 (1916).

Carter v GM Corp, 361 Mich 577, 106 NW2d 105 (1960).

Casimere v Herman, 28 Wis 2d 437, 137 NW2d 73 (1965).

Cody v SKF Industries, 447 Pa 558, 291 A2d 772 (1972).

Compensation of McGarrah, *In re,* 59 Or App 448, 651 P2d 153 (1982).

Consolidated Freightways v Drake, 678 P2d 874 (Wyo 1984).

Cook v State Industrial Court, 518 P2d 311 (Okla 1974).

Deadwyler v Industrial Commission, 86 Ill 106, 427 NE2d 560 (1981).

Detjen v Workman's Compensation Appeals Board, 422 Cal App 3d 470, 116 Cal Rptr 860 (1974).

Dillon v Legg, 68 Cal 2d 728, 441 P2d 912, 69 Cal Rptr 72 (1968).

Drake v Goodman, 386 Mass 88, 434 NE2d 1211 (1982).

Duncan v Railroad Retirement Board, 375 F2d 915 (4th Cir 1967).

Fischer v Famous—Barr Co, 618 SW2d 446 (Mo Ct App 1981).

Foley v Kibrick, 12 Mass App 382, 425 NE2d 376 (1981).

Followill v Emerson Electric Co, 234 Kan 791, 674 P2d 1050 (1984).

Forrest v Industrial Commission, 77 Ill 2d 86, 395 NE2d 576 (1979).

Gallagher v Industrial Commission, 9 Wis 2d 361, 101 NW2d 72 (1960).

Galovich v Hertz Corp, 513 SW2d 325 (Mo 1974).

Georgia Pacific Corp v McLaurin, 370 So 2d 1359 (Miss 1979).

Greenfarb v Arre, 2 NJ Super 420, 163 A2d 173 (1960).

Hedrick v Southland Corp, 41 NC App 431, 255 SE2d 198, *cert denied,* 298 NC 296 (1979).

Hess v Philadelphia Transportation Co, 358 Pa 144, 56 A2d 89 (1948).

Howard v Bloodworth, 137 Ga App 478, 224 SE2d 122 (1976).

Hughes v Moore, 214 Va 27, 197 SE2d 214 (1973).

Hunsley v Giard, 87 Wash 2d 424, 553 P2d 1096 (1976).

Hussey v May Department Stores, Inc, 238 Pa Super 431, 357 A2d 635 (1976).

Hyath v Sierra Boat Co, 79 Cal App 3d 325, 145 Cal Rptr 47 (1978).

Jones v Miller, 290 A2d 587 (DC 1972).

Kozaczka v Schweiker, 520 F Supp 1189 (WDNY 1981).

Kroger v Beck, 176 Ind App 202, 375 NE2d 640 (1978).

Laffoon v Califano, 558 F2d 253 (5th Cir 1973).

Landreth v Reed, 570 SW2d 486 (Tex Civ App 1976) (no writ).

Lewis v Weinberger, 541 F2d 417 (4th Cir 1976).

Lifshultz, In re, 2 Cal 3d 415, 467 P2d 557, 85 Cal Rptr 829 (1970).

Lindsay v Baltimore & Ohio R Co, 98 Ohio App 63, 128 NE2d 242 (1954).

Marshall v Papineau, 132 So 2d 786 (Fla Dist Ct App 1961).

Marston v Compensation Department, 252 Or 640, 452 P2d 311 (1969).

Martin v Secretary of Health, Education, & Welfare, 492 F2d 905 (4th Cir 1974)

Mental Health Association v Schweiker, 554 F Supp 157 (D Minn 1982), *affd in part, modified in part*, 720 F2d 965 (8th Cir 1983).

Mitchell v White Castle Systems, 290 NW2d 753 (Minn 1980).

Molien v Kaiser Foundation Hospital, 27 Cal 3d 916, 616 P2d 813, 167 Cal Rptr 831 (1980).

Murphy v Penn Fruit Co, 274 Pa Super 27, 418 A2d 480 (1980).

Nickerson v Hodges, 146 La 735, 84 So 37 (1920).

Oziokonshi v Babineau, 375 Mass 555, 380 NE2d 1295 (1978).

Pagan v Dewitt P Henry Co, 27 Pa Commw 495, 365 A2d 463 (1976).

Preveden v Metropolitan Life Insurance Co, 200 Minn 524, 274 NW 685 (1937).

Rayborn v Weinberger, 398 F Supp 1303 (ND Ind 1975).

Reyes v Harris, 482 F Supp 638 (SDNY 1979).

Richardson v Perales, 402 US 389 (1971).

Riddle v Dickens, 241 Md 579, 217 A2d 304 (1966).

Rodrigues v State, 52 Hawaii 156, 472 P2d 509 (1970).

Sanchez v Schindler, 651 SW2d 249 (Tex 1983).

Sandow v Weyerhaeuser Co, 252 Or 377, 449 P2d 426 (1969).

School Dist No 1 v Department of Industry, Labor & Human Relations, 62 Wis 2d 370, 215 NW2d 373 (1974).

Schope v Red Owl Stores, Inc, 323 NW2d 801 (Minn 1982).

Sewell v Roosevelt Hotel, 58 AD2d 924, 396 NYS2d 726 (1977).

Sinn v Byrd, 486 Pa 146, 404 A2d 672 (1979).

Sky Chefs, Inc v Rogers, 222 Va 800, 284 SE2d 605 (1985).

Smith v Schweiker, 646 F2d 1075 (5th Cir 1981).

Sutton Motor Co v Crysel, 289 SW2d 631 (Tex Civ App 1956), (no writ).

Swift & Co v Ware, 53 Ga App 500, 186 SE 452 (1936).

Texas Employers Associates v Thames, 236 SW2d 203 (Tex Civ App 1951) (no writ).

Texas Employers Associates v Wallace, 70 SW2d 832 (Tex Civ App 1934) (no writ).

Thom v Callahan, 97 Idaho 151, 540 P2d 1330 (1975).

Tobin v Grossman, 24 NY2d 609, 249 NE2d 419, 301 NYS2d 554 (1969).

Tramutola v Bortine, 63 NJ 9, 304 A2d 197 (1973).

Transportation Insurance Co v Makysun, 580 SW2d 334 (Tex 1979).

Underwood v Ribicoff, 298 F2d 850 (4th Cir 1962).

Vasquez v Schweiker, 701 F2d 733 (8th Cir 1983).

Walsh v Snyder, 295 Pa Super 94, 441 A2d 365 (1981).

Ware v Schweiker, 651 F2d 408 (5th Cir 1981), *cert denied*, 455 US 912 (1982).

Wiggins v Schweiker, 679 F2d 1387 (11th Cir 1982).

Wolfe v Sibley, Lindsay & Curr & Co, 36 NY 505, 330 NE2d 603, 369 NYS2d 637 (1975).

Statutes and Rules

5 USC §8337.

30 USC §901 *et seq.*

38 USC §1506 *et seq.*

42 USC §§405(b)(1), 416(i), 423, 1381.

45 USC §231.

Fed R Evid 801(d)(2), 803(4).

Regulations

20 CFR §404, subpt P, app 1 (1983).

20 CFR §§404.1508, 416.908.

20 CFR §1110 *et seq.*

§14.21   WESTLAW Search References

§14.01 *Personal Injury Litigation*
administrative /3 action decision /s jury

§14.02 *Mental and Emotional Consequences of Physical Injuries—The Legal Standard*
emotional mental /3 injury harm trauma stress suffering /p "physical injury" /s proximate** direct** /3 caus!

§14.03 *—The Role of the Expert*
digest, synopsis (emotional mental /3 injury harm trauma stress

suffering /s psychiatr*** psycholog! /3 testimony witness)
"post traumatic stress" /s physical** /3 injur** harm** impact

§14.04 *Emotional Assaults—The Legal Standard*
emotional** mental** /3 harm** injur** disorder** impact
trauma

landreth /s 570 +4 486 /p emotional** mental** /3 harm**
injur** disorder** impact trauma

(hunsley /s 553 +4 1096) (molien /s 167 +4 831) /p emotional** mental** /3 harm injur** disorder** impact trauma

§14.05 *—The Role of the Expert*
psychiatr*** psycholog! /p emotional** mental** /3 harm**
injur** disorder** impact trauma /p fabricat*** lying malinger*** % topic(110)

§14.06 *—Basis*
fi 181 se2d 549

§14.07 *—Limitations*
synopsis ("personal injury") & privilege* /s psychiatr*** psycholog!

§14.08 *—Testimony*
synopsis ("personal injury") & psychiatr*** psycholog! /4
testimony witness /s qualif!

§14.09 *Disability Claims in the Administrative Setting*
adjudication /p worker workman /3 compensation /p jury

§14.10 *Workers' Compensation—The Legal Standard*
worker workm*n /3 compensation /p mental** emotional** /3
injur** trauma! impact disorder** harm***

worker workm*n /3 compensation & "post traumatic stress"

§14.11 *—The Role of the Expert*
worker workm*n /3 compensation /s psycholog! psychiatr***
/6 testimony witness

§14.12 *—Basis*
worker workm*n /3 compensation /s psycholog! psychiatr***
/6 testimony opinion /5 based

§14.13 *—Limitations*
worker workm*n /3 compensation /p psycholog! psychiatr***
/p privilege*

§14.14 —*Testimony*
worker workm*n /s compensation /s proceeding /s (rule /3 evidence) hearsay

§14.15 *Social Security Disability Benefits—The Legal Standard*
"list*** of impairments" /p emotional mental /3 trauma injury impact disorder harm

"social security disability" /p emotional mental /3 trauma injury disorder impact harm

§14.16 —*The Role of the Expert*
"listing of impairments" & emotional mental /3 trauma injury impact disorder harm /p medical psycholog! psychiatr*** /5 testimony evidence witness

§14.17 —*Basis*
fi 91 sct 1420

§14.18 —*Limitations*
fi 706 f2d 564

§14.19 —*Testimony*
perales budds alvarado /p physician expert psycholog! psychiatr*** /p qualif! unqualif! credib!

15 Competence

§15.01 Guardianship and Conservatorship—The Legal Standard

Guardianship proceedings involve application of the parens patriae power of the state to protect the person or property of those thought to be unable to act responsibly for themselves.[1] In modern parlance, *guardianship* is used to refer to proceedings to protect the person and

---

[1] S. Brakel & R. Rock, The Mentally Disabled and the Law 250 (1971).

350

conservatorship is used to refer to proceedings to protect the property of the person or ward. A guardian of the person is typically empowered to decide such questions as where the incompetent should live and what medical care the incompetent should receive. A conservator is typically empowered to decide such questions as what encumbrance, sale, or investment of the incompetent's property should be made.

Plenary quardianship over both the person and estate as a standard matter in all cases is now thought to be overbroad.[2] The movement in guardianship law has been to restrict the use of guardianship to the narrowest finding of incapacity necessary to protect the incompetent. Selective incapacity, authorized by many guardianship laws, permits a finding of incapacity with respect to some, but not all, activities affected by a finding of incapacity.[3] Thus, for example, a person may be found to lack the capacity to operate an automobile but to retain the capacity to choose a residence. This approach is thought consistent with knowledge of the effects of mental disorder as well as legal doctrine limiting intrusion on individual liberty to the minimum necessary to accomplish a valid governmental purpose.[4]

The standard for appointment of a guardian or conservator articulated in those jurisdictions that have adopted the Uniform Probate Code[5] is that the person alleged to be incompetent "is impaired by reason of mental illness, mental deficiency or disability, advanced age, chronic use of drug, chronic intoxication or other cause (except minority) to the extent that he lacks sufficient understanding or capacity to make or communicate responsible decisions concerning his person."[6] This two-pronged test contemplates the use of psychiatric or psychological assistance in its first prong, the existence of conditions such as mental illness or deficiency. It is the second prong of the test that is more troublesome for the use of psychiatric and psychological assistance, for it raises problems of discriminating between differing value choices and the inability to make or communicate these choices responsibly.

The standard for civil commitment to a mental hospital, a mental

---

[2] Frolik, *Plenary Guardianship: An Analysis, a Critique and a Proposal for Reform,* 23 Ariz L Rev 599 (1981).

[3] *See* Unif Prob Code §5-306(c) (1983).

[4] *See* Chambers, *Alternatives to Civil Commitment of the Mentally Ill: Practical Guides and Constitutional Imperatives,* 70 Mich L Rev 1107 (1972).

[5] Alaska, Arizona, Colorado, Hawaii, Idaho, Montana, Nebraska, New Mexico, North Dakota, Oregon, and Utah.

[6] Unif Prob Code §5-103(7)(1983).

disorder plus dangerousness or a need for treatment,[7] does not address the same elements required for a finding of incompetence.[8] Thus, those committed are not thereby rendered incompetent to act in their own behalf unless a finding of incompetence accompanies the order of commitment. This issue raised by the disparity in these two tests arises frequently in the context of the right of committed patients to refuse treatment, particularly psychotropic medication.

§15.02   —The Role of the Expert

The standard for the appointment of a guardian or conservator, an inability to make or communicate responsible decisions based on a condition such as a mental disorder or deficiency,[9] implicates two roles for psychiatrists and psychologists in this decision. The first, diagnosis of a mental disorder or deficiency, is straight forward and limited only by the diagnostic abilities of the profession generally and the individual psychiatrist or psychologist.[10] The second, explaining the effect of that disorder on the capacity to make or communicate responsible decisions, is not so straightforward. It often involves discriminating between aberrant value choices resulting from individuality and those resulting from illness. Is an elderly woman's decision to take an expensive trip around the world with a young male friend, for example, at the cost of her own children's future inheritance, the result of a mental illness or a difference in value choices about parental responsibilities? Too often, the answer to this type of question turns on agreement with the decision made and not the process by which the decision was made.

To avoid this quagmire, it has been suggested that evaluation of the competence decision be broken down into the elements thought necessary to make a responsible choice.[11] First, is the alleged incompetent aware of situational factors? Does the elderly woman described above realize the amount of her funds, who her friends and relatives are, and what functional limitations, if any (e.g., heart disease), she suffers? Second, does she have a factual understanding of the issue in question?

---

[7] See §16.01.

[8] See, e.g., Rogers v Okin, 634 F2d 650 (1st Cir 1980), vacated & remanded sub nom Mills v Rogers, 457 US 291 (1982).

[9] Unif Prob Code §5-103(7)(1983).

[10] See ch 2.

[11] T. Gutheil & P. Appelbaum, Clinical Handbook of Psychiatry and the Law 217 (1982). For a discussion of several instruments available for use in competency evaluations, See T. Grisso, Evaluating Competencies: Forensic Assessments and Instruments 283-310 (1986).

Does she understand the facts relevant to the decision at hand—the cost of the trip, length of time it will take, and difficulties to be encountered. Third, does she possess an ability to manipulate this information rationally? Is she oriented in time, is there memory loss, intellectual function, alterations of mood, delusions, or hallucinations? Expert assistance in evaluating the decisional process in this fashion may be extremely helpful to the judge or jury.

The necessity for guardianship is a decision that lends itself to multidisciplinary analysis.[12] Psychological as well as psychiatric input is particularly appropriate in this decision. In many instances, social service studies will also be necessary. Thus a team, rather than an individual, approach to this issue is likely to be advantageous.

§15.03 —Basis

The basis for an opinion of the alleged incompetent's capacity could include a medical examination,[13] clinical psychiatric interview,[14] psychological testing,[15] and social service study. As the alleged incompetent is available for current examinations and testing, reliance principally on dated examinations and tests or those performed by others is not appropriate. The timing of these can be problematic, however.

As a guiding principle, the more recent the examination or test, the closer it is to the date of judicial decision, and thus the more probative. This principle has certain limitations, however. If the patient has recently been moved, from home to hospital or vice versa, for example, the confusion effected by this change in setting may not be an accurate reflection of "chronic" incapacity.[16]

Given the movement in favor of selective incapacity, the examining psychiatrist or psychologist should analyze the effect of any mental disorder on a variety of different functions the alleged incompetent might perform—e.g., driving an automobile, purchasing groceries, or paying rent. To perform this evaluation, the clinical information obtained by the witness must be supplemented by information about

---

[12] Hafemeister & Sales, *Interdisciplinary Evaluations for Guardianships & Conservatorships,* 8 Law & Hum Behav 335 (1984).

[13] *See* **§2.13.**

[14] *See* **§2.14.**

[15] *See* **§2.15.**

[16] T. Gutheil & P. Appelbaum, Clinical Handbook of Psychiatry and the Law 218 (1982).

current level of functioning in the relevant areas. Most typically, in public agency settings, a social service study will be the source of this information.

§15.04 —Limitations

The physician–patient privilege and its variants provide a potential limitation on the use of confidential patient communications as the basis for a treating psychiatrist or psychologist's opinion on the question of capacity.[17] It would be anomalous to permit a person alleged to be incapable of making responsible decisions to waive any applicable privilege. However, many of these privileges have specific exceptions for guardianship proceedings.[18] And, given the fact that the issue is current capacity, an examination by a nontreating psychiatrist or psychologist, with appropriate admonitions to the alleged incompetent, would appear to be an adequate alternative nonprivileged source of psychiatric and psychological testimony.

The hearsay rule may limit the admission of the alleged incompetent's statements to a psychiatrist or psychologist as the basis for an opinion on incapacity. However, various exceptions exist to moderate the rule's effect. Statements made to treating psychiatrists or psychologists may fall within the hearsay exception for statements made for medical diagnosis or treatment.[19] Statements of mind, otherwise hearsay, fit within a related hearsay exception.[20] And, statements of mind not introduced for the truth of the matter asserted (e.g., "I am the Pope") are not hearsay. Statements of the alleged incompetent, sought to be introduced against the alleged incompetent, constitute admissions and are thereby excluded from the limitations of the hearsay rule.[21]

§15.05 —Testimony

The context of the guardianship hearing affects the nature and form of expert testimony presented. In many jurisdictions, the hearing may be held without the alleged incompetent if a finding is made that this

---

[17] *See* §**10.02.**

[18] *See, e.g.,* Cal Evid Code §1005 (West 1966).

[19] Fed R Evid 803(4).

[20] Fed R Evid 803(3).

[21] Fed R Evid 801(d)(2).

is in the alleged incompetent's best interest.[22] These provisions are frequently utilized[23] and the preliminary finding largely determines the rigor of the hearing on the merits.

Although some states provide for the determination of incompetence to be made by a jury,[24] the use of juries in incompetence determinations is infrequent.[25] The absence of the jury results in a less formal proceeding in which adherence to the rules of evidence is less rigid. Although application of the rules of evidence is typically called for in model guardianship and conservatorship legislation,[26] hearsay, in the form of letters and affidavits from physicians, is frequently admitted in guardianship proceedings.[27]

The guardianship test involves the necessity for a careful discrimination between an inability to make or communicate responsible decisions as the result of a mental disorder and a difference in values manifesting themselves in different choices. Psychiatrists and psychologists are not immune from disputes over values, and their agreement with the values of the alleged incompetent may play a role in the resulting opinion. Moreover, the use of psychiatric jargon and unexplained conclusions poses a major risk that a difference in the psychiatrist's or psychologist's values may play a role in the expert's findings not appreciated by judge or jury. Thus, it is particularly important in this context that the basis and methodology used to arrive at an expert's opinions be explained, that values assumed by the expert be identified, and that conclusory testimony be limited. Since this is unlikely if the psychiatrist or psychologist is not present for direct and cross-examination, the admission of written reports and affidavits in lieu of live testimony in guardianship and conservatorship proceedings is particularly problematic.

---

[22] *See, e.g.,* Mich Comp Laws Ann §330.1617(4) (1980); 20 Pa Cons Stat Ann §5511(a) (Purdon 1979).

[23] *See generally* R. Allen, E. Ferster, & H. Weihofen, Mental Impairment and Legal Incompetency 83 (1968).

[24] Mo Ann Stat §475.075(1) (Vernon 1956); 20 Pa Cons Stat Ann §5511(a) (Purdon 1979).

[25] *See* Allen, Ferster, & Weihofen, *supra* note 23, at 84.

[26] *See, e.g.,* Guardianship and Conservatorship: Statutory Survey, ABA Commission on the Mentally Disabled, Model Statute (1979).

[27] *See* Allen, Ferster, & Weihofen, *supra* note 23, at 89.

§15.06   Testamentary Capacity—The Legal Standard

The right of an individual to provide testamentary direction for the disposition of property is contingent, inter alia, on the existence of testamentary capacity. The testator must be of *sound mind* at the time of the will.[28] Various articulations of the specific elements of the *sound mind* requirement exist,[29] but all follow in good measure from the English case of *Banks v Goodfellow.* [30] The court in *Banks* stated that testamentary capacity requires that at the time of the making of the will, the testator must know that he is making a will, know the nature and extent of his property subject to distribution by the will, know how the will would distribute that property, and know those blood relatives and others who would normally be expected to benefit from the distribution.[31]

The capacity requirements articulated in *Banks* and its progeny are functional, and require an evaluation of the testator's cognitive capacity with regard to this transaction. Thus, the requirements do not necessarily correspond to a psychiatric diagnosis or the absence of one. An individual diagnosed as schizophrenic may still be found to have the capacity to execute a will if the effects of that mental disorder at the time of the execution of the will are not incapacitating.[32] Lucid intervals may exist when an otherwise seriously mentally disordered individual is not deprived of sufficient capacity to execute a will.[33]

Just as a diagnosis of mental disorder does not automatically yield a finding of testamentary incapacity, so a judicial finding of mental disorder does not automatically yield a finding of testamentary incapacity. A judicial finding of incompetence in a guardianship proceeding[34] or an order of commitment[35] based on a mental disorder may be probative evidence of testamentary incapacity and may, if proximate in time, give rise to an inference of testamentary incapacity, but these

---

[28] Page on Wills §12.15 (1960).

[29] *Id* §12.21.

[30] [1870] 5 QB 549.

[31] *Id* 567-68.

[32] Dixon v Fillmore Cemetery, 608 SW2d 84 (Mo Ct App 1980); Kerr v O'Donovan, 389 Pa 614, 134 A2d 213 (1957).

[33] *In re* Cooke's, 231 Or 133, 372 P2d 520 (1962). *See* Note, *Testamentary Capacity in a Nutshell: A Psychiatric Reevaluation,* 18 Stan L Rev 1119, 1129 (1960).

[34] *See* §15.01.

[35] *See* §16.01.

findings are not dispositive of the issue.[36] The judicial finding of incompetence or commitability does not address the testator's capacity at the instant of the execution of the will. And, the standards for guardianship or commitment do not necessarily correspond to the standards for testamentary capacity.

The fact that an individual does not carry a psychiatric diagnosis or appear chronically mentally ill, however, does not guarantee that testamentary capacity exists. The existence of what courts call *insane delusions,* [37] irrational perceptions of particular persons or events, in a person otherwise seemingly normal may negate testamentary capacity if these delusions affect the testator's knowledge of property or relatives, for example, at the time of execution of the will. This may be manifested in irrational antipathy toward particular family members.[38] For example, if a testator, without any evidentiary basis, believes his wife has been unfaithful and accordingly disinherits his children because he thinks they are not his, incapacity based on an insane delusion would exist.[39]

§15.07   —The Role of the Expert

A challenge to a will based on testamentary incapacity requires that the mental status of the testator at some previous time, perhaps now long since past, be ascertained. Psychiatrists and psychologists may be useful in this attempt to reconstruct the testator's capacity at some past time. However, another use of these professionals is to examine the testator at the time proximate to the execution of the will if there is reason to suspect there will be a subsequent challenge because of either the testator's behavior or distribution of property in the will.[40] This examination may stave off challenges or provide important evidence to rebut a challenge to the testator's capacity.

Expert testimony is not necessary to mount or defuse a challenge to the testator's capacity. Lay witnesses who have observed the testator at a time relevant to the execution of the will may testify to their

---

[36] *See, e.g., In re* Dopkins, 34 Cal 2d 568, 212 P2d 886 (1949); *In re* Hastings, 479 Pa 122, 387 A2d 865 (1978).

[37] *See* Page on Wills §12.29 (1960).

[38] Galindo v Garcia, 145 Tex 507, 199 SW2d 499 (1947).

[39] *In re* Joslin, 4 Wis 2d 29, 89 NW2d 822 (1958).

[40] Slough, *Testamentary Capacity: Evidentiary Aspects,* 36 Tex L Rev 1, 4 (1957).

observations of the testator's behavior.[41] And, the weight to be given their testimony as against expert testimony is for the jury to decide based in part on the opportunity to observe the testator at a time proximate to the will's execution.[42]

Psychiatric and psychological testimony, while not controlling, is nonetheless important in challenges to testamentary capacity and is regarded as highly persuasive.[43] It may be useful in explaining the effects of particular events or conditions on the testator's cognitive capacity. For example, a psychiatrist or psychologist may explain the effects of a particular mental disorder on the cognitive process, the effects of drugs used to treat the disorder on the cognitive process, or the nature of the emotional ties between the testator and beneficiaries.

§15.08 —Basis

A challenge to the testator's capacity in a probate proceeding does not permit an opportunity to conduct a clinical psychiatric examination of the testator. Thus, information about the testator necessary to form the basis of a psychiatric or psychological opinion of testamentary capacity can come only from past events, either previous examinations of the testator or a reconstruction of a part of the testator's life. The opinion of a psychiatrist or psychologist who previously examined the patient at a time proximate to execution of the will is admissible and entitled to substantial weight.[44] In the absence of a prior examination of the testator, a hypothetical question may provide the basis for an opinion on testamentary capacity.[45]

The testator's other business dealings at a time proximate to the execution of the will may be highly reflective of cognitive abilities.[46]

---

[41] Speirer v Curtis, 312 Ill 152, 143 NE 427 (1927).

[42] Obold v Obold, 163 F2d 32 (DC Cir 1947). One author has gone so far as to suggest that the decision on testamentary capacity involves the sort of decisions laypersons make daily and that they have equal ability with psychiatrists or psychologists to evaluate cognitive capacity. Leifer, *The Competence of the Psychiatrist to Assist in the Determination of Incompetency: A Skeptical Inquiry into the Courtroom Functions of the Psychiatrist*, 14 Syracuse L Rev 564 (1973).

[43] *In re* Finkler, 3 Cal 2d 584, 46 P2d 149 (1935).

[44] Norton v Clark, 253 Ill 557, 97 NE 1079 (1912).

[45] Garrus v Davis, 234 Ill 326, 84 NE 924 (1908).

[46] DeMarco v McGill, 402 Ill 46, 83 NE2d 313 (1948); *In re* Slade, 106 AD2d 893, 483 NYS2d 513 (1984).

Idiosyncratic conduct alone is not dispositive of testamentary capacity.[47] However, aberrant conduct such as delusions of grandeur or persecution may be probative of testamentary capacity.[48] The use of drugs, for therapeutic or nontherapeutic reasons, may, depending on their effect, also be probative of testamentary capacity.[49]

Old age itself is not dispositive of testamentary capacity.[50] However, the effects of various diseases of the aging process such as dementia[51] or arteriosclerosis[52] are highly probative on the issue of testamentary capacity. Similarly, physical conditions causing temporary psychiatric impairments[53] may also be relevant to testamentary capacity.[54]

Prior psychiatric treatment, inpatient or outpatient, voluntary or involuntary, at a proximate time is relevant, but not dispositive of testamentary capacity. It is reasonable to expect these records, as well as other relevant medical records, to be relied on by the expert even if not independently introduced into evidence.[55]

§15.09   —Limitations

The protections against disclosure of confidential confidential communications of the physician–patient privilege and its variants do not end on the death of the patient.[56] As a general rule, a psychiatrist or psychologist may not be compelled to disclose confidential relational communications, privileged during the patient's life, when the patient dies. However, many jurisdictions assume that the testator would want any relevant communications disclosed to assure that intent is understood and effectuated. These jurisdictions, therefore, find an implied waiver of the privilege in will contest proceedings[57] or permit the

---

[47] *In re* Ellingson, 216 Or 373, 339 P2d 447 (1959). *See* Page on Wills §12.37 (1960).

[48] Green, *Judicial Tests of Mental Incompetency*, 6 Mo L Rev 141, 162-63 (1941).

[49] *See* §§3.05-.07.

[50] Cathey v Robertson, 395 SW2d 22 (Ark 1965).

[51] *See* §2.08.

[52] Johnson v Estate of Sullivan, 619 SW2d 232 (Tex Civ App 1981) (no writ).

[53] *See* §2.08. *See also* Page on Wills §12.27 (1960).

[54] *In re* Gill, 14 Cal App 2d 256, 58 P2d 734 (Ct App 1936).

[55] Manning v Mock, 119 Ill App 3d 788, 457 NE2d 447 (1983).

[56] Bassil v Ford Motor Co, 278 Mich 173, 270 NW 258 (1936), *overruled on other grounds, sub nom* Serafin v Serafin, 401 Mich 419, 258 NW2d 461 (1977); Prink v Rockefeller Center, Inc, 48 NY2d 309, 398 NE2d 517, 422 NYS2d 911 (1979).

[57] Cal Evid Code §1000 (West 1966); Winters v Winters, 102 Iowa 53, 71 NW 184 (1897).

personal representative or heirs to waive the privilege.[58]

Statements of the testator made to an examining psychiatrist or psychologist and introduced in support of the will are hearsay; however, they may fit within one of two exceptions to the hearsay rule. If the statements were made during the course of treatment and were pertinent to treatment, they fall within the hearsay exception for statements for purposes of medical diagnosis or treatment.[59] A related, and overlapping, exception applies to statements of existing state of mind.[60] Thus, a testator's statement, "I am upset with my daughter," would fit within the exception. Statements by the testator sought to be introduced in opposition to the will fall within the admission exception to the hearsay rule.[61] Many statements of the testator will not be introduced for a hearsay purpose because they are not introduced for the truth of the matter asserted therein. Thus, a testator's statement, "I am the Pope," would not be introduced to prove that the testator was the Pope, but that he believed he was and what that reflects about testamentary capacity.

The Dead Man's Statute, a vestige of the many common law rules of incompetence,[62] operates as another limit on the basis for an opinion on testamentary capacity. Where such statutes still exist,[63] they prevent persons interested in the estate from testifying on their own behalf to conversations with the testator in will contest proceedings. Thus, these conversations may not, in jurisdictions retaining a Dead Man's Statute, serve as the basis for an expert's opinion.

§15.10 —Testimony

The use of expert testimony in challenges to testamentary capacity has been plagued by the presentation of unhelpful testimony embracing the ultimate issue in the case.[64] Although a liberalization of the ultimate

---

[58] Haverstick v Banet, 267 Ind 351, 370 NE2d 341 (1977); Green v New England Mut Life Ins Co, 108 Misc 2d 540, 437 NYS2d 844 (Sup Ct 1981).

[59] Fed R Evid 803(4).

[60] Fed R Evid 803(3).

[61] Fed R Evid 801(d)(2).

[62] Ray, *Dead Man's Statutes*, 24 Ohio St LJ 89 (1963).

[63] *See, e.g.*, Ill Ann Stat ch 110, §8-201 (Smith-Hurd Supp 1985); Tex R Evid 601(b).

[64] Slough, *Testamentary Capacity: Evidentiary Aspects*, 36 Tex L Rev 1, 11 (1957).

issue[65] rule in most jurisdictions now permits the admission of expert testimony embracing an ultimate issue,[66] that testimony must still be helpful if it is to be admitted. Thus, for example, testimony by a psychiatrist or psychologist that the testator had the capacity to execute a will, which did not explore the legal criteria that make up this capacity, would be excludable as not helpful.[67] Conversely, if a psychiatrist or psychologist described the information relied on in reaching a diagnosis, the diagnosis of the testator, and the effects of any mental disorder diagnosed on the testator's knowledge of property, relatives, and the effect of the will, the expert's testimony otherwise embracing the ultimate issue would appear harmless in light of the other helpful testimony.

§15.11 Contractual Capacity—The Legal Standard

Binding legal agreements require the consent of the parties to the agreement. The intellectual capabilities and emotional constraints of individuals relevant to the capacity to consent vary widely, and the effect of permitting these variations to result in contract avoidance has a direct bearing on the stability of contracts generally. Thus, the traditional and current majority test for contractual incapacity based on mental disorder is a narrow, cognitive test. If, at the time of the transaction, as the result of a mental disorder, a party to the contract does not understand the nature or consequence of the transaction, contractual capacity does not exist.[68] If a party suffers from a mental disorder but that disorder does not affect knowledge or understanding of the contract, or if it would affect it, but a lucid interval exists at the time of the transaction, contractual capacity exists. Under this test, the other parties' knowledge of the incapacity is usually irrelevant.[69]

In parallel fashion to the expansion of the cognitive test for criminal responsibility,[70] a minority of courts have added a volitional prong to the test for contractual incapacity. This prong is most typically applied

---

[65] See §9.08.

[66] Fed R Evid 704.

[67] Fed R Evid 704 advisory committee notes, 56 FRD 183, 185 (1972).

[68] Green, *Judicial Tests of Mental Incompetency*, 6 Mo L Rev 141, 146-52 (1941); Weihofen, *Mental Incompetency to Contract or Convey*, 39 S Cal L Rev 211 (1966). *See, e.g.*, Krueger v Zoch, 285 Minn 332, 173 NW2d 18 (1969).

[69] E. Farnsworth, Contracts 226 (1982).

[70] See §12.02.

in cases of manic-depressive disorders.[71] In jurisdictions adopting this prong of the test, contractual incapacity exists when the contract is entered into "under the compulsion of a mental disease or disorder but for which the contract would not have been made."[72] The application of this test requires, in addition, that the other party knew or should have known of the incapacity.[73]

In all jurisdictions a finding of incompetence and appointment of a guardian contemporaneous with the transaction in question results in preclusion of relitigation on the question of contractual capacity.[74] However, since a contemporaneous finding is unusual, it is the subsequent effect of a finding of incompetence that is most often at issue. In some jurisdictions, contractual incapacity is conclusive at any time after a finding of incompetence until a finding of restoration to competence,[75] while in others an earlier finding of incompetence creates only a rebuttable presumption of contractual incapacity.[76] As the standards for civil commitment[77] and contractual capacity vary, and the timing of the commitment and contract may be disparate, evidence of commitment may be relevant, but is not conclusive on the question of contractual capacity.

§15.12 —The Role of the Expert

Lay testimony describing relevant behavior of the party alleged to be incapacitated is admissible, and contractual incapacity may be proved without expert testimony.[78] Competent expert testimony is also admissible, however, and may be extremely important in explaining the behavior of the party alleged to be incapacitated. As capacity at the time of the contract or transaction is the crucial question, the expert who, as a treating therapist, saw the party at the time of the transaction will be the most helpful.

---

[71] See §2.09.

[72] Faber v Sweet Mfg Corp, 40 Misc 2d 212, 215-16, 242 NYS2d 763, 767-68 (Sup Ct 1963).

[73] Ortelere v Teachers Retirement Bd, 25 NY2d 196, 250 NE2d 460, 303 NYS2d 362 (1969).

[74] Farnsworth, *supra* note 69, at 228.

[75] Board of Regents of the State Univ of Wis v Davis, 14 Cal 3d 33, 533 P2d 1047, 120 Cal Rptr 407 (1975); Pennsylvania Co for Banking & Trusts v Philadelphia Title Ins Co, 372 Pa 259, 93 A2d 687 (1953).

[76] Fugate v Walker, 204 Ky 767, 265 SW 331 (1924).

[77] See §16.01.

[78] Broida v Travelers Ins Co, 316 Pa 444, 175 A 492 (1934).

The role for the psychiatrist or psychologist that would be most helpful to the jury would be to describe the existence of any mental disorder suffered by the party and explain its effects or those of any drugs prescribed for its treatment on the cognitive, and, in some jurisdictions, volitional capacity of the contracting party. This permits an exploration of the decision-making capacity without merely evaluating the results of the choice.

§15.13 —Basis

A determination of contractual incapacity based on mental disorder requires an assessment of the party's mental status at the time of the contract or transaction at issue. This, in turn, requires that the basis for any expert opinion on this issue include information from this relevant time frame. If, for example, the expert, a treating psychiatrist or psychologist, only saw the party several months before or after the transaction, any resulting opinion may be deemed less valuable than the testimony of a lay witness who observed the party at the time of the transaction.[79] This will be particularly true in the case of those disorders that are cyclical in nature such as manic-depressive disorders.[80]

Because of the nature of the inquiry in these cases, performance of a current clinical psychiatric interview or the administration of psychological tests may be of limited utility. Thus, in the absence of a coincidental examination proximate to the contract or transaction, only circumstantial evidence will be available as a basis for an opinion on contractual capacity. Circumstantial evidence that courts have looked upon favorably includes the circumstances or negotiations surrounding this transaction and the party's behavior in similar transactions when contractual capacity was not questioned. Thus, if the party's negotiations were similar to those in other transactions when capacity was not questioned, the basis for an opinion of incapacity would be less persuasive.

§15.14 —Limitations

The physician-patient privilege and its variants are a potential limitation on the information that may form the basis for a psychiatrist's or psychologist's opinion on contractual capacity based on a mental disorder. However, the impact of the privilege in these proceedings may

---

[79] *In re* Meyers, 410 Pa 455, 189 A2d 852 (1963).
[80] *See* **§2.09.**

not be substantial. The party alleging incapacity may waive the privilege expressly by producing the treating therapist to support a finding of incapacity.[81] The party alleging incapacity may, in the alternative, under the patient-litigant exception, waive the privilege impliedly by asserting a mental disorder to avoid the contract.[82]

Statements of the contracting party made to an examining psychiatrist or psychologist and used to question contractual incapacity will, if pertinent to treatment, fall within the hearsay exception for statements for diagnosis or treatment.[83] Statements of the contracting party sought to be introduced in opposition to the party's claim of incapacity will fall within the admission exception to the hearsay rule.[84] And, some of the contracting party's statements may not be used for a hearsay purpose when not introduced for their truth, but instead for what they reflect about their maker. The classic example of this is the statement, "I am the Pope," introduced not to prove papal legitimacy, but as reflective of the maker's delusions.

§15.15 —Testimony

The tests for competence to stand trial, contract, execute a will, or appoint a guardian are not the same. Unfortunately, these differences are not always known and recognized by those who offer opinion testimony on the question of contractual incapacity.[85] Therefore, it is extremely important that psychiatrists and psychologists not be permitted to offer only conclusions about contractual capacity without first exploring the basis for those opinions and the standards for incapacity applied. Similarly, effective testimony should include the appropriate legal criteria along with clinical findings to support an opinion about whether the contracting party was competent.

---

[81] Litz v Wilson, 208 Neb 483, 304 NW2d 48 (1981).

[82] Ginsberg v Fifth Court of Appeals, 686 SW2d 105 (Tex 1985).

[83] Fed R Evid 803(4).

[84] Fed R Evid 801(d)(2).

[85] Weinstock, Copelan, & Bagtieri, *Physician Confusion Demonstrated by Competency Requests*, 30 J Forensic Sci 36 (1985).

§15.16 Suggested Reading

Books

R. Allen, E. Ferster, & H. Weihofen, *Mental Impairment and Legal Incompetency* (1968).

S. Brakel & R. Rock, *The Mentally Disabled and the Law* (1971).

E. Farnsworth, *Contracts* (1982).

T. Grisso, *Evaluating Competencies: Forensic Assessments and Instruments* (1986).

T. Gutheil & P. Appelbaum, *Clinical Handbook of Psychiatry and the Law* (1982).

Page on Wills (1960).

Articles

Chambers, *Alternatives to Civil Commitment of the Mentally Ill: Practical Guides and Constitutional Imperatives,* 70 Mich L Rev 1107 (1972).

Frolik, *Plenary Guardianship: An Analysis, a Critique and a Proposal for Reform,* 23 Ariz L Rev 599 (1981).

Green, *Judicial Tests of Mental Incompetency,* 6 Mo L Rev (1941).

Guardianship and Conservatorship: Statutory Survey, ABA Commission on the Mentally Disabled, Model Statute (1979).

Hafemeister & Sales, *Interdisciplinary Evaluations for Guardianships & Conservatorships,* 8 Law & Hum Behav 335 (1984).

Leifer, *The Competence of the Psychiatrist to Assist in the Determination of Incompetency: A Skeptical Inquiry into the Courtroom Functions of the Psychiatrist,* 14 Syracuse L Rev 564 (1973).

Note, *Testamentary Capacity in a Nutshell: A Psychiatric Reevaluation,* 18 Stan L Rev 1119 (1960).

Ray, *Dead Man's Statutes,* 24 Ohio St LJ 89 (1963).

Slough, *Testamentary Capacity: Evidentiary Aspects,* 36 Tex L Rev 1 (1957).

Weihofen, *Mental Incompetency to Contract or Convey,* 39 S Cal L Rev 211 (1966).

Weinstock, Copelan, & Bagtieri, *Physician Confusion Demonstrated by Competency Requests,* 30 J Forensic Sci 36 (1985).

Cases

Banks v Goodfellow, [1870] 5 QB 549.

Bassil v Ford Motor Co, 278 Mich 173, 270 NW 258 (1936), *overruled on other grounds sub nom Serafin v Serafin,* 401 Mich 419, 248 NW2d 461 (1977).

Board of Regents of the State University of Wisconsin v Davis, 14 Cal 3d 33, 533 P2d 1047, 120 Cal Rptr 407 (1975).

Broida v Travelers Insurance Co, 316 Pa 444, 175 A 492 (1934).

Cathey v Robertson, 395 SW2d 22 (Ark 1965).

Cooke, In re, 231 Or 133, 372 P2d 520 (1962).

DeMarco v McGill, 402 Ill 46, 83 NE2d 313 (1948).

Dixon v Fillmore Cemetery, 608 SW2d 84 (Mo Ct App 1980).

Dopkins, In re, 34 Cal 2d 568, 212 P2d 886 (1949).

Ellingson, In re, 216 Or 373, 339 P2d 447 (1959).

Faber v Sweet Manufacturing Corp, 40 Misc 2d 212, 242 NYS2d 763 (Sup Ct 1963).

Finkler, In re, 3 Cal 2d 584, 46 P2d 149 (1935).

Fugate v Walker, 204 Ky 767, 265 SW 331 (1924).

Galindo v Garcia, 145 Tex 507, 199 SW2d 499 (1947).

Garrus v Davis, 234 Ill 326, 84 NE 924 (1908).

Gill, In re, 14 Cal App 2d 256, 58 P2d 734 (1st Dst 1936).

Ginsberg v Fifth Court of Appeals, 686 SW2d 105 (Tex 1985).

Green v New England Mutual Life Insurance Co, 108 Misc 2d 540, 437 NYS2d 844 (Sup Ct 1981).

Hastings, In re, 479 Pa 122, 387 A2d 865 (1978).

Haverstick v Banet, 267 Ind 351, 370 NE2d 341 (1977).

Johnson v Estate of Sullivan, 619 SW2d 232 (Tex Civ App-Texarkana 1981) (no writ).

Joslin, In re, 4 Wis 2d 29, 89 NW2d 822 (1958).

Kerr v O'Donovan, 389 Pa 614, 134 A2d 213 (1957).

Krueger v Zoch, 285 Minn 332, 173 NW2d 18 (1969).

Litz v Wilson, 208 Neb 483, 304 NW2d 48 (1981).

Manning v Mock, 119 Ill App 3d 788, 457 NE2d 447 (1983).

Meyers, In re, 410 Pa 455, 189 A2d 852 (1963).

Norton v Clark, 253 Ill 557, 97 NE 1079 (1912).

Obold v Obold, 163 F2d 32 (DC Cir 1947).

Ortelere v Teachers Retirement Board, 25 NY2d 196, 250 NE2d 460, 303 NYS2d 362 (1969).

Pennsylvania Co for Banking & Trusts v Philadelphia Title Insurance Co, 372 Pa 259, 93 A2d 687 (1953).

Prink v Rockefeller Center, Inc, 48 NY2d 309, 398 NE2d 517, 422 NYS2d 911 (1979).

Rogers v Okin, 634 F2d 650 (1st Cir 1980), *vacated & remanded sub nom Mills v Rogers*, 457 US 291 (1982).

Speirer v Curtis, 312 Ill 152, 143 NE 427 (1927).

Will of Slade, In re, 483 NYS2d 513, 106 AD2d 893 (1984).

Winters v Winters, 102 Iowa 53, 71 NW 184 (1897).

Statutes and Rules

Cal Evid Code §1000 (West 1966).

Fed R Evid 704, advisory committee notes, 56 FRD 183, 185 (1972).

Fed R Evid 801(d)(2).

Fed R Evid 803(3) & (4).

Ill Ann Stat ch 110, §8-201 (Smith-Hurd Supp 1985).

Mich Comp Laws Ann §330.1617(4) (1980).

Mo Ann Stat §475.075(1) (Vernon 1956).

20 Pa Cons Stat Ann §5511(a) (Purdon 1979).

Tex R Evid 601(b).

Unif Prob Code §§5-103(7), 306(c) (1983).

§15.17 WESTLAW Search References

§15.01 *Guardianship and Conservatorship—The Legal Standard*
di parens patriae

digest (conservator! guardian! /s "parens patriae")

conservator! guardian! /p incapacity /p standard

§15.02 *—The Role of the Expert*
guardian! conservator! /p psycholog! psychiatr*** /5 witness testi! /s necess*** competen** incompeten**

§15.03 *—Basis*
guardian! conservator! /p psycholog! psychiatr*** /5 opinion testimony /5 based

§15.04 *—Limitations*
guardian! conservator! /p psycholog! psychiatr*** physician /p hearsay % "guardian ad litem"

§15.05 —*Testimony*
synopsis (incompetent) & guardianship conservatorship &?s proceeding hearing /p psychiatr*** psycholog! /s testimony opinion

§15.06 *Testamentary Capacity—The Legal Standard*
"testamentary capacity" /5 standard

digest (testamentary /3 capacity incapacity /s incompeten** (mental** /3 ill illness disorder defect***))

§15.07 —*The Role of the Expert*
digest (testamentary /3 capacity incapacity /s psychiatr*** psycholog! /5 testimony opinion)

§15.08 —*Basis*
testamentary /3 capacity incapacity /p psycholog! psychiatr*** /s testimony opinion /s based

§15.09 —*Limitations*
testamentary /3 capacity incapacity /p "dead man" +1 act statute

§15.10 —*Testimony*
testamentary /3 capacity incapacity /s "ultimate issue"

§15.11 *Contractual Capacity—The Legal Standard*
contract! /3 capacity incapacity /s standard test

§15.12 —*The Role of the Expert*
contract! /3 capacity incapacity /s expert psychiatr*** psycholog!

§15.13 —*Basis*
contract! /3 capacity incapacity /p examin! evidence

§15.14 —*Limitations*
fi 686sw2d105

§15.15 *Testimony*
contract! /3 capacity incapacity /s opinion testimony

16

Civil Commitment

§16.01 The Legal Standard

Statutory schemes authorizing the involuntary hospitalization of individuals suffering from a mental disability, who have not been charged with or convicted of a crime, exist in every state.[1] These statutory schemes address mentally ill and mentally retarded persons. They may have as their object the protection of the mentally disabled person, the protection of society from the disabled person, or the treatment or habilitation of the mentally disabled person.

Commitment of a mentally ill person is permitted in all states upon proof of the existence of a mental illness and consequential dangerousness to self or others.[2] Many states now require that this dangerousness be evidenced by a recent act or threat to address concerns about

---

[1] *See generally* S. Brakel & R. Rock, The Mentally Disabled and the Law (1971).

[2] Beis, *State Involuntary Commitment Statutes,* 7 Mental Disability L Rep 358 (1983).

369

erroneous predictions.[3] The nature of the dangerousness required typically is substantial, and the time period within which it will occur must not be remote.[4]

Statutory schemes for civil commitment of the mentally ill based on criteria other than dangerousness were rejected by courts and legislatures in the 1960s and 1970s because of concerns with the adequacy of treatment in public institutions and deprivations of liberty based on paternalistic considerations. However, a variety of conditions, including fears that a class of mentally disabled persons incapable of fending for themselves have been excluded from the system, have contributed to the reemergence of paternalistic commitment criteria in a number of jurisdictions.[5] The new generation of statutes permitting commitment under an *in need of treatment* standard require proof of a major mental disorder, a rejection of needed treatment by an incapacitated patient, and, in some jurisdictions, a showing that the required treatment will be available if commitment is ordered.[6] These new statutory schemes have not yet been tested for constitutionality.

Although civil commitment of the mentally ill does not require that the proposed patient have been charged with or convicted of a crime, one category of committed patients will have been charged with criminal conduct. This category is patients who have been found not guilty of criminal conduct by reason of insanity and subsequently civilly committed. In some jurisdictions individuals found not guilty by reason of insanity are subject to commitment under the same procedures applicable to all other civil committees,[7] while other jurisdictions provide for automatic commitment of insanity acquittees.[8] In *Jones v United States*[9] the United States Supreme Court held that persons found not guilty by reason of insanity may be confined without necessarily applying all the same procedural safeguards applicable to other committed patients.

---

[3] Dix, *Major Current Issues Concerning Civil Commitment Criteria*, 45 Law & Contemp Probs 137, 144-47 (1982).

[4] *Id.*

[5] *See* Stromberg & Stone, *A Model State Law on Civil Commitment*, 20 Harv J Legis 275 (1983).

[6] Tex Rev Civ Stat Ann art 5547-50(b) (Vernon Supp 1985); Wash Rev Code Ann §71.05.020(1) (Supp 1985).

[7] Note *Constitutional Law—Criminal Procedure Due Process and Release from Indefinite Commitment Following Acquittal By Reason of Insanity: Jones v. United States*, 32 U Kan L Rev 843, 844 n 13 (1984).

[8] *Id* 84.

[9] 463 US 354 (1983).

Most states provide for involuntary hospitalization of the mentally deficient or retarded under procedures that are the same or similar to those applicable to the mentally ill.[10] The definition of mental retardation or deficiency provided in these statutory schemes is typified by the Pennsylvania statute: "Mental Retardation means subaverage intelligence functioning which originates during the developmental period and is associated with impairment of one or more of the following: (1) maturation, (2) learning and (3) social adjustment."[11] Frequently, through the actions of court-appointed guardians, hospitalization of the mentally retarded is accomplished under procedures for voluntary hospitalization.[12]

§16.02   —The Role of the Expert

Statutory schemes for civil commitment of the mentally ill or retarded frequently require medical or psychiatric input in the commitment process as a prerequisite to commitment. This may entail the requirement of a certificate to institute the commitment process[13] or testimony at the commitment hearing.[14] In these jurisdictions, although lay testimony may be admissible, it is not an adequate substitute for the required medical input.

These statutory or constitutional requirements specifically mention physicians and psychiatrists; however, it is surprising that, in some instances, even in the absence of a psychiatrist, physicians are preferred over psychologists.[15] This preference cannot be justified by the relative expertise of these two professions or the issues raised in these proceedings. It appears to be an anachronism that does not reflect contemporary theory about mental disorders or the education and training of these professions.

In the absence of a statutory or constitutional requirement of expert medical testimony in commitment proceedings, such testimony is

---

[10] S. Brakel & R. Rock, *supra* note 1, at 37.

[11] Pa Cons Stat Ann 50 §4102 (Purdon 1969).

[12] S. Brakel & R. Rock, *supra* note 1, at 260. *See also* Gilboy & Schmidt, *Voluntary Hospitalization of the Mentally Ill*, 66 Nw L Rev 429 (1971). *But see* Pima Co Fiduciary v Superior Court, 26 Ariz App 85, 546 P2d 354 (1976).

[13] *See, e.g.,* W Va Code §27-5-3(a) (1980).

[14] *See, e.g.,* Tex Const art I, §15a.

[15] Dix & Poythress, *Propriety of Medical Dominance of Forensic Mental Health Practice: The Empirical Evidence*, 23 Ariz L Rev 961 (1981).

implicitly required by the commitment criteria.[16] Mental illness and mental retardation as criteria for involuntary hospitalization are utilized in a technical sense in these proceedings. Only if an individual has a diagnosed and treatable mental disorder does it make sense to confine that person for treatment in a mental hospital. The term *mental illness* in these proceedings is not utilized, for example, as *insanity* may be presented as an exculpating consideration in criminal law, which has significant moral overtones.[17]

Once it has been accepted that expert testimony must be presented, the role of the expert is a bit more troubling. The first issue to be addressed in proceedings for involuntary hospitalization is the existence of a mental disability of the requisite category and degree for the type of proceeding utilized—a substantial or severe mental disorder or deficiency. The difficulties that have characterized psychiatric diagnosis[18] should require, at minimum, that two independent diagnoses be obtained. In addition, a descriptive rendition of the disordered behavior observed by the testifying psychiatrist or psychologist and the applicable diagnostic criteria should be provided to the factfinder.

If the commitment is based on dangerousness to self or others, the role of the expert in predicting dangerousness presents particular problems. Psychiatric and psychological education and training does not typically include courses in the prediction of dangerousness,[19] and the professions have themselves disclaimed expertise of the prediction of dangerousness.[20] However, the United States Supreme Court has not found psychiatric testimony on future dangerousness, in the context of imposition of the death penalty, so unreliable that it should be excluded as a matter of constitutional law.[21] Instead, the Court relegated the inquiry to the expertise of the individual witness, scrutinized through cross-examination and the testimony of other experts. Thus, inquiry into the witness's education, training, or experience relevant to the

---

[16] *See, e.g., In re* Gannon, 123 NJ Super 104, 301 A2d 493 (1973).

[17] *See* Morse, *Crazy Behavior, Morals and Science: An Analysis of Mental Health Law,* 51 S Cal L Rev 527 (1978).

[18] *See* §2.11.

[19] *See* §§4.04, 4.10.

[20] American Psychiatric Assn, *Clinical Aspects of the Violent Individual* (1974); *Report of the Task Force on the Role of Psychology in the Criminal Justice System,* 33 Am Psychologist 1099, 1110 (1978).

[21] Barefoot v Estelle, 463 US 880 (1983).

prediction of future dangerousness is appropriate.[22] In the absence of any special expertise on this issue, the appropriate role of the psychiatric or psychological witness should be to identify to the factfinder those events or considerations that it may wish to consider on this issue.

§16.03   —Basis

In theory, the predicate to a diagnosis in a proceeding for involuntary hospitalization should be the same one utilized in private practice as a prerequisite to voluntary treatment in a psychiatric hospital. A thorough clinical psychiatric examination, history, psychological and intelligence tests, social service study, physical examination, and, when necessary, neurological examination are the appropriate bases for a psychiatric diagnosis.[23] In practice, the procedures often vary.[24] The absence of adequate private office space on the public hospital psychiatric ward may result in an abbreviated clinical psychiatric examination conducted in less than an ideal setting. The absence of adequate funding may result in inadequate social service staff and, as a result, an incomplete or cursory social service investigation. And, the requirement of an expeditious commitment hearing[25] may limit the opportunity to observe patient behavior on the ward for an extended period of time. Thus, it is important, to evaluate any diagnosis, that a thorough inquiry into its basis be made.

At minimum, courts have required an examination as a prerequisite to an expert opinion in involuntary hospitalization proceedings.[26] The adequacy of that examination is, however, an appropriate inquiry. The length of the exam, its location, the orientation of the examiner, and the information previously made known to the examiner about the patient are all relevant to the weight that should be given any resulting opinion.

One particularly problematic aspect of expert opinion in commitment proceedings based on dangerousness criteria is the basis for an opinion on this issue. Given the difficulty of making these predictions generally, some courts have required that any opinion of future dangerousness be based on a recent prior act, attempt, or threat to enhance the validity

---

[22] *See* **§7.06.**

[23] *See* **ch 2.**

[24] *See, e.g.,* Shuman & Hawkins, *The Use of Alternatives to Institutionalization of the Mentally Ill,* 33 Sw LJ 1181, 1191-1200 (1980).

[25] *See, e.g.,* Tex Rev Civ Stat Ann art 5547-42 (Vernon Supp 1985).

[26] *In re* Scott, 438 So 2d 728 (La Ct App 1983).

of the prediction.[27] Beyond that, an extensive history of the patient, the patient's family and social network, and the patient's use of drugs and alcohol are all extremely important data in predicting dangerousness.

§16.04 —Limitations

The principal potential limitations on the basis for a psychiatric or psychological opinion in a civil commitment proceeding are the privilege against self-incrimination, the physician-patient privilege and its variants, and the hearsay rule. The most controversial of these limitations is the privilege against self-incrimination.

Statutory schemes for civil commitment typically authorize court-ordered examinations of the proposed patient.[28] The results of this examination may then be a basis to order involuntary hospitalization. Although the object of these proceedings is not punishment as is the case in criminal proceedings, they may nonetheless result in a loss of liberty. On that basis, a minority of jurisdictions have held that the privilege against self-incrimination[29] applies to court-ordered examinations in commitment proceedings.[30] The majority of jurisdictions to address this issue have rejected the privilege's application in these proceedings on the ground that they are civil, not criminal, and their purpose is to treat, not punish; that the examination yields real—not testimonial—evidence; or that, as a practical necessity, informed commitment decisions could not be made without an examination of the proposed patient.[31]

By either statute or judicial ruling, the rules of evidence applicable in other judicial proceedings are typically applicable in civil commit-

---

[27] *See, e.g., In re* Johnston, 118 Ill App 2d 214, 454 NE2d 840 (1983). *But see* Mathew v Nelson, 461 F Supp 707 (ND Ill 1978).

[28] *See, e.g.,* Tex Rev Civ Stat Ann art 5547-46 (Vernon Supp 1985).

[29] US Const amend V.

[30] Lynch v Baxley, 386 F Supp 378 (MD Ala 1974); Lessard v Schmidt, 349 F Supp 1078 (ED Wis 1972), *vacated & remanded on other grounds,* 414 US 473, *on remand,* 379 F Supp 1078 (ED Wis 1974) *vacated & remanded on other grounds,* 421 US 957 (1975), *on remand,* 413 F Supp 1318 (ED Wis 1976). *See* Aronson, *Should the Privilege Against Self-Incrimination Apply to Compelled Psychiatric Examinations,* 26 Stan L Rev 55 (1973).

[31] Suzuki v Yuen, 617 F2d 173, 177 (9th Cir 1980); Gomes v Gaughan, 471 F2d 794 (1st Cir 1973); State v O'Neil, 274 Or 59, 545 P2d 97 (1976); *In re* Helvenston, 658 SW2d 99 (Tenn Ct App 1983); Moss v State, 539 SW2d 936 (Tex Civ App 1976) (no writ); Hawks v Lazaro, 202 SE2d 109 (W Va 1974).

ment proceedings.[32] One of the rules that is often at issue in these proceedings is the physician-patient privilege and its variants.[33] Because these proceedings turn on medical evidence, the use of communications between the proposed patient and a physician, psychiatrist, psychologist, or other psychotherapist are often highly relevant.

A major source of evidence in commitment proceedings is court-ordered examinations of the proposed patient. Court-ordered examinations of the proposed patient do not fit within the scope of privileged communications because their purpose is not the rendition of treatment, but the preparation of a report to the court.[34] Thus, so long as the patient is properly informed of the purpose of the examination, the privilege is inapplicable.[35]

More problematic is the subject of communications with a treating psychiatrist or psychologist when the patient's condition has deteriorated and the psychiatrist or psychologist or others conclude that commitment may be necessary. In this instance, if an applicable privilege exists, the communications were privileged at the outset, as the purpose of the relationship was treatment. Should this privilege give way to an exception in the face of a commitment proceeding?[36] A substantial number of jurisdictions have recognized statutory exceptions to the application of medical and related privileges in civil commitment proceedings.[37] Other jurisdictions have carved out judicially created exceptions to the privilege in commitment proceedings.[38] The assumption underlying these exceptions is that commitment will not occur in appropriate cases without this evidence, thereby denying proposed patients needed treatment or ineffectively protecting society from the dangerous mentally ill.[39]

Another potential limitation on the basis for an expert's opinion in

---

[32] Shuman, *The Road to Bedlam: Evidentiary Guideposts in Civil Commitment Proceedings*, 55 Notre Dame Law 53 (1979).

[33] *See* ch 10.

[34] *See* §10.04.

[35] Tex R Evid 510(d)(4); Commonwealth v Lamb, 365 Mass 265, 311 NE2d 47 (1974).

[36] Shuman, *supra* note 32, at 64-68.

[37] Ark Stat Ann §28-1001, Rule 503(d)(1) (1979); Cal Evid Code §1004 (West 1976); Fla Stat Ann §90.503(4)(a) (West Spec Pamphlet 1979); Kan Stat Ann §60-427(c)(1) (1976); Me R Evid 503(e)(1) (Supp 1978); Neb Rev Stat §27-504(4)(a) (1978).

[38] Metropolitan Life Ins Co v Ryan, 237 Mo App 464, 172 SW2d 269 (1943); *In re* Benson, 16 NYS 111 (1891).

[39] Shuman, *supra* note 32, at 65-68.

commitment proceedings is the hearsay rule. A psychiatrist or psychologist testifying in a commitment proceeding may seek to rely on statements made by the patient's friends or family or opinions of other psychiatrists or psychologists in reaching an opinion. In the absence of independent admission of this evidence, reliance on these extrajudicial sources presents a hearsay problem.

Although some jurisdictions limit either any reliance[40] or substantial reliance[41] on these extrajudicial sources where they are not independently excepted from the hearsay rule, the trend is to permit their utilization when customarily and reasonably relied on by experts in the field.[42] A thorough psychiatric diagnosis entails a "longitudinal study of behavior"[43] requiring information from the patient's friends and family, employers, and physicians. This information is typically compiled by a psychiatric social worker and relied upon in reaching psychiatric diagnoses without the judicial context. Whether this practice is reasonable depends on the specific investigatory techniques: Is the investigator well trained? Has the investigation been thorough? Have the informants' potential motives to falsify been identified and evaluated? Has any critical information been independently verified? Unfortunately, this sort of searching inquiry is rare.[44]

Statements by the proposed patient to a psychiatrist or psychologist utilized as the basis for an opinion may fit within one or more exceptions to the hearsay rule and, therefore, be independently admissible as nonhearsay. Communications by the proposed patient to a treating psychiatrist or psychologist that were pertinent to treatment will fall within the hearsay exception for statements made for purposes of medical diagnosis or treatment regardless of who offers them.[45] Statements by the proposed patient, whether made in the treatment context or elsewhere, are categorized as admissions and will not be barred by the hearsay rule when offered against the proposed patient.[46]

---

[40] Brackin v State, 417 So 2d 602 (Ala Crim App 1982).

[41] Moore v Graham, 599 SW2d 287 (Tex 1980).

[42] Fed R Evid 703. See §9.05.

[43] M. Guttmacher & H. Weihofen, Psychiatry and the Law 221 (1952).

[44] Note, *Hearsay Bases of Psychiatric Opinion Testimony: A Critique of Federal Rules of Evidence 703,* 51 S Cal L Rev 129 (1977).

[45] Fed R Evid 803(4).

[46] Fed R Evid 801(d)(2).

§16.05 —Testimony

Unfortunately, civil commitment hearings have provided some of the worst examples of unhelpful, conclusory psychiatric and psychological testimony.[47] Inquiries into the qualifications of these witnesses, the bases for their opinions, the process by which their opinions have been reached, or a descriptive version of their findings have tended to be the exception rather than the rule. Increasingly, however, courts have refused to accept conclusory expert testimony in commitment hearings as an adequate evidentiary basis to support the commitment.[48]

Minimally, the testimony of a psychiatrist or psychologist offered as an expert in a commitment proceeding should address the following issues: What are the witness's qualifications? Beyond basic education and licensure as a physician or clinical psychologist, is the witness board certified in a relevant specialty? What experience does the witness have in the diagnosis and treatment of the mental disorder alleged? If the commitment is based on dangerousness, what special education, training, or experience does the witness have to permit an opinion by the witness on the issue of dangerousness? What is the basis for the witness's opinion? When has the witness interviewed the proposed patient, for what length of time, and in what setting? What occurred during those interviews? Was the patient informed that any information revealed was not privileged? Does an exception to the privilege exist? What examinations or tests of the patient have been made to rule out the existence of physical disorders? Have psychological and intelligence tests been conducted and, if so, what did those tests reveal? Have the proposed patient's records of other treatments for physical or mental disorders been reviewed? Was a social service study prepared, by whom, what sources were contacted, and what did that study reveal?

What diagnosis has been reached? Have other experts independently examined the patient and have they reached the same diagnosis? What treatment is appropriate for this disorder? Does this treatment require inpatient hospitalization, and why? In what facilities is this treatment available? What insurance or other hospitalization benefits does the patient have? What family or friends does the patient have? What treatment program is recommended, and what treatment programs have been considered, not recommended, and why?

---

[47] *See, e.g.,* Wexler & Scoville, *Special Project—The Administration of Psychiatric Justice: Theory and Practice in Arizona,* 13 Ariz L Rev 1, 64-65 (1971).

[48] *See, e.g.,* State *ex rel* Mayberry, 685 SW2d 121 (Tex Civ App 1985).

§16.06   Suggested Reading

Books

S. Brakel & R. Rock, *The Mentally Disabled and the Law* (1971).

M. Guttmacher & H. Weihofen, *Psychiatry and the Law* (1952).

Articles

American Psychiatric Assn, *Clinical Aspects of the Violent Individual* (1974).

Aronson, *Should the Privilege Against Self-Incrimination Apply to Compelled Psychiatric Examinations,* 26 Stan L Rev 55 (1973).

Beis, *State Involuntary Commitment Statutes,* 7 Mental Disability L Rep 358 (1983).

Dix, *Major Current Issues Concerning Civil Commitment Criteria,* 45 Law & Contemp Probs 137 (1982).

Dix & Poythress, *Propriety of Medical Dominance of Forensic Mental Health Practice: The Empirical Evidence,* 23 Ariz L Rev 961 (1981).

Gilboy & Schmidt, *Voluntary Hospitalization of the Mentally Ill,* 66 Nw L Rev 429 (1971).

Morse, *Crazy Behavior, Morals, and Science: An Analysis of Mental Health Law,* 51 S Cal L Rev 527 (1978).

Note, *Constitutional Law—Criminal Procedure Due Process and Release from Indefinite Commitment Following Acquittal by Reason of Insanity: Jones v. United States,* 32 U Kan L Rev 843 (1984).

Note, *Hearsay Bases of Psychiatric Opinion Testimony: A Critique of Federal Rules of Evidence 703,* 51 S Cal L Rev 129 (1977).

Report of the Task Force on the Role of Psychology in the Criminal Justice System, 33 Am Psychologist 1099 (1978).

Shuman, *The Road to Bedlam: Evidentiary Guideposts in Civil Commitment Proceedings,* 55 Notre Dame Law 53 (1979).

Shuman & Hawkins, *The Use of Alternatives to Institutionalization of the Mentally Ill,* 33 Sw LJ 1181 (1980).

Stromberg & Stone, *A Model State Law on Civil Commitment,* 20 Harv J Legis 275 (1983).

Wexler & Scoville, *Special Project—The Administration of Psychiatric Justice: Theory and Practice in Arizona,* 13 Ariz L Rev 1 (1971).

Cases

Barefoot v Estelle, 463 US 880 (1983).

Benson, In re, 16 NYS 111 (1891).

Brackin v State, 417 So 2d 602 (Ala Crim App 1982).

Commonwealth v Lamb, 365 Mass 265, 311 NE2d 47 (1974).

Gannon, In re, 123 NJ Super 104, 301 A2d 493 (1973).

Gomes v Gaughan, 471 F2d 794 (1st Cir 1973).

Hawks v Lazaro, 202 SE2d 109 (W Va 1974).

Helvenston, In re, 658 SW2d 99 (Tenn Ct App 1983).

Johnston, In re, 118 Ill App 2d 214 454 NE2d 840 (1983).

Jones v United States, 463 US 354 (1983).

Lessard v Schmidt, 349 F Supp 1078 (ED Wis 1972), *vacated & remanded on other grounds*, 414 US 473 (1973), *on remand*, 379 F Supp 1078 (ED Wis 1974), *vacated & remanded on other grounds*, 421 US 957 (1975), *on remand*, 413 F Supp 1318 (ED Wis 1976).

Lynch v Baxley, 386 F Supp 378 (MD Ala 1974).

Mathew v Nelson, 461 F Supp 707 (ND Ill 1978).

Metropolitan Life Insurance Co v Ryan, 237 Mo App 464, 172 SW2d 269 (1943).

Moore v Graham, 599 SW2d 287 (Tex 1980).

Moss v State, 539 SW2d 936 (Tex Civ App 1976) (no writ).

Pima County Fiduciary v Superior Court, 26 Ariz App 85, 546 P2d 354 (1976).

Scott, In re, 438 So 2d 728 (La Ct App 1983).

State ex rel Mayberry, 685 SW2d 121 (Tex Civ App 1985).

State v O'Neil, 274 Or 59, 545 P2d 97 (1976).

Suzuki v Yuen, 617 F2d 173 (9th Cir 1980).

Constitutions, Statutes, and Rules

Ark Stat Ann §28-1001, Rule 503(d)(1)(1979).

Cal Evid Code §1004 (West 1976).

Fed R Evid 703.

Fed R Evid 801(d)(2).

Fed R Evid 803(4).

Fla Stat Ann §90.503(4)(a) (West Spec Pamphlet 1979).

Ha Rev Stat §334(b)(4)(G).

Kan Stat Ann §60-427(c)(1) (1976).

Me R Evid 503(e)(1) (Supp 1978).

Neb Rev Stat §27-504(4)(a) (1978).

Pa Cons Stat Ann 50 §4102 (Purdon 1969).

Tex Const art I, §15a.

Tex R Evid 510.

Tex Rev Civ Stat Ann art 5547-42, -46, -50(b) (Vernon Supp 1985).

US Const amend V.

W Va Code §27-5-3(a) (1980).

Wash Rev Code Ann §71.05.020(1) (Supp 1985).

§16.07   WESTLAW Search References

§16.01 *The Legal Standard*
> "civil commitment" /5 standard test
>
> "civil commitment" /p jones /s 103 +5 3043

§16.02 —*The Role of the Expert*
> "civil commitment" /s psychiatrist psychologist physician

§16.03 —*Basis*
> "civil commitment" /s testimony opinion /5 bas**

§16.04 —*Limitations*
> "civil commitment" /p "self incrimination"
>
> "civil commitment" /p hearsay
>
> "civil commitment" /p privilege*

§16.05 —*Testimony*
> "civil commitment" /p psychiatr*** psycholog! conclusory /5 testimony opinion

17

Novel Applications of Psychiatric and Psychological Evidence

§17.01 Testimonial Credibility—The Legal Standard

Eyewitness testimony is often critical in resolving issues of fact in civil and criminal trials. It has been argued, however, that this testimony is frequently less reliable than it is assumed to be, and that there is a body of research available to assist judges and jurors in evaluating eyewitness testimony more carefully. Thus, some have argued that juries should receive assistance, through expert testimony, in the evaluation of eyewitness testimony.

In addition to research bearing on the weight that should be given the testimony of all eyewitnesses, it has been suggested that evidence of mental disorders suffered by a particular eyewitness should be admitted as relevant to witness credibility. Limits on the ability of a witness to testify accurately have implications for the admissibility of the testimony (testimonial competence) and the weight of the testimony (testimonial credibility). Although considerations such as mental illness or drug addiction might once have rendered a witness incompetent to give testimony,[1] these considerations are now often relegated to the weight rather than the admissibility of the testimony.[2] A witness with a mental disability that may affect perception, memory, sincerity, or narration may now testify, and the existence or effects of this disability on credibility may, without more, be unknown or incompletely understood by the judge or jury. Thus, expert testimony bearing on the mental disability of an individual witness that affects perception, memory, sincerity, or narration may provide important information that is highly relevant in determining the credibility of a witness.

Although expert testimony on witness credibility may be relevant, its probative value may be counterbalanced by other considerations.[3] The potential counterweights to admissibility of this testimony are several. The decision to admit this type of testimony entails additional trial time spent in the examination and cross-examination of these expert witnesses. The use of these expert witnesses adds an additional expense to the trial, as both sides will wish to present expert evidence when one side has opened the door. Fear of overkill exists; in the case of testimony about eyewitness research, for example, the effect of admitting this testimony may be to make jurors more skeptical of eyewitness testimony than they ought to be.[4] And, the applicability of the laboratory research

---

[1] Weihofen, *Testimonial Competence and Credibility*, 34 Geo Wash L Rev 53 (1965).

[2] Fed R Evid 601 provides, in part, that "[e]very person is competent to be a witness." Arizona, Arkansas, Delaware, Hawaii, Oklahoma, and Wyoming adopted this portion of the federal rule. J. Weinstein & M. Berger, Weinstein's Evidence ¶601[06] (1982). Other jurisdictions such as Ohio and Michigan retain insanity as a functional limitation on competence, disqualifying witnesses whose mental capacity prevents truthful or understandable testimony. *Id.*
Even though a general rule of incompetence may not exclude the witness's testimony, a witness must still be capable of taking the oath and appreciating its requirements. A mental disability may have an impact on this capacity. In addition, if the consequence of a mental disability is to reduce the probative value of the testimony so that it is substantially outweighed by confusion or delay, its exclusion may be justified on other grounds. *See* Fed R Evid 403.

[3] *See* Fed R Evid 403. "Although relevant, evidence may be excluded if its probative value is substantially outweighed by the danger of unfair prejudice, confusion of the issues, or misleading the jury, or by considerations of undue delay, waste of time, or needless presentation of cumulative evidence."

[4] Wells, Lindsay, & Tousignant, *Effects of Expert Psychological Advice on Human Performance in Judging the Validity of Eyewitness Testimony*, 4 Law & Hum Behav 275 (1980).

on eyewitness identification to actual identifications may be inappropriate.[5] Finally, the use of experts telling jurors whom they ought and ought not to believe poses a threat to the independence of the jury.[6]

The result of the judicial balancing of these considerations is that expert testimony providing general information about the reliability of eyewitness testimony is admissible or excludable largely at the discretion of the trial court judge.[7] Appellate courts have not rebuked trial courts for admitting this evidence, nor, similarly, have they, in the main, reversed trial courts for excluding this evidence. There is, however, a trend in favor of admissibility and several appellate courts have reversed trial court decisions excluding this testimony.[8] These decisions in which reversals occurred involved attempts to present well-qualified experts who were to present experimentally derived data, in cases where the facts were close and the case turned on the accuracy of eyewitness identification.

The admissibility of psychiatric or psychological testimony about the mental disability of a particular witness has turned on the degree of the disability and its effect on testimonial credibility. Evidence of a major mental illness that may have an impact on perception of a relevant event and expert testimony explaining its effects is admissible to challenge the credibility of the witness.[9] Conversely, evidence concerning mental disorders not likely to affect perception or memory has been excluded.[10] The question in each individual case is whether the disorder is merely an aberration in behavior or of a degree that may affect the witness's ability to perceive, remember, or narrate accurately and sincerely.

---

[5] McCloskey & Egeth, *Eyewitness Identification: What Can a Psychologist Tell a Jury?*, 38 Am Psychologist 550 (1983).

[6] State v Caldwell, 267 Ark 1053, 594 SW2d 24 (1980); Jones v State, 232 Ga 762, 208 SE2d 850 (1974).

[7] *See, e.g.*, United States v Watson, 587 F2d 365 (7th Cir 1978), *cert denied*, 439 US 1132 (1979); United States v Brown, 540 F2d 1048 (10th Cir 1976); United States v Amaral, 488 F2d 1148 (9th Cir 1973).

[8] United States v Downing, 753 F2d 1224 (3d Cir 1985); State v Chapple, 135 Ariz 281, 660 P2d 1208 (1983); People v McDonald, 37 Cal 3d 351, 690 P2d 709, 208 Cal Rptr 236 (1984).

[9] *See, e.g.*, United States v Partin, 493 F2d 750, 762-64 (5th Cir 1974), *cert denied*, 434 US 903 (1977) (auditory hallucinations).

[10] *See, e.g.*, United States v Brumbaugh, 471 F2d 1128 (6th Cir), *cert denied*, 412 US 918 (1973) (depression).

§17.02 —The Role of the Expert

Psychiatrists and psychologists have provided two types of evidence about testimonial credibility. The first type is testimony that a particular witness is not credible because of a mental or emotional disorder. The second type involves providing general information from the research literature about the factors that affect perception and memory of all witnesses, which the jury or judge may then apply to determine the credibility of a particular witness.

The first major trial in which a psychiatrist was used to provide evidence of the credibility of a witness involved the first type of evidence. In the trial of Alger Hiss for passing government secrets to the Russians, the defendant sought to impeach the credibility of the government's chief eyewitness, Whittaker Chambers, with the testimony of a psychiatrist, Dr. Carl Binger.[11] Dr. Binger testified, based on his observations of Chambers while testifying, that Chambers was a "psychopath with a tendency toward making false accusations."[12] Although an effective cross-examination of Dr. Binger resulted in the defense strategy backfiring, this trial signaled the dawning of a new use of psychiatrists and psychologists in judicial proceedings.

One attempted use of this type of attack on witness credibility has occurred in drug prosecutions involving the testimony of government informants who are themselves drug users. The use of these drugs may affect perception of the incident at issue, memory of that incident, susceptibility to manufacture testimony sympathetic to the government's efforts to convict, and an ability to appreciate the oath or affirmation requirement at trial. Thus, evidence that a witness was under the effects of narcotic drugs when perceiving a relevant event or while testifying is admissible, and the effect of those drugs may be explained by a qualified expert.[13] Conversely, evidence of drug use not specifically related to the event at issue or the time of trial has been excluded.

A recent use of psychiatric and psychological testimony that has a bearing on testimonial credibility is evidence about *rape trauma syndrome.*[14] This syndrome describes the symptoms of a post-traumatic

---

[11] United States v Hiss, 88 F Supp 559 (SDNY 1950), *cert denied*, 340 US 948 (1951).

[12] R. Slovenko, Psychiatry and the Law 45 (1973).

[13] United States v Banks, 520 F2d 627 (7th Cir 1975).

[14] Burgess & Holstrom, *Rape Trauma Syndrome* 131 Am J Psychiatry 981 (1974). *See also Testimony on Rape Trauma Syndrome: Admissibility and Effective Use in Criminal Rape Prosecutions* 33 Am U L Rev 417 (1984).

stress disorder[15] found in women who have been sexually assaulted. Some common responses include fear of retaliation, fear of another sexual assault, fear of men, fear of being alone, sleep and appetite disturbance, shame, and embarrassment. A slight majority of courts that have considered the admissibility of this evidence in rape prosecutions have permitted the testimony of highly qualified experts that the prosecutrix displayed behaviors consistent with this syndrome, to respond to a defense of consent.[16] It is not clear whether courts view this evidence as corroboration or as rehabilitation of the prosecutrix's credibility that was implicitly impeached by raising or giving evidence on the defense of consent. When expert evidence has been rejected on this issue, rejection has been based on a fear that the syndrome is not sufficiently reliable because of the sample used in the original research, that the symptoms of rape trauma syndrome are not distinguishable from other post-traumatic stress disorders, and that victim behaviors vary widely.[17]

The use of experts to provide information derived from research about the problems of eyewitness testimony generally has been more recent. It has grown out of a body of research conducted by experimental psychologists. Its thrust has been to explain that perception is not a photographic process and that memory is affected by a multitude of factors beyond the mere passage of time.[18] The role of the expert in describing these findings is not to suggest that a particular witness is credible, but rather to provide information to the jury from the research literature about circumstances that increase or decrease the reliability of eyewitness testimony and to permit the jury to apply that information to the facts of the individual case to determine the reliability of the testimony.

Some examples of the research findings follow. This research has suggested that the importance of an item at the time of the original

---

[15] American Psychiatric Assn, Diagnostic and Statistical Manual of Mental Disorders 309.30 & 309.81 (3d ed 1980) (DSM-III).

[16] State v Huey, 145 Ariz 59, 699 P2d 1290 (1985); State v Marks, 231 Kan 645, 647 P2d 1292 (1982); State v Liddell, 685 P2d 918 (Mont 1984). Even in jurisdictions admitting this evidence on the issue of consent, where consent is not an issue and the defendant denies any sexual contact with the prosecutrix, rape trauma syndrome evidence is not admissible to prove that the rape occurred. State v Bressman, 236 Kan 296, 689 P2d 901 (1984).

[17] State v Saldana, 324 NW2d 227 (Minn 1982); State v Taylor, 663 SW2d 235 (Mo 1984).

[18] Buckhout, *Eyewitness Testimony*, 231 Sci Am 23 (1974).

perception increases the likelihood that perception will be accurate.[19] Conversely, the fact that an item was not important at the time decreases the likelihood that recollection will be accurate. The amount of exposure at the time of perception is directly proportional to the likelihood that subsequent recollection will be accurate.[20] Stress does not increase the accuracy of perception, but instead tends to decrease it and narrow attention.[21] Perceptions frequently correspond to expectations about what the observer thinks should have happened.[22] Memory of perceptions is affected by postevent occurrences such as interrogation by the police.[23] Eyewitness testimony tends to be less reliable in cases of cross-racial identification.[24] And, the confidence of an eyewitness's testimony tends to be unrelated to poor witnessing conditions.[25]

§17.03 —Basis

When the testimony of the expert provides general information from the research literature, the expert need only be aware of the facts of the case in a general way. The expert may need to know whether the witness and the defendant were of the same race or whether the police interrogated the witness afterwards to know which body of research applies in the case, but there is no need for the expert to interview the eyewitness in these instances. The expert need not apply the body of scientific knowledge provided to the facts of the case, but rather may leave that to the judge or jury.[26]

---

[19] Leippe, Wells, & Ostram, *Crime Seriousness as a Determinant of Accuracy in Eyewitness Identification*, 63 J Applied Psychology 345 (1978).

[20] Deffenbacher, *The Influence of Arousal on Reliability of Testimony*, in Evaluating Witness Evidence: Recent Psychological Research and New Perspectives (1983).

[21] *Id.*

[22] Powers, Adricks, & Loftus, *Eyewitness Accounts of Females and Males*, 64 J Applied Psychology 399 (1979).

[23] Lipton, *On the Psychology of Eyewitness Testimony*, 62 J Applied Psychology 90 (1977).

[24] Brigham & Barkowitz, *Do "they all look alike?": The Effect of Race, Sex, Experience, and Attitudes and the Ability to Recognize Faces*, 8 J Applied Soc Psychology 306 (1978).

[25] Deffenbacher, *Eyewitness Accuracy and Confidence: Can We Infer Anything About Their Relationship?*, 4 Law & Hum Behav 243 (1980).

[26] *See* Fed R Evid 702 advisory committee notes, 56 FRD 183, 282 (1972):

Much of the literature assumes that experts testify only in the form of opinions. The assumption is logically unfounded. The Rule accordingly

When, however, the expert testifies that a particular witness is not credible because that witness suffers from some mental disorder or defect that affects testimonial credibility, the basis for that opinion is problematic. Rendering a psychiatric diagnosis without a physical examination, clinical psychiatric examination and history, or psychological tests, but instead based exclusively on an observation of the witness or in response to a hypothetical question, is extremely suspect.[27] It fails to conform to standard psychiatric or psychological diagnostic techniques, and the weight of any such opinion is questionable. How is the expert to know, for example, whether observed behaviors result from a physical disorder or the effects of medication? If an opinion without an examination is inappropriate, may a psychiatric or psychological examination of an adverse party or a witness on the issue of credibility be compelled?

Rule 35 of the Federal Rules of Civil Procedure[28] and its state counterparts[29] permit an examination of a party whose physical or mental condition is in controversy. The *in controversy* requirement has been interpreted to relate not to the party's credibility as a witness, but directly to proof of the claim or defense.[30] The examination of a nonparty witness is not generally permitted under the authority of this rule.[31]

Although courts have found the inherent authority to order the examination of a witness whose competence to testify is at issue in a civil

---

recognizes that an expert on the stand may give a dissertation or exposition of scientific or other principles relevant to the case, leaving the trier of fact to apply them to the facts.

[27] *See* **§2.14.**

[28] Fed R Civ P 35(a) provides:

(a)   Order for Examination. When the mental or physical condition (including the blood group) of a party, or of a person in the custody or under the legal control of a party, is in controversy, the court in which the action is pending may order the party to submit to a physical or mental examination by a physician or to produce for examination the person in his custody or legal control. The order may be made only on motion for good cause shown and upon notice to the person to be examined and to all parties and shall specify the time, place, manner, conditions, and scope of the examination and the person or persons by whom it is to be made.

[29] *See, e.g.,* Ill Sup Ct R 215; Tex R Civ P 167(a).

[30] Schlagenhauf v Holder, 379 US 104 (1964).

[31] Scharf v United States Attorney Gen, 597 F2d 1240 (9th Cir 1979). *But see* State v Butler, 27 NJ 560, 143 A2d 530 (1958).

or criminal proceeding,[32] they have generally refrained from ordering it when the only issue was one of credibility.[33] The reasons courts have advanced for refusing to order an examination of a witness include the witness's right to privacy and the risk of deterring individuals from volunteering information to law enforcement officials. This rule is not absolute. For example, when, in the case of a complaint for sexual abuse, little corroboration exists and the complaining witness's mental condition is raised in relation to veracity, the majority of jurisdictions will permit the court to order an examination of that witness.[34]

§17.04   —Limitations

The provision of general information derived from research about perception or memory does not require that the expert providing the information utilize statements made by the eyewitness. Thus, the physician–patient privilege and its variants will not apply to limit the basis for this type of testimony. The privilege against self-incrimination will be inapplicable, as the evidence provided does not rest on compelled statements by an accused. And, the hearsay rule will not come into play as a limit on specific statements constituting the basis for the expert's testimony.

Testimony that a witness suffers from a particular mental disorder or defect, describing the effects of that disorder on the witness's credibility, does require reliance on information provided by the witness. If this information is derived exclusively from observing the witness while testifying or from performing a court-ordered examination, no privilege attaches. If, however, the information is derived from a relationship in which the witness was treated by the testifying psychiatrist or psychologist, an applicable privilege will prevent the use of information gained in this relationship as the basis for an attack on the witness/patient's

---

[32] Gurleski v United States, 405 F2d 253, 267 (5th Cir 1968), *cert denied,* 395 US 977 (1969); Mell v State, 133 Ark 197, 202 SW 33 (1918); State v Teager, 22 Iowa 391, 269 NW 348 (1936); Miller v State, 295 P 403 (Okla Crim App 1930); Rice v State, 195 Wis 181, 217 NW 697 (1928); State v Butler, 27 NJ 560, 143 A2d 530 (1958).

[33] *See, e.g.,* United States v Jackson, 576 F2d 46, 49 (5th Cir 1978).

[34] *See, e.g.,* State v Wahrlich, 105 Ariz 103, 459 P2d 727 (1969); Ballard v Superior Court, 64 Cal 2d 159, 410 P2d 838, 49 Cal Rptr 302 (1966); State v Gregg, 226 Kan 481, 602 P2d 85 (1979); State v Maestas, 190 Neb 312, 207 NW2d 699 (1973); Washington v State, 96 Nev 305, 608 P2d 1101 (1980). *But see* Commonwealth v Widrick, 392 Mass 884, 467 NE2d 1353 (1984); People v Souvenir, 83 Misc 2d 1038, 373 NYS2d 824 (Crim Ct 1975).

credibility.[35] Although disclosure of the witness's criminal behavior bearing on credibility, such as the use of narcotic drugs, may incriminate the witness, when the witness testifies for the government under a grant of immunity, this problem may be resolved. If the witness testifies for the defense and the government seeks to impeach the witness based on illegal drug use, the limits on compelled disclosure of this information imposed by the Fifth Amendment remain.

§17.05   —Testimony

In those instances in which courts have permitted expert testimony based on research about eyewitness testimony, they have limited the extent of the testimony to general information.[36] The witness may describe what is known about the effects of stress on perception, for example, but may not then testify that the stress in this particular case was sufficient to affect that perception or that the witness should not be believed. Fear that the jury may fail to exercise independent scrutiny of the evidence has resulted in limiting the expert's drawing of inferences from the research as applied to the facts of the case.

Experts testifying about the effects of a particular mental disease or disorder on credibility have not been limited in similar fashion. In the first recognized use of this type of testimony, the trial of Alger Hiss, a psychiatrist was permitted to testify that the witness was a "psychopath with a tendency toward making false accusations."[37] Yet, the risks present with this form of testimony, no less than in the case of more general testimony about the accuracy of eyewitness testimony, caution in favor of descriptive rather than conclusory testimony.

§17.06   The Psychiatric Autopsy—The Legal Standard

The behavior of someone now deceased is often of legal consequence in determining such issues as the cause of death—accident or suicide, or the circumstances surrounding the death—self-defense or an unjustified use of force. In the early 1950s, Dr. Edwin Schneidman and his colleagues at the Los Angeles Suicide Prevention Center investigating

---

[35] *See* **§10.02.**

[36] United States v Downing, 753 F2d 1224 (3d Cir 1985); State v Chapple, 135 Ariz 281, 660 P2d 1208 (1983); People v McDonald, 37 Cal 3d 351, 690 P2d 709, 208 Cal Rptr 236 (1984).

[37] R. Slovenko, Psychiatry and the Law 45 (1973).

deaths from equivocal causes developed a technique called a psychological autopsy to ascertain whether a death was the result of suicide.[38] The theory underlying the technique is that most suicide victims communicate their intentions in some way. The psychological autopsy technique they developed entails the reconstruction of a psychological profile of the decedent from information gleaned from interviews with family and friends of the decedent. Subsequently, the psychological autopsy was renamed a psychiatric autopsy because of the addition of medical data—toxicology, pharmacology, and anatomical pathology—in the analysis.[39]

Although the validity of the psychiatric autopsy has been touted in a variety of therapeutic and investigative contexts,[40] its accuracy has not been systematically studied. Indeed, it is used only when it is impossible to ascertain with certainty the circumstances surrounding the death of the decedent. It is principally a clinical technique. Thus, its reliability will turn on the skills and techniques of the clinician utilizing it.

The potential for use of the psychiatric autopsy exists whenever the issues raised in a case concern the behavior of the decedent and direct evidence is absent or incomplete. This would include, for example, life insurance policy suicide defenses[41] and self-defense of battered wives.[42] Life insurance policies frequently exclude coverage for suicide. Thus, when the circumstances of death suggest the possibility of suicide, payment may be denied and a defense of suicide asserted to a claim on the policy. Without much careful scrutiny by the courts of the research on the psychiatric autopsy or the qualifications of the expert, testimony by a psychiatrist or psychologist who never met or examined the decedent has been admitted on the issue that the insured committed suicide.[43]

Another potential use of the psychiatric autopsy is in criminal cases

---

[38] N. Faberow & E. Schneidman, The Cry for Help 12 (1961). *See also* Widman, *The Use of a Suicidologist in Accidental Death Litigation,* 47 Ins Couns J 219 (1980).

[39] Bendheim, *The Psychiatric Autopsy: Its Legal Implications,* 7 Bull Am Acad Psychiatry 400 (1979).

[40] *See, e.g.,* Litman, Curphey, Schneidman, Faberow, & Tabachnick, *Investigations of Equivocal Suicides,* 184 JAMA 924 (1963); Sanborn & Sanborn, *The Psychological Autopsy as a Therapeutic Tool,* 37 Diseases Nervous Sys 4 (1976).

[41] Widman, *supra* note 38.

[42] Bendheim, *supra* note 39.

[43] Starkey Paint Co v Springfield Life Ins Co, 24 NC App 507, 211 SE2d 498 (1975). *See also* Biro v Prudential Ins Co, 110 NJ Super 391, 265 A2d 830, *revd,* 57 NJ 204, 271 A2d 1 (1970).

to substantiate a claim of self-defense by a battered wife.[44] The testimony here may be used to corroborate the defendant/wife's belief that the threats made by her victim/husband were likely to be carried out unless deadly force was used.

§17.07 —The Role of the Expert

Lay testimony describing the last events of the decedent's life or the conditions surrounding the decedent's death is admissible to prove that the death was an accident or a suicide, or that the decedent attacked the defendant without provocation.[45] No requirement exists that expert testimony be presented to sustain a claim that the cause of death was suicide or an unprovoked attack. However, expert testimony is admissible as to the cause or circumstances of death.[46] The benefit of psychiatric or psychological testimony on this issue is in explaining the significance of the events described by the lay witnesses that might otherwise go unnoticed or be misunderstood.

The psychiatric autopsy is a clinical investigative technique. Unlike the results of an MMPI, a standardized psychological test, the skills and techniques of the clinician will determine the reliability of the results of the psychiatric autopsy. Thus, qualification as an expert on this issue should be carefully scrutinized. Minimally, in addition to qualification as a psychiatrist or psychologist, the witness should be familiar with the literature on the psychiatric autopsy, and should have received training and be experienced in its use.

The psychiatric autopsy is based on an evaluation of events in the decedent's life. Thus, the psychiatrist or psychologist performing the autopsy must first insure that a thorough investigation of these events has taken place. Absent a thorough investigation, evidence of the decedent's true intentions may be lost and the resulting opinion worthless.

---

[44] State v Jones, Cr No 98666 (Ariz 1978). *See* Note *Diagnosing the Dead: The Admissibility of the Psychiatric Autopsy,* 18 Am Crim L Rev 617 (1981). See discussion of the Battered Wife Syndrome in **§12.01.**

[45] Starkey Paint Co v Springfield Life Ins Co, 24 NC App 507, 211 SE2d 498 (1975).

[46] *See* A. Moenssens & F. Inbau, Scientific Evidence in Criminal Cases §5.06 (1978).

§17.08 —Basis

Although a psychiatrist or psychologist may have treated the decedent shortly before death, this typically is not the case in the psychiatric autopsy. Most often, the psychiatric autopsy is performed by a psychiatrist or psychologist who never met or examined the decedent, but who has received information about the decedent from a variety of other sources. Although a clinical examination is obviously the ideal as a diagnostic technique,[47] it is not feasible in these circumstances. Because the ability to gather information will be severely limited, all other available information must be gathered as a prerequisite to a helpful opinion.

The information recommended as the basis for a psychiatric autopsy includes a multitude of sources that may shed light on the decedent's death.[48] The coroner's findings as to the specific cause of death are extremely important. Relevant medical records of treatments for physical illness that may have afflicted the decedent and have been the cause of pain or were likely to have been terminal must be discovered. Similarly, records of any treatment for mental disorders are important information in a psychological autopsy to reveal the existence of any acute or chronic disorders. Interviews with survivors—friends, relatives, and business acquaintences—to learn about the decedent are necessary. The financial and personal stakes of these sources in the autopsy findings must be considered in utilizing the information they provide.[49] Letters written by the decedent may also provide valuable information.

§17.09 —Limitations

The protections of the physician-patient privilege and its variants do not end with the death of the patient.[50] In the absence of an authorized waiver or exception, the testimony of the decedent's therapist on confidential relational communications with the decedent may not be compelled. The decedent's representative may waive the privilege

---

[47] *See* §2.12.

[48] N. Faberow & E. Schneidman, The Cry for Help 12 (1961).

[49] Selkin & Loya, *Issues in Psychological Autopsy of a Controversial Public Figure,* 10 Prof Psychology 87 (1979).

[50] Bassil v Ford Motor Co, 278 Mich 173, 270 NW 258 (1936), *overruled on other grounds sub nom* Serafin v Serafin, 401 Mich 419, 258 NW2d 461 (1977); Prink v Rockefeller Center, Inc, 48 NY2d 309, 398 NE2d 517, 422 NYS2d 911 (1979).

under certain circumstances,[51] and this may be recognized to respond to a defense of suicide on an application for life insurance benefits.

The basis for a psychiatric autopsy—medical records, interviews with survivors, coroner's report—may not have been admitted or be admissible in evidence. If this information has been admitted, it may be presented to the expert in the form of a hypothetical question.[52] If this information has not been admitted and is relied on for its truth, a hearsay problem exists. Although psychiatrists and psychologists may customarily and reasonably use these sources in their professional practice and may thus seek to avoid the bar of the hearsay rule,[53] there is a critical difference between the two situations. It is one thing to utilize these sources to supplement a patient interview. It is quite another thing to use these same sources without ever having met or interviewed the decedent. Thus, the hearsay rule should not be stretched so far in these cases as to permit the utilization of sources not directly available to the factfinder. The sources on which the psychiatrist or psychologist relies should be presented to the judge or jury for examination in person.

§17.10 —Testimony

The psychiatric autopsy is accomplished through a reconstruction of the decedent's character or personality from information gained from a variety of sources. This reconstructed character or personality is then used to make a retrospective prediction of the likelihood of the decedent's having committed a particular act. A problem raised by this reconstruction is that rules of evidence generally prohibit the use of character evidence to show conformity with that character.[54]

---

[51] Haverstick v Banet, 267 Ind 351, 370 NE2d 341 (1977); Greene v New England Mut Life Ins Co, 108 Misc 2d 540, 437 NYS2d 844 (Sup Ct 1981).

[52] Starkey Paint Co v Springfield Life Ins Co, 24 NC App 507, 211 SE2d 498 (1975).

[53] Fed R Evid 703 permits an expert to use an inadmissible basis for an opinion if it is customary and reasonable for other experts to do so in similar circumstances in their professional practice.

[54] Fed R Evid 404(a) provides:

(a)   Character Evidence Generally. Evidence of a person's character or a trait of his character is not admissible for the purpose of proving that he acted in conformity therewith on a particular occasion, except:
(1)   Character of Accused. Evidence of a pertinent trait of his character offered by an accused, or by the prosecution to rebut the same;
(2)   Character of Victim. Evidence of a pertinent trait of character of the victim of the crime offered by an accused, or by the prosecution to rebut the same, or evidence of a character trait of peacefulness of the victim

An exception to this general rule is recognized in criminal cases to permit the accused to introduce evidence of a pertinent trait of the accused's character or the victim's.[55] This exception would apply in the case of a psychiatric autopsy to substantiate a claim of self-defense made by a battered wife. Character evidence suggesting that the victim was likely to act violently toward his wife would be a pertinent trait of character of the victim to substantiate a claim of self-defense.

When these exceptions are not applicable, character evidence may not be introduced to show conformity, according to the general rule. However, character as contemplated by the rules of evidence is not defined in those rules, and it may be argued that it does not include personality or psychological predisposition.[56] The writers and rules seem in a state of confusion on this point. For example, while Wigmore defined character as "moral or psysical disposition,"[57] he also recognized that proof of insanity has not generally been restricted under the rule prohibiting proof of character to show conformity.[58] In a related area, the use of the *battering parent syndrome*,[59] a cluster of behaviors common in abusing parents, most courts that have addressed its admissibility have excluded evidence by the prosecution of this syndrome to prove that the defendant conformed to the syndrome and was, therefore, more likely to have abused the victim, as violative of the rule prohibiting the use of character to show conformity.[60] Thus, the proponent of the psychiatric autopsy in civil cases will be required to prove that the development of this technique justifies an exclusion of this evidence from the concept of character contemplated by the rules.

---

offered by the prosecution in a homicide case to rebut evidence that the victim was the first aggressor;

(3)   Character Witness. Evidence of the character of a witness, as provided in Rules 607, 608, and 609.

Arkansas, Arizona, Colorado, New Mexico, North Dakota, South Dakota, Washington, and Wyoming have adopted a rule identical to the federal rule. J. Weinstein & M. Berger, Weinstein's Evidence ¶404[01] (1988). Alaska, Florida, Michigan, Minnesota, Montana, Nevada, North Carolina, Ohio, Oklahoma, and Wisconsin have adopted similar rules. *Id.*

[55] *Id.*

[56] *See* C. Wright & K. Graham, Federal Practice and Procedure §5233 (1978).

[57] 1 J. Wigmore, Evidence §52, at 488 (3d ed 1940)

[58] *Id* §86.

[59] *See* §13.10.

[60] *In re* Cheryl, 153 Cal App 3d 1098, 200 Cal Rptr 789 (1984); State v Loebach, 310 NW2d 58 (Minn 1981).

An indirect reference in the Advisory Committee Notes to Federal Rule of Evidence 404 may make this argument more difficult.

> Much of the force of the position of those favoring greater use of character evidence in civil cases is dissipated by their support of Uniform Rule 48 which excludes the evidence in negligence cases, where it could be expected to achieve its maximum usefulness. Moreover, expanding concepts of "character," which seem of necessity to extend into such areas as psychiatric evaluation and psychological testing, coupled with expanded admissibility, would open up such vistas of mental examinations as caused the Court concern in Schlagenhauf v. Holder, 379 U.S. 104, 85 S.Ct. 234, 13 L.Ed.2d 152 (1964). It is believed that those espousing change have not met the burden of persuasion.[61]

§17.11 Suggested Reading

Books

American Psychiatric Assn, *Diagnostic and Statistical Manual of Mental Disorders* (3d ed 1980) (DSM-III).

N. Faberow & E. Schneidman, *The Cry for Help* (1961).

A. Moenssens & F. Inbau, *Scientific Evidence in Criminal Cases* (1978).

R. Slovenko, *Psychiatry and the Law* (1973).

J. Weinstein & M. Berger, *Weinstein's Evidence* (1982).

1 J. Wigmore, *Evidence* (3d ed 1940).

C. Wright & K. Graham, *Federal Practice and Procedure* (1978).

Articles

Bendheim, *The Psychiatric Autopsy: Its Legal Implications,* 7 Bull Am Acad Psychiatry 400 (1979).

Brigham & Barkowitz, *Do "they all look alike?": The Effect of Race, Sex, Experience, and Attitudes on the Ability to Recognize Faces,* 8 J Applied Soc Psychology 306 (1978).

Burgess & Holstrom, *Rape Trauma Syndrome* 131 Am J Psychiatry 981 (1974).

Deffenbacher, *Eyewitness Accuracy and Confidence: Can We Infer Anything About Their Relationship?,* 4 Law & Hum Behavior 243 (1980).

---

[61] Fed R Evid 404 advisory committee notes, 56 FRD 183, 219-21 (1972).

Deffenbacher, *The Influence of Arousal on Reliability of Testimony*, in Evaluating Witness Evidence: Recent Psychological Research and New Perspectives (1983).

Leippe, Wells, & Ostram, *Crime Seriousness as a Determinant of Accuracy in Eyewitness Identification*, 63 J Applied Psychology 345 (1978).

Lipton, *On the Psychology of Eyewitness Testimony*, 62 J Applied Psychology 90 (1977).

Litman, Curphey, Schneidman, Faberow, & Tabachnick, *Investigation of Equivocal Suicides*, 184 JAMA 924 (1963).

Mcloskey & Egeth, *Eyewitness Identification: What Can a Psychologist Tell a Jury?*, 83 Am Psychologist 550 (1983).

Note, *Diagnosing the Dead: The Admissibility of the Psychiatric Autopsy*, 18 Am Crim L Rev 617 (1981).

Note, *Testimony on Rape Trauma Syndrome: Admissibility and Effective Use in Criminal Rape Prosecutions* 33 Am U L Rev 417 (1984).

Powers, Adricks, & Loftus, *Eyewitness Accounts of Females and Males*, 64 J Applied Psychology 399 (1979).

Sanborn & Sanborn, *The Psychological Autopsy as a Therapeutic Tool*, 37 Dis Nervous Sys 4 (1976).

Selkin & Loya, *Issues in Psychological Autopsy of a Controversial Public Figure*, 10 Prof Psychology 87 (1979).

Weihofen, *Testimonial Competence and Credibility*, 34 Geo Wash L Rev 53 (1965).

Wells, Lindsay, & Tousignant, *Effects of Expert Psychological Advice on Human Performance in Judging the Validity of Eyewitness Testimony*, 4 Law & Hum Behav 275 (1980).

Widman, *The Use of a Suicidologist in Accidental Death Litigation*, 47 Ins Couns J 219 (1980).

Cases

Ballard v Superior Court, 64 Cal 2d 159, 410 P2d 838, 49 Cal Rptr 302 (1966).

Bassil v Ford Motor Co, 278 Mich 173, 270 NW 258 (1936), *overruled on other grounds sub nom Serafin v Serafin*, 401 Mich 419, 258 NW2d 461 (1977).

Biro v Prudential Insurance Co, 110 NJ Super 391, 265 A2d 830, *revd*, 57 NJ 204, 271 A2d 1 (1970).

Cheryl, In re, 153 Cal App3d 1098, 200 Cal Rptr 789 (1984).

Commonwealth v Widrick, 392 Mass 884, 467 NE2d 1353 (1984).

Greene v New England Mutual Life Insurance Co, 108 Misc 2d 540, 437 NYS2d 844 (1981).

Gurleski v United States, 405 F2d 253 (5th Cir 1968), *cert denied,* 395 US 977 (1969).

Haverstick v Banet, 267 Ind 351, 370 NE2d 341 (1977).

Jones v State, 232 Ga 762, 208 SE2d 850 (1974).

Mell v State, 133 Ark 197, 202 SW 33 (1918).

Miller v State, 295 P 403 (Okla Crim App 1930).

People v McDonald, 37 Cal 3d 351, 690 P2d 709, 208 Cal Rptr 236 (1984).

People v Souvenir, 83 Misc 2d 1038, 373 NYS2d 824 (1975).

Prink v Rockefeller Center, Inc, 48 NY2d 309, 398 NE2d 517, 422 NYS2d 911 (1979).

Rice v State, 195 Wis 181, 217 NW 697 (1928).

Scharf v United States Attorney General, 597 F2d 1240 (9th Cir 1979).

Schlagenhauf v Holder, 379 US 104 (1964).

Starkey Point Co v Springfield Life Insurance Co, 24 NC App 507, 211 SE2d 498 (1975).

State v Bressman, 236 Kan 296, 689 P2d 901 (1984).

State v Butler, 27 NJ 560, 143 A2d 530 (1958).

State v Caldwell, 267 Ark 1053, 594 SW2d 24 (1980).

State v Chapple, 235 Ariz 281, 660 P2d 1208 (1983).

State v Gregg, 226 Kan 481, 602 P2d 85 (1979).

State v Huey, 145 Ariz 59, 699 P2d 1290 (1985).

State v Jones, Cr No 98666 (Ariz 1978).

State v Liddell, 685 P2d 918 (Mont 1984).

State v Loebach, 310 NW2d 58 (Minn 1981).

State v Maestas, 190 Neb 312, 207 NW2d 699 (1973).

State v Marks, 231 Kan 645, 647 P2d 1292 (1982).

State v Saldana, 324 NW2d 277 (Minn 1982).

State v Taylor, 663 SW2d 235 (Mo 1984).

State v Teager, 22 Iowa 391, 269 NW 348 (1936).

State v Wahrlich, 105 Ariz 103, 459 P2d 727 (1969).

United States v Amaral, 488 F2d 1148 (9th Cir 1973).

United States v Banks, 520 F2d 627 (7th Cir 1975).

United States v Brown, 540 F2d 1048 (10th Cir 1976).

United States v Brumbaugh, 471 F2d 1128 (6th Cir), *cert denied,* 412 US 918 (1973)

United States v Downing, 753 F2d 1224 (3d Cir 1985).

United States v Hiss, 88 F Supp 559 (SDNY), 185 F2d 822 (2d Cir 1950), *cert denied,* 340 US 958 (1951).

United States v Jackson, 576 F2d 46 (5th Cir 1978).

United States v Partin, 493 F2d 750 (5th Cir 1974), *cert denied,* 434 US 903 (1977).

United States v Watson, 587 F2d 365 (7th Cir 1978), *cert denied,* 439 US 1132 (1979).

Washington v State, 96 Nev 305, 608 P2d 1101 (1980).

Statutes and Rules

Fed R Civ P 35(a).

Fed R Evid 403.

Fed R Evid 404 advisory committee notes, 56 FRD 183, 219-21 (1972).

Fed R Evid 601.

Fed R Evid 702 advisory committee notes, 56 FRD 183, 282 (1972).

Fed R Evid 703.

Ill Sup Ct R 215.

Tex R Civ P 167(a).

§17.12   WESTLAW Search References

§17.01 *Testimonial Credibility—The Legal Standard*
   expert /3 opinion testimony /s credib! reliab! /5 witness
   eyewitness victim /s mental** /3 ill**** disorder defect***

§17.02 *—The Role of the Expert*
   fi 520f2d627

§17.03 *—Basis*
   expert /3 opinion testimony /5 bas** /s credib! reliab! /5
   witness eyewitness

§17.04 *—Limitations*
   fi 372nw2d151

§17.05 *—Testimony*
   expert /3 opinion testimony /p credib! reliab! /5 witness
   eyewitness victim /p downing chapple

§17.06 *The Psychiatric Autopsy—The Legal Standard*
    fi 684p2d1101

§17.07 —*The Role of the Expert*
    suicid** /s psycholog! psychiatr*** expert /5 testimony opinion % topic(110)

§17.08 —*Basis*
    suicid** /p psycholog! psychiatr*** expert /5 testimony opinion /5 bas** % topic(110)

§17.09 —*Limitations*
    fi 270nw258

§17.10 —*Testimony*
    psycholog! psychiatr*** /5 testimony opinion /p act** /3 conform***

Nontestimonial Uses of Psychiatric and Psychological Evidence

§18.01 Case Preparation and Review

The use of a psychiatrist or psychologist to assist an attorney in evaluating, preparing, and presenting the case, without an appearance on the witness stand, offers many benefits to the attorney and often provides a more palatable role for the psychiatrist or psychologist in the litigation. Nontestimonial assistance avoids involving the psychiatrist or psychologist as a witness in that part of the adversary process that is often uncomfortable for nonattorneys. It also avoids for the psychiatrist or psychologist many of the ethical dilemmas raised by becoming a witness. And, it can be a good use of a knowledgeable psychiatrist or psychologist who would not be an effective witness.

A preliminary evaluation by an attorney when a client seeks to institute or defend an action—is there a cognizable claim or defense—may be materially aided by a psychiatrist or psychologist. This assistance may take the form of a review of relevant medical records or an examination of the client to determine the extent of any mental disorder prior to raising an insanity defense or instituting a personal injury action, for example. Assistance may also come in the form of an evaluation of the client's sincerity when the client's story leaves the attorney less than convinced of its veracity. This may be critical given the increasing judicial concern that attorneys scrutinize their clients' stories before instituting litigation.[1] A psychiatrist or psychologist may also be useful in breaking down barriers to effective communication between counsel and client.

After the institution of litigation, psychiatric and psychological assistance may help to explain the behavior of an adverse party. Why is the opponent refusing to settle this case in which damages are so small or liability so obvious? What else drives the pursuit of the litigation? This same analysis may also provide fertile ground for cross-examination.

A psychiatrist or psychologist may be useful in identifying other psychiatrists or psychologists who may be effective witnesses,[2] contacting these individuals, and soliciting their assistance. In addition, the nontestifying psychiatrist or psychologist may be useful in suggesting appropriate questions for examination of these witnesses. Similarly, the psychiatrist or psychologist may be useful in evaluating an opponent's psychiatrists or psychologists and suggesting questions for their cross-examination.

The nontestifying psychiatrist or psychologist may be helpful in planning the presentation of the case. This individual may help to evaluate the effect of testifying on the client and the effect of the client's testimony on the judge or jury. If, following this evaluation, the client is to testify, the psychiatrist or psychologist may assist the client in preparing for testifying—presenting a favorable image on the witness stand, dealing with the anxiety of testifying, and withstanding cross-examination. In addition, the psychiatrist or psychologist may provide advice on the overall structuring of the presentation of the case and its effect on the judge or jury.

Beyond presentation of the case at trial, a psychiatrist or psychologist may be helpful in the settlement process. One avenue of assistance may be in understanding the opponent's motivation in bringing or defending an action. Another potential avenue for assistance in settlement may be the preparation of a community survey of responses to the case. The psychiatrist or psychologist may prepare a brief questionnaire, describing the case most favorable to the opponent, and present it, in person or by telephone, to members of the community selected as representative of typical jury panels in the jurisdiction where the case would be tried. The sampling technique, questionnaire, and results may then be recorded on a videotape of the psychiatrist or psychologist who conducted it, and presented to the opponent to encourage settlement.

---

[1] Fed R Civ P 11 (as amended Apr 28, 1983).

[2] *See* §§6.03-6.08.

If the only role the psychiatrist or psychologist plays is assisting the attorney in evaluating, preparing, or presenting the case, the physician–patient privilege and its variants provide no limitation on disclosure of information gained in this process by the psychiatrist or psychologist.[3] Instead, any protection that exists will come from the attorney-client or work product privilege,[4] viewing the psychiatrist or psychologist as the attorney's assistant. These protections limit disclosure of these communications in the absence of a showing that these individuals possess a unique fund of knowledge not reasonably obtainable elsewhere. This condition permitting disclosure might be satisfied in the rare situation when the issues in the case turned on the expertise possessed by only one person, already retained as a nontestifying consultant by one of the litigants.[5]

The protections of the attorney–client or work product privilege governing nontestifying experts may also be waived. For example, in a minority of jurisdictions, raising the insanity defense waives any applicable privilege as to nontestifying psychiatrists or psychologists who have examined the defendant.[6] A more direct form of waiver would occur if a portion of the results of the psychiatrist or psychologist's report were utilized, for example, to support a motion to find the defendant incompetent to stand trial. Beyond this type of waiver, Rule 35 of the Federal Rules of Civil Procedure provides for the waiver of applicable privileges and reciprocal exchange of reports as a condition of requesting a copy of the report of an opponent's examination of a party under authority of the rule.[7]

---

[3] *See* **§10.02.**

[4] *See* **§10.06.**

[5] *See, e.g.,* Dixon v Cappellini, 88 FRD 1 (MD Pa 1980).

[6] *See, e.g.,* People v Al-Kanani, 33 NY2d 260, 307 NE2d 43, 351 NYS2d 969 (1973), *cert denied,* 417 US 916 (1974).

[7] Fed R Civ P 35 provides:

Rule 35.   Physical and Mental Examination of Persons

(a)   Order for Examination.   When the mental or physical condition (including the blood group) of a party, or of a person in the custody or under the legal control of a party, is in controversy, the court in which the action is pending may order the party to submit to a physical or mental examination by a physician or to produce for examination the person in his custody or legal control. The order may be made only on motion for good cause shown and upon notice to the person to be examined and to all parties and shall specify the time, place, manner, conditions, and scope of the examination and the person or persons by whom it is to be made.

(b)   Report of Examining Physician.

(1)   If requested by the party against whom an order is made under

§18.02 Jury Selection

The right to trial by jury recognized in the federal[8] and state constitutions[9] includes the right to a fair and impartial jury chosen from a cross-section of the community.[10] Various mechanisms including peremptory challenges,[11] challenges for cause,[12] challenges to the panel,[13] and change of venue[14] exist to increase the probability of obtaining a fair and imparital jury. To utilize these mechanisms, attorneys and judges have often relied on intuitive judgments about the behavior of prospective jurors. Research analyzing the use of this intuition, however, has found that it is often not effective and that social scientists have much to offer to improve the efficacy of these decisions.[15] What follows is a description of various techniques utilizing the

---

Rule 35(a) or the person examined, the party causing the examination to be made shall deliver to him a copy of a detailed written report of the examining physician setting out his findings, including results of all tests made, diagnoses and conclusions, together with like reports of all earlier examinations of the same condition. After delivery the party causing the examination shall be entitled upon request to receive from the party against whom the order is made a like report of any examination, previously or thereafter made, of the same condition, unless, in the case of a report of examination of a person not a party, the party shows that he is unable to obtain it. The court on motion may make an order against a party requiring delivery of a report on such terms as are just, and if a physician fails or refuses to make a report the court may exclude his testimony if offered at the trial.

(2) By requesting and obtaining a report of the examination so ordered or by taking the deposition of the examiner, the party examined waives any privilege he may have in that action or any other involving the same controversy, regarding the testimony of every other person who has examined or may thereafter examine him in respect of the same mental or physical condition.

(3) This subdivision applies to examinations made by agreement of the parties, unless the agreement expressly provides otherwise. This subdivision does not preclude discovery of a report of an examining physician or the taking of a deposition of the physician in accordance with the provisions of any other rule.

[8] US Const amend VI & VII.

[9] *See, e.g.,* Tex Const art 1, §15.

[10] Thiel v Southern Pac Co, 328 US 217 (1946).

[11] Fed R Crim P 24(b).

[12] Irvin v Dowd, 366 US 717 (1961).

[13] Swain v Alabama, 380 US 202 (1965).

[14] Fed R Crim P 21(a).

[15] *See, e.g.,* Broeder, *Voir Dire Examinations: An Empirical Study,* 38 S Cal L Rev

assistance of social scientists to achieve a fair and impartial jury.[16] The development and application of these techniques to jury selection is rather recent. Use of these techniques first occurred in the early 1970s in the trial of the antiwar activists, the Berrigans, and subsequently in the trial of Angela Davis, a Black Panther, and Joan Little, a black woman accused of murdering a white male jailer she alleged sexually assaulted her in jail.[17]

Evaluation of individual jurors utilizing clinical techniques involves an assessment of the individual juror based on various perspectives. One set of techniques involves observation of the prospective juror's verbal (language content), paralinguistic (speech patterns), kinesic ("body language") and group behavior to predict behavior as a juror.[18] Another involves an assessment of various demographic attributes (e.g., age, sex, race, employment) and what they suggest about the juror's values relevant to the issues in the case. Extrajudicial observations of the juror's home or automobile may reveal information such as an alarm system or bumper sticker thought to manifest important values or beliefs. And, assessment of personality types for observable behavior (e.g., authoritarianism) is also thought to be aided by the clinical skills of social scientists.[19]

Another technique utilized to predict juror behavior is the public opinion survey.[20] This involves a psychological survey of a sample of the community from which the jury will be drawn to ascertain representative attitudes about issues raised by the case (e.g., divorce, homosexuality, physicians, or large damage awards). From this survey, the attributes of those jurors in the geographic area most and least sympathetic on these issues can be identified (e.g., age, sex, race, marital status, or employment) and each prospective juror can be compared to these models to decide on the use of challenges. Although this technique is used with much confidence, it can cost upwards of $30,000.

Another popular technique does not involve the selection of actual

---

503 (1965).

[16] See generally Lees-Haley, The Psychology of Jury Selection, 47 Tex BJ 918 (1984).

[17] McConahay, Mullin, & Frederick, The Uses of Social Science in Trials with Political and Racial Overtones: The Trial of Joan Little, 41 Law & Contemp Probs 205 (1977).

[18] Suggs & Sales, Using Communication Cues to Evaluate Prospective Jurors During the Voir Dire, 20 Ariz L Rev 629 (1978).

[19] Frederick, Jury Behavior: A Psychologist Examines Jury Selection, 5 Ohio NUL Rev 571, 581-82 (1978).

[20] Id 578.

jurors, but, instead, testing the case with a mock jury.[21] Utilizing demographic data about typical juries in the forum, a panel representative of the jury likely to be chosen is selected and compensated by a party. This panel is then presented with the entire case, to evaluate the effect of trial strategy, theories for recovery, arguments, witness persuasiveness, and case value.[22] A related technique involves a shadow jury. The shadow jury is also privately selected and compensated. This panel is present during the actual trial and reports on reactions to the case on an ongoing basis so that adjustments may be made in strategy and presentation before substantial damage is done or the opportunity to capitalize on advantages lost.

In opposition to these techniques, it has been argued both that they do not work and that they work too well. The argument that they do not work or that a competent attorney should be capable of making the same assessments without social scientists[23] is not troubling. No one forces an attorney to use these techniques. An attorney who remains unconvinced of their efficacy need not use them.

The argument in opposition to the use of social science in jury selection that assumes these techniques are effective is more troubling. A major thrust of this argument is that the effect of these techniques is not to obtain a fair and impartial jury, but instead to stack the deck.[24] Only if both sides utilize these techniques will the desired fair and impartial jury result, and this requires the addition of substantial costs to the litigation. Moreover, because not all litigants will be able to afford a $30,000 public opinion survey, for example, one side may enjoy a decided advantage in jury selection. This point is well taken; however, it highlights a flaw in the system not limited to jury selection. Wealthy litigants have more money for attorneys, experts, and discovery than poor litigants. In the absence of a decision to make systemic changes to limit the effects of a litigant's wealth on the quality of justice, is there cogent basis for singling out jury selection to limit the impact of a litigant's wealth on the litigation?

Even when the litigants are evenly matched financially, many of these techniques intrude on the privacy of individual jurors. Observations of a prospective juror's home or automobile, investigation of credit

---

[21] Vinson, *The Shadow Jury: An Experiment in Litigation Science*, 68 ABA J 1242 (1982).

[22] V. Starr & M. McCormick, Jury Selection §6.0 (1985).

[23] Saks, *The Limits of Scientific Jury Selection: Ethical and Empirical*, 17 Jurimetrics 3 (1976).

[24] Etzioni, *Creating An Imbalance*, 10(6) Trial 28 (1974).

records, or psychological analysis of behavior to predict behavior as a juror adds costs to service as a juror beyond those inherent in the process. Thus, some courts limit extrajudicial inquiry into the private affairs of individual jurors.[25]

§18.03   Suggested Reading

Books

V. Starr & M. McCormick, *Jury Selection* (1985).

Articles

Broeder, *Voir Dire Examinations: An Empirical Study*, 38 S Cal L Rev 503 (1965).

Etzioni, *Creating an Imbalance*, 10(6) Trial 28 (1974).

Frederick, *Jury Behavior: A Psychologist Examines Jury Selection*, 5 Ohio NUL Rev 571 (1978).

Lees-Haley, *The Psychology of Jury Selection*, 47 Tex BJ 918 (1984).

McConahay, Mullin, & Frederick, *The Uses of Social Science in Trials with Political and Racial Overtones: The Trial of Joan Little*, 41 Law & Contemp Probs 205 (1977).

Saks, *The Limits of Scientific Jury Selection: Ethical and Empirical*, 17 Jurimetrics 3 (1976).

Suggs & Sales, *Using Communication Cues to Evaluate Prospective Jurors During the Voir Dire*, 20 Ariz L Rev 629 (1978).

Vinson, *The Shadow Jury: An Experiment in Litigation Science*, 68 ABA J 1242 (1982).

Cases

Commonwealth v Allen, 379 Mass 564, 400 NE2d 229 (1980).

Dixon v Cappellini, 88 FRD 1 (MD Pa 1980)

Irvin v Dowd, 366 US 717 (1961).

People v Al-Kanani, 33 NY2d 260, 307 NE2d 43, 351 NYS2d 969 (1973), *cert denied*, 417 US 916 (1974).

Swain v Alabama, 380 US 202 (1965).

Thiel v Southern Pacific Co, 328 US 217 (1946).

---

[25] *See, e.g.*, Commonwealth v Allen, 379 Mass 564, 400 NE2d 229 (1980).

Constitutions, Statutes, and Rules

Fed R Civ P 11 (as amended Apr 28, 1983).

Fed R Civ P 35.

Fed R Crim P 21(a).

Fed R Crim P 24(b).

Tex Const art 1, §15.

US Const amend VI.

US Const amend VII.

Appendix A
Using WESTLAW with
Psychiatric and
*Psychological Evidence**
By Kevin T. Jackson, J.D., M.A.

I. Introduction

This informational appendix is designed to aid the reader in the general use of the WESTLAW system and more specifically to demonstrate how WESTLAW can be used in conjunction with this text to help make research in the area of psychiatric and psychological evidence swift and complete.

II. The WESTLAW System

WESTLAW is a computer-assisted legal research service of West Publishing Company. It is accessible through a number of different types of computer terminals. The materials available through WESTLAW are contained in databases stored at the central computer in St. Paul, Minnesota.

To use the WESTLAW service a "query" or search request, is typed into the terminal and sent to the central computer. There it is processed and all of the documents that satisfy the search request are identified. The text of each of these documents is then stored on disks and transmitted to the user via a telecommunication network. This data then appears on the user's terminal, where it may be reviewed and evaluated. The user must then decide if the displayed documents are pertinent or if further research is desired. If further research is necessary, the query may be recalled for editing, or an entirely new query may

---

be sent. Documents displayed on the terminal may be printed or, on some terminals, the text may be stored on its own disks.

III.   Improving Legal Research with WESTLAW

The WESTLAW service is designed for use in conjunction with the more traditional tools of legal research. In principle, WESTLAW works as an index to primary and secondary legal materials. Yet it differs from traditional digests and indexes in that more terms can be researched, and more documents retrieved.

Through WESTLAW it is possible to index, or search for any significant term or combination of terms in an almost infinite variety of grammatical relationships by formulating a query composed of those terms. Unlike manual systems of secondary legal sources that reference only a few key terms in each document, WESTLAW is capable of indexing every key word. This enables documents to be located using terms not even listed in manual reference systems.

In addition to its expanded search term capabilities, WEST-LAW, through its numerous databases, enables the user to research issues in any and every jurisdiction quickly and efficiently. Most of the queries that appear in this text are designed to search WESTLAW's Connecticut case law database. However, WESTLAW provides access to many other libraries as well. For example, WESTLAW contains comprehensive federal and state case law databases as well as separate topical databases for areas of federal and state law such as tax, securities, energy, and government contracts.

WESTLAW also includes the text of the United States Code and the Code of Federal Regulations, the Federal Register, West's INSTA-CITE™, Shepard's ® Citations, *Black's Law Dictionary*, the Forensic Services Directory and many other legal sources. Furthermore, because new cases are continuously being added to the WESTLAW databases as they are decided by the courts, the documents retrieved will include the most current law available on any given issue.

In addition, WESTLAW queries augment the customary role of footnotes to the text by directing the user to a wider range of supporting authorities. Readers may use the preformulated queries supplied in this edition "as is" or formulate their own queries in order to retrieve cases relevant to the points of law discussed in the text.

IV. Query Formulation

a. General Principles

The art of query formulation is the heart of WESTLAW research. Although the researcher can gain technical skills by using the terminal, there is no strictly mechanical procedure for formulating queries. One must first comprehend the meaning of the legal issue to be researched before beginning a search on WESTLAW. Then the user will need to supply imagination, insight, and legal comprehension with knowledge of the capabilities of WESTLAW to formulate a useful query. Effective query formulation requires an alternative way of thinking about the legal research process.

Using WESTLAW is a constant balancing between generating too many documents and missing important documents. In general, it is better to look through a reasonable number of irrelevant documents than it is to be too restrictive and miss important material. The researcher should take into consideration at the initial query formulation stage what he or she will do if too many, or not enough documents are retrieved. Thought should be given as to how the query might be narrowed or the search broadened, and what can be done if the initial search retrieves zero documents.

Some issues by their very nature will require more lengthy queries than others; however, it is best to strive for efficiency in structuring the query. Look for unique search terms that will eliminate the need for a lengthy query. Keep in mind that WESTLAW is literal. Consider all possible alternative terms. Especially consider inherent limitations of the computer. It does not think, create, or make analogies. The researcher must do that for the computer. The computer is designed to look for the terms in the documents in relationships specified by the query. The researcher should know what he or she is looking for, at least to the extent of knowing how the terms are likely to show up in relevant documents. Always keep in mind the parameters of the system as to date and database content.

The WESTLAW Reference Manual should be consulted for more information on query formulation and WESTLAW commands. The Reference Manual is updated periodically to reflect new enhancements of WESTLAW. It provides detailed and comprehensive instructions on all aspects of the WESTLAW system and offers numerous illustrative examples on the proper format for various types of queries. Material contained in the Reference Manual enables the user to benefit from all of the system's capabilities in an effective and efficient manner.

b. The WESTLAW Query

The query is a message to WESTLAW. It instructs the computer to retrieve documents containing terms in the grammatical relationships specified by the query. The terms in a query are made up of words and/or numbers that pinpoint the legal issue to be researched.

An example of the kind of preformulated queries that appear in this publication is reproduced below. The queries corresponding to each section of the text appear at the end of the section.

The query appearing below is taken from Chapter 9, Section 9.03 and appears at the end of this section of the text.

expert /s witness testimony /p psychiatr! psycholog! /p hearsay

This query instructs WESTLAW to retrieve documents containing the word EXPERT within the same sentence as either the word WITNESS or the word TESTIMONY, all within the same paragraph as either a form of the root PSYCHIATR or a form of the root PSYCHOLOG, all within the same paragraph as HEARSAY.

This query illustrates what a standard request to WESTLAW looks like - words or numbers describing an issue, tied together by connectors. These connectors tell WESTLAW in what relationships the terms must appear. WESTLAW will retrieve all documents from the database that contain the terms appearing in those relationships.

The material that follows explains the methods by which WESTLAW queries are formulated, and shows how users of *Psychiatric and Psychological Evidence* can employ the preformulated queries in this publication in thier research. In addition, there are instructions that will enable readers to modify their queries to fit the particular needs of their research.

c. Selection of Terms

After determining the legal issue that is to be researched, the first step in query formulation is to select the key terms from the issue that will be used as search terms in the query. Words, numbers, and various other symbols may be used as search terms.

The goal in choosing search terms is to select the most unique terms for the issue. In selecting such terms it is frequently helpful to imagine how the terms might appear in the language of the documents that will be searched by the query. Moreover, it is necessary to consider the grammatical and editorial structure of the document. This involves a consideration of how the writer of the document (i.e., judge or headnote and synopsis writer) has worded both the factual and legal components of the issue involved in the case.

Although traditional book research generally starts with a consideration of the general legal concepts under which particular problems are subsumed, WESTLAW research starts with a consideration of specific terms that are likely to appear in documents that have addressed those problems. This is so because documents are retrieved from WESTLAW on the basis of the terms they contain. The more precise the terms, the more relevant the search results will be. For example, in researching the Fourteenth Amendment, inclusion of the unique terms "Fourteenth Amendment" or "due process" rather than the common term "constitution," would retrieve more specific, and hopefully more pertinent documents.

Once the initial search terms have been selected for a query, it is important to consider synonyms, antonyms, and other alternatives for the search terms. A space left between each of these alternative terms will be read as an "or" in WESTLAW. (See section e: Query Formulation: Proximity Connectors.) The nature of the legal issue will determine which alternative terms are desirable.

d. The Format of Search Terms
Once the key search terms have been selected, it is necessary to consider the proper form in which the term should appear in the query. As WESTLAW is literal in its search for terms, and as a term may appear in a variety of ways, derivative forms of each search term must be considered. There are

two devices available on WESTLAW for automatically generating alternative forms of search terms in a query. The first of these is the Unlimited Root Expander, the symbol (!). Placement of the ! symbol at the end of the root term generates other forms containing the same root. For example, adding the ! symbol to the root contract in the following query:

contract! /3 incapacity capacity

instructs the computer to generate the words CONTRACT, CONTRACTS, CONTRACTING, and CONTRACTUAL as search terms for the query. Yet time and space are saved by not having to include each of these alternatives in the query.

The second device used to automatically generate alternative forms of search terms is the Universal Character, the symbol *. This symbol permits the generation of all possible characters by placing one or more asterisks at the location in the term where the universal character is desired. For example, placing an asterisk on the root SCHIZOPHRENI in the following query:

schizophreni* /s delusion

instructs the computer to generate all forms of the root term with one additional character. Thus, the terms SCHIZOPHRENIA and SCHIZOPHRENIC would be generated by this query. (Note, however, that words with more than three letters following the root, other than plurals, will not be generated. Thus, the above query would not generate SCHIZOPHRENICALLY.) The symbol * may also be embedded inside of a term, as in the following query:

m*naghten /s rule test standard

This will generate the alternative terms M'NAGHTEN and MCNAGHTEN without the need to enter both terms. As WESTLAW automatically generates plural forms for search terms (e.g., the endings -s -es and -ies) it is generally unnecessary to use the root expansion devices to obtain plural forms of search terms.

e. Proximity Connectors

Once the search terms and alternate search terms have been selected the next consideration is how these terms may be ordered so as to retrieve the most relevant documents. The connectors and their meanings appear below.

1. Space (or). A space between search terms is read as an "or" by WESTLAW. For example, leaving a space between the query terms PSYCHIATRIST and PSYCHOLO-GIST:

    psychiatrist psychologist

    instructs the computer to retrieve documents that contain either the word PSYCHIATRIST or the word PSYCHOLOGIST or both.

2. & (ampersand). The symbol & means "and." Placing it between two terms instructs the computer to retrieve documents that contain both of the terms without regard to word order. For example, inserting the & between the terms PSYCHIATRIST and EXPERT:

    psychiatrist & expert

    commands the computer to retrieve documents that contain both the term PSYCHIATRIST and the term EXPERT anywhere in the text. The ampersand may also be placed between groups of alternative terms. By placing an & between PSYCHIATRIST or PSYCHOLO-GIST and EXPERT or SPECIALIST:

    psychiatrist psychologist & expert specialist

    documents containing the terms PSYCHIATRIST and/or PSYCHOLOGIST and the terms EXPERT and/or SPECIALIST may be retrieved.

3. /p (same paragraph). The /p symbol means "within the same paragraph." It requests that the terms to the left of the /p appear within the same paragraph as the terms to the right of the connector. For example, placing the /p between WITNESS and EVIDENCE:

    witness /p evidence

    instructs the computer to retrieve documents in which both the terms WITNESS and EVIDENCE appear in the same paragraph. The terms on each side of the /p connector may appear in the document in any order within the paragraph. As with the & connector the /p may be placed between groups of alternative terms. Thus, the query

    witness eyewitness /p evidence data

will succeed in retrieving all documents in which the terms WITNESS and/or EYEWITNESS appear in the same paragraph as EVIDENCE and/or DATA.

4. _____/s (same sentence)._____ The /s symbol requires that the search terms so connected occur within the same sentence. A /s placed between EYEWITNESS and EVI-DENCE.

eyewitness /s evidence

will retrieve documents that contain the words EYEWIT-NESS and EVIDENCE in the same sentence, without regard to which of these terms occur first in the sentence. As with the previous connectors, the /s may be placed between groups of alternative terms. Inserting the /s between the terms WITNESS or EYEWITNESS and EVIDENCE or DATA

witness eyewitness /s evidence data

instructs the computer to retrieve documents with the terms WITNESS and/or EYEWITNESS in the same sentence as the terms EVIDENCE and/or DATA regard-less of which terms appear first.

5. _____+s (precedes within sentence)._____ The +s symbol requires that the terms to the left of the +s connector precede the terms to the right of the connector within the same sentence. The query

durham +s test

instructs the computer to retrieve all documents in which the word DURHAM precedes the word TEST where both words appear in the same sentence. This connector may also be used between groups of alternative terms. Thus, the query

durham +s test standard rule

commands the computer to retrieve all documents in which the term DURHAM precedes the terms TEST and/or STANDARD and/or RULE in the same sen-tence.

6. _____/n (numerical proximity-within n words)._____ The /n symbol means "within n words," where n represents any whole number between 1 and 255, inclusive. It requests that the term to the left of the /n appear within the

designated number of words as terms to the right of the connector. For example, in the following query:

expert /3 testimony

the computer is instructed to retrieve all documents in which the term EXPERT appears within 3 words of the term TESTIMONY, without regard to word order. In addition, the + symbol may be used to require that the terms to the left of the numerical proximity connector precede the terms to the right of the connector. Thus, the query above could be altered to require that EXPERT precede TESTIMONY by no more than 3 words by replacing the /3 connector with the +3 connector.

expert +3 testimony

Both the /n and the +n connectors may also be used between groups of alternative search terms. For example:

expert ⎸3 testimony opinion witness

instructs the computer to retrieve all documents in which the word EXPERT occurs within the three words preceding the words TESTIMONY or OPINION or WITNESS.

7. " " (quotation marks). The " " (quotation marks) symbol is the most restrictive grammatical connector. When used to enclose search terms it requires that the computer retrieve only those documents in which enclosed terms appear exactly as they do within the quotation marks. For example, placing the following words within quotation marks

"hypothetical question"

commands the computer to retrieve all documents in which the terms HYPOTHETICAL and QUESTION occur in precisely the same order as they do within the quotation marks.

The quotation marks symbol is especially effective when searching for legal terms of art, legal concepts, or legal entities that occur together as multiple terms. Some examples are:

"parens patriae" "guardian ad litem" "mens rea"

8. _____ % (exclusion/but not). _____ The % symbol may be translated as "but not." It instructs the computer to

exclude documents that contain terms appearing after the percentage symbol. For example, to retrieve documents containing the term EXPERT within the three words of TESTIMONY but not the topic 110 (Criminal Law), the following query would be used:

expert /3 testimony % topic(110)

Any document containing topic 110 would automatically be excluded in the document search.

The connectors described above may be used in a variety of combinations, enabling the user to fine-tune a query to meet his or her specific research needs.

V. Advanced Search Techniques

a. The Field Search

Within any given database a more specialized search may be conducted. Rather than searching the entire text of a case for a designated query term, the search may be limited to specific portions of the case by conducting a "field search." A search may be restricted to a particular field (or portion) of a document by incorporating the field name into the query, followed by the field search terms enclosed in parentheses.

The fields available for WESTLAW case law databases are described below.

1. *Title Field:* The title field may be used to retrieve a particular case on WESTLAW. The ampersand, rather than the v. is used between the names of the parties. Thus, to retrieve the case entitled *Dixon v. Cappellini* the following query would be used:

   title(dixon & cappellini)

2. *Citation Field:* The citation field may be used for any document for which a citation exists in the WESTLAW databases. The proper database must first be selected. A numerical proximity connector is then used instead of the publication name to separate volume and page number. For example, to retrieve the case appearing at 706 F.2d 564, the Courts of Appeals (cta) database must be selected. The following query may then be used:

   citation(706 +5 564)

3. *Court Field:* The court field permits searches for case law to be restricted to particular states, districts, or courts.

The correct database in which to conduct the search must be chosen. For example, to restrict a search to cases appearing in the Atlantic Reporter from Connecticut and Maryland, the following query could be used in the "atl" database:

court(dc md) & 157k535

4. *Judge Field:* A search may be limited to the individual or majority opinion of a particular judge. To retrieve all cases in which Justice Powell has authored an opinion the following query would be used:

judge(powell)

5. *Synopsis Field:* The synopsis field consists of the editorially prepared summary of the case found immediately after the title. By reading the synopsis it may be determined if the decision generally encompasses the legal issue being researched without reading the entire decision.

The synopsis field search can be especially useful in focusing broad queries which might retrieve too many cases if the entire case was searched. For example, the following query would limit retrieval to cases in which emotional harm was a key element:

synopsis(emotional mental /3 injury harm trauma stress suffering)

6. *Topic Field:* The topic field contains the West topics and Key Numbers assigned to the headnotes in a case. A search in this field may be conducted by using either the West topic name or by using the West topic number designated for that topic. For example, the West digest topic of Evidence has been given the number 157. Thus, in order to retrieve cases classified under the digest topic Evidence either of these two queries could be used:

topic(evidence) /p psychiatr! psycholog! /p report record writ***

or

topic(157) /p psychiatr! psycholog! /p report record writ***

7. *Digest Field:* The digest field contains digest paragraphs prepared by West editors. It includes headnotes, corresponding digest topics and Key Numbers, the title and citation of the case, court, and year of decision. The

digest field can be used to search for terms which are not among the West topic headings. For example, the following query may be used to research cases involving parens patriae even though this is not one of the West topic headings.

digest(conservator! guardian! /p "parens patriae")

8. *Headnote Field:* A headnote search limits the search to the language of the headnote, exclusive of the digest topic and Key Number lines and case identification information. Thus, the headnote field is useful in conducting a search where exclusion of the topic name, the Key Number or the title of the case is necessary to retrieve only the most pertinent cases. For example, if the query includes statute or rule numbers the headnote field can be helpful to exclude unwanted citation and key numbers. The query found below is an illustration of this function. The search, run in the United States Court of Appeals database will retrieve cases construing Rule 706, Federal Rules of Evidence.

headnote(evidence /s rule +1 706)

9. *Opinion Field:* The opinion field contains the text of the case, court and docket numbers, and the names of the attorneys and judges participating. The opinion field search is useful in retrieving cases in which a particular attorney, judge or witness has been involved. The following format can be used to retrieve this information:

opinion(clarence /2 darrow)

NOTE:

Terms may be searched for in clusters of fields by joining any number of field names by commas. This technique is illustrated below:

synopsis, digest(civil /s discovery /s psychiatr!
psycholog!)

With this query, documents containing the terms CIVIL, DISCOVERY and PSYCHIATR! or PSYCHOLOG! in either the synopsis or digest portions of the case will be retrieved.

b. Field Browsing

The WESTLAW fields listed above may be used in yet

another way. This second method, known as field browsing, may be used with any query. Once a search has been completed, the documents retrieved may be scanned by entering the "f" command. A list of fields available for browsing is then displayed. Once a field has been selected, WESTLAW will display only the specified field(s).

The WESTLAW Reference Manual should be consulted for further instruction on using WESTLAW fields for searching or browsing.

c. Date Restrictions

WESTLAW may be instructed to retrieve documents appearing before, after or on a specified date, as well as within a range of dates. To use the date restriction the term DATE, followed in parentheses by the words BEFORE and/or AFTER, or the abbreviations BEF and/or AFT, or the symbols < and > must be included in the query. Note that the month, day and year may be included to further restrict the search. Date restrictions should be placed at the beginning or end of the query and connected to the query by an ampersand. The following are examples of how the date restriction may be used within a query:

date(after 1965) & worker workm*n /3 compensation & "post traumatic stress"

date(aft 1965) & worker workm*n /3 compensation & "post traumatic stress"

worker workm*n /3 compensation & "post traumatic stress" & date(bef 1975)

worker workm*n /3 compensation & "post traumatic stress" & date(aft may 10, 1965 and bef feb 28, 1981)

d. Key Number Searching

Searches may be performed using West Digest Topic and Key Numbers as search terms. When using this search technique, the query consists of the West Digest Topic Number followed by the letter k and then the Key Number classified as a subheading under the Digest Topic and Key Number. For example, to retrieve cases under the Digest Topic classification of Evidence (Digest Topic number 157), and under its subsection or Key Number for Necessity of Qualification, (Key Number 535), the following query would be used.

157k535

A complete list of Digest Topics and their numerical equivalents appears in the WESTLAW Reference Manual and is also available online in the WESTLAW database directory.

e. The Find Command

The FIND command may be used at any point in a search to retrieve a particular case from WESTLAW. No matter what the database, a case may be displayed by typing FIND followed by the case citation. For example:

find 88 frd 1

will retrieve the case of *Dixon v. Cappellini* no matter what the database. To return to the original screen, the GOBACK command is then entered.

f. The Locate Command

The LOCATE command may be used when viewing documents retrieved by a search query to identify documents within the search results which contain certain words. To locate a term, LOCATE or LOC is typed followed by the ENTER key. On the screen which follows the LOCATE terms are then typed. The terms LOCATE terms are then typed. The terms may or may not be words contained in the query. WESTLAW will then search the documents retrieved by the query to find the LOCATE terms. For example, to search the documents retrieved by the query:

contract! /3 capacity incapacity /s standard test

for those documents containing the term GUARDIAN type LOCATE followed by the term GUARDIAN. Documents containing the term will then be displayed.

VI. Citation Research with WESTLAW

a. Shepard's ® Citations on WESTLAW

From any point in WESTLAW, case citations may be entered to retrieve Shepard's listings for those citations. To enter a citation to be Shepardized, the following format is used:

sh 88 frd 1

or

sh 88 f.r.d. 1

or

sh 88frd1

When the citation is entered, Shepard's listings for the citation will be displayed. To shepardize a citation it is not necessary to be in the same database as that of the citation. For example, a Supreme Court citation may be entered from the Pacific Reporter database.

b. WESTLAW as a Citator

It is possible to retrieve new cases citing previous decisions by using WESTLAW itself as a citator. Using WESTLAW as a citator complements Shepard's Citations by retrieving very recent decisions not yet included in Shepard's. Because citation styles are not always uniform, special care must be taken to identify variant forms of citations.

Retrieving Cases that Cite Other Court Decisions

WESTLAW can be used as a citator of other court decisions if the title of the decision, its citation, or both, are known. When only the title of the case is known, use the following format:

frye /7 "united states"

This query instructs the computer to retrieve all documents citing the case of *Frye v. "United States"*. The /7 numerical connector requires that the term FRYE occur within seven words of the term "UNITED STATES".

If the citation of the case is known, it may be added to the query to retrieve only those documents citing the correct case name and case citation. For example, to retrieve cases that have referred to the *Frye* decision by its citation, 293 Fed. 1013, the following format may be used:

293 +7 1013

If both the citation and the case title are known, one or both of the case name terms may be used to retrieve all documents citing this case. The queries below illustrate this format.

frye /7 "united states" /15 293 + 1013

or

frye /15 293 +7 1013

West's INSTA-CITE

INSTA-CITE, West Publishing Company's case history system, allows users to quickly verify the accuracy of case citations and the validity of decisions. It contains prior and subsequent case histories in sequential listings, parallel citations and precedential treatment.

Some examples of the kind of direct case history provided by INSTA-CITE are: "affirmed," "certiorari denied," "decision reversed and remanded," and "judgment vacated." A complete list of INSTA-CITE case history and precedential treatment notations appears in the WESTLAW Reference Manual.

The format for entering a case citation into Insta-Cite consists of the letters IC followed by the citation, with or without spaces and periods:

706 f.2d 564

or

706 f2d 564

or

706f2d564

VII. Special Features

a. Black's Law Dictionary

WESTLAW contains an on-line version of Black's Law Dictionary. The dictionary incorporates definitions of terms and phrases of English and American law.

The dictionary may be accessed at any point while using WESTLAW by typing DI followed by the term to be defined:

di

To obtain definitions of a phrase, enter the command DI followed by the phrase without quotation marks:

di expert witness

If the precise spelling of a term to be defined is not known, or a list of dictionary terms is desired, a truncated form of the words may be entered with the root expansion symbol (!) attached to it:

di bar!

This example will produce a list of dictionary terms beginning with the root BAR. From the list of terms a number corresponding to the desired term can be entered to obtain the appropriate definition of BARRISTER.

VIII. WESTLAW Hornbook Queries

a. Query Format

There is seldom only one "correct" way to formulate a query

for a particular problem. There is a wide range of alternative ways that queries may be structured for effective research. Such variance in query style reflects the great flexibility that the WESTLAW system affords its users in formulating search strategies.

For some research problems, it may be necessary to make a series of refinements to a query, such as the addition of search terms or the substitution of different grammatical connectors, to adequately fit the particular needs of the individual researcher's problem. The responsibility remains with the researcher to "fine-tune" his or her queries in accordance with his or her own research requirements.

If a query does not retrieve any cases in a given database, it is because there are no documents in that database which satisfy the proximity requirements of the query. In this situation, to search another database with the same query, enter the letter S followed by the initials DB, followed by the new database identifier. Thus, if a query was initially addressed to the CONNECTICUT (ct-cs) database, but retrieved no documents, the user could then search the Vermont cases database (vt-cs) with the same query by entering the following command:

s db vt-cs

The maximum number of cases retrieved by a query in any given database will vary, depending on a variety of factors, including the relative generality of the search terms and proximity connectors, the frequency of litigation or discussion of the issue in the courts and administrative bodies, and the number of documents comprising the database.

b. Textual Illustrations

Examples from the text of this edition have been selected to illustrate how readers may formulate WESTLAW queries to meet the specific needs of research in the area of psychiatric and psychological evidence. A portion of Chapter 16 (Civil Commitment) section 16.02 of this text appears below. The footnotes have been omitted for purposes of brevity.

The Role of the Expert

Statutory schemes for civil commitment of the mentally ill or retarded frequently require medical or psychiatric input in the commitment process as a prerequisite to commitment. This may entail the requirement of a certificate to institute the commitment process or testimony at the commitment hearing. In these jurisdictions, although lay testimony may be admissible, it is not an adequate substitute for the required medical input.

Although these statutory or constitutional requirements mention physicians and psychiatrists, it is surprising that in some instances, even in the absence of a psychiatrist, physicians are preferred over psychologists. This preference cannot be justified by the relative expertise of these two professions or the issues raised in these proceedings. It appears to be an anachronism that does not reflect contemporary theory about mental disorders or the education and training of these professions.

In the absence of a statutory or constitutional requirement of expert medical testimony in commitment proceedings, it is implicitly required by the commitment criteria. Mental illness and mental retardation as criteria for involuntary hospitalization are utilized in a technical sense in these proceedings. They are not utilized, for example, as insanity may be contemplated as as exculpating consideration in criminal law which has significant moral overtones.

Once it has been accepted that expert testimony must be presented, the role of the expert is a bit more troubling. The first issue to be addressed in proceedings for involuntary hospitalization is the existence of a mental disability of the requisite category and degree for the type of proceeding utilized, a substantial severe mental disorder or deficiency. The difficulties that have characterized psychiatric diagnosis should require at minimum that two independent diagnoses be obtained. In addition, a descriptive rendition of the disordered behavior observed by the testifying psychiatrist or psychologist and the applicable diagnostic criteria set forth should be provided to the factfinder.

If the commitment is based upon dangerousness to self or others, the role of the expert in predicting dangerousness presents particular roblems. Psychiatric and psychological education and training does not typically include courses in the prediction of dangerousness and the professional have themselves disclaimed expertise on the prediction of dangerousness. However, the United States Supreme Court has not found psychiatric testimony on future dangerousness, in the context of imposition of the death penalty, so unreliable that it should be excluded as a matter of constitutional law. Instead, the Court relegated the inquiry to the expertise of the individual witness, scrutinized through cross examination and the testimony of other experts. Thus inquiry into the witnesses' particular education, training, or experience relevant to the prediction of future dangerousness is appropriate. In the absence of any special expertise on this issue, the appropriate role of the psychiatric or psychological witness should be to identify to the factfinder those events or considerations that it may wish to consider on this issue.

This excerpt discusses the use of medical and mental health professionals in the civil commitment process. In order to retrieve documents discussing this topic, the following preformulated query is given as a suggested search strategy on WESTLAW.

"civil commitment" /s psychiatrist psychologist physician

In the text of a case retrieved by the query, the paragraph below appears.

372 P.2d 154 R 2 OF 13   P 3 OF 11   PAC   T
(1)
257ak41
MENTAL HEALTH
k.   Hearing and determination in general.
Ariz.App. 1984
Civil commitments cannot occur solely on strength of physicians' recommendations. A.R.S. §36-539, subd. 8.
Matter of Appeal in Pima County Mental Health Matter No. MH 8621
693 P.2d 993, 143 Ariz. 338

The query can be altered in a number of ways to tailor it to the needs of the individual researcher. For example, to research civil commitment cases on the above topic involving issues of dangerousness in particular, the following query could be used:

"civil commitment" /s psychiatrist psychologist physician /p dangerous!

By adding DANGEROUS! within the same paragraph as "CIVIL COMMITMENT" /S PSYCHIATRIST PSYCHOLOGIST PHYSICIAN, the query retrieves documents which discuss the use of medical and mental health professionals in civil commitment cases involving dangerousness. One such document retrieved from the Pacific Reporter (pac) database is shown below.

578 P.2d 1   R 12 OF 15   P 3 OF 6   PAC   T
257Ak41
MENTAL HEALTH
k.   Hearing and determination in general.
Or.App. 1978.
Testimony of psychologist that alleged mentally ill person did not do anything that might be considered dangerous but that he "might be dangerous if this pattern of thinking continued as it seemed to be developing" was not sufficient, in absence of any evidence or threats or voilent actions, to support a finding that the subject was dangerous to himself or others, so as to warrant civil commitment. ORS 426.005 426.170, 426.005(2).
Matter of Conrad
578 P.2d 1, 34 Or.App. 119

IX.   Ranking Documents Retrieved on WESTLAW: Age and Term Options

Documents retrieved by a query can be ordered in either of two ways. One way is to order documents by their dates, with the most recent documents displayed first. This is ranking by AGE. Using the AGE option is suggested when the user's highest priority is to retrieve the most recent decisions from a search.

Alternatively, documents can be ranked by the frequency of appearance of query terms. This is ranking by TERMS. When a search is performed with the TERMS option, the cases containing the greatest number of different search terms will be displayed first.

When a database is accessed by entering a database identifier, WESTLAW responds with a screen requesting that the query be entered. At this point the user may select which type of ranking, AGE or TERMS, is desired.

X.   Conclusion

This appendix has demonstrated methods that can be used to obtain the most effective research results in the area of psychiatric and psychological evidence. The addition of WEST-LAW references for most sections of the text opens the door to a powerful and easily accessed computerized law library.

WESTLAW queries may be formulated as needed to meet the needs of researcher's specific problems. The power and flexibility of WESTLAW affords users of this publication a unique opportunity to greatly enhance their access to and understanding of psychiatric and psychological evidence.

Cases

F

Faber v Sweet Mfg Corp, 40
Misc 2d 212, 242 NYS2d 763
(Sup Ct 1963) **§15.11**

Feguer v United States, 302 F2d
214 (8th Cir), *cert denied,* 371
US 872 (1962) **§11.06**

Felber v Foote, 321 F Supp 85
(D Conn 1970) **§10.09**

Field v State, 370 So 2d 408 (Fla
1980) **§13.05**

Finkler, *In re,* 3 Cal 2d 584, 46
P2d 149 (1935) **§15.07**

Fino v McCollum Mining Co, 93
FRD 455 (ND Tex 1982)
§6.15

Fischer v Famous-Barr Co, 618
SW2d 446 (Mo Ct App 1981)
§14.05

Fitzgibbon v Fitzgibbon, 197 NJ
Super 63, 484 A2d 46 (1984)
§§13.01, 13.04

Foley v Kibrick, 12 Mass App
382, 425 NE2d 376 (1981)
§14.03

Followill v Emerson Elec Co,
234 Kan 791, 674 P2d 1050
(1984) **§14.10**

Forrest v Industrial Commn, 77
Ill 2d 86, 395 NE2d 576
(1979) **§14.14**

Fred J, *In re,* 89 Cal App 3d 168,
152 Cal Rptr 327 (1979)
§13.04

Frederick v Federal Life Ins Co,
57 P2d 235 (Cal 1936) **§10.02**

Fritz v Parke Davis & Co, 277
Minn 210, 152 NW2d 129
(1967) **§7.02**

Frye v United States, 293 F 1013
(DC Cir 1923) **§12.08**

Fugate v Walker, 204 Ky 767,
265 SW 331 (1924) **§15.11**

Furman v Georgia, 408 US 238
(1972) **§12.08**

G

Galindo v Garcia, 145 Tex 507,
199 SW2d 499 (1947) **§15.06**

Gallagher v Ind Commn, 9 Wis
2d 361, 101 NW2d 72 (1960)
§14.10

Galovich v Hertz Corp, 513
SW2d 325 (Mo 1974) **§14.02**

Gannon, *In re,* 123 NJ Super
104, 301 A2d 493 (1973)
§16.02

Garrus v Davis, 234 Ill 326, 84
NE 924 (1908) **§15.08**

Gault, *In re,* 387 US 1 (1967)
§11.09

Gaynier v Johnson, 673 SW2d
899 (Tex Civ App 1984)
§§10.03, 10.04

Georgia Pac Corp v McLaurin,
370 So 2d 1359 (Miss 1979)
§14.14

Gill, *In re,* 14 Cal App 256, 58
P2d 734 (1936) **§15.08**

Ginsberg v Fifth Court of
Appeals, 686 SW2d 105 (Tex
1985) **§15.14**

Glawe v Rulon, 284 F2d 495
(8th Cir 1960) **§9.10**

Goldade v State, 674 P2d 721
(Wyo 1983) **§13.10**

Gomes v Gaughan, 471 F2d 794
(1st Cir 1973) **§16.04**

U

Statutes

United States Code

5 USC §8337 **§14.15**

18 USC §4241 **§§11.01, 11.04, 11.06**

18 USC §4244 **§6.14**

18 USC §4247 **§§11.01, 11.04, 11.06**

30 USC §901 *et seq* **§14.15**

38 USC §1506 *et seq* **§14.15**

38 USC §3142 **§§11.01, 11.02**

42 USC §290dd-3 **§10.09**

42 USC §290ee-3 **§10.09**

42 USC §405(b)(1) **§§9.10, 14.15**

42 USC §416(i) **§14.15**

42 USC §423 **§14.15**

42 USC §1381 **§14.15**

45 USC §231 **§14.15**

State Statutes

Ala Code §34-26-2 (Supp 1984) **§10.05**

Alaska R Crim P 16 **§6.19**

Ariz Const art 2, §22 **§11.01**

Ariz R Crim P 15.1 & .2 **§6.19**

Ariz Rev Stat §8-533(b)(3) (1974-84 Supp) **§13.01**

Ariz Rev Stat Ann §13-502 (West 1985) **§12.02**

Ark Stat Ann §28-1001, Rule 503(d)(1) (1979) **§16.04**

Ark Stat Ann §43-2011.2 (1985) **§6.19**

Cal Bus & Prof Code §2263 (West Supp 1984) **§10.01**

Cal Civ Code §4608 (West 1985) **§13.01**

Cal Const art 1, §12 **§11.01**

Cal Evid Code §§990-1007, 110-1026 (West 1966 & Supp 1984) **§10.05**

Cal Evid Code §1000 (West 1966) **§§15.04, 15.09**

Cal Evid Code §1004 (West 1976) **§16.04**

Cal Penal Code §25(b) (West 1985) **§12.02**

Cal Penal Code §29 (West Supp 1985) **§§9.08, 12.06**

Cal Penal Code §11171(b) (West 1982) **§13.09**

Colo Rev Stat §13-25-129 (1984 Supp) **§13.10**

Conn Gen Stat §52-146d (1983) **§10.05**

Conn Gen Stat §54-86a (1983) **§6.19**

Conn Gen State Ann §52-146(c) (West Supp 1983) **§10.05**

Fla Stat Ann §90.503 (West 1979) **§10.05**

Fla Stat Ann §90.503(4)(a) (West 1979) **§16.04**

Idaho Code §19-2515(g)(8) (Supp 1984) **§12.08**

Ill Ann Stat ch 38 §104-16(b) (Smith-Hurd 1980) **§§11.07, 11.10**

Ill Ann Stat ch 38 §114-13 (Smith-Hurd 1985) **§6.19**

Ill Ann Stat ch 40, §602 (Smith-Hurd 1980) **§13.01**

Ill Ann Stat ch 110, §8-201 (Smith-Hurd Supp 1985) **§15.09**

Ill Ann Stat ch 111, §5306 (Smith-Hurd 1978 & Supp 1984-85) **§10.05**

Ill Rev Stat ch 38, §6-2 (1985) **§12.02**

Ill Rev Stat ch 51, §5.2 (1966) **§10.02**

Ind Code Ann §35-37-4-3 (Burns 1985) **§6.19**

Ind Code Ann §35-41-3-6 (Burns 1985) **§12.02**

Kan Stat Ann §60-427(c)(1) (1976) **§16.04**

Kan Stat Ann §60-460(dd) (Supp 1982) **§13.10**

Md Cts & Judic Proc Ann §9-109 (1984) **§10.05**

Mich Comp Laws Ann §330.1017(4) (1980) **§15.05**

Mich Comp Laws Ann §338.1043 (West 1976) **§10.05**

Model Penal Code §201(1) (1962) **§12.02**

Mo Ann Stat §337.055 (Vernon Supp 1984) **§10.05**

Mo Ann Stat §475.075(1) (Vernon 1956) **§15.05**

NC Gen Stat §§8-53, 53.1 (1981) **§10.04**

NC Gen Stat §15A-903 (1983) **§6.19**

Neb Rev Stat §27-504(4)(a) (1978) **§16.04**

Neb Rev Stat §29-1912 (1979) **§6.19**

Neb Rev Stat §29-1916 (1979) **§6.19**

Neb Rev Stat §29-1917 (1979) **§6.19**

Nev Rev Stat §49.215.2 (1979) **§10.05**

Nev Rev Stat §174.235 (1979) **§6.19**

Nev Rev Stat §174.255 (1979) **§6.19**

NY Dom Rel Laws §§240 *et seq* (McKinney 1985) **§13.01**

NY Fam Ct Act §320.5(3)(b) (Consol 1984) **§11.01**

NY Mental Hyg Law §9.27 (1978) **§8.02**

NY Penal Law §30.05 (McKinney 1985) **§12.02**

Rules and Regulations

Index

A

AFFECTIVE DISORDERS
Definition §2.09
Diagnosis. See PSYCHIATRIC
AND PSYCHOLOGICAL
DIAGNOSIS
Treatment. See TREATMENT
OF MENTAL DISORDER

B

BAIL
Basis for expert opinion
§11.03
Legal standard §11.01
Limitations on basis for expert
opinion §11.04
Role of the expert §11.02
Testimony of the expert
§11.05

BASIS FOR EXPERT OPINION
Generally §9.02
–extrajudicial sources §9.05
–hypothetical question §9.04
–personal knowledge §9.03
Particular proceedings

BASIS FOR EXPERT OPINION,
continued
–bail §11.03
–child abuse proceedings
§13.08
–child custody litigation
§13.03
–civil commitment proceedings
§16.03
–contractual capacity
determinations §15.03
–guardianship proceedings
§15.03
–insanity defense §12.04
–personal injury litigation
§14.06
–psychiatric autopsy §17.08
–sentencing §12.11
–social security disability
claims §14.17
–testamentary capacity
determinations §15.08
–testimonial credibility §17.03
–workers' compensation
§14.12

453

O

P